6/11/21 $5.00

Upgrading and Repairing PCs Quick Reference

Que Quick Reference Series

Scott Mueller

que

Upgrading and Repairing PCs Quick Reference

Copyright © 1994 by Que® Corporation

Library of Congress Catalog No.: 94-65316

ISBN: 1-56529-736-9

97 96 95   4 3

Interpretation of the printing code: the rightmost double-digit number is the year of the book's printing; the rightmost single-digit number, the number of the book's printing. For example, a printing code of 94-1 shows that the first printing of the book occurred in 1994.

Screen reproductions in this book were created with Collage Plus from Inner Media, Inc., Hollis, NH

Publisher
David P. Ewing

Publishing Manager
Brad Koch

Product Director
Robin Drake

Production Editors
Mike La Bonne
Thomas F. Hayes

Book Designer
Amy Peppler-Adams

Production Team
Angela Bannan
Claudia Bell
Anne Dickerson
Michael Hughes
Elizabeth Lewis
G. Alan Palmore
Tina Trettin
Donna Winter

Composed in *Stone* and *MCPdigital* by Que Corporation

Table of Contents

Introduction

This book has a great deal of useful information, primarily reference information, designed not to be read but to be looked up. This type of information can be very useful in troubleshooting or upgrading sessions, but usually is spread out among many sources. In this *Upgrading and Repairing PCs Quick Reference*, you'll find quickly and easily virtually every type of reference information you'll need for troubleshooting and upgrading systems.

The information in this *Quick Reference* is in the form of many charts and tables—in particular, information about the default interrupt, DMA channel, I/O port, and memory use of the primary system and most standard options. This information is invaluable whether you install new boards or upgrade a system in any way. This information also can be important when you troubleshoot a conflict between two devices.

This book has information about various system connectors—from the serial and parallel ports to the power-supply connections. Diagrams for making serial and parallel wrap (test) plugs are also shown.

Tables indicate the hard disk drive parameters found in XT, AT, PS/2, and other IBM-compatible systems. Many compatible BIOS drive tables are included. This information is often necessary when adding a hard disk to a system.

One of the most useful tables is a concise listing of the IBM diagnostics error codes. These codes can be generated by the POST and by the disk-based diagnostics programs. These error codes are not documented by IBM in tabular form; this compilation is the result of poring over hardware-maintenance service, technical-reference, and other manuals that IBM produces. Some of the codes come from reading the commented ROM listings in the technical-reference manuals. This information can be very useful in deciphering the codes quickly and efficiently, without having to look through a stack of books.

This book also has a listing of all the available IBM technical manuals and a description of all the documentation available. The listing has part-number and pricing information, as well as information useful in ordering this documentation.

Although all of this information comes from a wide range of sources, most of it comes from the technical-reference manuals and hardware-maintenance service manuals available for various systems from IBM and other manufacturers. These documents are invaluable if you want to pursue this topic more extensively.

Chapter 1

General Information

ASCII Character Code Charts

Figures 1.1 through 1.3 show ASCII control, standard, and extended character values. Figure 1.4 shows the IBM extended ASCII line-drawing characters in an easy-to-use format. I frequently use these extended ASCII line-drawing characters for visual enhancement in documents I create.

ASCII Control Codes:

DEC	HEX	CHAR	NAME		CONTROL CODE
0	00		Ctrl-@	NUL	Null
1	01	☺	Ctrl-A	SOH	Start of Heading
2	02	●	Ctrl-B	STX	Start of Text
3	03	♥	Ctrl-C	ETX	End of Text
4	04	♦	Ctrl-D	EOT	End of Transmit
5	05	♣	Ctrl-E	ENQ	Enquiry
6	06	♠	Ctrl-F	ACK	Acknowledge
7	07	●	Ctrl-G	BEL	Bell
8	08	◘	Ctrl-H	BS	Back Space
9	09	○	Ctrl-I	HT	Horizontal Tab
10	0A	◙	Ctrl-J	LF	Line Feed
11	0B	♂	Ctrl-K	VT	Vertical Tab
12	0C	♀	Ctrl-L	FF	Form Feed
13	0D	♪	Ctrl-M	CR	Carriage Return
14	0E	♫	Ctrl-N	SO	Shift Out
15	0F	☼	Ctrl-O	SI	Shift In
16	10	►	Ctrl-P	DLE	Data Line Escape
17	11	◄	Ctrl-Q	DC1	Device Control 1
18	12	↕	Ctrl-R	DC2	Device Control 2
19	13	‼	Ctrl-S	DC3	Device Control 3
20	14	¶	Ctrl-T	DC4	Device Control 4
21	15	§	Ctrl-U	NAK	Negative Acknowledge
22	16	▬	Ctrl-V	SYN	Synchronous Idle
23	17	↨	Ctrl-W	ETB	End of Transmit Block
24	18	↑	Ctrl-X	CAN	Cancel
25	19	↓	Ctrl-Y	EM	End of Medium
26	1A	→	Ctrl-Z	SUB	Substitute
27	1B	←	Ctrl-[	ESC	Escape
28	1C	∟	Ctrl-\	FS	File Separator
29	1D	↔	Ctrl-]	GS	Group Separator
30	1E	▲	Ctrl-^	RS	Record Separator
31	1F	▼	Ctrl-_	US	Unit Separator

Fig. 1.1   ASCII control codes.

Standard ASCII Characters (Including Control Codes):

DEC	HEX	CHAR	DEC	HEX	CHAR	DEC	HEX	CHAR	DEC	HEX	CHAR
0	0		32	20		64	40	@	96	60	`
1	1	☺	33	21	!	65	41	A	97	61	a
2	2	●	34	22	"	66	42	B	98	62	b
3	3	♥	35	23	#	67	43	C	99	63	c
4	4	♦	36	24	$	68	44	D	100	64	d
5	5	♣	37	25	%	69	45	E	101	65	e
6	6	♠	38	26	&	70	46	F	102	66	f
7	7	•	39	27	'	71	47	G	103	67	g
8	8	◘	40	28	(	72	48	H	104	68	h
9	9	○	41	29	)	73	49	I	105	69	i
10	A	■	42	2A	*	74	4A	J	106	6A	j
11	B	♂	43	2B	+	75	4B	K	107	6B	k
12	C	♀	44	2C	,	76	4C	L	108	6C	l
13	D	♪	45	2D	-	77	4D	M	109	6D	m
14	E	♫	46	2E	.	78	4E	N	110	6E	n
15	F	✿	47	2F	/	79	4F	O	111	6F	o
16	10	►	48	30	0	80	50	P	112	70	p
17	11	◄	49	31	1	81	51	Q	113	71	q
18	12	↕	50	32	2	82	52	R	114	72	r
19	13	‼	51	33	3	83	53	S	115	73	s
20	14	¶	52	34	4	84	54	T	116	74	t
21	15	§	53	35	5	85	55	U	117	75	u
22	16	▬	54	36	6	86	56	V	118	76	v
23	17	↨	55	37	7	87	57	W	119	77	w
24	18	↑	56	38	8	88	58	X	120	78	x
25	19	↓	57	39	9	89	59	Y	121	79	y
26	1A	→	58	3A	:	90	5A	Z	122	7A	z
27	1B	←	59	3B	;	91	5B	[	123	7B	{
28	1C	∟	60	3C	<	92	5C	\	124	7C		
29	1D	↔	61	3D	=	93	5D	]	125	7D	}
30	1E	▲	62	3E	>	94	5E	^	126	7E	~
31	1F	▼	63	3F	?	95	5F	_	127	7F	⌂

Fig. 1.2   Standard ASCII characters (including control codes).

Extended ASCII Characters:

DEC	HEX	CHAR	DEC	HEX	CHAR	DEC	HEX	CHAR	DEC	HEX	CHAR
128	80	Ç	160	A0	á	192	C0	└	224	E0	α
129	81	ü	161	A1	í	193	C1	┴	225	E1	ß
130	82	é	162	A2	ó	194	C2	┬	226	E2	Γ
131	83	â	163	A3	ú	195	C3	├	227	E3	π
132	84	ä	164	A4	ñ	196	C4	─	228	E4	Σ
133	85	à	165	A5	Ñ	197	C5	┼	229	E5	σ
134	86	å	166	A6	ª	198	C6	╞	230	E6	µ
135	87	ç	167	A7	º	199	C7	╟	231	E7	τ
136	88	ê	168	A8	¿	200	C8	╚	232	E8	Φ
137	89	ë	169	A9	⌐	201	C9	╔	233	E9	Θ
138	8A	è	170	AA	¬	202	CA	╩	234	EA	Ω
139	8B	ï	171	AB	½	203	CB	╦	235	EB	δ
140	8C	î	172	AC	¼	204	CC	╠	236	EC	∞
141	8D	ì	173	AD	¡	205	CD	═	237	ED	φ
142	8E	Ä	174	AE	«	206	CE	╬	238	EE	ε
143	8F	Å	175	AF	»	207	CF	╧	239	EF	∩
144	90	É	176	B0	░	208	D0	╨	240	F0	≡
145	91	æ	177	B1	▒	209	D1	╤	241	F1	±
146	92	Æ	178	B2	▓	210	D2	╥	242	F2	≥
147	93	ô	179	B3	│	211	D3	╙	243	F3	≤
148	94	ö	180	B4	┤	212	D4	╘	244	F4	⌠
149	95	ò	181	B5	╡	213	D5	╒	245	F5	⌡
150	96	û	182	B6	╢	214	D6	╓	246	F6	÷
151	97	ù	183	B7	╖	215	D7	╫	247	F7	≈
152	98	ÿ	184	B8	╕	216	D8	╪	248	F8	°
153	99	Ö	185	B9	╣	217	D9	┘	249	F9	∙
154	9A	Ü	186	BA	║	218	DA	┌	250	FA	·
155	9B	¢	187	BB	╗	219	DB	█	251	FB	√
156	9C	£	188	BC	╝	220	DC	▄	252	FC	ⁿ
157	9D	¥	189	BD	╜	221	DD	▌	253	FD	²
158	9E	₧	190	BE	╛	222	DE	▐	254	FE	■
159	9F	ƒ	191	BF	┐	223	DF	▀	255	FF	

Fig. 1.3 Extended ASCII characters.

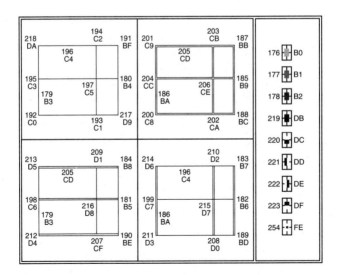

Fig. 1.4 Extended ASCII line-drawing characters.

Hexadecimal/ASCII Conversion Table

DEC	HEX	OCTAL	BINARY	NAME	CHARACTER
0	00	000	0000 0000	blank	
1	01	001	0000 0001	happy face	☺
2	02	002	0000 0010	inverse happy face	●
3	03	003	0000 0011	heart	♥
4	04	004	0000 0100	diamond	♦
5	05	005	0000 0101	club	♣
6	06	006	0000 0110	spade	♠
7	07	007	0000 0111	bullet	•
8	08	010	0000 1000	inverse bullet	◘
9	09	011	0000 1001	circle	○
10	0A	012	0000 1010	inverse circle	◙
11	0B	013	0000 1011	male sign	♂
12	0C	014	0000 1100	female sign	♀
13	0D	015	0000 1101	single note	♪
14	0E	016	0000 1110	double note	♫
15	0F	017	0000 1111	sun	☼
16	10	020	0001 0000	right triangle	►
17	11	021	0001 0001	left triangle	◄
18	12	022	0001 0010	up/down arrow	b
19	13	023	0001 0011	double exclamation	‼
20	14	024	0001 0100	paragraph sign	¶
21	15	025	0001 0101	section sign	§
22	16	026	0001 0110	rectangular bullet	■
23	17	027	0001 0111	up/down to line	↨
24	18	030	0001 1000	up arrow	↑
25	19	031	0001 1001	down arrow	↓
26	1A	032	0001 1010	right arrow	→
27	1B	033	0001 1011	left arrow	←
28	1C	034	0001 1100	lower left box	L
29	1D	035	0001 1101	left/right arrow	↔
30	1E	036	0001 1110	up triangle	▲
31	1F	037	0001 1111	down triangle	▼
32	20	040	0010 0000	space	Space
33	21	041	0010 0001	exclamation point	!
34	22	042	0010 0010	quotation mark	"
35	23	043	0010 0011	number sign	#
36	24	044	0010 0100	dollar sign	$
37	25	045	0010 0101	percent sign	%
38	26	046	0010 0110	ampersand	&
39	27	047	0010 0111	apostrophe	'
40	28	050	0010 1000	opening parenthesis	(
41	29	051	0010 1001	closing parenthesis	)
42	2A	052	0010 1010	asterisk	*
43	2B	053	0010 1011	plus sign	+
44	2C	054	0010 1100	comma	,
45	2D	055	0010 1101	hyphen or minus sign	-
46	2E	056	0010 1110	period	.
47	2F	057	0010 1111	slash	/
48	30	060	0011 0000	zero	0
49	31	061	0011 0001	one	1
50	32	062	0011 0010	two	2
51	33	063	0011 0011	three	3
52	34	064	0011 0100	four	4
53	35	065	0011 0101	five	5
54	36	066	0011 0110	six	6
55	37	067	0011 0111	seven	7
56	38	070	0011 1000	eight	8
57	39	071	0011 1001	nine	9
58	3A	072	0011 1010	colon	:
59	3B	073	0011 1011	semicolon	;
60	3C	074	0011 1100	less than sign	<
61	3D	075	0011 1101	equal sign	=
62	3E	076	0011 1110	greater than sign	>
63	3F	077	0011 1111	question mark	?

DEC	HEX	OCTAL	BINARY	NAME	CHARACTER
64	40	100	0100 0000	at sign	@
65	41	101	0100 0001	capital A	A
66	42	102	0100 0010	capital B	B
67	43	103	0100 0011	capital C	C
68	44	104	0100 0100	capital D	D
69	45	105	0100 0101	capital E	E
70	46	106	0100 0110	capital F	F
71	47	107	0100 0111	capital G	G
72	48	110	0100 1000	capital H	H
73	49	111	0100 1001	capital I	I
74	4A	112	0100 1010	capital J	J
75	4B	113	0100 1011	capital K	K
76	4C	114	0100 1100	capital L	L
77	4D	115	0100 1101	capital M	M
78	4E	116	0100 1110	capital N	N
79	4F	117	0100 1111	capital O	O
80	50	120	0101 0000	capital P	P
81	51	121	0101 0001	capital Q	Q
82	52	122	0101 0010	capital R	R
83	53	123	0101 0011	capital S	S
84	54	124	0101 0100	capital T	T
85	55	125	0101 0101	capital U	U
86	56	126	0101 0110	capital V	V
87	57	127	0101 0111	capital W	W
88	58	130	0101 1000	capital X	X
89	59	131	0101 1001	capital Y	Y
90	5A	132	0101 1010	capital Z	Z
91	5B	133	0101 1011	opening bracket	[
92	5C	134	0101 1100	backward slash	\
93	5D	135	0101 1101	closing bracket	]
94	5E	136	0101 1110	caret	^
95	5F	137	0101 1111	underscore	_
96	60	140	0110 0000	grave	`
97	61	141	0110 0001	lowercase A	a
98	62	142	0110 0010	lowercase B	b
99	63	143	0110 0011	lowercase C	c
100	64	144	0110 0100	lowercase D	d
101	65	145	0110 0101	lowercase E	e
102	66	146	0110 0110	lowercase F	f
103	67	147	0110 0111	lowercase G	g
104	68	150	0110 1000	lowercase H	h
105	69	151	0110 1001	lowercase I	i
106	6A	152	0110 1010	lowercase J	j
107	6B	153	0110 1011	lowercase K	k
108	6C	154	0110 1100	lowercase L	l
109	6D	155	0110 1101	lowercase M	m
110	6E	156	0110 1110	lowercase N	n
111	6F	157	0110 1111	lowercase O	o
112	70	160	0111 0000	lowercase P	p
113	71	161	0111 0001	lowercase Q	q
114	72	162	0111 0010	lowercase R	r
115	73	163	0111 0011	lowercase S	s
116	74	164	0111 0100	lowercase T	t
117	75	165	0111 0101	lowercase U	u
118	76	166	0111 0110	lowercase V	v
119	77	167	0111 0111	lowercase W	w
120	78	170	0111 1000	lowercase X	x
121	79	171	0111 1001	lowercase Y	y
122	7A	172	0111 1010	lowercase Z	z
123	7B	173	0111 1011	opening brace	{
124	7C	174	0111 1100	vertical line		
125	7D	175	0111 1101	closing brace	}
126	7E	176	0111 1110	tilde	~
127	7F	177	0111 1111	small house	

(continues)

Hexadecimal/ASCII Conversion Table (continued)

DEC	HEX	OCTAL	BINARY	NAME	CHARACTER
128	80	200	1000 0000	C cedilla	Ç
129	81	201	1000 0001	u umlaut	Ü
130	82	202	1000 0010	e acute	é
131	83	203	1000 0011	a circumflex	â
132	84	204	1000 0100	a umlaut	ä
133	85	205	1000 0101	a grave	à
134	86	206	1000 0110	a ring	å
135	87	207	1000 0111	c cedilla	ç
136	88	210	1000 1000	e circumflex	ê
137	89	211	1000 1001	e umlaut	ë
138	8A	212	1000 1010	e grave	è
139	8B	213	1000 1011	I umlaut	ï
140	8C	214	1000 1100	I circumflex	î
141	8D	215	1000 1101	I grave	ì
142	8E	216	1000 1110	A umlaut	Ä
143	8F	217	1000 1111	A ring	Å
144	90	220	1001 0000	E acute	É
145	91	221	1001 0001	ae ligature	æ
146	92	222	1001 0010	AE ligature	Æ
147	93	223	1001 0011	o circumflex	ô
148	94	224	1001 0100	o umlaut	ö
149	95	225	1001 0101	o grave	ò
150	96	226	1001 0110	u circumflex	û
151	97	227	1001 0111	u grave	ù
152	98	230	1001 1000	y umlaut	ÿ
153	99	231	1001 1001	O umlaut	Ö
154	9A	232	1001 1010	U umlaut	Ü
155	9B	233	1001 1011	cent sign	¢
156	9C	234	1001 1100	pound sign	£
157	9D	235	1001 1101	yen sign	¥
158	9E	236	1001 1110	Pt	₧
159	9F	237	1001 1111	function	ƒ
160	A0	240	1010 0000	a acute	á
161	A1	241	1010 0001	I acute	í
162	A2	242	1010 0010	o acute	ó
163	A3	243	1010 0011	u acute	ú
164	A4	244	1010 0100	n tilde	ñ
165	A5	245	1010 0101	N tilde	Ñ
166	A6	246	1010 0110	a macron	ª
167	A7	247	1010 0111	o macron	º
168	A8	250	1010 1000	opening question mark	¿
169	A9	251	1010 1001	upper left box	⌐
170	AA	252	1010 1010	upper right box	¬
171	AB	253	1010 1011	1/2	½
172	AC	254	1010 1100	1/4	¼
173	AD	255	1010 1101	opening exclamation	¡
174	AE	256	1010 1110	opening guillemets	«
175	AF	257	1010 1111	closing guillemets	»
176	B0	260	1011 0000	light block	░
177	B1	261	1011 0001	medium block	▒
178	B2	262	1011 0010	dark block	▓
179	B3	263	1011 0011	single vertical	│
180	B4	264	1011 0100	single right junction	┤
181	B5	265	1011 0101	2 to 1 right junction	╡
182	B6	266	1011 0110	1 to 2 right junction	╢
183	B7	267	1011 0111	1 to 2 upper right	╖
184	B8	270	1011 1000	2 to 1 upper right	╕
185	B9	271	1011 1001	double right junction	╣
186	BA	272	1011 1010	double vertical	║
187	BB	273	1011 1011	double upper right	╗
188	BC	274	1011 1100	double lower right	╝
189	BD	275	1011 1101	1 to 2 lower right	╜
190	BE	276	1011 1110	2 to 1 lower right	╛
191	BF	277	1011 1111	single upper right	┐

DEC	HEX	OCTAL	BINARY	NAME	CHARACTER
192	C0	300	1100 0000	single lower left	└
193	C1	301	1100 0001	single lower junction	┴
194	C2	302	1100 0010	single upper junction	┬
195	C3	303	1100 0011	single left junction	├
196	C4	304	1100 0100	single horizontal	─
197	C5	305	1100 0101	single intersection	┼
198	C6	306	1100 0110	2 to 1 left junction	╞
199	C7	307	1100 0111	1 to 2 left junction	╟
200	C8	310	1100 1000	double lower left	╚
201	C9	311	1100 1001	double upper left	╔
202	CA	312	1100 1010	double lower junction	╩
203	CB	313	1100 1011	double upper junction	╦
204	CC	314	1100 1100	double left junction	╠
205	CD	315	1100 1101	double horizontal	═
206	CE	316	1100 1110	double intersection	╬
207	CF	317	1100 1111	1 to 2 lower junction	╧
208	D0	320	1101 0000	2 to 1 lower junction	╨
209	D1	321	1101 0001	1 to 2 upper junction	╤
210	D2	322	1101 0010	2 to 1 upper junction	╥
211	D3	323	1101 0011	1 to 2 lower left	╙
212	D4	324	1101 0100	2 to 1 lower left	╘
213	D5	325	1101 0101	2 to 1 upper left	╒
214	D6	326	1101 0110	1 to 2 upper left	╓
215	D7	327	1101 0111	2 to 1 intersection	╫
216	D8	330	1101 1000	1 to 2 intersection	╪
217	D9	331	1101 1001	single lower right	┘
218	DA	332	1101 1010	single upper right	┌
219	DB	333	1101 1011	inverse space	█
220	DC	334	1101 1100	lower inverse	▄
221	DD	335	1101 1101	left inverse	▌
222	DE	336	1101 1110	right inverse	▐
223	DF	337	1101 1111	upper inverse	▀
224	E0	340	1110 0000	alpha	α
225	E1	341	1110 0001	beta	β
226	E2	342	1110 0010	Gamma	Γ
227	E3	343	1110 0011	pi	Π
228	E4	344	1110 0100	Sigma	Σ
229	E5	345	1110 0101	sigma	σ
230	E6	346	1110 0110	mu	μ
231	E7	347	1110 0111	tau	τ
232	E8	350	1110 1000	Phi	Φ
233	E9	351	1110 1001	theta	θ
234	EA	352	1110 1010	Omega	Ω
235	EB	353	1110 1011	delta	δ
236	EC	354	1110 1100	infinity	∞
237	ED	355	1110 1101	phi	σ
238	EE	356	1110 1110	epsilon	ε
239	EF	357	1110 1111	intersection of sets	$\cap$
240	F0	360	1111 0000	is identical to	
241	F1	361	1111 0001	plus/minus sign	$\pm$
242	F2	362	1111 0010	greater/equal sign	$\geq$
243	F3	363	1111 0011	less/equal sign	$\leq$
244	F4	364	1111 0100	top half integral	$\lceil$
245	F5	365	1111 0101	lower half integral	$\rfloor$
246	F6	366	1111 0110	divide by sign	$\div$
247	F7	367	1111 0111	approximately	$\approx$
248	F8	370	1111 1000	degree	$\cdot$
249	F9	371	1111 1001	filled in degree	$\cdot$
250	FA	372	1111 1010	small bullet	$\cdot$
251	FB	373	1111 1011	square root	$\sqrt{}$
252	FC	374	1111 1100	superscript n	n
253	FD	375	1111 1101	superscript 2	ε
254	FE	376	1111 1110	box	∎
255	FF	377	1111 1111	phantom space	

EBCDIC Character Codes

DEC	HEX	OCTAL	BINARY	NAME	CHARACTER
0	00	000	0000 0000	NUL	
1	01	001	0000 0001	SOH	
2	02	002	0000 0010	STX	
3	03	003	0000 0011	ETX	
4	04	004	0000 0100	SEL	
5	05	005	0000 0101	HT	
6	06	006	0000 0110	RNL	
7	07	007	0000 0111	DEL	
8	08	010	0000 1000	GE	
9	09	011	0000 1001	SPS	
10	0A	012	0000 1010	RPT	
11	0B	013	0000 1011	VT	
12	0C	014	0000 1100	FF	
13	0D	015	0000 1101	CR	
14	0E	016	0000 1110	SO	
15	0F	017	0000 1111	SI	
16	10	020	0001 0000	DLE	
17	11	021	0001 0001	DC1	
18	12	022	0001 0010	DC2	
19	13	023	0001 0011	DC3	
20	14	024	0001 0100	RES/ENP	
21	15	025	0001 0101	NL	
22	16	026	0001 0110	BS	
23	17	027	0001 0111	POC	
24	18	030	0001 1000	CAN	
25	19	031	0001 1001	EM	
26	1A	032	0001 1010	UBS	
27	1B	033	0001 1011	CU1	
28	1C	034	0001 1100	IFS	
29	1D	035	0001 1101	IGS	
30	1E	036	0001 1110	IRS	
31	1F	037	0001 1111	IUS/ITB	
32	20	040	0010 0000	DS	
33	21	041	0010 0001	SOS	
34	22	042	0010 0010	FS	
35	23	043	0010 0011	WUS	
36	24	044	0010 0100	BYP/INP	
37	25	045	0010 0101	LF	
38	26	046	0010 0110	ETB	
39	27	047	0010 0111	ESC	
40	28	050	0010 1000	SA	
41	29	051	0010 1001	SFE	
42	2A	052	0010 1010	SM/SW	
43	2B	053	0010 1011	CSP	
44	2C	054	0010 1100	MFA	
45	2D	055	0010 1101	ENQ	
46	2E	056	0010 1110	ACK	
47	2F	057	0010 1111	BEL	
48	30	060	0011 0000		
49	31	061	0011 0001		
50	32	062	0011 0010	SYN	
51	33	063	0011 0011	IR	
52	34	064	0011 0100	PP	
53	35	065	0011 0101	TRN	
54	36	066	0011 0110	NBS	
55	37	067	0011 0111	EOT	
56	38	070	0011 1000	SBS	
57	39	071	0011 1001	IT	
58	3A	072	0011 1010	RFF	
59	3B	073	0011 1011	CU3	
60	3C	074	0011 1100	DC4	
61	3D	075	0011 1101	NAK	
62	3E	076	0011 1110		
63	3F	077	0011 1111	SUB	

DEC	HEX	OCTAL	BINARY	NAME	CHARACTER
64	40	100	0100 0000	SP	
65	41	101	0100 0001	RSP	
66	42	102	0100 0010		
67	43	103	0100 0011		
68	44	104	0100 0100		
69	45	105	0100 0101		
70	46	106	0100 0110		
71	47	107	0100 0111		
72	48	110	0100 1000		
73	49	111	0100 1001		
74	4A	112	0100 1010		¢
75	4B	113	0100 1011		.
76	4C	114	0100 1100		<
77	4D	115	0100 1101		(
78	4E	116	0100 1110		+
79	4F	117	0100 1111		|
80	50	120	0101 0000		&
81	51	121	0101 0001		
82	52	122	0101 0010		
83	53	123	0101 0011		
84	54	124	0101 0100		
85	55	125	0101 0101		
86	56	126	0101 0110		
87	57	127	0101 0111		
88	58	130	0101 1000		
89	59	131	0101 1001		
90	5A	132	0101 1010		!
91	5B	133	0101 1011		$
92	5C	134	0101 1100		*
93	5D	135	0101 1101		)
94	5E	136	0101 1110		;
95	5F	137	0101 1111		¬
96	60	140	0110 0000		−
97	61	141	0110 0001		/
98	62	142	0110 0010		
99	63	143	0110 0011		
100	64	144	0110 0100		
101	65	145	0110 0101		
102	66	146	0110 0110		
103	67	147	0110 0111		
104	68	150	0110 1000		
105	69	151	0110 1001		
106	6A	152	0110 1010		|
107	6B	153	0110 1011		,
108	6C	154	0110 1100		%
109	6D	155	0110 1101		-
110	6E	156	0110 1110		>
111	6F	157	0110 1111		?
112	70	160	0111 0000		
113	71	161	0111 0001		
114	72	162	0111 0010		
115	73	163	0111 0011		
116	74	164	0111 0100		
117	75	165	0111 0101		
118	76	166	0111 0110		
119	77	167	0111 0111		
120	78	170	0111 1000		
121	79	171	0111 1001		'
122	7A	172	0111 1010		:
123	7B	173	0111 1011		#
124	7C	174	0111 1100		@
125	7D	175	0111 1101		'
126	7E	176	0111 1110		=
127	7F	177	0111 1111		"

(continues)

EBCDIC Character Codes (continued)

DEC	HEX	OCTAL	BINARY	NAME	CHARACTER
128	80	200	1000 0000		
129	81	201	1000 0001		a
130	82	202	1000 0010		b
131	83	203	1000 0011		c
132	84	204	1000 0100		d
133	85	205	1000 0101		e
134	86	206	1000 0110		f
135	87	207	1000 0111		g
136	88	210	1000 1000		h
137	89	211	1000 1001		i
138	8A	212	1000 1010		
139	8B	213	1000 1011		
140	8C	214	1000 1100		
141	8D	215	1000 1101		
142	8E	216	1000 1110		
143	8F	217	1000 1111		
144	90	220	1001 0000		
145	91	221	1001 0001		j
146	92	222	1001 0010		k
147	93	223	1001 0011		l
148	94	224	1001 0100		m
149	95	225	1001 0101		n
150	96	226	1001 0110		o
151	97	227	1001 0111		p
152	98	230	1001 1000		q
153	99	231	1001 1001		r
154	9A	232	1001 1010		
155	9B	233	1001 1011		
156	9C	234	1001 1100		
157	9D	235	1001 1101		
158	9E	236	1001 1110		
159	9F	237	1001 1111		
160	A0	240	1010 0000		
161	A1	241	1010 0001		~
162	A2	242	1010 0010		s
163	A3	243	1010 0011		t
164	A4	244	1010 0100		u
165	A5	245	1010 0101		v
166	A6	246	1010 0110		w
167	A7	247	1010 0111		x
168	A8	250	1010 1000		y
169	A9	251	1010 1001		z
170	AA	252	1010 1010		
171	AB	253	1010 1011		
172	AC	254	1010 1100		
173	AD	255	1010 1101		
174	AE	256	1010 1110		
175	AF	257	1010 1111		
176	B0	260	1011 0000		
177	B1	261	1011 0001		
178	B2	262	1011 0010		
179	B3	263	1011 0011		
180	B4	264	1011 0100		
181	B5	265	1011 0101		
182	B6	266	1011 0110		
183	B7	267	1011 0111		
184	B8	270	1011 1000		
185	B9	271	1011 1001		
186	BA	272	1011 1010		
187	BB	273	1011 1011		
188	BC	274	1011 1100		
189	BD	275	1011 1101		
190	BE	276	1011 1110		
191	BF	277	1011 1111		

DEC	HEX	OCTAL	BINARY	NAME	CHARACTER
192	C0	300	1100 0000		{
193	C1	301	1100 0001		A
194	C2	302	1100 0010		B
195	C3	303	1100 0011		C
196	C4	304	1100 0100		D
197	C5	305	1100 0101		E
198	C6	306	1100 0110		F
199	C7	307	1100 0111		G
200	C8	310	1100 1000		H
201	C9	311	1100 1001		I
202	CA	312	1100 1010	SHY	
203	CB	313	1100 1011		
204	CC	314	1100 1100		
205	CD	315	1100 1101		
206	CE	316	1100 1110		
207	CF	317	1100 1111		
208	D0	320	1101 0000		}
209	D1	321	1101 0001		J
210	D2	322	1101 0010		K
211	D3	323	1101 0011		L
212	D4	324	1101 0100		M
213	D5	325	1101 0101		N
214	D6	326	1101 0110		O
215	D7	327	1101 0111		P
216	D8	330	1101 1000		Q
217	D9	331	1101 1001		R
218	DA	332	1101 1010		
219	DB	333	1101 1011		
220	DC	334	1101 1100		
221	DD	335	1101 1101		
222	DE	336	1101 1110		
223	DF	337	1101 1111		
224	E0	340	1110 0000		\
225	E1	341	1110 0001	NSP	
226	E2	342	1110 0010		S
227	E3	343	1110 0011		T
228	E4	344	1110 0100		U
229	E5	345	1110 0101		V
230	E6	346	1110 0110		W
231	E7	347	1110 0111		X
232	E8	350	1110 1000		Y
233	E9	351	1110 1001		Z
234	EA	352	1110 1010		
235	EB	353	1110 1011		
236	EC	354	1110 1100		
237	ED	355	1110 1101		
238	EE	356	1110 1110		
239	EF	357	1110 1111		
240	F0	360	1111 0000		0
241	F1	361	1111 0001		1
242	F2	362	1111 0010		2
243	F3	363	1111 0011		3
244	F4	364	1111 0100		4
245	F5	365	1111 0101		5
246	F6	366	1111 0110		6
247	F7	367	1111 0111		7
248	F8	370	1111 1000		8
249	F9	371	1111 1001		9
250	FA	372	1111 1010		
251	FB	373	1111 1011		
252	FC	374	1111 1100		
253	FD	375	1111 1101		
254	FE	376	1111 1110		
255	FF	377	1111 1111	EO	

Metric System (SI) Prefixes

Multiplier Symbol	Exponent Form	Prefix	SI
1 000 000 000 000 000 000	10^{18}	exa	E
1 000 000 000 000 000	10^{15}	peta	P
1 000 000 000 000	10^{12}	tera	T
1 000 000 000	10^{9}	giga	G
1 000 000	10^{6}	mega	M
1 000	10^{3}	Kilo	k
100	10^{2}	hecto	h
10	10^{1}	deca	da
0.1	10^{-1}	deci	d
0.01	10^{-2}	centi	c
0.001	10^{-3}	milli	m
0.000 001	10^{-6}	micro	m
0.000 000 001	10^{-9}	nano	n
0.000 000 000 001	10^{-12}	pico	p
0.000 000 000 000 001	10^{-15}	femto	f
0.000 000 000 000 000 001	10^{-18}	atto	a

Powers of 2

n	2^n	Hexadecimal
0	1	1
1	2	2
2	4	4
3	8	8
4	16	10
5	32	20
6	64	40
7	128	80
8	256	100
9	512	200
10	1,024	400
11	2,048	800
12	4,096	1000
13	8,192	2000
14	16,384	4000
15	32,768	8000
16	65,536	10000
17	131,072	20000
18	262,144	40000

n	2^n	Hexadecimal
19	524,288	80000
20	1,048,576	100000
21	2,097,152	200000
22	4,194,304	400000
23	8,388,608	800000
24	16,777,216	1000000
25	33,554,432	2000000
26	67,108,864	4000000
27	134,217,728	8000000
28	268,435,456	10000000
29	536,870,912	20000000
30	1,073,741,824	40000000
31	2,147,483,648	80000000
32	4,294,967,296	100000000
33	8,589,934,592	200000000
34	17,179,869,184	400000000
35	34,359,738,368	800000000
36	68,719,476,736	1000000000
37	137,438,953,472	2000000000
38	274,877,906,944	4000000000
39	549,755,813,888	8000000000
40	1,099,511,627,776	10000000000
41	2,199,023,255,552	20000000000
42	4,398,046,511,104	40000000000
43	8,796,093,022,208	80000000000
44	17,592,186,044,416	100000000000
45	35,184,372,088,832	200000000000
46	70,368,744,177,664	400000000000
47	140,737,488,355,328	800000000000
48	281,474,976,710,656	1000000000000
49	562,949,953,421,312	2000000000000
50	1,125,899,906,842,624	4000000000000
51	2,251,799,813,685,248	8000000000000
52	4,503,599,627,370,496	10000000000000
53	9,007,199,254,740,992	20000000000000
54	18,014,398,509,481,984	40000000000000
55	36,028,797,018,963,968	80000000000000
56	72,057,594,037,927,936	100000000000000
57	144,115,188,075,855,872	200000000000000
58	288,230,376,151,711,744	400000000000000
59	576,460,752,303,423,488	800000000000000
60	1,152,921,504,606,846,976	1000000000000000
61	2,305,843,009,213,693,952	2000000000000000
62	4,611,686,018,427,387,904	4000000000000000
63	9,223,372,036,854,775,808	8000000000000000
64	18,446,744,073,709,551,616	10000000000000000

Chapter 2

DOS Information

Tables 2.1 through 2.3 show all the resident, batch, and tran-
sient DOS commands and in which DOS version they are
supported. If you are responsible for providing technical
support, you should know what DOS commands are available to the users at the other end of the phone. These tables
identify which commands are supported in any version of
DOS released to date.

Table 2.1   Resident DOS Commands

Command Name	1.0	1.1	2.0	2.1	3.0	3.1	3.2	3.3	4.x	5.x	6.x
					DOS Version Number						
CD/CHDIR			×	×	×	×	×	×	×	×	×
CHCP								×	×	×	×
CLS			×	×	×	×	×	×	×	×	×
COPY	×	×	×	×	×	×	×	×	×	×	×
CTTY			×	×	×	×	×	×	×	×	×
DATE			×	×	×	×	×	×	×	×	×
DEL/ERASE	×	×	×	×	×	×	×	×	×	×	×
DIR	×	×	×	×	×	×	×	×	×	×	×
EXIT			×	×	×	×	×	×	×	×	×
EXPAND										×	×
Loadhigh/LH										×	×
MD/MKDIR			×	×	×	×	×	×	×	×	×
PATH			×	×	×	×	×	×	×	×	×
PROMPT			×	×	×	×	×	×	×	×	×
RD/RMDIR			×	×	×	×	×	×	×	×	×
REN/RENAME	×	×	×	×	×	×	×	×	×	×	×
SET			×	×	×	×	×	×	×	×	×
TIME	×	×	×	×	×	×	×	×	×	×	×
TYPE	×	×	×	×	×	×	×	×	×	×	×
VER				×	×	×	×	×	×	×	×
VERIFY			×	×	×	×	×	×	×	×	×
VOL			×	×	×	×	×	×	×	×	×

Table 2.2 DOS Batch File Commands

Command Name	DOS Version Number										
	1.0	1.1	2.0	2.1	3.0	3.1	3.2	3.3	4.x	5.x	6.x
CALL								X	X	X	X
ECHO	X	X	X	X	X	X	X	X	X	X	X
FOR	X	X	X	X	X	X	X	X	X	X	X
GOTO	X	X	X	X	X	X	X	X	X	X	X
IF	X	X	X	X	X	X	X	X	X	X	X
PAUSE	X	X	X	X	X	X	X	X	X	X	X
REM	X	X	X	X	X	X	X	X	X	X	X
SHIFT	X	X	X	X	X	X	X	X	X	X	X

Table 2.3 Transient DOS Commands

Command Name	DOS Version Number										
	1.0	1.1	2.0	2.1	3.0	3.1	3.2	3.3	4.x	5.x	6.x
APPEND								X	X	X	X
ASSIGN			X	X	X	X	X	X	X	X	X
ATTRIB					X	X	X	X	X	X	X
BACKUP			X	X	X	X	X	X	X	X	X
BASIC	X	X	X	X	X	X	X	X	X	X	X
BASICA	X	X	X	X	X	X	X	X	X	X	X
CHCP								X	X	X	X

(continues)

Table 2.3   Continued

Command Name	DOS Version Number

Command Name	1.0	1.1	2.0	2.1	3.0	3.1	3.2	3.3	4.x	5.x	6.x
CHKDSK	X	X	X	X	X	X	X	X	X	X	X
COMMAND	X		X	X	X	X	X	X	X	X	X
COMP	X	X	X	X	X	X	X	X	X	X	X
DEBUG	X	X	X	X	X	X	X	X	X	X	X
DISKCOMP	X	X	X	X	X	X	X	X	X	X	X
DISKCOPY	X	X	X	X	X	X	X	X	X	X	X
DOSKEY										X	X
DOSSHELL									X	X	X
EDIT										X	X
EDLIN	X	X	X	X	X	X	X	X	X	X	X
EMM386										X	X
EXE2BIN			X	X	X	X	X	X	X	X	X
FASTOPEN								X	X	X	X
FC								X	X	X	X
FDISK			X	X	X	X	X	X	X	X	X
FIND			X	X	X	X	X	X	X	X	X
FORMAT	X	X	X	X	X	X	X	X	X	X	X
GRAFTABL					X	X	X	X	X	X	X
GRAPHICS			X	X	X	X	X	X	X	X	X
HELP										X	X
JOIN						X	X	X	X		
KEYB								X	X	X	X
KEYBFR					X	X	X				
KEYBGR					X	X	X				

Command Name	DOS Version Number										
	1.0	1.1	2.0	2.1	3.0	3.1	3.2	3.3	4.x	5.x	6.x
KEYBIT					X	X	X				
KEYBSP					X	X	X				
KEYBUK					X	X	X				
LABEL								X	X	X	X
LIB	X	X	X	X	X	X	X				
LINK	X	X	X	X	X	X	X				
MEM									X	X	X
MIRROR										X	
MODE	X	X	X	X	X	X	X	X	X	X	X
MORE			X	X	X	X	X	X	X	X	X
NLSFUNC								X	X	X	X
PRINT			X	X	X	X	X	X	X	X	X
QBASIC										X	X
RECOVER			X	X	X	X	X	X	X	X	
REPLACE							X	X	X	X	X
RESTORE			X	X	X	X	X	X	X	X	X
SETVER										X	X
SHARE					X	X	X	X	X	X	X
SORT			X	X	X	X	X	X	X	X	X
SUBST						X	X	X	X	X	X
SYS	X	X	X	X	X	X	X	X	X	X	X
TREE			X	X	X	X	X	X	X	X	X
UNDELETE										X	X
UNFORMAT										X	X
XCOPY							X	X	X	X	X

LIB, LINK, and EXE2BIN are included with the DOS technical-reference manual for DOS versions 3.3 and higher. EXE2BIN is included with DOS 5.0.

DOS History

IBM and MS-DOS 1.x to 3.x Versions

Table 2.4   IBM and MS-DOS 1.x to 3.x Versions

System File Sizes:

DOS Version	File Dates	COMMAND.COM	IO.SYS IBMBIO.COM	MSDOS.SYS IBMDOS.COM
IBM PC 1.0	08-04-81	3,231	1,920	6,400
IBM PC 1.1	05-07-82	4,959	1,920	6,400
IBM PC 2.0	03-08-83	17,792	4,608	17,152
IBM PC 2.1	10-20-83	17,792	4,736	17,024
IBM PC 3.0	08-14-84	22,042	8,964	27,920
IBM PC 3.1	03-07-85	23,210	9,564	27,760
IBM PC 3.2	12-30-85	23,791	16,369	28,477
MS 3.2	07-07-86	23,612	16.138	28,480
IBM PC 3.3	03-17-87	25,307	22,100	30,159
MS 3.3	07-24-87	25,276	22,357	30,128

IBM DOS 4.xx Versions

DOS 4.xx has had many revisions since being introduced in mid-1988. Since the first release, IBM has released different Corrective Service Diskettes (CSDs), which fix a variety of problems with DOS 4. Each CSD is cumulative, which means that the later ones include all previous fixes. Note that these fixes are for IBM DOS and not for any other manfacturer's version.

Table 2.5 shows a summary of the different IBM DOS 4.xx releases and specific information about the system files and shell so you can identify the release you are using. To obtain the latest Corrective Service Diskettes (CSD) that update you to the latest release, contact your dealer—the fixes are free.

Table 2.5 IBM DOS 4.xx Releases

File name	Size	Date	Version	SYSLEVEL	Comments
IBMBIO.COM	32810	06/17/88	4.00		Original release
IBMDOS.COM	35984	06/17/88			
COMMAND.COM	37637	06/17/88			
IBMBIO.COM	32816	08/03/88	4.01	CSD UR22624	EMS fixes
IBMDOS.COM	36000	08/03/88			
COMMAND.COM	37637	06/17/88			
IBMBIO.COM	32816	08/03/88	4.01	CSD UR24270	Date change fixed
IBMDOS.COM	36000	11/11/88			
COMMAND.COM	37652	11/11/88			
IBMBIO.COM	33910	04/06/89	4.01	CSD UR25066	Death disk fixed

File name	Size	Date	Version	SYSLEVEL	Comments
IBMDOS.COM	37136	04/06/89			
COMMAND.COM	37652	11/11/88			
IBMBIO.COM	34660	03/20/90	4.01	CSD UR29015	SCSI support added
IBMDOS.COM	37248	02/20/90			
COMMAND.COM	37765	03/20/90			
IBMBIO.COM	34660	04/27/90	4.01	CSD UR31300	HPFS compatibility
IBMDOS.COM	37264	05/21/90			
COMMAND.COM	37765	06/29/90			
IBMBIO.COM	34692	04/08/91	4.01	CSD UR35280	HPFS and CHKDSK
IBMDOS.COM	37280	11/30/90			
COMMAND.COM	37762	09/27/91			

IBM DOS 5.xx Versions

DOS 5.xx has had several revisions following its introduction in mid-1991. Since the first release, IBM has released various Corrective Service Diskettes (CSDs), which fix a variety of problems with DOS 5. Each CSD is cumulative, which means that the later ones include all previous fixes. You should notice that these fixes are for IBM DOS and not any other manufacturer's version. IBM typically provides more support in the way of fixes and updates than any other manufacturer. Notice, also, that IBM now supports the installation of IBM DOS on clone systems.

Table 2.6 shows a summary of the different IBM DOS 5.xx releases and specific information about the system files and shell so that you can identify the release you are using. To obtain the latest Corrective Service Diskettes (CSD) that update you to the latest release, get in touch with your dealer—the fixes are free.

Table 2.6 IBM DOS 5.xx Releases

File name	Size	Date	Version	SYSLEVEL	Comments
IBMBIO.COM	33430	05/09/91	5.00		Original release
IBMDOS.COM	37378	05/09/91			
COMMAND.COM	47987	05/09/91			
IBMBIO.COM	33430	05/09/91	5.00	CSD UR35423	XCOPY fixed
IBMDOS.COM	37378	05/09/91			QEDIT fixed
COMMAND.COM	48005	08/16/91			
IBMBIO.COM	33430	05/09/91	5.00	CSD UR35748	SYS fixed
IBMDOS.COM	37378	05/09/91			
COMMAND.COM	48006	10/25/91			
IBMBIO.COM	33446	11/29/91	5.00	CSD UR35834	EMM386, FORMAT,
IBMDOS.COM	37378	11/29/91			BACKUP fixed
COMMAND.COM	48006	11/29/91			
IBMBIO.COM	33446	02/28/92	5.00.1	CSD UR36603	Many Fixes,
IBMDOS.COM	37378	11/29/91	Rev. A		Clone support,
COMMAND.COM	48006	02/28/92			New retail version
IBMBIO.COM	33446	05/29/92	5.00.1	CSD UR37387	RESTORE,
IBMDOS.COM	37362	05/29/92	Rev. 1		UNDELETE fixed,
COMMAND.COM	48042	09/11/92			>1GB HD fix
IBMBIO.COM	33718	09/01/92	5.02		New retail version
IBMDOS.COM	37362	09/01/92	Rev. 0		Several new
COMMAND.COM	47990	09/01/92			commands added.

IBM and MS-DOS 6.xx Versions

Microsoft and IBM have produced several different versions
of DOS 6.x. The original release of MS-DOS 6.0 came from
Microsoft. One of the features included in MS-DOS 6.0 was
the new DoubleSpace disk compression. Unfortunately,
DoubleSpace had some problems with certain system configurations and hardware types. In the meantime, IBM updated the program to fix several small problems, removed
the disk compression, and sold the program as IBM DOS 6.1.
IBM also selected a different type of compression program.
But the company held off including the program with 6.1
until it was free of problems like DoubleSpace. However, IBM
included a coupon in 6.1 that was good for a free copy of the
compression program after it was fixed. The later versions of
IBM's DOS 6.1 (now called PC DOS 6.1) included the compression software. Also included in the updated 6.1 release
were enhanced PCMCIA commands. Microsoft later released
MS-DOS 6.2 as a free upgrade for MS-DOS 6.0 users. The new
6.2 version had fixes to several programs, especially the
DoubleSpace compression program.

Table 2.7 IBM and Microsoft DOS 6.xx Releases

File name	Size	Date	Version	SYSLEVEL	Comments
IO.SYS	40470	03/10/93	MS		Original Microsoft release
MSDOS.SYS	38138	03/10/93	6.00		
COMMAND.COM	52925	03/10/93	Rev. A		
IBMBIO.COM	40694	06/29/93	IBM		Original IBM release has fixes over MS version
IBMDOS.COM	38138	06/29/93	6.10		
COMMAND.COM	52589	06/29/93	Rev. 0		
IBMBIO.COM	40964	09/30/93	PC		SuperStor/DS compression, enhanced PCMPIA
IBMDOS.COM	38138	09/30/93	6.10		
COMMAND.COM	52797	09/30/93	Rev. 0		
IO.SYS	40566	09/30/93	MS		DoubleSpace fixes Enhanced cleanboot and data recovery
MSDOS.SYS	38138	09/30/93	6.20		
COMMAND.COM	54619	09/30/93	Rev. A		

Chapter 3

System Information

CPU Types and Specifications

Table 3.1   Intel Processor Specifications

Processor	CPU Clock	Internal Register Size	Data Bus Width	Address Bus Width	Integral Cache	Integral FPU	Maximum Memory	No. of Transistors	Date Introduced
8088	1x	16-bit	8-bit	20-bit	-	-	1MB	29,000	Jun. '79
8086	1x	16-bit	16-bit	20-bit	-	-	1MB	29,000	Jun. '78
286	1x	16-bit	16-bit	24-bit	-	-	16MB	130,000	Feb. '82
386 SX	1x	32-bit	16-bit	24-bit	-	-	16MB	275,000	Jun. '88
386 SL	1x	32-bit	16-bit	24-bit	0K	-	16MB	855,000	Oct. '90
386 DX	1x	32-bit	32-bit	32-bit	-	-	4GB	275,000	Oct. '85
486 SX	1x	32-bit	32-bit	32-bit	8K	-	4GB	1,185,000	Apr. '91
487 SX	1x	32-bit	32-bit	32-bit	8K	Yes	4GB	1,200,000	Apr. '91
486 DX	1x	32-bit	32-bit	32-bit	8K	Yes	4GB	1,200,000	Apr. '89
486 SL	1x	32-bit	32-bit	32-bit	8K	Optional	4GB	1,400,000	Nov. '92

Processor	CPU Clock	Internal Register Size	Data Bus Width	Address Bus Width	Integral Cache	Integral FPU	Maximum Memory	No. of Transistors	Date Introduced
486 DX2	2x	32-bit	32-bit	32-bit	8K	Yes	4GB	1,100,000	Mar. '92
Pentium	1x	32-bit	64-bit	32-bit	2x8K	Yes	4GB	3,100,000	May. '93

Note: The 386 SL contains an integral cache controller; however, cache memory is external to the chip.

Table 3.2 IBM Processor Specifications

Processor	CPU Clock	Internal Register Size	Data Bus Width	Address Bus Width	Integral Cache	Integral FPU	Maximum Memory	No. of Transistors	Date Introduced
386 SLC	1x	32-bit	16-bit	24-bit	8K	No	16MB	N/A	Oct. '91
486 SLC	1x	32-bit	16-bit	24-bit	16K	No	16MB	N/A	1992
486 SLC2	2x	32-bit	16-bit	24-bit	16K	No	16MB	N/A	Jun. '92
486 BL2	2x	32-bit	32-bit	32-bit	16K	No	4GB	N/A	1992
486 BL3	3x	32-bit	32-bit	32-bit	16K	No	4GB	N/A	1992

FPU=Floating Point Unit (Math Coprocessor)

Hardware and ROM BIOS Data

This section has an enormous amount of detailed reference information covering a variety of hardware and ROM BIOS topics. These figures and tables cover very useful information, such as IBM PC and XT motherboard switch settings (see fig. 3.1), AT CMOS RAM addresses, and diagnostic status-byte information. This section also has a variety of other hardware information, such as BIOS version data, keyboard scan codes, and a great deal of information about the expansion buses—pinouts, resources such as interrupts, DMA channels, and I/O port addresses. Finally, this section has a number of connector pinouts for serial, parallel, keyboard, video, and other connectors.

IBM PC and XT Motherboard Switch Settings

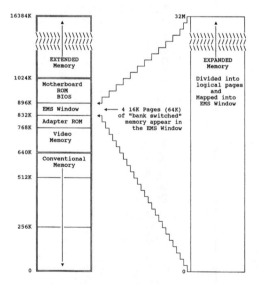

Fig. 3.1 IBM PC and XT motherboard switch settings.

AT CMOS RAM Addresses

Table 3.3 shows the information maintained in the 64-byte AT CMOS RAM module. This information controls the configuration of the system much like the switches control the PC and XT configurations. This memory is read and written by the system SETUP program.

Table 3.3 AT CMOS RAM Addresses

Offset Hex	Offset Dec	Field size	Function
00h	0	1 byte	Current second in binary coded decimal (BCD)
01h	1	1 byte	Alarm second in BCD
02h	2	1 byte	Current minute in BCD
03h	3	1 byte	Alarm minute in BCD
04h	4	1 byte	Current hour in BCD
05h	5	1 byte	Alarm hour in BCD
06h	6	1 byte	Current day of week in BCD
07h	7	1 byte	Current day in BCD
08h	8	1 byte	Current month in BCD
09h	9	1 byte	Current year in BCD

Offset Hex	Offset Dec	Field size	Function

0Ah	10	1 byte	Status register A
			Bit 7 = Update in progress
			    0 = Date and time can be read
			    1 = Time update in progress
			Bits 6-4 = Time frequency divider
			    010 = 32.768KHz
			Bits 3-0 = Rate selection frequency
			    0110 = 1.024KHz square wave frequency

0Bh	11	1 byte	Status register B
			Bit 7 = Clock update cycle
			    0 = Update normally
			    1 = Abort update in progress
			Bit 6 = Periodic interrupt
			    0 = Disable interrupt (default)
			    1 = Enable interrupt
			Bit 5 = Alarm interrupt
			    0 = Disable interrupt (default)
			    0 = Disable interrupt (default)
			    1 = Enable interrupt
			Bit 4 = Update-ended interrupt
			    0 = Disable interrupt (default)
			    1 = Enable interrupt
			Bit 3 = Status register A square wave frequency
			    0 = Disable square wave (default)
			    1 = Enable square wave

(continues)

Table 3.3 Continued

Offset Hex	Offset Dec	Field size	Function
			Bit 2 = Date format
			0 = Calendar in BCD format (default)
			1 = Calendar in binary format
			Bit 1 = 24-hour clock
			0 = 24-hour mode (default)
			1 = 12-hour mode
			Bit 0 = Daylight Savings Time
			0 = Disable Daylight Savings (default)
			1 = Enable Daylight Savings
0Ch	12	1 byte	Status register C
			Bit 7 = IRQF flag
			Bit 6 = PF flag
			Bit 5 = AF flag
			Bit 4 = UF flag
			Bits 3-0 = Reserved
0Dh	13	1 byte	Status register D
			Bit 7 = Valid CMOS RAM bit
			0 = CMOS battery dead
			1 = CMOS battery power good
			Bits 6-0 = Reserved

Offset Hex	Offset Dec	Field size	Function

0Eh	14	1 byte	Diagnostic status
			Bit 7 = Real-time clock power status
			    0 = CMOS *has not* lost power
			    1 = CMOS *has* lost power
			Bit 6 = CMOS checksum status
			    0 = Checksum is good
			    1 = Checksum is bad
			
			Bit 5 = POST configuration information status
			    0 = Configuration information is valid
			    1 = Configuration information is invalid
			Bit 4 = Memory size compare during POST
			    0 = POST memory equals configuration
			    1 = POST memory *not equal* to configuration
			Bit 3 = Fixed disk/adapter initialization
			    0 = Initialization good
			    1 = Initialization failed
			Bit 2 = CMOS time status indicator
			    0 = Time is valid
			    1 = Time is Invalid
			Bits 1-0 = Reserved

(continues)

Table 3.3 Continued

Offset Hex	Offset Dec	Field size	Function
0Fh	15	1 byte	Shutdown code 00h = Power on or soft reset 01h = Memory size pass 02h = Memory test pass 03h = Memory test fail 04h = POST end; boot system 05h = JMP double word pointer with EOI 06h = Protected mode tests pass 07h = Protected mode tests fail 07h = Protected mode tests fail 08h = Memory size fail 09h = Int 15h block move 0Ah = JMP double word pointer without EOI 0Bh = used by 80386
10h	16	1 byte	Floppy disk drive types Bits 7-4 = Drive 0 type Bits 3-0 = Drive 1 type 0000 = None 0001 = 360K 0010 = 1.2M 0011 = 720K 0100 = 1.44M

Offset Hex	Offset Dec	Field size	Function
11h	17	1 byte	Reserved
12h	18	1 byte	Hard disk types Bits 7-4 = Hard disk 0 type (0-15) Bits 3-0 = Hard disk 1 type (0-15)
13h	19	1 byte	Reserved
14h	20	1 byte	Installed equipment Bits 7-6 = Number of floppy disk drives 00 = 1 floppy disk drive 01 = 2 floppy disk drives Bits 5-4 = Primary display 00 = Use display adapter BIOS 01 = CGA 40-column 10 = CGA 80-column 11 = Monochrome Display Adapter Bits 3-2 = Reserved Bit 1 = Math coprocessor present Bit 0 = Floppy disk drive present
15h	21	1 byte	Base memory low-order byte

(continues)

Table 3.3 Continued

Offset Hex	Offset Dec	Field size	Function
16h	22	1 byte	Base memory high-order byte
17h	23	1 byte	Extended memory low-order byte
18h	24	1 byte	Extended memory high-order byte
19h	25	1 byte	Hard Disk 0 Extended Type (0-255)
1Ah	26	1 byte	Hard Disk 1 Extended Type (0-255)
1Bh	27	9 bytes	Reserved
2Eh	46	1 byte	CMOS checksum high-order byte
2Fh	47	1 byte	CMOS checksum low-order byte

Offset Hex	Offset Dec	Field size	Function
30h	48	1 byte	Actual extended memory low-order byte
31h	49	1 byte	Actual extended memory high-order byte
32h	50	1 byte	Date century in BCD

33h	51	1 byte	POST information flag
			Bit 7 = Top 128K base memory status
			  0 = Top 128K base memory not installed
			  1 = Top 128K base memory installed
			Bit 6 = Setup program flag
			  0 = Normal (default)
			  1 = Put out first user message
			Bits 5-0 = Reserved

34h	52	2 bytes	Reserved

Table 3.4 shows the values that may be stored by your system BIOS in a special CMOS byte called the *diagnostics status byte*. By examining this location with a diagnostics program, you can determine whether your system has set "trouble codes," which indicate that a problem previously has occurred.

Table 3.4   CMOS RAM (AT and PS/2) Diagnostic Status Byte Codes

Bit number 7 6 5 4 3 2 1 0	Hex	Function
1	80	Real-time clock (RTC) chip lost power
. 1	40	CMOS RAM checksum is bad
. . 1	20	Invalid configuration information found at POST
. . . 1	10	Memory size compare error at POST
. . . . 1 . . .	08	Fixed disk or adapter failed initialization
. . . . . 1 . .	04	Real-time clock (RTC) time found invalid
. . . . . . 1 .	02	Adapters do not match configuration
. . . . 1	01	Time-out reading an adapter ID
. . . .	00	No errors found (Normal)

IBM BIOS Model, Submodel and Revision Codes

Table 3.5 shows information about the different ROM BIOS versions that have appeared in various IBM systems.

The ID byte, Submodel byte, and Revision numbers are in hexadecimal.

—	=	This feature is not supported.
None	=	Only SCSI drives are supported.
?	=	Information unavailable.

IBM BIOS Model, Submodel and Revision Codes

Table 3.5 IBM BIOS Model, Submodel, and Revision Codes			
System description	CPU	Clock speed	Bus type/width
PC	8088	4.77 MHz	ISA/8
PC	8088	4.77 MHz	ISA/8
PC	8088	4.77 MHz	ISA/8
PC-XT	8088	4.77 MHz	ISA/8
PC-XT	8088	4.77 MHz	ISA/8
PC-XT	8088	4.77 MHz	ISA/8
PC*jr*	8088	4.77 MHz	ISA/8
PC Convertible	80C8	4.77 MHz	ISA/8
PS/2 25	8086	8 MHz	ISA/8
PS/2 30	8086	8 MHz	ISA/8
PS/2 30	8086	8 MHz	ISA/8
PS/2 30	8086	8 MHz	ISA/8
PC-AT	286	6 MHz	ISA/16
PC-AT	286	6 MHz	ISA/16
PC-AT	286	8 MHz	ISA/16
PC-XT 286	286	6 MHz	ISA/16
PS/1	286	10 MHz	ISA/16
PS/2 25 286	286	10 MHz	ISA/16
PS/2 30 286	286	10 MHz	ISA/16
PS/2 30 286	286	10 MHz	ISA/16
PS/2 35 SX	386SX	20 MHz	ISA/16
PS/2 35 SX	386SX	20 MHz	ISA/16
PS/2 40 SX	386SX	20 MHz	ISA/16
PS/2 40 SX	386SX	20 MHz	ISA/16
PS/2 L40 SX	386SX	20 MHz	ISA/16
PS/2 50	286	10 MHz	MCA/16
PS/2 50	286	10 MHz	MCA/16

ROM BIOS date	ID byte	Sub-model byte	Rev.	ST506 drive types
04/24/81	FF	—	—	—
10/19/81	FF	—	—	—
10/27/82	FF	—	—	—
11/08/82	FE	—	—	—
01/10/86	FB	00	01	—
05/09/86	FB	00	02	—
06/01/83	FD	—	—	—
09/13/85	F9	00	00	—
06/26/87	FA	01	00	26
09/02/86	FA	00	00	26
12/12/86	FA	00	01	26
02/05/87	FA	00	02	26
01/10/84	FC	—	—	15
06/10/85	FC	00	01	23
11/15/85	FC	01	00	23
04/21/86	FC	02	00	24
12/01/89	FC	0B	00	44
06/28/89	FC	09	02	37
08/25/88	FC	09	00	37
06/28/89	FC	09	02	37
03/15/91	F8	19	05	37
04/04/91	F8	19	06	37
03/15/91	F8	19	05	37
04/04/91	F8	19	06	37
02/27/91	F8	23	02	37
02/13/87	FC	04	00	32
05/09/87	FC	04	01	32

(continues)

Table 3.5   Continued

PS/2 50Z	286	10 MHz	MCA/16
PS/2 50Z	286	10 MHz	MCA/16
PS/2 55 SX	386SX	16 MHz	MCA/16
PS/2 55 LS	386SX	16 MHz	MCA/16
PS/2 57 SX	386SX	20 MHz	MCA/16
PS/2 60	286	10 MHz	MCA/16
PS/2 65 SX	386SX	16 MHz	MCA/16
PS/2 70 386	386DX	16 MHz	MCA/32
PS/2 70 386	386DX	16 MHz	MCA/32
PS/2 70 386	386DX	16 MHz	MCA/32
PS/2 70 386	386DX	20 MHz	MCA/32
PS/2 70 386	386DX	20 MHz	MCA/32
PS/2 70 386	386DX	20 MHz	MCA/32
PS/2 70 386	386DX	25 MHz	MCA/32
PS/2 70 386	386DX	25 MHz	MCA/32
PS/2 70 486	486DX	25 MHz	MCA/32
PS/2 70 486	486DX	25 MHz	MCA/32
PS/2 P70 386	386DX	16 MHz	MCA/32
PS/2 P70 386	386DX	20 MHz	MCA/32
PS/2 P75 486	486DX	33 MHz	MCA/32
PS/2 80 386	386DX	16 MHz	MCA/32
PS/2 80 386	386DX	20 MHz	MCA/32
PS/2 80 386	386DX	25 MHz	MCA/32
PS/2 90 XP 486	486SX	20 MHz	MCA/32
PS/2 90 XP 486	487SX	20 MHz	MCA/32
PS/2 90 XP 486	486DX	25 MHz	MCA/32
PS/2 90 XP 486	486DX	33 MHz	MCA/32
PS/2 90 XP 486	486DX	50 MHz	MCA/32
PS/2 95 XP 486	486SX	20 MHz	MCA/32
PS/2 95 XP 486	487SX	20 MHz	MCA/32
PS/2 95 XP 486	486DX	25 MHz	MCA/32

01/28/88	FC	04	02	33
04/18/88	FC	04	03	33
11/02/88	F8	0C	00	33
?	F8	1E	00	33
07/03/91	F8	26	02	None
02/13/87	FC	05	00	32
02/08/90	F8	1C	00	33
01/29/88	F8	09	00	33
04/11/88	F8	09	02	33
12/15/89	F8	09	04	33
01/29/88	F8	04	00	33
04/11/88	F8	04	02	33
12/15/89	F8	04	04	33
06/08/88	F8	0D	00	33
02/20/89	F8	0D	01	33
12/01/89	F8	0D	?	?
09/29/89	F8	1B	00	?
?	F8	50	00	?
01/18/89	F8	0B	00	33
10/05/90	F8	52	00	33
03/30/87	F8	00	00	32
10/07/87	F8	01	00	32
11/21/89	F8	80	01	?
?	F8	2D	00	?
?	F8	2F	00	?
?	F8	11	00	?
?	F8	13	00	?
?	F8	2B	00	?
?	F8	2C	00	?
?	F8	2E	00	?
?	F8	14	00	?

System Memory

The following maps show where memory is located logically within a system. The first map shows the standard processor-addressable memory in real and/or protected mode. The second map shows how expanded memory fits into the reserved space between 640K and 1M, and how it is not directly addressable by the processor. Expanded memory can be addressed only a small piece (*page*) at a time through a small window of memory. These maps can be useful for mapping out the logical locations of any adapter in your system. All memory locations must be uniquely supplied by a single device; the potential for conflicts does exist if two devices are mapped into the same logical locations.

16-Megabyte Memory Map

The following map shows the logical address locations for an IBM-compatible system. If the processor is running in Real Mode, then only the first megabyte would be accessible. If the processor is in Protected Mode, then the full 16M would be accessible. Notice that while this map shows 16M, 386DX and higher, processors can actually access up to 4,096M in Protected Mode.

. = Program-accessible memory (standard RAM)

G = Graphics Mode Video RAM

M= Monochrome Text Mode Video RAM

C = Color Text Mode Video RAM

V = Video ROM BIOS (would be "a" in PS/2)

a = Adapter board ROM and special-purpose RAM

r = Additional PS/2 Motherboard ROM BIOS (unused in non-PS/2 systems)

R = Motherboard ROM BIOS

b = IBM Cassette BASIC (would be "R" in IBM
    compatibles)

h = High memory area (HMA), if HIMEM.SYS is loaded

Conventional (Base) Memory:

```
      : 0---1---2---3---4---5---6---7---8---9---A---B---C---D---E---F----
000000: ................................................................
010000: .....                          .....................
020000: ................................................................
030000: ................................................................
040000: ................................................................
050000: ................................................................
060000: ................................................................
070000: ................................................................
080000: ................................................................
090000: ................................................................
```

Upper Memory Area (UMA):

```
      : 0---1---2---3---4---5---6---7---8---9---A---B---C---D---E---F----
0A0000: GGGGGGGGGGGGGGGGGGGGGGGGGGGGGGGGGGGGGGGGGGGGGGGGGGGGGGGGGGGGGGGGG
0B0000: MMMMMMMMMMMMMMMMMMMMMMMMMMMMMMMMMMMCCCCCCCCCCCCCCCCCCCCCCCCCCCCCCCC
```

```
      : 0---1---2---3---4---5---6---7---8---9---A---B---C---D---E---F----
0C0000: VVVVVVVVVVVVVVVVVVVVVVVVVVVVVVVVVaaaaaaaaaaaaaaaaaaaaaaaaaaaaaaaaa
0D0000: aaaaaaaaaaaaaaaaaaaaaaaaaaaaaaaaaaaaaaaaaaaaaaaaaaaaaaaaaaaaaaaaa
```

```
      : 0---1---2---3---4---5---6---7---8---9---A---B---C---D---E---F----
0E0000: rrrrrrrrrrrrrrrrrrrrrrrrrrrrrrrrrrrrrrrrrrrrrrrrrrrrrrrrrrrrrrrrrr
0F0000: RRRRRRRRRRRRRRRRRRRRRRRRRRRbbbbbbbbbbbbbbbbbbbbbbbbbbbbbbbbRRRRRRRR
```

Extended Memory:

```
      : 0---1---2---3---4---5---6---7---8---9---A---B---C---D---E---F----
100000: hhhhhhhhhhhhhhhhhhhhhhhhhhhhhhhhhhhhhhhhhhhhhhhhhhhhhhhhhhhhhhhhhh
```

Extended Memory Specification (XMS) Memory:

```
110000: ..........................................................
120000: ..........................................................
130000: ..........................................................
140000: ..........................................................
150000: ..........................................................
160000: ..........................................................
170000: ..........................................................
180000: ..........................................................
190000: ..........................................................
1A0000: ..........................................................
1B0000: ..........................................................
1C0000: ..........................................................
1D0000: ..........................................................
1E0000: ..........................................................
1F0000: ..........................................................
      : 0---1---2---3---4---5---6---7---8---9---A---B---C---D---E---F---
200000: ..........................................................
210000: ..........................................................
220000: ..........................................................
230000: ..........................................................
240000: ..........................................................
250000: ..........................................................
260000: ..........................................................
270000: ..........................................................
280000: ..........................................................
290000: ..........................................................
2A0000: ..........................................................
2B0000: ..........................................................
2C0000: ..........................................................
2D0000: ..........................................................
2E0000: ..........................................................
2F0000: ..........................................................
      : 0---1---2---3---4---5---6---7---8---9---A---B---C---D---E---F---
300000: ..........................................................
310000: ..........................................................
320000: ..........................................................
330000: ..........................................................
340000: ..........................................................
350000: ..........................................................
360000: ..........................................................
370000: ..........................................................
380000: ..........................................................
390000: ..........................................................
3A0000: ..........................................................
3B0000: ..........................................................
3C0000: ..........................................................
3D0000: ..........................................................
3E0000: ..........................................................
3F0000: ..........................................................
      : 0---1---2---3---4---5---6---7---8---9---A---B---C---D---E---F---
```

```
400000:  ................................................................
410000:  ................................................................
420000:  ................................................................
430000:  ................................................................
440000:  ................................................................
450000:  ................................................................
460000:  ................................................................
470000:  ................................................................
480000:  ................................................................
490000:  ................................................................
4A0000:  ................................................................
4B0000:  ................................................................
4C0000:  ................................................................
4D0000:  ................................................................
4E0000:  ................................................................
4F0000:  ................................................................
      :  0---1---2---3---4---5---6---7---8---9---A---B---C---D---E---F----
500000:  ................................................................
510000:  ................................................................
520000:  ................................................................
530000:  ................................................................
540000:  ................................................................
550000:  ................................................................
560000:  ................................................................
570000:  ................................................................
580000:  ................................................................
590000:  ................................................................
5A0000:  ................................................................
5B0000:  ................................................................
5C0000:  ................................................................
5D0000:  ................................................................
5E0000:  ................................................................
5F0000:  ................................................................
      :  0---1---2---3---4---5---6---7---8---9---A---B---C---D---E---F----
600000:  ................................................................
610000:  ................................................................
620000:  ................................................................
630000:  ................................................................
640000:  ................................................................
650000:  ................................................................
660000:  ................................................................
670000:  ................................................................
680000:  ................................................................
690000:  ................................................................
6A0000:  ................................................................
6B0000:  ................................................................
6C0000:  ................................................................
6D0000:  ................................................................
6E0000:  ................................................................
6F0000:  ................................................................
```

```
        : 0---1---2---3---4---5---6---7---8---9---A---B---C---D---E---F----
700000: ................................................................
710000: ................................................................
720000: ................................................................
730000: ................................................................
740000: ................................................................
750000: ................................................................
760000: ................................................................
770000: ................................................................
780000: ................................................................
790000: ................................................................
7A0000: ................................................................
7B0000: ................................................................
7C0000: ................................................................
7D0000: ................................................................
7E0000: ................................................................
7F0000: ................................................................
        : 0---1---2---3---4---5---6---7---8---9---A---B---C---D---E---F----
800000: ................................................................
810000: ................................................................
820000: ................................................................
830000: ................................................................
840000: ................................................................
850000: ................................................................
860000: ................................................................
870000: ................................................................
880000: ................................................................
890000: ................................................................
8A0000: ................................................................
8B0000: ................................................................
8C0000: ................................................................
8D0000: ................................................................
8E0000: ................................................................
8F0000: ................................................................
        : 0---1---2---3---4---5---6---7---8---9---A---B---C---D---E---F----
900000: ................................................................
910000: ................................................................
920000: ................................................................
930000: ................................................................
940000: ................................................................
950000: ................................................................
960000: ................................................................
970000: ................................................................
980000: ................................................................
990000: ................................................................
9A0000: ................................................................
9B0000: ................................................................
9C0000: ................................................................
9D0000: ................................................................
9E0000: ................................................................
9F0000: ................................................................
```

```
        : 0---1---2---3---4---5---6---7---8---9---A---B---C---D---E---F----
A00000: ................................................................
A10000: ................................................................
A20000: ................................................................
A30000: ................................................................
A40000: ................................................................
A50000: ................................................................
A60000: ................................................................
A70000: ................................................................
A80000: ................................................................
A90000: ................................................................
AA0000: ................................................................
AB0000: ................................................................
AC0000: ................................................................
AD0000: ................................................................
AE0000: ................................................................
AF0000: ................................................................
        : 0---1---2---3---4---5---6---7---8---9---A---B---C---D---E---F----
B00000: ................................................................
B10000: ................................................................
B20000: ................................................................
B30000: ................................................................
B40000: ................................................................
B50000: ................................................................
B60000: ................................................................
B70000: ................................................................
B80000: ................................................................
B90000: ................................................................
BA0000: ................................................................
BB0000: ................................................................
BC0000: ................................................................
BD0000: ................................................................
BE0000: ................................................................
BF0000: ................................................................
        : 0---1---2---3---4---5---6---7---8---9---A---B---C---D---E---F----
C00000: ................................................................
C10000: ................................................................
C20000: ................................................................
C30000: ................................................................
C40000: ................................................................
C50000: ................................................................
C60000: ................................................................
C70000: ................................................................
C80000: ................................................................
C90000: ................................................................
CA0000: ................................................................
CB0000: ................................................................
CC0000: ................................................................
CD0000: ................................................................
CE0000: ................................................................
CF0000: ................................................................
```

```
        : 0---1---2---3---4---5---6---7---8---9---A---B---C---D---E---F----
D00000: ................................................................
D10000: ................................................................
D20000: ................................................................
D30000: ................................................................
D40000: ................................................................
D50000: ................................................................
D60000: ................................................................
D70000: ................................................................
D80000: ................................................................
D90000: ................................................................
DA0000: ................................................................
DB0000: ................................................................
DC0000: ................................................................
DD0000: ................................................................
DE0000: ................................................................
DF0000: ................................................................
        : 0---1---2---3---4---5---6---7---8---9---A---B---C---D---E---F----
E00000: ................................................................
E10000: ................................................................
E20000: ................................................................
E30000: ................................................................
E40000: ................................................................
E50000: ................................................................
E60000: ................................................................
E70000: ................................................................
E80000: ................................................................
E90000: ................................................................
EA0000: ................................................................
EB0000: ................................................................
EC0000: ................................................................
ED0000: ................................................................
EE0000: ................................................................
EF0000: ................................................................
        : 0---1---2---3---4---5---6---7---8---9---A---B---C---D---E---F----
F00000: ................................................................
F10000: ................................................................
F20000: ................................................................
F30000: ................................................................
F40000: ................................................................
F50000: ................................................................
F60000: ................................................................
F70000: ................................................................
F80000: ................................................................
F90000: ................................................................
FA0000: ................................................................
FB0000: ................................................................
FC0000: ................................................................
FD0000: ................................................................
FE0000: ................................................................
FF0000: ................................................................
```

Expanded Memory

The map in figure 3.2 shows how expanded memory fits with conventional and extended memory.

A. IBM PC and XT Motherboard Switch Settings

SWITCH BLOCK 1 (PC and XT)			SWITCH BLOCK 2 (PC only)

Switch Block #1
1 2 34 56 78

```
         NO. FLOPPY DRIVES:
         11 = 1 floppy drive
         01 = 2 floppy drives
         10 = 3 floppy drives
         00 = 4 floppy drives

      VIDEO ADAPTER:
      00 = Monochrome Display Adapter
      01 = Color Graphics Adapter - 40x25
      10 = Color Graphics Adapter - 80x25
      11 = Video Adapter w/onboard BIOS

    FILLED MOTHERBOARD MEMORY BANKS:
    11 = Bank 0 only
    01 = Banks 0 and 1
    10 = Banks 0, 1 and 2
    00 = All 4 Banks

   MATH CO-PROCESSOR:
   0 = Installed
   1 = Not Installed

  IBM PC:
  0 = Boot From Floppy Drive
  1 = Do Not Boot From Floppy Drive

  IBM XT:
  0 = Normal POST (Power-On Self Test)
  1 = Continuous Looping POST
```

Total Memory (K)	Switch Block #2 1	2	3	4	5	6	7	8
16	1	1	1	1	1	0	0	0
32	1	1	1	1	0	0	0	0
48	1	1	1	1	0	0	0	0
64	1	1	1	1	0	0	0	0
96	0	1	1	1	0	0	0	0
128	1	0	1	1	1	0	0	0
160	0	0	1	1	1	0	0	0
192	1	1	0	1	1	0	0	0
224	0	1	0	1	1	0	0	0
256	1	0	0	1	1	0	0	0
288	0	0	0	1	1	0	0	0
320	1	1	1	0	1	0	0	0
352	0	1	1	0	1	0	0	0
384	1	0	1	0	1	0	0	0
416	0	0	1	0	1	0	0	0
448	1	1	0	0	1	0	0	0
480	0	1	0	0	1	0	0	0
512	1	0	0	0	1	0	0	0
544	0	0	0	0	1	0	0	0
576	1	1	1	1	0	0	0	0
608	0	1	1	1	0	0	0	0
640	1	0	1	1	0	0	0	0

LEGEND:
0 = Off
1 = On

Fig. 3.2   The relationship between conventional, extended, and expanded memory.

Memory SIMMs

SIMM Types

With regard to the interface, PC systems today contain the following two main types of SIMMs (Single Inline Memory Modules):

- 9-Bit (30-Pin) SIMMs

- 36-Bit (72-Pin) SIMMs

Two different styles of 9-bit (30-pin) SIMMs are available: an industry standard version used by most PC compatible systems, and a version used by IBM in some of the older PS/2 systems. The IBM 9-bit variant is no longer used by IBM. Instead, it uses only industry standard 36-bit (72-pin) SIMMs.

The 36-bit (72-pin) SIMMs are available in one common connector type, which is an industry standard. These SIMMs are vastly preferred over the 9-bit variety, because 36-bit SIMMs contain an entire bank of memory for a 32-bit system (32 data bits plus 4 parity bits). This means that in most 386, 486, or Pentium systems, these SIMMs can be installed or removed one at a time (unlike the 9-bit SIMMs, which must be used in groups of 4 to make up a full bank in a 32-bit system). This makes the 9-bit SIMMs clumsy and much more difficult to work with, plus they take up much more motherboard real estate. I recommend purchasing systems today that use only the 36-bit SIMMs.

Notice that some low-end systems use versions of SIMMs that do not contain parity bits. These SIMMs would be known as 8-bit (30-pin) and 32-bit (72-pin) SIMMs. Systems that use SIMMs without parity must disable parity checking or errors will result. I do not recommend running PC systems without parity-checked memory.

SIMM Interface Connectors

The following tables show the interface connector pinouts for both 9-bit (30-pin) varieties, and the standard 36-bit SIMM. Also included is a special presence detect table that shows the configuration of the presence detect pins on various 36-bit SIMMs. The presence detect pins are used by the motherboard to detect exactly what size and speed SIMM is installed. Industry standard 9-bit SIMMs do not have a presence detect feature.

Table 3.6   Industry Standard and IBM 30-Pin (9-bit) SIMM Pinouts***

Pin	Standard SIMM Signal Names	IBM SIMM Signal Names
1	+5 Vdc	+5 Vdc
2	Column Address Strobe	Column Address Strobe
3	Data Bit 0	Data Bit 0
4	Address Bit 0	Address Bit 0
5	Address Bit 1	Address Bit 1
6	Data Bit 1	Data Bit 1
7	Address Bit 2	Address Bit 2
8	Address Bit 3	Address Bit 3
9	Ground	Ground
10	Data Bit 2	Data Bit 2
11	Address Bit 4	Address Bit 4
12	Address Bit 5	Address Bit 5
13	Data Bit 3	Data Bit 3
14	Address Bit 6	Address Bit 6
15	Address Bit 7	Address Bit 7
16	Data Bit 4	Data Bit 4
17	Address Bit 8	Address Bit 8
18	Address Bit 9	Address Bit 9
19	Address Bit 10	Row Address Strobe 1
20	Data Bit 5	Data Bit 5
21	Write Enable	Write Enable
22	Ground	Ground
23	Data Bit 6	Data Bit 6
24	No Connection	Presence Detect (Ground)
25	Data Bit 7	Data Bit 7
26	Data Bit 8 (Parity) Out	Presence Detect (1M = Ground)
27	Row Address Strobe	Row Address Strobe
28	Column Address Strobe Parity	No Connection
29	Data Bit 8 (Parity) In	Data Bit 8 (Parity) I/O
30	+5 Vdc	+5 Vdc

Table 3.7   Standard 72-Pin (36-bit) SIMM Pinout***

Pin	SIMM Signal Name
1	Ground
2	Data Bit 0
3	Data Bit 16
4	Data Bit 1
5	Data Bit 17
6	Data Bit 2
7	Data Bit 18
8	Data Bit 3
9	Data Bit 18
10	+5 Vdc
11	Column Address Strobe Parity
12	Address Bit 0
13	Address Bit 1
14	Address Bit 2
15	Address Bit 3
16	Address Bit 4
17	Address Bit 5
18	Address Bit 6
19	Reserved
20	Data Bit 4
21	Data Bit 20
22	Data Bit 5
23	Data Bit 21
24	Data Bit 6
25	Data Bit 22
26	Data Bit 7
27	Data Bit 23
28	Address Bit 7
29	Block Select 0
30	+5 Vdc
31	Address Bit 8
32	Address Bit 9
33	Row Address Strobe 3
34	Row Address Strobe 2
35	Parity Data Bit 2
36	Parity Data Bit 0
37	Parity Data Bit 1
38	Parity Data Bit 3
39	Ground
40	Column Address Strobe 0
41	Column Address Strobe 2
42	Column Address Strobe 3
43	Column Address Strobe 1
44	Row Address Strobe 0
45	Row Address Strobe 1
46	Block Select 1
47	Write Enable
48	Reserved
49	Data Bit 8
50	Data Bit 24
51	Data Bit 9
52	Data Bit 25
53	Data Bit 10
54	Data Bit 26
55	Data Bit 11
56	Data Bit 27

Pin	SIMM Signal Name
57	Data Bit 12
58	Data Bit 28
59	+5 Vdc
60	Data Bit 29
61	Data Bit 13
62	Data Bit 30
63	Data Bit 14
64	Data Bit 31
65	Data Bit 15
66	Block Select 2
67	Presence Detect Bit 0
68	Presence Detect Bit 1
69	Presence Detect Bit 2
70	Presence Detect Bit 3
71	Block Select 3
72	Ground

Table 3.8 72-Pin (36-bit) SIMM Presence Detect Pins

70	69	68	67	SIMM Type	IBM Part Number
N/C	N/C	N/C	N/C	Not a valid SIMM	N/A
N/C	N/C	N/C	Gnd	1 MB 120ns	N/A
N/C	N/C	Gnd	N/C	2 MB 120ns	N/A
N/C	N/C	Gnd	Gnd	2 MB 70ns	92F0102
N/C	Gnd	N/C	N/C	8 MB 70ns	64F3606
N/C	Gnd	N/C	Gnd	Reserved	N/A
N/C	Gnd	Gnd	N/C	2 MB 80ns	92F0103
N/C	Gnd	Gnd	Gnd	8 MB 80ns	64F3607
Gnd	N/C	N/C	N/C	Reserved	N/A
Gnd	N/C	N/C	Gnd	1 MB 85ns	90X8624
Gnd	N/C	Gnd	N/C	2 MB 85ns	92F0104
Gnd	N/C	Gnd	Gnd	4 MB 70ns	92F0105
Gnd	Gnd	N/C	N/C	4 MB 85ns	79F1003 (square notch) L40-SX
Gnd	Gnd	N/C	Gnd	1 MB 100ns	N/A
Gnd	Gnd	N/C	Gnd	8 MB 80ns	79F1004 (square notch) L40-SX
Gnd	Gnd	Gnd	N/C	2 MB 100ns	N/A
Gnd	Gnd	Gnd	Gnd	4 MB 80ns	87F9980
Gnd	Gnd	Gnd	Gnd	2 MB 85ns	79F1003 (square notch) L40SX

N/C = No Connection (open)   Gnd = Ground
Pin 67 = Presence detect bit 0   Pin 68 = Presence detect bit 1
Pin 69 = Presence detect bit 2   Pin 70 = Presence detect bit 3

Bus Information

System Bus Pinouts

The following section details the interface connector pinouts for all of the PC bus architectures available today. These pinout tables can be useful when you troubleshoot problems with devices plugged into the bus.

ISA Bus (8-Bit and 16-Bit) Interface Connectors

The following tables show the pinouts for the Industry Standard Architecture (ISA) PC, XT, and AT 8-bit and 16-bit expansion slot connectors.

Table 3.9   ISA (Industry Standard Architecture) 8-Bit and 16-Bit Bus Connectors

Signal	Pin	Pin	Signal	Signal	Pin	Pin	Signal
Ground	B1	A1	-I/O CH CHK	Ground	B1	A1	-I/O CH CHK
RESET DRV	B2	A2	Data Bit 7	RESET DRV	B2	A2	Data Bit 7
+5 Vdc	B3	A3	Data Bit 6	+5 Vdc	B3	A3	Data Bit 6
IRQ 2	B4	A4	Data Bit 5	IRQ 9	B4	A4	Data Bit 5
-5 Vdc	B5	A5	Data Bit 4	-5 Vdc	B5	A5	Data Bit 4
DRQ 2	B6	A6	Data Bit 3	DRQ 2	B6	A6	Data Bit 3
-12 Vdc	B7	A7	Data Bit 2	-12 Vdc	B7	A7	Data Bit 2
-CARD SLCTD	B8	A8	Data Bit 1	-0 WAIT	B8	A8	Data Bit 1
+12 Vdc	B9	A9	Data Bit 0	+12 Vdc	B9	A9	Data Bit 0
Ground	B10	A10	-I/O CH RDY	Ground	B10	A10	-I/O CH RDY
-SMEMW	B11	A11	AEN	-SMEMW	B11	A11	AEN
-SMEMR	B12	A12	Address 19	-SMEMR	B12	A12	Address 19
-IOW	B13	A13	Address 18	-IOW	B13	A13	Address 18
-IOR	B14	A14	Address 17	-IOR	B14	A14	Address 17
-DACK 3	B15	A15	Address 16	-DACK 3	B15	A15	Address 16
DRQ 3	B16	A16	Address 15	DRQ 3	B16	A16	Address 15
-DACK 1	B17	A17	Address 14	-DACK 1	B17	A17	Address 14
DRQ 1	B18	A18	Address 13	DRQ 1	B18	A18	Address 13
-Refresh	B19	A19	Address 12	-Refresh	B19	A19	Address 12
CLK(4.77MHz)	B20	A20	Address 11	CLK(8.33MHz)	B20	A20	Address 11
IRQ 7	B21	A21	Address 10	IRQ 7	B21	A21	Address 10
IRQ 6	B22	A22	Address 9	IRQ 6	B22	A22	Address 9
IRQ 5	B23	A23	Address 8	IRQ 5	B23	A23	Address 8
IRQ 4	B24	A24	Address 7	IRQ 4	B24	A24	Address 7
IRQ 3	B25	A25	Address 6	IRQ 3	B25	A25	Address 6
-DACK 2	B26	A26	Address 5	-DACK 2	B26	A26	Address 5
T/C	B27	A27	Address 4	T/C	B27	A27	Address 4
BALE	B28	A28	Address 3	BALE	B28	A28	Address 3
+5 Vdc	B29	A29	Address 2	+5 Vdc	B29	A29	Address 2
OSC(14.3MHz)	B30	A30	Address 1	OSC(14.3MHz)	B30	A30	Address 1
Ground	B31	A31	Address 0	Ground	B31	A31	Address 0

Signal	Pin	Pin	Signal
-MEM CS16	D1	C1	-SBHE
-I/O CS16	D2	C2	Latch Address 23
IRQ 10	D3	C3	Latch Address 22
IRQ 11	D4	C4	Latch Address 21
IRQ 12	D5	C5	Latch Address 20
IRQ 15	D6	C6	Latch Address 19
IRQ 14	D7	C7	Latch Address 18
-DACK 0	D8	C8	Latch Address 17
DRQ 0	D9	C9	-MEMR
-DACK 5	D10	C10	-MEMW
DRQ 5	D11	C11	Data Bit 8
-DACK 6	D12	C12	Data Bit 9
DRQ 6	D13	C13	Data Bit 10
-DACK 7	D14	C14	Data Bit 11
DRQ 7	D15	C15	Data Bit 12
+5 Vdc	D16	C16	Data Bit 13
-Master	D17	C17	Data Bit 14
Ground	D18	C18	Data Bit 15

EISA Bus (32-Bit) Interface Connector

Table 3.10   EISA (Extended Industry Standard Architecture) 32-Bit Bus Connector

Lower Signal	Upper Signal	Pin	Pin	Upper Signal	Lower Signal
Ground	Ground	B1	A1	-I/O CH CHK	-CMD
+5 Vdc	RESET DRV	B2	A2	Data Bit 7	-START
+5 Vdc	+5 Vdc	B3	A3	Data Bit 6	EXRDY
Reserved	IRQ 9	B4	A4	Data Bit 5	-EX32
Reserved	-5 Vdc	B5	A5	Data Bit 4	Ground
KEY	DRQ 2	B6	A6	Data Bit 3	KEY
Reserved	-12 Vdc	B7	A7	Data Bit 2	-EX16
Reserved	-0 WAIT	B8	A8	Data Bit 1	-SLBURST
+12 Vdc	+12 Vdc	B9	A9	Data Bit 0	-MSBURST
M-IO	Ground	B10	A10	-I/O CH RDY	W-R
-LOCK	-SMEMW	B11	A11	AEN	Ground
Reserved	-SMEMR	B12	A12	Address 19	Reserved
Ground	-IOW	B13	A13	Address 18	Reserved
Reserved	-IOR	B14	A14	Address 17	Reserved
-BE 3	-DACK 3	B15	A15	Address 16	Ground
KEY	DRQ 3	B16	A16	Address 15	KEY
-BE 2	-DACK 1	B17	A17	Address 14	-BE 1
-BE 0	DRQ 1	B18	A18	Address 13	-Latch Address 31
Ground	-Refresh	B19	A19	Address 12	Ground
+5 Vdc	CLK(8.33MHz)	B20	A20	Address 11	-Latch Address 30
-Latch Address 29	IRQ 7	B21	A21	Address 10	-Latch Address 28
Ground	IRQ 6	B22	A22	Address 9	-Latch Address 27
-Latch Address 26	IRQ 5	B23	A23	Address 8	-Latch Address 25
-Latch Address 24	IRQ 4	B24	A24	Address 7	Ground
KEY	IRQ 3	B25	A25	Address 6	KEY
Latch Address 16	-DACK 2	B26	A26	Address 5	Latch Address 15
Latch Address 14	T/C	B27	A27	Address 4	Latch Address 13
+5 Vdc	BALE	B28	A28	Address 3	Latch Address 12
+5 Vdc	+5 Vdc	B29	A29	Address 2	Latch Address 11
Ground	OSC(14.3MHz)	B30	A30	Address 1	Ground
Latch Address 10	Ground	B31	A31	Address 0	Latch Address 9
Latch Address 8	-MEM CS16	D1	C1	-SBHE	Latch Address 7
Latch Address 6	-I/O CS16	D2	C2	Latch Address 23	Ground
Latch Address 5	IRQ 10	D3	C3	Latch Address 22	Latch Address 4
+5 Vdc	IRQ 11	D4	C4	Latch Address 21	Latch Address 3
Latch Address 2	IRQ 12	D5	C5	Latch Address 20	Ground
KEY	IRQ 15	D6	C6	Latch Address 19	KEY
Data Bit 16	IRQ 14	D7	C7	Latch Address 18	Data Bit 17
Data Bit 18	-DACK 0	D8	C8	Latch Address 17	Data Bit 19
Ground	DRQ 0	D9	C9	-MEMR	Data Bit 20
Data Bit 21	-DACK 5	D10	C10	-MEMW	Data Bit 22
Data Bit 23	DRQ 5	D11	C11	Data Bit 8	Ground
Data Bit 24	-DACK 6	D12	C12	Data Bit 9	Data Bit 25
Ground	DRQ 6	D13	C13	Data Bit 10	Data Bit 26
Data Bit 27	-DACK 7	D14	C14	Data Bit 11	Data Bit 28
KEY	DRQ 7	D15	C15	Data Bit 12	KEY
Data Bit 29	+5 Vdc	D16	C16	Data Bit 13	Ground
+5 Vdc	-MASTER	D17	C17	Data Bit 14	Data Bit 30
+5 Vdc	Ground	D18	C18	Data Bit 15	Data Bit 31
-MAKx		D19	C19		-MREQx

VESA VL-Bus Interface Connectors

64-Bit	32-Bit	Pin	Pin	32-Bit	64-Bit
Table 3.11 VESA VL-Bus (Video Local-Bus) Connector pinouts (Rev. 2.0p)					
	DAT 00	A01	B01	DAT 01	
	DAT 02	A02	B02	DAT 03	
	DAT 04	A03	B03	GND	
	DAT 06	A04	B04	DAT 05	
	DAT 08	A05	B05	DAT 07	
	GND	A06	B06	DAT 09	
	DAT 10	A07	B07	DAT 11	
	DAT 12	A08	B08	DAT 13	
	VCC	A09	B09	DAT 15	
	DAT 14	A10	B10	GND	
	DAT 16	A11	B11	DAT 17	
	DAT 18	A12	B12	VCC	
	DAT 20	A13	B13	DAT 19	
	GND	A14	B14	DAT 21	
	DAT 22	A15	B15	DAT 23	
	DAT 24	A16	B16	DAT 25	
	DAT 26	A17	B17	GND	
	DAT 28	A18	B18	DAT 27	
	DAT 30	A19	B19	DAT 29	
	VCC	A20	B20	DAT 31	
DAT 63	ADR 31	A21	B21	ADR 30	DAT 62
	GND	A22	B22	ADR 28	DAT 60
DAT 61	ADR 29	A23	B23	ADR 26	DAT 58
DAT 59	ADR 27	A24	B24	GND	
DAT 57	ADR 25	A25	B25	ADR 24	DAT 56
DAT 55	ADR 23	A26	B26	ADR 22	DAT 54
DAT 53	ADR 21	A27	B27	VCC	
DAT 51	ADR 19	A28	B28	ADR 20	DAT 52
	GND	A29	B29	ADR 18	DAT 50
DAT 49	ADR 17	A30	B30	ADR 16	DAT 48
DAT 47	ADR 15	A31	B31	ADR 14	DAT 46
	VCC	A32	B32	ADR 12	DAT 44
DAT 45	ADR 13	A33	B33	ADR 10	DAT 42
DAT 43	ADR 11	A34	B34	ADR 08	DAT 40
DAT 41	ADR 09	A35	B35	GND	
DAT 39	ADR 07	A36	B36	ADR 06	DAT 38
DAT 37	ADR 05	A37	B37	ADR 04	DAT 36
	GND	A38	B38	WBACK#	
DAT 35	ADR 03	A39	B39	BE 0#	BE 4#
DAT 34	ADR 02	A40	B40	VCC	
LBS64#	NC	A41	B41	BE 1#	BE 5#
	RESET#	A42	B42	BE 2#	BE 6#
	D/C#	A43	B43	GND	
	M/IO#	A44	B44	BE 3#	BE 7#
	W/R#	A45	B45	ADS#	

(continues)

Table 3.11 Continued

64-Bit	32-Bit	Pin	Pin	32-Bit	64-Bit
KEY	KEY	A46	B46	KEY	KEY
KEY	KEY	A47	B47	KEY	KEY
	RDYRTN#	A48	B48	LRDY#	
	GND	A49	B49	LDEV<x>#	
	IRQ 9	A50	B50	LREQ<x>#	
	BRDY#	A51	B51	GND	
	BLAST#	A52	B52	LGNT<x>#	
DAT 32	ID 0	A53	B53	VCC	
DAT 33	ID 1	A54	B54	ID 2	
	GND	A55	B55	ID 3	
	LCLK	A56	B56	ID 4	ACK64#
	VCC	A57	B57	NC	
	LBS16#	A58	B58	LEADS#	

Table 3.12 PCI Local Bus Interface Connectors

Pin	5V Side-B	5V Side-A	3.3V Side-B	3.3V Side-A	Comments
1	-12V	TRST#	-12V	TRST#	32-bit connector start
2	TCK	+12V	TCK	+12V	
3	Ground	TMS	Ground	TMS	
4	TDO	TDI	TDO	TDI	
5	+5V	+5V	+5V	+5V	
6	+5V	INTA#	+5V	INTA#	
7	INTB#	INTC#	INTB#	INTC#	
8	INTD#	+5V	INTD#	+5V	
9	PRSNT1#	Reserved	PRSNT1#	Reserved	
10	Reserved	+5V (I/O)	Reserved	+3.3V (I/O)	
11	PRSNT2#	Reserved	PRSNT2#	Reserved	
12	Ground	Ground	KEY	KEY	3.3 volt key
13	Ground	Ground	KEY	KEY	3.3 volt key
14	Reserved	Reserved	Reserved	Reserved	
15	Ground	RST#	Ground	RST#	
16	CLK	+5V (I/O)	CLK	+3.3V (I/O)	
17	Ground	GNT#	Ground	GNT#	
18	REQ#	Ground	REQ#	Ground	
19	+5V (I/O)	Reserved	+3.3V (I/O)	Reserved	
20	AD[31]	AD[30]	AD[31]	AD[30]	
21	AD[29]	+3.3V	AD[29]	+3.3V	
22	Ground	AD[28]	Ground	AD[28]	
23	AD[27]	AD[26]	AD[27]	AD[26]	
24	AD[25]	Ground	AD[25]	Ground	
25	+3.3V	AD[24]	+3.3V	AD[24]	
26	C/BE[3]#	IDSEL	C/BE[3]#	IDSEL	
27	AD[23]	+3.3V	AD[23]	+3.3V	
28	Ground	AD[22]	Ground	AD[22]	

Pin	5V Side-B	5V Side-A	3.3V Side-B	3.3V Side-A	Comments
29	AD[21]	AD[20]	AD[21]	AD[20]	
30	AD[19]	Ground	AD[19]	Ground	
31	+3.3V	AD[18]	+3.3V	AD[18]	
32	AD[17]	AD[16]	AD[17]	AD[16]	
33	C/BE[2]#	+3.3V	C/BE[2]#	+3.3V	
34	Ground	FRAME#	Ground	FRAME#	
35	IRDY#	Ground	IRDY#	Ground	
36	+3.3V	TRDY#	+3.3V	TRDY#	
37	DEVSEL#	Ground	DEVSEL#	Ground	
38	Ground	STOP#	Ground	STOP#	
39	LOCK#	+3.3V	LOCK#	+3.3V	
40	PERR#	SDONE	PERR#	SDONE	
41	+3.3V	SBO#	+3.3V	SBO#	
42	SERR#	Ground	SERR#	Ground	
43	+3.3V	PAR	+3.3V	PAR	
44	C/BE[1]#	AD[15]	C/BE[1]#	AD[15]	
45	AD[14]	+3.3V	AD[14]	+3.3V	
46	Ground	AD[13]	Ground	AD[13]	
47	AD[12]	AD[11]	AD[12]	AD[11]	
48	AD[10]	Ground	AD[10]	Ground	
49	Ground	AD[09]	Ground	AD[09]	
50	KEY	KEY	Ground	Ground	5 volt key
51	KEY	KEY	Ground	Ground	5 volt key
52	AD[08]	C/BE[0]#	AD[08]	C/BE[0]#	
53	AD[07]	+3.3V	AD[07]	+3.3V	
54	+3.3V	AD[06]	+3.3V	AD[06]	
55	AD[05]	AD[04]	AD[05]	AD[04]	
56	AD[03]	Ground	AD[03]	Ground	
57	Ground	AD[02]	Ground	AD[02]	
58	AD[01]	AD[00]	AD[01]	AD[00]	
59	+5V (I/O)	+5V (I/O)	+3.3V (I/O)	+3.3V (I/O)	
60	ACK64#	REQ64#	ACK64#	REQ64#	
61	+5V	+5V	+5V	+5V	
62	+5V	+5V	+5V	+5V	32-bit connector end
	KEY	KEY	KEY	KEY	64-bit spacer
	KEY	KEY	KEY	KEY	64-bit spacer
63	Reserved	Ground	Reserved	Ground	64-bit connector start
64	Ground	C/BE[7]#	Ground	C/BE[7]#	
65	C/BE[6]#	C/BE[5]#	C/BE[6]#	C/BE[5]#	
66	C/BE[4]#	+5V (I/O)	C/BE[4]#	+3.3V (I/O)	
67	Ground	PAR64	Ground	PAR64	
68	AD[63]	AD[62]	AD[63]	AD[62]	
69	AD[61]	Ground	AD[61]	Ground	
70	+5V (I/O)	AD[60]	+3.3V (I/O)	AD[60]	
71	AD[59]	AD[58]	AD[59]	AD[58]	

(continues)

Table 3.12 Continued

Pin	5V Side-B	5V Side-A	3.3V Side-B	3.3V Side-A	Comments
72	AD[57]	Ground	AD[57]	Ground	
73	Ground	AD[56]	Ground	AD[56]	
74	AD[55]	AD[54]	AD[55]	AD[54]	
75	AD[53]	+5V (I/O)	AD[53]	+5V (I/O)	
76	Ground	AD[52]	Ground	AD[52]	
77	AD[51]	AD[50]	AD[51]	AD[50]	
78	AD[49]	Ground	AD[49]	Ground	
79	+5V (I/O)	AD[48]	+3.3V (I/O)	AD[48]	
80	AD[47]	AD[46]	AD[47]	AD[46]	
81	AD[45]	Ground	AD[45]	Ground	
82	Ground	AD[44]	Ground	AD[44]	
83	AD[43]	AD[42]	AD[43]	AD[42]	
84	AD[41]	+5V (I/O)	AD[41]	+3.3V (I/O)	
85	Ground	AD[40]	Ground	AD[40]	
86	AD[39]	AD[38]	AD[39]	AD[38]	
87	AD[37]	Ground	AD[37]	Ground	
88	+5V (I/O)	AD[36]	+3.3V (I/O)	AD[36]	
89	AD[35]	AD[34]	AD[35]	AD[34]	
90	AD[33]	Ground	AD[33]	Ground	
91	Ground	AD[32]	Ground	AD[32]	
92	Reserved	Reserved	Reserved	Reserved	
93	Reserved	Ground	Reserved	Ground	
94	Ground	Reserved	Ground	Reserved	64-bit connector end

MCA (16-Bit and 32-Bit) Interface Connectors

The following tables show the pinouts for the Micro Channel Architecture (MCA) bus connectors in the PS/2 systems. Shown are the 16-bit connector with an optional auxiliary video-extension connector (AVEC), and the 32-bit connector with the optional matched memory extension.

Table 3.13   16-Bit Connector with optional Auxiliary Video

Signal	Pin	Pin	Signal
ESYNC	BV10	AV10	VSYNC
Ground	BV9	AV9	HSYNC
P5	BV8	AV8	BLANK
P4	BV7	AV7	Ground
P3	BV6	AV6	P6
Ground	BV5	AV5	EDCLK
P2	BV4	AV4	DCLK

Signal	Pin	Pin	Signal
P1	BV3	AV3	Ground
P0	BV2	AV2	P7
Ground	BV1	AV1	EVIDEO
KEY	KEY	KEY	KEY
AUDIO GND	B1	A1	-CD SETUP
AUDIO	B2	A2	MADE 24
Ground	B3	A3	Ground
OSC (14.3MHz)	B4	A4	Address 11
Ground	B5	A5	Address 10
Address 23	B6	A6	Address 9
Address 22	B7	A7	+5 Vdc
Address 21	B8	A8	Address 8
Ground	B9	A9	Address 7
Address 20	B10	A10	Address 6
Address 19	B11	A11	+5 Vdc
Address 18	B12	A12	Address 5
Ground	B13	A13	Address 4
Address 17	B14	A14	Address 3
Address 16	B15	A15	+5 Vdc
Address 15	B16	A16	Address 2
Ground	B17	A17	Address 1
Address 14	B18	A18	Address 0
Address 13	B19	A19	+12 Vdc
Address 12	B20	A20	-ADL
Ground	B21	A21	-PREEMPT
-IRQ 9	B22	A22	-BURST
-IRQ 3	B23	A23	-12 Vdc
-IRQ 4	B24	A24	ARB 00
Ground	B25	A25	ARB 01
-IRQ 5	B26	A26	ARB 02
-IRQ 6	B27	A27	-12 Vdc
-IRQ 7	B28	A28	ARB 03
Ground	B29	A29	ARB/-GNT

(continues)

Table 3.13	Continued		
Signal	**Pin**	**Pin**	**Signal**
Reserved	B30	A30	-TC
Reserved	B31	A31	+5 Vdc
-CHCK	B32	A32	-S0
Ground	B33	A33	-S1
-CMD	B34	A34	M/-IO
CHRDYRTN	B35	A35	+12 Vdc
-CD SFDBK	B36	A36	CD CHRDY
Ground	B37	A37	Data Bit 0
Data Bit 1	B38	A38	Data Bit 2
Data Bit 3	B39	A39	+5 Vdc
Data Bit 4	B40	A40	Data Bit 5
Ground	B41	A41	Data Bit 6
CHRESET	B42	A42	Data Bit 7
Reserved	B43	A43	Ground
Reserved	B44	A44	-DS 16 RTN
Ground	B45	A45	-REFRESH
KEY	B46	A46	KEY
KEY	B47	A47	KEY
Data Bit 8	B48	A48	+5 Vdc
Data Bit 9	B49	A49	Data Bit 10
Ground	B50	A50	Data Bit 11
Data Bit 12	B51	A51	Data Bit 13
Data Bit 14	B52	A52	+12 Vdc
Data Bit 15	B53	A53	Reserved
Ground	B54	A54	-SBHE
-IRQ 10	B55	A55	-CD DS 16
-IRQ 11	B56	A56	+5 Vdc
-IRQ 12	B57	A57	-IRQ 14
Ground	B58	A58	-IRQ 15
Reserved	B59	A59	Reserved
Reserved	B60	A60	Reserved

Signal	Pin	Pin	Signal
Ground	BM4	AM4	Reserved
Reserved	BM3	AM3	-MMC CMD
-MMCR	BM2	AM2	Ground
Reserved	BM1	AM1	-MMC
AUDIO GND	B1	A1	-CD SETUP
AUDIO	B2	A2	MADE 24
Ground	B3	A3	Ground
OSC (14.3MHz)	B4	A4	Address 11
Ground	B5	A5	Address 10
Address 23	B6	A6	Address 9
Address 22	B7	A7	+5 Vdc
Address 21	B8	A8	Address 8
Ground	B9	A9	Address 7
Address 20	B10	A10	Address 6
Address 19	B11	A11	+5 Vdc
Address 18	B12	A12	Address 5
Ground	B13	A13	Address 4
Address 17	B14	A14	Address 3
Address 16	B15	A15	+5 Vdc
Address 15	B16	A16	Address 2
Ground	B17	A17	Address 1
Address 14	B18	A18	Address 0
Address 13	B19	A19	+12 Vdc
Address 12	B20	A20	-ADL
Ground	B21	A21	-PREEMPT
-IRQ 9	B22	A22	-BURST
-IRQ 3	B23	A23	-12 Vdc
-IRQ 4	B24	A24	ARB 00
Ground	B25	A25	ARB 01
-IRQ 5	B26	A26	ARB 02
-IRQ 6	B27	A27	-12 Vdc
-IRQ 7	B28	A28	ARB 03

Table 3.14   MCA 32-Bit Connector with Optional Matched Memory Extension

(continues)

Table 3.14 Continued

Signal	Pin	Pin	Signal
Ground	B29	A29	ARB/-GNT
Reserved	B30	A30	-TC
Reserved	B31	A31	+5 Vdc
-CHCK	B32	A32	-SO
Ground	B33	A33	-S1
-CMD	B34	A34	M/-IO
CHRDYRTN	B35	A35	+12 Vdc
-CD SFDBK	B36	A36	CD CHRDY
Ground	B37	A37	Data Bit 0
Data Bit 1	B38	A38	Data Bit 2
Data Bit 3	B39	A39	+5 Vdc
Data Bit 4	B40	A40	Data Bit 5
Ground	B41	A41	Data Bit 6
CHRESET	B42	A42	Data Bit 7
Reserved	B43	A43	Ground
Reserved	B44	A44	-DS 16 RTN
Ground	B45	A45	-REFRESH
KEY	B46	A46	KEY
KEY	B47	A47	KEY
Data Bit 8	B48	A48	+5 Vdc
Data Bit 9	B49	A49	Data Bit 10
Ground	B50	A50	Data Bit 11
Data Bit 12	B51	A51	Data Bit 13
Data Bit 14	B52	A52	+12 Vdc
Data Bit 15	B53	A53	Reserved
Ground	B54	A54	-SBHE
-IRQ 10	B55	A55	-CD DS 16
-IRQ 11	B56	A56	+5 Vdc
-IRQ 12	B57	A57	-IRQ 14
Ground	B58	A58	-IRQ 15
Reserved	B59	A59	Reserved
Reserved	B60	A60	Reserved
Reserved	B61	A61	Ground

Signal	Pin	Pin	Signal
Reserved	B62	A63	Reserved
Ground	B63	A63	Reserved
Data Bit 16	B64	A64	Reserved
Data Bit 17	B65	A65	+12 Vdc
Data Bit 18	B66	A66	Data Bit 19
Ground	B67	A67	Data Bit 20
Data Bit 22	B68	A68	Data Bit 21
Data Bit 23	B69	A69	+5 Vdc
Reserved	B70	A70	Data Bit 24
Ground	B71	A71	Data Bit 25
Data Bit 27	B72	A72	Data Bit 26
Data Bit 28	B73	A73	+5 Vdc
Data Bit 29	B74	A74	Data Bit 30
Ground	B75	A75	Data Bit 31
-BE 0	B76	A76	Reserved
-BE 1	B77	A77	+12 Vdc
-BE 2	B78	A78	-BE 3
Ground	B79	A79	-DS 32 RTN
TR 32	B80	A80	-CD DS 32
Address 24	B81	A81	+5 Vdc
Address 25	B82	A82	Address 26
Ground	B83	A83	Address 27
Address 29	B84	A84	Address 28
Address 30	B85	A85	+5 Vdc
Address 31	B86	A86	Reserved
Ground	B87	A87	Reserved
Reserved	B88	A88	Reserved
Reserved	B89	A89	Ground

PCMCIA Interface Connector

The PCMCIA (Personal Computer Memory Card International Association) bus also is known as the credit card adapter bus because the cards are approximately the same shape and size as a credit card. Although originally designed for memory cards only, the PCMCIA has been adapted to work with virtually any type of peripheral. The following table shows the PCMCIA Interface connector specification.

Table 3.15 PCMCIA (Personal Computer Memory Card International Association) Bus Pinout

Pin	PCMCIA Signal
1	Ground
2	Data Bit 3
3	Data Bit 4
4	Data Bit 5
5	Data Bit 6
6	Data Bit 7
7	-Card Enable 1
8	Address Bit 10
9	-Output Enable
10	Address Bit 11
11	Address Bit 9
12	Address Bit 8
13	Address Bit 13
14	Address Bit 14
15	-Write Enable /-Program
16	Ready/-Busy (IREQ)
17	+5 Vdc
18	Vpp1
19	Address Bit 16
20	Address Bit 15
21	Address Bit 12
22	Address Bit 7
23	Address Bit 6
24	Address Bit 5
25	Address Bit 4
26	Address Bit 3
27	Address Bit 2
28	Address Bit 1
29	Address Bit 0
30	Data Bit 0
31	Data Bit 1
32	Data Bit 2
33	Write Protect (-IOIS16)

Pin	PCMCIA Signal
33	Write Protect (-IOIS16)
34	Ground
35	Ground
36	-Card Detect 1
37	Data Bit 11
38	Data Bit 12
39	Data Bit 13
40	Data Bit 14
41	Data Bit 15
42	-Card Enable 2
43	Refresh
44	RFU (-IOR)
45	RFU (-IOW)
46	Address Bit 17
47	Address Bit 18
48	Address Bit 19
49	Address Bit 20
50	Address Bit 21
51	+5 Vdc
52	Vpp2
53	Address Bit 22
54	Address Bit 23
55	Address Bit 24
56	Address Bit 25
57	RFU
58	RESET
59	-WAIT
60	RFU (-INPACK)
61	-Register Select
62	Battery Voltage Detect 2 (-SPKR)
63	Battery Voltage Detect 1 (-STSCHG)
64	Data Bit 8
65	Data Bit 9
66	Data Bit 10
67	-Card Detect 2
68	Ground

Table 3.16   MicroChannel Architecture Adapter ID Codes

ID	Adapter Name
001D	DR-one SC306 Video Standards Converter
0101	p1840 ProNET-4 Network Adapter for PS/2
0425	Pacific Image Superfax Adapter
04DC	Omninet/4 PS/2 Transporter
04FF	Viking PS2 Display Controller
0503	Kurzweil Discoverer SCSI Adapter
0803	Madge MC Ringnode
0EFF	Northern Telecom Lanstar/MC Card
0F1F	Adaptec AHA-1640 SCSI Host Adapter
0F7F	PScomm4
0FC7	Wizard i860 Attached Processor Adapter
0FCC	D-Link Ethernet Card
0FDF	NI9210 Micro Channel Network Controller
1185	VEN-TEL 2400 modem
5022	Online CDI-210S (Sony) CD ROM Controller
5023	PCM Audio Record/Playback Unit
5025	Online CDI-210H (Hitachi) CD ROM Controller
5028	Emerald SCSI / Micro Channel(tm) Tape Adapter
5035	Panasonic FX-RS505/RS506 Image Scanner Adapter
5039	Kurzweil Flatbed Scanner Adapter
503A	Kurweil Discover 7320 Model 115 Optical Character Recognition
50C1	Data Translation 2901 Data Aquisition Board
5101	AMS IOSIX-7 Adapter
511F	NetWorth, Inc. - v Series
5125	Tecmar QIC-60 QT-60, QT-90, QT-125 Tape Drive
5126	Tecmar Floppy Tape Controller
5152	Intel Micro-Channel Connection CoProcessor
5156	Intel Micro-Channel Connection CoProcessor with Modem Option
5186	Daitoh SCSI Interface Adapter
5323	3 Plus SCSI Adapter
5333	National Instruments MC-GPIB IEEE-488 Interface
5349	Invisible Network Model 200/A
5353	National Instruments MC-DIO-32F
5356	TOPS FlashCard/MC LocalTalk Adapter
5500	COREtape Controller
5607	Cabletron Ethernet Board E3010-X
568B	MaynStream QIC-02 Tape Adapter

ID	Adapter Name
568B	MaynStream QIC-02 Tape Adapter
568D	MaynStream SCSI Tape Adapter
57DF	DFI Handy Scanner HS-3000-II
57FE	Micro Channel Tape Drive Host Adapter
5822	Small 4 Port Chase Research Intelligent Serial I/O Controller
5823	4 Port Chase Research Intelligent Serial I/O Controller
5824	8 Port Chase Research Intelligent Serial I/O Controller
5825	16 Port Chase Research Intelligent Serial I/O Controller
5C0F	Land Computer SCSI Interface Adapter
5CC1	MAP 3.0 Adapter, Type 1410 Concord Communications, Inc.
5CEC	CEC PS< >488 GPIB Adapter
5CED	PS< >488 IEEE-488 Adapter from CEC (rev D)
5CFF	GammaFax CMPC Communications Adapter
5DEF	AGA Micro Channel SCSI Adapter
5DFF	GammaFax PS/2 Communication Adapter
5EDF	National Instruments MC-MIO-16 Data Acquisition Card
5EEE	HITACHI CD-ROM Adapter
5F60	Tiara Local Area Networks LANcard/A-II ARCnet Adapter
5F77	Future Domain SCSI Adapter
5FE1	MXI-1000 GPIB interface adapter
5FE5	Qua Tech GPA-1000 Game port adapter
5FE8	QUA TECH SP-1000 Parallel printer adapter
5FE9	QUA TECH SP-1050 Serial/Parallel port adapter
5FF8	PLUS PASSPORT MC ADAPTER BOARD
6000	Tiara LanCard/EII ETHERNET/CHEAPERNET Adapter
6001	Tiara LanCard/E*MC TWISTED PAIR Adapter
6011	Computer Logics Ltd. - MicroLogic II Adapter
6014	Standard Microsystems Corporation ARCNET-PS110
6018	Gateway Communications G/Ethernet Controller
601C	Multi-Tech Systems MT224PS/ES
601F	Hewlett-Packard Scanner Interface Adapter
6029	MetraByte UCDAS-8PGA Data Acquisition Board
6040	Intel 2400B Modem 2
6042	3Com EtherLink/MC Ethernet Adapter
6060	IDEAcomm 5251 4 LU short card
6092	Rabbit RB78 Coax Adapter
609E	MICROTEK MS-PS/2 Interface Adapter
60C2	Boca Research Dual Async/Parallel Adapter
60C9	Boca Research Bidirectional Parallel Adapter
60D0	Hayes JT Fax 4800P

(continues)

Table 3.16	Continued
ID	**Adapter Name**
60E5	Boca Research Dual Async/Parallel Adapter 2
6106	Altera LP5 Logic Programmer
611B	Raster Devices Controller
611F	NetWorth, Inc. - EtherNext/MC Network Adapter
6147	Micro Channel Compatible Key Card
6180	LavaLink Dual Async Adapter
6205	Excelan EXOS 215T Intelligent Ethernet Adapter
6221	The ITI LinkUp COAX - 3270 Emulation Adapter
6247	Lasergraphics RASCOL IV
6262	p1800 ProNET-10 Network Adapter for PS/2
62FC	The Quadram MainLink IIM - 3270 Connection
62FE	The Quadram MainLink IIM - 3270 Connection
63CA	Hewlett Packard StarLAN-10 Adapter Rev 1.1
64B6	Thomas-Conrad ARC-CARD/MC
64FF	The Quadram MainLink IIM - 3270 Connection
6508	PDIUC508 Microchannel ARCNET Interface Adapter
655B	Wang Microchannel Local Office Connection (MCLOC)
6600	Ziatech GPIB adapter
6612	Evercom 24/2 Modem
6666	SYSTEM GOLD COMMUNICATIONS CARD
6674	DayStar LocalTalk/MCA AppleTalk Adapter - DayStar Digital
677F	ATTACHMATE - Advanced 3270 Adapter/2
6780	NEOTECH FOUR CHANNEL SERIAL ADAPTER
6781	NEOTECH SERIAL ADAPTER
6782	NEOTECH PARALLEL ADAPTER
6783	NEOTECH SERIAL/PARALLEL ADAPTER
6784	NEOTECH DUAL RS-422/RS-485 SERIAL ADAPTER
6786	NEOTECH TWO CHANNEL PARALLEL ADAPTER
678F	BBS GPIB-3000
6A93	ISDN-S/2 Adapter
6AB4	Mayze Systems Ltd - Syncro 24PS V26 bis Modem
6AB5	Mayze Systems Ltd - Syncro 48PS V27 ter Modem
6AE7	Dacom Asyncronous Modem Version 1.0
6AFB	Miracom Keycard/PS Modem
6B0F	Siemens BAM Adapter (FM9750 Emulation)
6B1B	REDIO/2 RAMPA Engineering Digital I/O
6B28	Mainlan Network Adapter
6B29	Techland Sync Comms Adapter

ID	Adapter Name
6B80	Dataflex Design MCA Biscom Modem
6B94	CORE ESDI Fixed Disk Controller
6B95	CORE ESDI Fixed Disk Controller
6BBA	Internal Ethernet Controller
6BBC	Internal Synchronous Communications
6BCB	CONNECT ARCnet Adapter
6BF8	Serial Communications Card
6C06	Sanyo CD-ROM Adapter
6C0F	Roland MIDI Processing Unit - MPU-IMC
6C67	OPTO 22 Isolated RS-485 Serial Port
6C68	OPTO 22 Dual RS-485 Serial Port
6C69	OPTO 22 Pamux 4 Adapter
6CEC	GAT PS2 Coprocessor
6D6D	EICON TECHNOLOGY : Laser Printer Adapter / Micro Channel
6DAC	Logitech ScanMan, hand-held scanner
6DD6	Sync-Up 2/201
6DE0	Sync-Up 2/V.32
6DE1	Sync-Up 2/T9628B
6DE2	Fastalk 2/V.32
6DE3	Fastalk 2/2400
6DE4	Fastalk 2/1200
6DE5	Sync-Up 2/V.22 bis
6DE6	Sync-Up 2/201/212
6DE7	Sync-Up 2/208/201
6DED	U.S. Robotics Courier 2400 eps
6DEF	Digital Ethernet Micro Channel Adapter
6DF0	Emerald Technology, Inc.3XTwin/2
6DF1	Emerald Technology, Inc.3XPlus/2
6DF4	Emerald Technology, Inc.3XPlus/2 Rev. B
6E6C	IBM Audio Capture & Playback Adapter/A
6E6E	EICON Technology Single Port Communication Adapter Level 2
6E78	IRMA2-MCA Adapter
6E79	IRMA 3 3270 Coax Adapter
6E7A	DCA MCA Link
6E7C	DCA Intelligent Comm Adapter
6EE7	IMC Networks CorporationPCnic II Ethernet Controller
6EEE	Sync-Up 2/Multi-Protocol Adapter
6EF0	10NET/STARLAN LAN Adapter
6F01	Hayes 2400 bps Smartmodem Model 2400P

(continues)

ID	Adapter Name
Table 3.16 Continued	
6F04	Hayes Enhanced serial port adapter
6F6F	EICON Technology Single Port Communication Adapter Level 1
6F7E	Street Electronics "ECHO" Speech Synthesiser
6FBF	WATSON Board By Natural MicroSystems Corp.
6FC0	Western Digital WD8003ET/A Ethernet Adapter
6FC1	Western Digital WD8003ST/A Starlan Adapter
6FC2	WD EtherCard PLUS 10T/A (WD8003W/A)
6FC9	Applied Digital Parallel Adapter
6FCB	PM2400 PS/2 Internal Modem
6FCB	Practical Peripherals PM2400 Internal Modem
6FD7	CHI Communications Adapter
6FE4	DigiBoard PS-COM/16
6FE5	DigiBoard PS-COM/8
6FE6	DigiBoard PS-COM/4
6FE9	DigiBoard Open-Ender
6FEA	DigiBoard Open-Ender RS422
6FF6	Modem DIGICOM SNM
6FFC	Jovian Logic Corp. VIA
6FFF	Interactive Images Touch Screen Adapter
7000	AST Advantage/2 286 0-8M memory adapter
7001	AST Advantage/2 286 with Dual Serial Port Option
7002	AST Advantage/2 286 with Serial & Parallel Port Option
7010	Tecmar MicroRAM 386 Multifunction Board
7011	Tecmar MicroRAM AD Multifunction Board
7012	Ungermann-Bass PC3030 Ethernet Adapter
701A	TrueScan Version: PS/2 MCA. Calera Recognition Systems Inc.
7020	Cumulus 2 Meg Expanded/Extended Memory Multifunction Adapter
7048	EDSUN Memory board
7049	EDSUN Memory board
704E	IBM AVC Video Capture Adapter/A
7050	AST RampagePlus/MC
7051	AST RampagePlus/MC With I/O Pak/MC-S Option
7052	AST RampagePlus/MC With I/O Pak/MC-SP Option
706F	Aox MicroMASTER 386
7074	Video Capture Adapter/A
707E	Irwin 4100MC Controller

ID	Adapter Name
7081	AST Advantage/2 -386 Adapter
7082	AST Advantage/2 386 with Serial & Parallel Port Option
7083	AST Advantage/2 386 0-8M memory adapter
7086	CRi "Coherent Processor" Content Addressable Memory
708E	Kingston KTM-8000/286 Expansion Memory Adapter
708F	Kingston KTM-8000/386 Expansion Memory Adapter
7090	AST-5251/11A Enhanced Adapter
7091	AST-3270/CoaxIIA Adapter
7092	AST-CC423/A Adapter
70B0	Intel Above Board MC32
70C3	PS2 HIGH SPEED COMM
70C4	Excalibur EXC-1553 PS2/E card
70CE	Video Capture Adapter/A with PAL
70D7	AdLib MC Music Synthesizer Adapter
7154	NetWare NE/2 NIC
7188	Mountain QIC-02 Adapter
7283	Bit3 Adapter
7401	QIC80 Tape Drive Controller
7430	Paragon Enhanced 80386 4-16MB Memory Expansion (34F3011)
76DA	QUADMEG PS/Q Memory Adapter (primary)
76DE	QUADMEG PS/Q Memory Adapter (secondary)
7788	Above Board 2 Plus
7CEC	OS/RAM4 Memory Adapter
7CED	OS/RAM8 Memory Adapter, Capital Equipment Corp.
7CEE	OS/RAM32 Memory Adapter, Capital Equipment Corp.
7D7F	Orchid Ramquest Extra 16/32
7DF0	SYSGEN PST100 Tape Adapter
7E76	Overland Data 9 Track Tape Coupler Model XL/2
7F4F	NCR SCSI Host Adapter Board
7F7E	ORCHID RamQuest EXTRA
7F7F	PS/2 SBCA Communication Adapter Board / on-card intel 80188
7FF9	IOMEGA PC4 Host Adapter Board
7FFA	IOMEGA PC4B-50 SCSI Host Adapter Board
8002	AHEAD SYSTEMS INC., VGA ENHANCER-Z, Rev. A
8009	Vermont MicrosystemsCOBRA /2
800D	PIXELWORKS PS/2 Ultra Clipper Graphics Subsystem V1.1
800F	Microcomp DR-one MultiVGA
807F	MICRO DISPLAY SYSTEMS Video Adapter

(continues)

Table 3.16 Continued

ID	Adapter Name
8080	Control Systems Artist 10 MC
8081	Telesensory Systems Inc. Vista/2 Adapter for the Visually
8099	Number Nine Pepper PRO1024 MCA Graphics Adapter
80A9	Intel ActionMedia i750 DVI card
80AF	Cornerstone DualPage Hi-Res Monitor and Adapter
80B3	M-Motion Video Adapter
80CB	Arlunya SC306 Standards Converter
80CC	Microfield T8/2 High Resolution Graphics Controller
80F8	Matrox PG2-1281 Hi-res Graphics Controller
8102	Colorgraphics Corp. Dual VGA/MicroChannel
8202	AHEAD SYSTEMS INC., VGA ENHANCER-Z, Rev. A
8484	IBM 5080 Serial Link Adapter
8888	Metaphor WS2XP/MCA
8DF0	IBM Image Adapter/A
8DF1	IBM Image Adapter/A and Printer/Scanner Option
8DF2	DSS and sub card 2
8DF3	DSS and sub card 3
8DF3	DSS and sub card 3
8DF4	IBM Image Adapter/A
8DF5	IBM Image Adapter/A and Printer/Scanner Option
8EF7	IBM Gearbox Model 800 System Resource Card
8EFD	IBM Gearbox Model 800 Cached SCSI Adapter
8EFE	IBM PS/2 SCSI Adapter (16 bit)
8EFF	IBM PS/2 SCSI Adapter with Cache (32/16 bit)
8F70	IBM Realtime Interface Co-Processor Portmaster Adapter
8FC4	IBM Personal/370 Processor
8FC8	Token-Ring Busmaster Adapter/A
8FCF	IBM Remote 5250 Adapter/A
8FDB	XGA Video Adapter
8FFF	IBM Gearbox Model 800 Processor Card
A980	Intel ActionMedia i750 DVI card
D77F	IBM 4755 Cryptographic Adapter
DDFF	IBM ESDI Fixed Disk Controller
DEFF	IBM Multi-Protocol Communications Adapter
DF3F	IBM IEEE488 Adapter/A
DF7F	3363 Optical Disk Controller
DF9F	IBM Integrated Fixed Disk Controller 60/120 Mb
DFAF	IBM 4250 Printer Adapter/A
DFBF	IBM 6157 Streaming Tape Adapter Card

ID	Adapter Name
DFF6	IBM 3890/XP Interface Adapter
DFFA	5.25-inch Diskette Drive Adapter
DFFC	IBM INFOWINDOW GPIB2 CARD
DFFD	ST506 Fixed Disk Controller
E000	IBM Token-Ring Network Adapter/A
E001	IBM Token-Ring Network 16/4 Adapter/A (or Trace & Performance)
E014	IBM S/370 Channel Emulator/A
E016	IBM 300/1200/2400 Internal Modem/A
E04F	3119 High Speed Scanner Adapter
E1FF	IBM 3270 Connection Version B (Short card)
E7FF	IBM 3270 Connection Version A (Long Card)
EAA8	Engineering Graphics Display (IBM, Internal use only)
EAFF	IBM 4 port serial adapter
ECCE	IBM Display Adapter 1.10
ECEC	IBM Display Adapter 1.00
EDAF	IBM P70 Plasma Display controller
EDD7	IBM RAS Adapter
EDFF	IBM PS/2 1200/2400 Internal Modem/A
EECE	IBM 4684 Device Channel Adapter
EEE7	Serial Port 2
EEFF	IBM Dual Async Adapter
EF7F	IBM 8514/A Display Adapter
EF8F	IBM Extended Async Communication Adapter/A
EFB0	IBM ISDN Interface Co-Processor/2 Model 2
EFBF	InfoWindow VGA Control Card
EFCF	IBM Store Loop Adapter
EFE0	IBM ISDN Interface Co-Processor/2
EFE2	IBM FAX Server Card
EFE5	PS/2 Adapter for Ethernet Networks/A
EFEF	PC Network Adapter
EFF0	IBM Realtime Interface (Co-processor Multiport/2 or X.25/2
EFF2	IBM G3 Adapter/A
EFF3	IBM MSR-J Adapter/A
EFF5	Ungermann-Bass NICps/2 Ethernet LAN Adapter
EFF6	IBM Personal Pageprinter (4216) Adapter/A
EFF8	IBM TTL Async Communication Adapter
EFFE	IBM Display Adapter II 1.10
EFFF	IBM Video Adapter-J 1.10
F04F	IBM 3117 Scanner Adapter/A
F7CE	IBM EMS Support Card (For PS/55 5530Zxx)

(continues)

ID	Adapter Name
	Table 3.16 Continued
ID	**Adapter Name**
F7F7	IBM Memory Expansion Adapter 2-8M 80286
F7FE	IBM XMA/A Memory adapter (2M or 0-8M)
FA74	IBM 7437 PS/2 Interface Adapter Card
FAFF	IBM Memory Expansion Adapter 2-6M 80386
FCF0	Serial/Parallel Adapter
FCFF	IBM Memory Expansion Adapter 2-8M 80386
FDDF	Enhanced Memory Expansion 16M 80386
FEFE	IBM Memory Expansion Adapter 1-2M 80286
FF7F	Built In Features
FFAF	Built In Features
FFCF	IBM Store Loop Adapter
FFDE	IBM Gearbox Model {800-0-16MB Extended Memory Adapter
FFF8	S36/38 Workstation Emulation Adapter

System Resources

Hardware Interrupts

Interrupt request channels (IRQ), or hardware interrupts, are used by various hardware devices to signal the motherboard that a request must be fulfilled. These channels are represented by wires on the motherboard and in the slot connectors. When a particular interrupt is invoked, a special routine takes over the system, which first saves all the CPU register contents on a stack and then directs the system to the interrupt vector table. In this vector table is a list of program locations or addresses that correspond to each interrupt channel. Depending on which interrupt was invoked, the program corresponding to that channel is run. The pointers in this vector table point to the address of whatever software driver is used to service the card that generated the interrupt. For a network card, for example, the vector may point to the address of the network drivers that have been loaded to operate the card; for a hard disk controller, the vector may point to the ROM BIOS code that operates the controller. After the particular software routine is finished performing whatever function the card needed, the interrupt control software returns the stack contents to the CPU registers, and the system then continues whatever it was doing before the interrupt occurred.

By using interrupts, your system can respond in a timely fashion to external events. Each time a serial port presents a byte to your system, an interrupt is generated to ensure that the system responds immediately to read that byte before another comes in. Hardware interrupts are prioritized by their number, with the highest-priority interrupts having the lowest numbers. Higher-priority interrupts take precedence over lower-priority interrupts by interrupting them. In this way, several interrupts can occur concurrently in your system, each nesting within the other. If you overload the system, in this case by running out of stack resources, an `internal stack overflow` message results. By increasing the available stack resources through the STACKS parameter in CONFIG.SYS, you can handle such situations.

The Industry Standard Architecture (ISA) bus uses *edge-triggered interrupt sensing*, in which the interrupt is sensed by a signal sent on a particular wire located in the slot connector. A different wire corresponds to each hardware interrupt. Because the motherboard cannot recognize which slot contains the card that signalled the interrupt line and, therefore, generated the interrupt, if more than one card were set to use a particular interrupt, confusion would result. Each interrupt, therefore, usually is designated for a single hardware device, and most of the time cannot be "shared."

A device can be designed to share interrupts, and a few devices allow this; most cannot, however, because of the way interrupts are signaled in the ISA bus. Systems with the Micro Channel Architecture (MCA) bus use *level-sensitive interrupts*, which allows complete interrupt sharing to occur. In fact, all boards could be set to the same interrupt with no conflicts or problems. For maximum performance, however, interrupts should be staggered as much as possible. By eliminating interrupt conflicts as a problem, the MCA bus makes configuring boards much simpler than the ISA bus, and allows for more expansion, because you can never "run out of" interrupts.

Because interrupts usually cannot be shared in the ISA bus systems, you often will run out of interrupts when you are adding boards to a system. If two boards use the same interrupt level to signal the system, a conflict causes neither board to operate properly. The tables in the following sections show you the interrupt channels (IRQ) any standard devices use, and what may be free in your system. The AT systems have twice the number of interrupts and usually can be expanded much more easily than 8-bit ISA (PC or XT) systems.

8-Bit ISA Bus Interrupts

The PC and XT have eight standard prioritized levels of interrupt, with the lower priority 6 (numbered 2-7) being bused to the system expansion slots. A special Non-Maskable Interrupt (NMI) has the highest priority. The interrupts are used as follows, in order of priority:

Table 3.17   XT-bus (8-bit ISA) Default Interrupt Assignment

IRQ	Function	Bus Slot
0	System Timer	No
1	Keyboard Controller	No
2	Available	Yes (8-bit)
3	Serial Port 2 (COM2:)	Yes (8-bit)
4	Serial Port 1 (COM1:)	Yes (8-bit)
5	Hard Disk Controller	Yes (8-bit)
6	Floppy Disk Controller	Yes (8-bit)
7	Parallel Port 1 (LPT1:)	Yes (8-bit)

ISA (16-bit), EISA, and MCA Bus Interrupts

The AT supports 16 standard levels of interrupts, with 11 channels bused to the expansion slots. A special Non-Maskable Interrupt (NMI) has the highest priority. Two Intel 8259A controllers are used, with 8 channels per chip. The interrupts from the second chip are cascaded through IRQ 2 on the first chip.

Because IRQ 2 now is used directly by the motherboard, the wire for IRQ 9 has been rerouted to the same position in the slot that IRQ 2 normally would occupy. Therefore, any board you install that is set to IRQ 2 is really using IRQ 9. The interrupt vector table has been adjusted accordingly to enable this deception to work. This adjustment to the system enables greater compatibility with the PC interrupt structure and enables cards set to IRQ 2 to work properly. Note that Interrupts 0, 1, 2, 8, and 13 are *not* on the bus connectors and are not accessible to adapter cards. Interrupts 10, 11, 12, 14, and 15 are from the second interrupt controller and are accessible only by boards that use the 16-bit extension connector, because this is where these wires are found. IRQ 9 is rewired to the 8-bit slot connector in place of IRQ 2, which means that IRQ 9 replaces IRQ 2 and, therefore, is available to 8-bit cards (as IRQ 2). Although the 16-bit ISA bus has twice as many interrupts as systems with the 8-bit ISA bus, you still will run out of available interrupts because only 16-bit adapters can use any of the new interrupts.

As before, although the MCA bus does follow this scheme, the interrupts can be shared without conflict. The interrupts are used as shown in this table:

Table 3.18   ISA, EISA, and MCA Default Interrupt Assignments

IRQ	Standard Function	Bus Slot
0	System Timer	No
1	Keyboard Controller	No
2	Second IRQ Controller	No
8	Real-Time Clock	No
9	Available (Redirected IRQ 2)	Yes (8-bit)
10	Available	Yes (16-bit)
11	Available	Yes (16-bit)
12	Motherboard Mouse Port	Yes (16-bit)
13	Math Coprocessor	No
14	Hard Disk Controller	Yes (16-bit)
15	Available	Yes (16-bit)
3	Serial Port 2 (COM2:)	Yes (8-bit)
4	Serial Port 1 (COM1:)	Yes (8-bit)
5	Parallel Port 2 (LPT2:)	Yes (8-bit)
6	Floppy Disk Controller	Yes (8-bit)
7	Parallel Port 1 (LPT1:)	Yes (8-bit)

DMA Channels

DMA channels are used by any high-speed communications devices that must send information to and receive information from the motherboard at high speed. A serial or parallel port does not use a DMA channel, but a network adapter often does. DMA channels sometimes can be shared if the devices are not of the type that would need them simultaneously. For example, you can have a network adapter and a tape backup adapter both sharing DMA channel 1, but you cannot back up while the network is running. To back up during network operation, you must ensure that each adapter uses a unique DMA channel. Note that twice as many DMA channels are available in an AT-type system.

8-Bit ISA DMA Channels

Four DMA (direct memory access) channels support high-speed data transfers between I/O devices and memory. Three of the channels are bused to the expansion slots and are used as follows:

Table 3.19 XT-bus (8-bit ISA) Default DMA Channel Assignments			
DMA	**Standard Function**	**Bus Slot**
0	Dynamic RAM Refresh	No
1	Available	Yes (8-bit)
2	Floppy Disk Controller	Yes (8-bit)
3	Hard Disk Controller	Yes (8-bit)

ISA (16-bit), EISA, and MCA Bus DMA Channels

The system supports seven direct memory access (DMA) channels, with six bused to the expansion slots. DMA channel 4 is used to cascade channels 0 through 3 to the microprocessor. Channels 1-3 are available for 8-bit transfers, and DMA 0 and 5-7 are for 16-bit transfers only. The channels are used as shown in the following table:

Table 3.20   ISA, EISA, and MCA Default DMA Channel Assignments

DMA	Standard Function	Bus Slot
0	Available	Yes (16-bit)
1	Available	Yes (8-bit)
2	Floppy Disk Controller	Yes (8-bit)
3	Available	Yes (8-bit)
4	First DMA Controller	No
5	Available	Yes (16-bit)
6	Available	Yes (16-bit)
7	Available	Yes (16-bit)

I/O Port Addresses

Input-output ports are addresses used by the processor to communicate directly with devices. These addresses are like memory addresses but are not for storage; 64K I/O ports are available in the IBM system design for both XT- and AT-type systems. Because the ports must be uniquely assigned to only a single board or device, the potential for conflicts exists. Plenty of I/O ports generally are available, but many boards do not allow their default port addresses to be changed. Note that the I/O addresses hex 000 to 0FF are reserved for the motherboard. Ports from 100 on up are available to adapter cards.

The following table lists all the default motherboard port addresses for any 8-bit ISA bus system.

Table 3.21   8-Bit ISA Motherboard I/O Port Addresses

Hex Addresses	Device
000-00F	8237 DMA Controller
020-021	8259 Interrupt Controller
040-043	8253 Timer chip
060-063	8255 Programmable Peripheral Interface chip
080	Manufacturer POST code port
080-083	DMA page registers
0A0	NMI mask register

The following table lists all the default motherboard port addresses for any 16-bit ISA bus system.

Table 3.22 16-bit ISA Motherboard I/O Port Addresses	
Hex Addresses	**Device**
000-01F	8237 DMA Controller 1
020-03F	8259 Interrupt Controller 1
040-05F	8254 Timer chip
060	8042 Keyboard/Auxiliary Device (Mouse) Controller
061	System board I/O port
064	8042 Keyboard/Auxiliary Device (Mouse) Controller
070	CMOS RAM Index Register, NMI mask
071	CMOS RAM Data Register
080	Manufacturer POST Code output port
080-08F	DMA page registers, 74LS612
0A0-0BF	8237 Interrupt Controller 2
0C0-0DF	8237 DMA Controller 2
0F0-0FF	Math Coprocessor

The following table lists the standard I/O Port Address usage of several common adapters.

Table 3.23 Common Adapter Card I/O Port Address Usage	
Hex Addresses	**Device**
1F0-1F7	16-Bit (AT) Hard disk controller
200-20F	Game (Joystick) Adapter I/O and Control
210-217	Expansion Unit
21F	Voice Communications Adapter
258-25F	Intel Above Board (EMS Adapter)
278-27F	Parallel Port 2 or 3 (LPT:2 or LPT:3)
2B0-2BF	Alternate Enhanced Graphics Adapter (EGA)
2E1	GPIB (Adapter 0)

Hex Addresses	Device
2E2-2E3	Data Acquisition (Adapter 0)
2E8-2EF	Serial Port 4 (COM:4)
2F8-2FF	Serial Port 2 (COM:2)
300-31F	Prototype card
320-32F	8-Bit (XT) Hard disk controller
348-357	DCA 3278 Terminal Emulator
360-367	PC Network (primary)
368-36F	PC Network (alternate)
378-37F	Parallel Port 1 or 2 (LPT:1 or LPT:2)
380-38F	SDLC, Bisynchronous Port 2
390-393	Cluster Adapter
3A0-3AF	Bisynchronous Port 1
3B0-3BF	Monochrome Display and Printer Adapter (MDA)
3BC-3BE	Parallel Port 1 (LPT:1)
3C0-3CF	Enhanced Graphics Adapter (EGA)
3D0-3DF	Color Graphics Adapter (CGA)
3E8-3EF	Serial Port 3 (COM:3)
3F0-3F7	Floppy Disk Controller
3F8-3FF	Serial Port 1 (COM:1)
A20-A23	Token Ring Network Adapter (primary)
A24-A27	Token Ring Network Adapter (secondary)

Power Supply Connectors

XT/AT (Standard Compatible) Style

The following table shows the pinouts for most standard AT
or PC/XT compatible systems. Some systems may have more
or fewer drive connectors; for example, IBM's AT system
power supplies had only three disk drive power connectors,
although most compatible power supplies have four. If you
are adding drives and need additional disk drive power

connectors, you may purchase "Y" splitter cables from many electronics supply houses (including Radio Shack) that will adapt a single power connector to serve two drives. Be sure that your total power supply output is capable of supplying the additional power as a precaution.

Table 3.24   Typical PC Compatible Power-Supply Connections

Connector	AT Type	PC/XT Type
P8-1	Power Good (+5 Vdc)	Power Good (+5 Vdc)
P8-2	+5 Vdc	Key (No connect)
P8-3	+12 Vdc	+12 Vdc
P8-4	−12 Vdc	−12 Vdc
P8-5	Ground (0)	Ground (0)
P8-6	Ground (0)	Ground (0)
P9-1	Ground (0)	Ground (0)
P9-2	Ground (0)	Ground (0)
P9-3	−5 Vdc	−5 Vdc
P9-4	+5 Vdc	+5 Vdc
P9-5	+5 Vdc	+5 Vdc
P9-6	+5 Vdc	+5 Vdc
P10-1	+12 Vdc	+12 Vdc
P10-2	Ground (0)	Ground (0)
P10-3	Ground (0)	Ground (0)
P10-4	+5 Vdc	+5 Vdc
P11-1	+12 Vdc	+12 Vdc
P11-2	Ground (0)	Ground (0)
P11-3	Ground (0)	Ground (0)
P11-4	+5 Vdc	+5 Vdc
P12-1	+12 Vdc	—
P12-2	Ground (0)	—
P12-3	Ground (0)	—
P12-4	+5 Vdc	—
P13-1	+12 Vdc	—
P13-2	Ground (0)	—
P13-3	Ground (0)	—
P13-4	+5 Vdc	—

Acceptable voltage ranges are 4.5 to 5.4 for 5 volts, and 10.8 to 12.9 for 12 volts.

Table 3.25 Disk Drive Power Connector		
Pin	Wire Color	Signal
1	Yellow	+12v
2	Black	Gnd
3	Black	Gnd
4	Red	+5v

Motherboard Connectors

Table 3.26 Battery Connector	
Pin	Signal
1	Gnd
2	Unused
3	KEY
4	+6v

Table 3.27 LED and Keylock Connector	
Pin	Signal
1	LED Power (+5v)
2	KEY
3	Gnd
4	Keyboard Inhibit
5	Gnd

Table 3.28 Speaker Connector	
Pin	Signal
1	Audio
2	KEY
3	Gnd
4	+5v

System Video Information

MDA	=	Monochrome Display Adapter
CGA	=	Color Graphics Adapter
EGA	=	Enhanced Graphics Adapter
PGA	=	Professional Graphics Adapter
MCGA	=	Multi-Color Graphics Array
VGA	=	Video Graphics Array
8514	=	8514/A Adapter
XGA	=	eXtended Graphics Array
APA	=	All Points Addressable (Graphics)
DBL	=	Double Scan
IL	=	Interlaced
-	=	Not Supported

Note

The 8514/A adapter allows the System Board VGA signals to pass through via the Auxiliary Video Connector (slot); therefore, all VGA modes will function normally. The XGA Adapter shuts down the System Board VGA and contains a full 16-bit VGA adapter circuit on board.

Table 3.29 Video Adapter & Display Modes & Standards

Video Std.	Introduced	Resolution	No. of Colors	Mode Type	BIOS Modes	Char. Format	Char. Box	Vert. (Hz)	Horiz. (KHz)	Scan Mode
									Scan Freq.	
MDA	08/12/81	720x350	4	Text	07h	80x25	9x14	50	8.432	Std
CGA	08/12/81	320x200	16	Text	00/01h	40x25	8x8	60	15.75	Std
		640x200	16	Text	02/03h	80x25	8x8	60	15.75	Std
		160x200	16	APA	-	-	-	60	15.75	Std
		320x200	4	APA	04/05h	40x25	8x8	60	15.75	Std
		640x200	2	APA	06h	80x25	8x8	60	15.75	Std
EGA	09/10/84	320x350	16	Text	00/01h	40x25	8x14	60	21.85	Std
		640x350	16	Text	02/03h	80x25	8x14	60	21.85	Std
		720x350	4	Text	07h	80x25	9x14	50	18.432	Std
		320x200	16	APA	0Dh	40x25	8x8	60	15.75	Std

(continues)

Table 3.29 Continued

Video Std.	Introduced	Resolution	No. of Colors	Mode Type	BIOS Modes	Char. Format	Char. Box	Scan Freq. Vert. (Hz)	Scan Freq. Horiz. (KHz)	Scan Mode
		640x200	16	APA	0Eh	80x25	8x8	15.75	Std	
		640x350	4	APA	0Fh	80x25	8x14	50	18.432	Std
		640x350	16	APA	10h	80x25	8x14	60	21.85	Std
PGA	09/10/84	320x200	16	Text	00/01h	40x25	8x8	60	15.75	Std
		640x200	16	Text	02/03h	80x25	8x8	60	15.75	Std
		320x200	4	APA	04/05h	40x25	8x8	60	15.75	Std
		640x200	2	APA	06h	80x25	8x8	60	15.75	Std
		640x480	256	APA	-	-	-	60	30.48	Std
MCGA	04/02/87	320x400	16	Text	00/01h	40x25	8x16	70	31.5	Std
		640x400	16	Text	02/03h	80x25	8x16	70	31.5	Std

								Scan Freq.	
Video Std.	Introduced	Resolution	No. of Colors	Mode Type	BIOS Modes	Char. Format	Char. Box	Vert. (Hz)	Horiz. (KHz)	Scan Mode
		320x200	4	APA	04/05h	40x25	8x8	70	31.5	DBL
		640x200	2	APA	06h	80x25	8x8	70	31.5	DBL
		640x480	2	APA	11h	80x30	8x16	60	31.5	Std
		320x200	256	APA	13h	40x25	8x8	70	31.5	DBL
VGA	04/02/87	360x400	16	Text	00/01h	40x25	9x16	70	31.5	Std
		720x400	16	Text	02/03h	80x25	9x16	70	31.5	Std
		320x200	4	APA	04/05h	40x25	8x8	70	31.5	DBL
		640x200	2	APA	06h	80x25	8x8	70	31.5	DBL
		720x400	16	Text	07h	80x25	9x16	70	31.5	Std
		320x200	16	APA	0Dh	40x25	8x8	70	31.5	DBL
		640x200	16	APA	0Eh	80x25	8x8	70	31.5	DBL

(continues)

Table 3.29 Continued

Video Std.	Introduced	Resolution	No. of Colors	Mode Type	BIOS Modes	Char. Format	Char. Box	Scan Freq.		
								Vert. (Hz)	Horiz. (KHz)	Scan Mode
		640x350	4	APA	0Fh	80x25	8x14	70	31.5	Std
		640x350	16	APA	10h	80x25	8x14	70	31.5	Std
		640x480	2	APA	11h	80x30	8x16	60	31.5	Std
		640x480	16	APA	12h	80x30	8x16	60	31.5	Std
		320x200	256	APA	13h	40x25	8x8	70	31.5	DBL
8514	04/02/87	1024x768	256	APA	H-0h	85x38	12x20	43.48	35.52	IL
		640x480	256	APA	H-1h	80x34	8x14	60	31.5	Std
		1024x768	256	APA	H-3h	146x51	7x15	43.48	35.52	IL
XGA	10/30/90	360x400	16	Text	00/01h	40x25	9x16	70	31.5	Std
		720x400	16	Text	02/03h	80x25	9x16	70	31.5	Std
		320x200	4	APA	04/05h	40x25	8x8	70	31.5	DBL

Video Std.	Introduced	Resolution	No. of Colors	Mode Type	BIOS Modes	Char. Format	Char. Box	Scan Freq. Vert. (Hz)	Horiz. (KHz)	Scan Mode
		640x200	2	APA	06h	80x25	8x8	70	31.5	DBL
		640x350	4	APA	0Fh	80x25	8x14	70	31.5	Std
		640x350	16	APA	10h	80x25	8x14	70	31.5	Std
		640x480	2	APA	11h	80x30	8x16	60	31.5	Std
		640x480	16	APA	12h	80x30	8x16	60	31.5	Std
		320x200	256	APA	13h	40x25	8x8	70	31.5	DBL
8514	04/02/87	1024x768	256	APA	H-0h	85x38	12x20	43.48	35.52	IL
		640x480	256	APA	H-1h	80x34	8x14	60	31.5	Std
		1024x768	256	APA	H-3h	146x51	7x15	43.48	35.52	IL
XGA	10/30/90	360x400	16	Text	00/01h	40x25	9x16	70	31.5	Std
		720x400	16	Text	02/03h	80x25	9x16	70	31.5	Std

(continues)

Table 3.29 Continued

Video Std.	Introduced	Resolution	No. of Colors	Mode Type	BIOS Modes	Char. Format	Char. Box	Vert. (Hz)	Horiz. (KHz)	Scan Mode
									Scan Freq.	
		320x200	4	APA	04/05h	40x25	8x8	70	31.5	DBL
		640x200	2	APA	06h	80x25	8x8	70	31.5	DBL
		720x400	16	Text	07h	80x25	9x16	70	31.5	Std
		320x200	16	APA	0Dh	40x25	8x8	70	31.5	DBL
		640x200	16	APA	0Eh	80x25	8x8	70	31.5	DBL
		640x350	4	APA	0Fh	80x25	8x14	70	31.5	Std
		640x350	16	APA	10h	80x25	8x14	70	31.5	Std
		640x480	2	APA	11h	80x30	8x16	60	31.5	Std
		640x480	16	APA	12h	80x30	8x16	60	31.5	Std
		320x200	256	APA	13h	40x25	8x8	70	31.5	DBL

Video Std.	Introduced	Resolution	No. of Colors	Mode Type	BIOS Modes	Char. Format	Char. Box	Scan Freq.		Scan Mode
								Vert. (Hz)	Horiz. (KHz)	
		1056x400	16	Text	14h	132x25	8x16	70	31.5	Std
		1056x400	16	Text	14h	132x43	8x9	70	31.5	Std
		1056x400	16	Text	14h	132x56	8x8	70	31.5	Std
		1056x400	16	Text	14h	132x60	8x6	70	31.5	Std
		1024x768	256	APA	H-0h	85x38	12x20	43.48	35.52	IL
		640x480	65536	APA	H-1h	80x34	8x14	60	31.5	Std
		1024x768	256	APA	H-2h	128x54	8x14	43.48	35.52	IL
		1024x768	256	APA	H-3h	146x51	7x15	43.48	35.52	IL

Video Connector Pinouts

Monochrome Display Adapter (MDA) Connector

The following table shows the Monochrome Display Adapter connector pinout.

Table 3.30   9-Pin Monochrome Display Adapter (MDA) Connector

Pin	Description	I/O
1	Ground	—
2	Ground	—
3	Not Used	—
4	Not Used	—
5	Not Used	—
6	+Intensity	Out
7	+Video	Out
8	+Horizontal	Out
9	—-Vertical	Out

Color Graphics Adapter (CGA) Connector

The following table shows the Color Graphics Adapter connector pinout.

Table 3.31   9-Pin color Graphics Adapter (CGA) Connector

Pin	Description	I/O
1	Ground	—
2	Ground	—
3	Red	Out
4	Green	Out
5	Blue	Out
6	+Intensity	Out
7	RESERVED	—
8	+Horizontal drive	Out
9	–Vertical drive	Out

Enhanced Graphics Adapter (EGA) Connector

The following table shows the EGA (Enhanced Graphics Adapter) connector pinout.

Table 3.32   9-Pin Enhanced Graphics Adapter (EGA) Connector

Pin	Description	I/O
1	Ground	—
2	Secondary Red	Out
3	Red	Out
4	Green	Out
5	Blue	Out
6	Secondary Green/Intensity	Out
7	Secondary Blue/Mono	Out
8	Horizontal Retrace	Out
9	Vertical Retrace	Out

Video Graphics Array (VGA) Connector

The following table shows the VGA (Video Graphics Array) or XGA (eXtended Graphics Array) connector pinouts. Also shown are typical pinouts for Monochrome or Color Displays that may be attached to the video adapter. Notice that when the display adapter detects a monochrome display, it performs a color summing function and sends the sum signal out pin 2 (green). This is how the monochrome displays can display colors as different shades.

Table 3.33   15-Pin Video Graphics Array (VGA) Connector

Pin	VGA Signal	I/O	Mono Display	Color Display
1	Red	Out	No Pin	Red
2	Green	Out	Mono	Green
3	Blue	Out	No Pin	Blue
4	Monitor ID 2	In	No Pin	No Pin/Ground
5	Digital Ground	—	Self Test	Self Test
6	Red Ground	—	Not Connected	Red Ground

Table 3.33	**Continued**			
Pin	VGA Signal	I/O	Mono Display	Color Display
7	Green Ground	—	Mono Ground	Green Ground
8	Blue Ground	—	No Pin	Blue Ground
9	KEY (plug)	—	KEY (No Pin)	KEY (No Pin)
10	Sync Ground	—	Ground	Ground
11	Monitor ID 0	In	No Pin	Ground/No Pin
12	Monitor ID 1	In	Ground	No Pin
13	Horizontal Sync	Out	Horizontal Sync	Horizontal Sync
14	Vertical Sync	Out	Vertical Sync	Vertical Sync
15	Monitor ID 3	In	No Pin	No Pin/Ground

Monitor ID Pins

The following table shows the settings used for the Monitor ID bits for several different IBM displays. By sensing which of these four pins is grounded, the video adapter can determine what type of display is attached. This is especially used with regards to Monochrome or Color display detection. In this manner, the VGA or XGA circuitry can properly select the color mapping and image size to suit the display.

Table 3.34	**IBM Display Monitor ID Settings**					
Display	Size	Type	ID0	ID1	ID2	ID3
8503	12-inch	Mono	No Pin	Ground	No Pin	No Pin
8512	13-inch	Color	Ground	No Pin	No Pin	No Pin
8513	12-inch	Color	Ground	No Pin	No Pin	No Pin
8514	15-inch	Color	Ground	No Pin	Ground	No Pin
8515	14-inch	Color	No Pin	No Pin	Ground	No Pin
9515	14-inch	Color	No Pin	No Pin	Ground	No Pin
9517	17-inch	Color	Ground	No Pin	Ground	Ground
9518	14-inch	Color	Ground	No Pin	Ground	No Pin

PS/2 System Specific Information

Table 3.35	IBM PS/2 System Models with ISA Bus									
Part number	CPU	MHz	PLANAR MEMORY Std.	Max.	STANDARD Floppy Drive	Hard Disk	Bus Type	Total/ Available Slots	STANDARD Video	Key Board	Date Introduced	Date Withdrawn
25												
8525-001	8086	8	512K	640K	1x720K		ISA/8	2/2	MCGA	SS	08/04/87	
8525-G01	8086	8	512K	640K	1x720K		ISA/8	2/2	MCGA	Enh	08/04/87	
8525-004	8086	8	512K	640K	1x720K		ISA/8	2/2	MCGA	SS	08/04/87	
8525-G04	8086	8	512K	640K	1x720K		ISA/8	2/2	MCGA	Enh	08/04/87	
25 LS												
8525-L01	8086	8	640K	640K	1x720K		ISA/8	2/1	MCGA	Enh	06/02/88	
8525-L04	8086	8	640K	640K	1x720K		ISA/8	2/1	MCGA	Enh	06/02/88	

(continues)

Table 3.35 Continued

Part number	CPU	MHz	PLANAR MEMORY Std.	Max.	STANDARD Floppy Drive	Hard Disk	Bus Type	Total/ Available Slots	STANDARD Video	Key Board	Date Introduced	Date Withdrawn
30												
8530-001	8086	8	640K	640K	1x720K		ISA/8	3/3	MCGA	Enh	04/04/89	12/27/90
8530-002	8086	8	640K	640K	2x720K		ISA/8	3/3	MCGA	Enh	04/02/87	07/05/89
8530-021	8086	8	640K	640K	1x720K	20M	ISA/8	3/3	MCGA	Enh	04/02/87	12/27/90
PS/1 286												
2011-M01	286	10	512K	2.5M	1x1.44M		ISA/16	0	VGA	Enh	06/26/90	
2011-C01	286	10	512K	2.5M	1x1.44M		ISA/16	0	VGA	Enh	06/26/90	
2011-M34	286	10	1M	2.5M	1x1.44M	30M	ISA/16	0	VGA	Enh	06/26/90	
2011-C34	286	10	1M	2.5M	1x1.44M	30M	ISA/16	0	VGA	Enh	06/26/90	
PS/1 SX												
2121-C42	386SX	16	2M	6M	1x1.44M	40M	ISA/16	0	VGA	Enh	10/07/91	

Part number	CPU	MHz	PLANAR MEMORY Std.	Max.	STANDARD Floppy Drive	Hard Disk	Bus Type	Total/ Available Slots	STANDARD Video	Key Board	Date Introduced	Date Withdrawn
2121-B82	386SX	16	2M	6M	1x1.44M	80M	ISA/16	2/2	VGA	Enh	10/07/91	
2121-C92	386SX	16	2M	6M	1x1.44M	129M	ISA/16	2/2	VGA	Enh	10/07/91	
25 286												
8525-006	286	10	1M	4M	1x1.44M		ISA/16	2/2	VGA	SS	05/10/90	
8525-G06	286	10	1M	4M	1x1.44M		ISA/16	2/2	VGA	Enh	05/10/90	
8525-036	286	10	1M	4M	1x1.44M	30M	ISA/16	2/2	VGA	SS	05/10/90	
8525-G36	286	10	1M	4M	1x1.44M	30M	ISA/16	2/2	VGA	Enh	05/10/90	
25 SX												
8525-K00	386SX	16	1M	16M	1x1.44M		ISA/16	2/1	VGA	Enh	01/21/92	
8525-K01	386SX	16	4M	16M	1x1.44M		ISA/16	2/2	VGA	Enh	01/21/92	
8525-L01	386SX	16	4M	16M	1x1.44M		ISA/16	2/1	VGA	Enh	01/21/92	

(continues)

Table 3.35 Continued

Part number	CPU	MHz	PLANAR MEMORY Std.	Max.	STANDARD Floppy Drive	Hard Disk	Bus Type	Total/Available Slots	Video	Key Board	Date Introduced	Date Withdrawn
30 286												
8530-E01	286	10	1M	4M	1x1.44M		ISA/16 3/3		VGA	Enh	09/13/87	05/04/92
8530-E21	286	10	1M	4M	1x1.44M	20M	ISA/16 3/3		VGA	Enh	09/13/88	09/11/91
8530-E31	286	10	1M	4M	1x1.44M	30M	ISA/16 3/3		VGA	Enh	09/26/89	01/17/92
8530-E41	286	10	1M	4M	1x1.44M	45M	ISA/16 3/3		VGA	Enh	04/23/91	05/04/92
35 SX												
8535-040	386SX	20	2M	16M	1x1.44M		ISA/16 3/3		VGA	Any	06/11/91	
8535-043	386SX	20	2M	16M	1x1.44M	40M	ISA/16 3/3		VGA	Any	06/11/91	

Part number	CPU	MHz	PLANAR MEMORY Std.	Max.	STANDARD Floppy Drive	Hard Disk	Bus Type	Total/ Available Slots	STANDARD Video	Key Board	Date Introduced	Date Withdrawn
35 LS												
8535-14X	386SX 20	2M	16M				ISA/16 3/2		VGA	Any	10/17/91	
8535-24X	386SX 20	2M	16M				ISA/16 3/2		VGA	Any	06/11/91	
40 SX												
8540-040	386SX 20	2M	16M		1x1.44M		ISA/16 5/5		VGA	Any	06/11/91	
8540-043	386SX 20	2M	16M		1x1.44M	40M	ISA/16 5/5		VGA	Any	06/11/91	
8540-045	386SX 20	2M	16M		1x1.44M	80M	ISA/16 5/5		VGA	Any	06/11/91	
L40 SX												
8543-044	386SX 20	2M	18M		1x1.44M	60M	ISA/16 0		VGA	SS	03/26/91	07/21/92

Table 3.36   IBM PS/2 System Models with MCA Bus

Part number	CPU	MHz	PLANAR MEMORY Std.	Max.	Floppy Drive	STANDARD Hard Disk	STANDARD Bus Type	Total/ Available Slots	STANDARD Key Video	Date Board	Date Introduced	Withdrawn
50												
8550-021	286	10	1M	1M	1x1.44M	20M	MCA/16	4/3	VGA	Enh	04/02/87	05/03/89
50Z												
8550-031	286	10	1M	2M	1x1.44M	30M	MCA/16	4/3	VGA	Enh	06/07/88	07/23/91
8550-061	286	10	1M	2M	1x1.44M	60M	MCA/16	4/3	VGA	Enh	06/07/88	07/23/91
55 SX												
8555-031	386SX	16	2M	8M	1x1.44M	30M	MCA/16	3/3	VGA	Enh	05/09/89	09/11/91
8555-041	386SX	16	4M	8M	1x1.44M	40M	MCA/16	3/3	VGA	Enh	06/11/91	05/25/92
8555-061	386SX	16	2M	8M	1x1.44M	60M	MCA/16	3/3	VGA	Enh	05/09/89	09/11/91
8555-081	386SX	16	4M	8M	1x1.44M	80M	MCA/16	3/3	VGA	Enh	06/11/91	05/25/92

Part number	CPU	MHz	PLANAR MEMORY Std.	Max.	Floppy Drive	STANDARD Hard Disk	Bus Type	Total/ Available Slots	STANDARD Key Video	Date Board	Date Introduced	Withdrawn
55 LS												
8555-LT0	386SX	16	4M	8M			MCA/16	3/2	VGA	Enh	10/09/90	05/25/92
8555-LE0	386SX	16	4M	8M			MCA/16	3/2	VGA	Enh	10/09/90	05/25/92
56 SX												
8556-043	386SX	20	4M	16M	1x2.88M	40M	MCA/16	3/3	VGA	Any	02/25/92	
8556-045	386SX	20	4M	16M	1x2.88M	80M	MCA/16	3/3	VGA	Any	02/25/92	
56 SLC												
8556-055	386SLC	20	4M	16M	1x2.88M	80M	MCA/16	3/3	VGA	Any	02/25/92	
8556-059	386SLC	20	4M	16M	1x2.88M	160M	MCA/16	3/3	VGA	Any	02/25/92	
56 LS												
8556-14x	386SX	20	4M	16M			MCA/16	3/2	VGA	Any	02/25/92	

(continues)

Table 3.36 Continued

Part number	CPU	MHz	PLANAR MEMORY Std.	Max.	Floppy Drive	STANDARD Hard Disk	Bus Type	Total/ Available Slots	STANDARD Key Video	Date Board	Date Introduced	Withdrawn
8556-24x	386SX	20	4M	16M			MCA/16	3/2	VGA	Any	02/25/92	
56 SLC LS												
8556-15x	386SLC	20	4M	16M			MCA/16	3/2	VGA	Any	02/25/92	
8556-25x	386SLC	20	4M	16M			MCA/16	3/2	VGA	Any	02/25/92	
57 SX												
8557-045	386SX	20	4M	16M	1x2.88M	80M	MCA/16	5/5	VGA	Any	06/11/91	12/21/92
8557-049	386SX	20	4M	16M	1x2.88M	160M	MCA/16	5/5	VGA	Any	06/11/91	12/21/92
57 SLC												
8557-055	386SLC	20	4M	16M	1x2.88M	80M	MCA/16	5/5	VGA	Any	02/25/92	
8557-059	386SLC	20	4M	16M	1x2.88M	160M	MCA/16	5/5	VGA	Any	02/25/92	

Part number	CPU	MHz	PLANAR MEMORY Std.	Max.	Floppy Drive	STANDARD Hard Disk	Bus Type	Total/Available Slots	STANDARD Key Video	Date Board	Date Introduced	Withdrawn
M57 SLC												
8557-255	386SLC	20	4M	16M	1x2.88M	80M	MCA/16	5/3	XGA	Any	10/17/91	02/25/92
8557-259	386SLC	20	4M	16M	1x2.88M	160M	MCA/16	5/3	XGA	Any	02/25/92	
60												
8560-041	286	10	1M	1M	1x1.44M	44M	MCA/16	8/7	VGA	Enh	04/02/87	10/31/90
8560-071	286	10	1M	1M	1x1.44M	70M	MCA/16	8/7	VGA	Enh	04/02/87	10/31/90
65 SX												
8565-061	386SX	16	2M	8M	1x1.44M	60M	MCA/16	8/7	VGA	Enh	03/20/90	07/23/91
8565-121	386SX	16	2M	8M	1x1.44M	120M	MCA/16	8/7	VGA	Enh	03/20/90	07/23/91
8565-321	386SX	16	2M	8M	1x1.44M	320M	MCA/16	8/7	VGA	Enh	10/30/90	07/23/91

(continues)

Table 3.36 Continued

70 386

Part number	CPU	MHz	PLANAR MEMORY Std.	Max.	Floppy Drive	STANDARD Hard Disk	Bus Type	Total/ Available Slots	STANDARD Key Video	Date Board	Date Introduced	Withdrawn
8570-E61	386DX	16	2M	6M	1x1.44M	60M	MCA/32	3/3	VGA	Enh	06/07/88	07/23/91
8570-061	386DX	20	2M	6M	1x1.44M	60M	MCA/32	3/3	VGA	Enh	09/26/89	09/11/91
8570-081	386DX	20	4M	6M	1x1.44M	80M	MCA/32	3/3	VGA	Enh	06/11/91	
8570-121	386DX	20	2M	6M	1x1.44M	120M	MCA/32	3/3	VGA	Enh	09/26/89	09/11/91
8570-161	386DX	20	4M	6M	1x1.44M	160M	MCA/32	3/3	VGA	Enh	06/11/91	
8570-A61	386DX	25	2M	8M	1x1.44M	60M	MCA/32	3/3	VGA	Enh	09/26/89	09/11/91
8570-A81	386DX	25	4M	8M	1x1.44M	80M	MCA/32	3/3	VGA	Enh	06/11/91	01/17/92
8570-A21	386DX	25	2M	8M	1x1.44M	120M	MCA/32	3/3	VGA	Enh	09/26/89	09/11/91
8570-A16	386DX	25	4M	8M	1x1.44M	160M	MCA/32	3/3	VGA	Enh	06/11/91	

Part number	CPU	MHz	PLANAR MEMORY Std.	Max.	Floppy Drive	STANDARD Hard Disk	STANDARD Bus Type	Total/Available Slots	STANDARD Key Video	Date Board	Date Introduced	Withdrawn
70 486												
8570-B61	486DX	25	2M	8M	1x1.44M	60M	MCA/32	3/3	VGA	Enh	09/26/89	09/11/91
8570-B21	486DX	25	2M	8M	1x1.44M	120M	MCA/32	3/3	VGA	Enh	06/20/89	09/11/91
P70 386												
8573-031	386DX	16	2M	8M	1x1.44M	30M	MCA/32	2/2	VGA	Enh	03/20/90	07/23/91
8573-061	386DX	20	4M	8M	1x1.44M	60M	MCA/32	2/2	VGA	Enh	05/09/89	07/23/91
8573-121	386DX	20	4M	8M	1x1.44M	120M	MCA/32	2/2	VGA	Enh	05/09/89	
P75 486												
8573-161	486DX	33	8M	16M	1x1.44M	160M	MCA/32	4/4	XGA	Enh	11/12/90	12/15/92
8573-401	486DX	33	8M	16M	1x1.44M	400M	MCA/32	4/4	XGA	Enh	11/12/90	04/30/93

(continues)

Table 3.36 Continued

Part number	CPU	MHz	PLANAR MEMORY Std.	Max.	Floppy Drive	STANDARD Hard Disk	STANDARD Bus Type	Total/ Available Slots	STANDARD Key Video	Date Board	Date Introduced	Withdrawn
80 386												
8580-041	386DX	16	1M	4M	1x1.44M	44M	MCA/32	8/7	VGA	Enh	04/02/87	10/31/90
8580-071	386DX	16	2M	4M	1x1.44M	70M	MCA/32	8/7	VGA	Enh	04/02/87	10/31/90
8580-081	386DX	20	4M	4M	1x1.44M	80M	MCA/32	8/7	VGA	Enh	10/30/90	
8580-111	386DX	20	2M	4M	1x1.44M	115M	MCA/32	8/7	VGA	Enh	04/02/87	12/27/90
8580-121	386DX	20	2M	4M	1x1.44M	120M	MCA/32	8/7	VGA	Enh	03/20/90	01/29/91
8580-161	386DX	20	4M	4M	1x1.44M	160M	MCA/32	8/7	VGA	Enh	10/30/90	
8580-311	386DX	20	2M	4M	1x1.44M	314M	MCA/32	8/7	VGA	Enh	08/04/87	12/27/90
8580-321	386DX	20	4M	4M	1x1.44M	320M	MCA/32	8/7	VGA	Enh	03/20/90	
8580-A21	386DX	25	4M	8M	1x1.44M	120M	MCA/32	8/7	VGA	Enh	03/20/90	01/29/91
8580-A16	386DX	25	4M	8M	1x1.44M	160M	MCA/32	8/7	VGA	Enh	10/30/90	

Part number	CPU	MHz	PLANAR MEMORY Std.	Max.	Floppy Drive	STANDARD Hard Disk	Bus Type	Total/Available Slots	STANDARD Key Video	Date Board	Date Introduced	Withdrawn
8580-A31	386DX	25	4M	8M	1x1.44M	320M	MCA/32	8/7	VGA	Enh	03/20/90	
90 XP 486												
8590-0G5	486SX	20	4M	64M	1x1.44M	80M	MCA/32	4/3	XGA	Enh	04/23/91	01/17/92
8590-0G9	486SX	20	4M	64M	1x1.44M	160M	MCA/32	4/3	XGA	Enh	04/23/91	01/17/92
8590-0H5	486SX	25	4M	64M	1x1.44M	80M	MCA/32	4/3	XGA	Enh	10/17/91	
8590-0H9	486SX	25	4M	64M	1x1.44M	160M	MCA/32	4/3	XGA	Enh	10/17/91	
8590-0J5	486DX	25	8M	64M	1x1.44M	80M	MCA/32	4/3	XGA	Enh	10/30/90	01/17/92
8590-0J9	486DX	25	8M	64M	1x1.44M	160M	MCA/32	4/3	XGA	Enh	10/30/90	01/17/92
8590-0K9	486DX	33	8M	64M	1x1.44M	320M	MCA/32	4/3	XGA	Enh	10/17/91	07/28/92
8590-0KD	486DX	33	8M	64M	1x1.44M	320M	MCA/32	4/3	XGA	Enh	10/30/90	07/17/92
8590-0KF	486DX	33	8M	64M	1x1.44M	400M	MCA/32	4/3	XGA	Enh	10/17/91	07/28/92

(continues)

Table 3.36 Continued

95 XP 486

Part number	CPU	MHz	PLANAR MEMORY Std.	Max.	Floppy Drive	STANDARD Hard Disk	Bus Type	Total/ Available Slots	STANDARD Key Video	Date Board	Date Introduced	Withdrawn
8595-0G9	486SX	20	4M	64M	1x1.44M	160M	MCA/32	8/6	XGA	Enh	04/23/91	01/17/92
8595-0GF	486SX	20	4M	64M	1x1.44M	400M	MCA/32	8/6	XGA	Enh	04/23/91	01/17/92
8595-0H9	486SX	25	8M	64M	1x1.44M	160M	MCA/32	8/6	XGA	Enh	10/17/91	
8595-0HF	486SX	25	8M	64M	1x1.44M	400M	MCA/32	8/6	XGA	Enh	10/17/91	
8595-0J9	486DX	25	8M	64M	1x1.44M	160M	MCA/32	8/6	XGA	Enh	10/30/90	01/17/92
8595-0JD	486DX	25	8M	64M	1x1.44M	320M	MCA/32	8/6	XGA	Enh	10/30/90	01/17/92
8595-0JF	486DX	25	8M	64M	1x1.44M	400M	MCA/32	8/6	XGA	Enh	04/23/91	01/17/92
8595-0KD	486DX	33	8M	64M	1x1.44M	320M	MCA/32	8/6	XGA	Enh	10/30/90	01/17/92
8595-0KF	486DX	33	8M	64M	1x1.44M	400M	MCA/32	8/6	XGA	Enh	04/23/91	

Table 3.37 Standard PS/2 Accessories

Description	Part number	Notes
PS/2 mouse	6450350	2-button mouse
Trackpoint	1397040	Mouse/trackball
Dual Serial adapter/A	6451013	For 50-95, NS16550, 9-pin plug
Serial/parallel adapter	6450215	25-40 (not L40), NS16450, 9-pin
Floor stand	92F5606	Vertical mount for 35 LS/SX

Table 3.38 PS/2Memory Modules and Adapters

Description	Part number	Notes
ISA 8-bit memory adapter		
Expanded memory adapter	2685193	2M RAM , LPT (XMA) port, XT/AT/30
ISA bus 16-bit memory adapters		
0-12M multifunction adapter	30FS364	COM/LPT port, 30 286
All Charge Card	34F2863	Memory manager for 25/30 286
3M expanded memory adapter	34F2864	ChargeCard, 0-12M card, 3M RAM
4M expanded memory kit	34F2866	ChargeCard, 4M system-board RAM
MCA bus 16-bit memory adapters		
1-8M 80286 memory optional/85ns	6450685	M, EMS 4.0 for 50 55/60/65
2-8M 80286 memory optional/85ns	6450609	2M, EMS 4.0 for 50 55/60/65
MCA bus 32-bit adapters		
2-14M enhanced adapters	87F9856	2M, for 70/P70/80 /85ns
4-14M enhanced adapter	87F9860	4M, for 70/P70/80 /85ns

(continues)

Table 3.38 Continued

Description	Part number	Notes
Memory module kits (SIMMs)		
25 system board	78X8955	128K kit (6chips) memory/ 120Nns for 25
512K memory module kit	30F5348	2-256K SIMMs for /120ns 30F5364/1497259, 25/30 286 system board
2M memory module kit 120 ns	30F5360	2-1M SIMMs for 30F5364/ 1497259, 34F2866 25/30 286 System board
1M memory module kit/85ns	6450603	1M SIMM for 6450605/ 6450609, 6450685/34F30771/ 34F3011, 50Z/55/65/70 386 (Not Axx/Bxx)/P70 386
2M memory module kit/85ns	6450604	2M SIMM for 6450605/ 6450609, 6450685/3$F3077/ 34F3011, 50Z/55/65/70 (Not Axx/Bxx)/P70 386
4M memory module kit/85ns	87F9977	4M SIMM for 35/40/55/ 6534F3011/34F3077
2M memory module kit/80ns	6450608	2M SIMM for 35/40/70 -Axx/ Bxx
8M memory module kit/80ns	6450129	8M SIMM for 35/40
2M memory module kit/70ns	6450902	2M SIMM for 57/90/95
4M memory module kit/70ns	6450128	4M SIMM for 57/p75/90/95
8M memory module kit/70ns	6450130	8M SIMM for 35/40/57/P75/90/ 95
2M memory module kit/80ns	79F0999	2M CMOS SIMM for L40 (keyed)
4M memory module kit/80ns	79F1000	4M CMOS SIMM for L40 (keyed)
8M memory module kit/80ns	79F1001	8M CMOS SIMM for L40 (keyed)
1M system board kit/80ns	6450375	1M card for 80-041
2M system board kit/80ns	6450379	2M card for 80 (except Axx)
4M system board kit/80ns	6451060	4M card for 80-A21/A31

Table 3.39 PS/2 Floppy Drives, Adapters, and Cables

Description	Part number	Notes
5 1/4-inch floppy drives		
5 1/4-inch external 360K drive	4869001	For all PS/2s
5 1/4-inch external 1.2M drive	4869002	For 50-95, requires 6451007
5 1/2-inch internal 1.2M drive	6451006	For 60/65/80
5 1/4-inch internal 1.2M slim drive	6451066	For 35/40/57/90/95
3 1/2-inch floppy drives		
3 1/2-inch internal 720K drive	78X8956	For 25 S/N<100,000
3 1/2-inch internal 720K 1/3-height drive	6451056	For 25 S/N>100,000
3 1/2-inch internal 720K 1/3-height drive	6451027	For 30-001
3 1/2 inch internal1.44M 1/3-height drive	6451063	For 25-006/G06
3 1/2-inch internal 1.44M drive 386	6450353	For 30-E01/50-80, not 55/P70
3 1/2-inch internal 1.44M slim drive	6451130	35/40/57, not L40, media-sense
3 1/2-inch internal 1.44M 1/3-height drive	6451072	50-95, not 55/P70 30-E01
3 1/2-inch internal 2.88M slim drive	6451106	35/40/547, not L40, media-sense
Floppy disk drive adapters		
5 1/4-inch external adapter L40	6450244	360K for 25-40, not drive
5 1/4-inch external drive adapter/A	6450245	360K for 50-80, not 55/P70 386
5 1/4-inch floppy disk drive adapter/A	6451007	For 1.2M/360K in 50-95
Cables and miscellaneous		
5 1/4-inch external 360K cable external drive	6451033	For 30-001/021
5 1/4-inch external 360K cable	27F4245	For 30-Exx external drive
5 1/4-inch external drive adapter cable	6451124	For 35/40 and 4869001
External storage device cable	23F2716	P70 360K,P75 360K/ 1.2M
3 1/2-inch internal drive kit	6451037	Cable/Bezel for 6451353

(continues)

Description	Part number	Notes
Cables and miscellaneous		
3 1/2-inch internal 1/3 height drive kit	6451034	Cable/Bezel for 6451072
3 1/2-inch internal 1/3-height drive kit B	6451035	For 6451026 in 55 LS
Drive upgrade kit for 35 LS	6451127	For 6451130/6451106/ 6451066
IBM preformatted floppy disks		
5 1/4-inch 10 360K disks	6023450	Carboard slipcase
5 1/4-inch 10 360K disks with case	6069769	Plastic library case/ stand
5 1/4-inch 10 1.2M disks	6109660	Cardboard slipcase
5 1/4-inch 10 1.2M disks with case	6109661	Plastic library case/ stand
3 1/2-inch 10 720K disks with case	6404088	Plastic library case/ stand
3 1/2-inch 10 1.44M disks with case	6404083	Plastic library case/ stand
3 1/2-inch 10 2.88M disks with case	72X6111	Plastic library case/ stand

Table 3.40 PS/2 Hard Disks, Adapters, and Cables

Description	Part number	Notes
IDE hard disk drives		
20M 3 1/2-inch 80ms IDE drive	78X8958	for 25
20M 3 1/2-inch 27ms IDE drive	6451075 6451071	For 25-xx6, Req
30M 3 1/2-inch 19ms IDE drive 6451071	6451076	For 25-xx6, Req
40M 3 1/2-inch 17ms IDE drive	6451047	For 55 LS
40M 3 1/2-inch 17 ms IDE drive	6451073	For 35/40
80M 3 1/2-inch 17 ms IDE drive	6451043	For 55 LS
80M 3 1/2-inch 17ms IDE drive	6451074	For 35/40

Description	Part number	Notes
SCSI hard disk drives		
60M 3 1/2-inch 23ms, 32K cache	6451049	Async, 1.25M/sec Xfer rate
80M 3 1/2-inch 17ms, 32K cache	6451045	Async, 1.25M/sec Xfer rate
120M 3 1/2-inch 23 ms, 32K cache	6451050	Async, 1.5M/sec Xfer rate
160M 3 1/2-inch 116ms, 32K cache	6451046	Async, 1.5M/sec Xfer rate
320M 3 1/2-inch 12.5ms, 64K cache	6451234	Sync, 2.0M/sec Xfer rate
400M 3 1/2-inch 11.5ms, 128K cache	6451235	Sync, 2.0M/sec Xfer rate
IG 3 1/2-inch 11ms, 256K cache	0451052	Sync, 2.0M/sec Xfer rate
SCSI host adapter		
SCSI ADapter/A	6451109	375 16-bit Bus Master
SCSI Adapter/A with 512K cache	6451133	32/16-bit Bus Master
SCSI external terminator	6451039	For Adapter with Cache
Cables and miscellaneous		
Fixed Disk Drive Kit A	6451071	Installation kit for 25-xx6
Fixed Disk Upgrade Kit/35	6451128 35 LS	For 6451073/6451074 in
SCSI Installation Kit A	6451053	For 3 1/2-inch drive in 60/65/80
Fixed Disk Drive Kit D	6451120	For 60/120M drives in 90/95
SCSI card to option cable	6451139	Includes terminator, replaces 6451041
SCSI option to option cable	6451042	Connect external options

(continues)

Table 3.40 Continued

Description	Part number	Notes
CD-ROM drives		
Internal 600M CD-ROM drive	6451113	Requires SCSI adapter
External 600M CD-ROM drive	3510001	Requires SCSI adapter
CD-ROM installation kit/A	6450847	Install in 5 1/4-inch bay
3 1/2-inch 128 rewritable drive	6450162	Requires SCSI adapter
OPtical drive Kit A	6451126	For 6450162 in 60/80 (non-SCSI)
3 1/2-inch rewritable cartridge	38F8645	128M cartridge for 6451062
3 1/2-inch rewritable cartridge	38F8646	5-128M cartridges for 6450162
8mm tape backup drives and accessories		
2.3G internal SCSI drive	6451121	For 95/3511, requires SYTOS
2.3G external SCSI drive	6451121	Requires SCSI adapter and SYTOS
SCSI cable for external drive	31F4187	Connects tape drive to system
SCSI device-to-device cable	31F4186	Chains tape to other devices
8mm data cartridge	21F8595	Stores 2.3 gigabytes
8mm cleaning cartridge	21F8593	For cleaning heads
SYTOS plus v1.3 for DOS	04G3375	Data compression
SYTOS plus v1.3 for OS/2 PM FAT/HPFS	04G3374	Data compression,
SCSI expansion units		
3510 external SCSI storage unit	35100V0	1 half-height, 3 1/2-inch, 5 1/4-inch bay
3511 external SCSI storage unit	3511003	7 bays, 3 1/2-inch, 5 1/4-inch, 320M drive

Table 3.41   IBM-Installed ST-506/412 Hard Drives Used in the XT, AT, and PS/2 Model 25

Drive form factor	5 1/4	5 1/4	5 1/4	5 1/4	3 1/2
Capacity	10MB	20MB	20MB	30MB	20MB
Physical/logical interface	ST506	ST506	ST506	ST506	ST506
Average access rate (ms)	85	65	40	40	38
Read-ahead cache (k)	—	—	—	—	—
Encoding scheme	MFM	MFM	MFM	MFM	RLL
BIOS drive type number	1	2	2	2	36
Cylinders	306	615	615	733	402
Heads	4	4	4	5	4
Sectors/track	17	17	17	17	26
Rotational speed (RPM)	3600	3600	3600	3600	3600
Standard interleave factor	6:1	3:1	3:1	3:1	3:1
Data transfer rate (K/second)	85	170	170	170	260
Automatic head parking	No	No	Yes	Yes	Yes

Table 3.42   IBM-Installed ST-506/412 Hard Drvides Used in the XT, AT, and PS/2 Models 50, 60, and 80

Drive form factor	3 1/2	5 1/4	5 1/4
Capacity	20MB	44MB	44MB
Physical/logical interface	ST506	ST506	ST506
Average access rate (ms)	80	40	40
Read-ahead cache (K)	—	—	—
Encoding scheme	MFM	MFM	MFM
BIOS drive type number	30	31	32
Cylinders	611	732	1023
Heads	4	7	5
Sectors/track	17	17	17
Rotational speed (RPM)	3600	3600	3600
Standard interleave factor	1:1	1:1	1:1
Data transfer rate (K/second)	510	510	510
Automatic head parking	No	Yes	Yes

Table 3.43   IBM-Installed XT IDE Drives Used in the PS/2 Models 25, 30, 25 286 and 30 286

Drive form factor	3 1/2	3 1/2	3 1/2	3 1/2	3 1/2
Capacity	20MB	20MB	30MB	30MB	45MB
Physical interface	IDE	IDE	IDE	IDE	IDE
Logical interface	XT	XT	XT	XT	XT
Average access rate (ms)	80	27	27	19	32
Read-ahead cache (k)	—	—	—	—	—
Encoding scheme	MFM	RLL	RLL	RLL	RLL
BIOS drive type number	26	34	33	35	37
Cylinders	612	775	614	921	580
Heads	4	2	4	2	6
Sectors/track	17	27	25	33	26
Rotational speed (RPM)	3600	3600	3600	3600	3600
Standard interleave factor	2:1	3:1	3:1	4:1	3:1
Data transfer rate (K/second)	255	270	250	248	260
Automatic head parking	No	No	No	Yes	Yes

Table 3.44   IBM-Installed ATA IDE Drives Used in the Models 35, 40, and L40

Drive for fact	2 1/2	3 1/2	3 1/2
Capacity	60MB	40MB	80MB
Physical interface	IDE	IDE	IDE
Logical interface	ATA	ATA	ATA
Average access rate (ms)	19	17	17
Read ahead cache (K)	—	32K	32K
Encoding scheme	RLL	RLL	RLL
BIOS drive type number	—	—	—
Cylinders	822	1038	1021
Heads	4	2	4
Sectors/track	38	39	39
Rotational speed (RPM)	3600	3600	3600
Standard interleave factor	1:1	1:1	1:1
Data transfer rate (K/second)	1140	1170	1170
Automatic head parking	Yes	Yes	Yes

Table 3.45   IBM-Installed MCA IDE Drives Used in the PS/2 Models 50Z, 55, 70 386, and P70 386

Drive form factor	3 1/2	3 1/2	3 1/2	3 1/2	3 1/2	3 1/2	3 1/2	3 1/2
Capacity	30MB	30MB	30MB	40MB	60MB	80MB	120MB	160MB
Physical interface	IDE	IDE	IDE	IDE	IDE	IDE	IDE	IDE
Logical interface	ST506	ST506	ESDI	ESDI	ESDI	ESDI	ESDI	ESDI
Average access rate (ms)	39	27	19	17	27	17	23	16
Read-ahead cache (K)	—	—	—	32K	—	32K	—	32K
Encoding scheme	RLL	RLL	RLL	RLL	RLL	RLL	RLL	RLL
BIOS drive type number	33	33	—	—	—	—	—	—
Cylinder	614	614	920	1038	762	1021	920	1021
Heads	4	4	2	2	6	4	8	8
Sectors/track	25	25	32	39	26	39	32	39
Rotational speed (RPM)	3600	3600	3600	3600	3600	3600	3600	3600

Table 3.46   IBM-Installed MCA IDE Drives Used in the PS/2 Models 50Z, 55, 70 386, and P70 386

Drive form factor	3 1/2	3 1/2	3 1/2	3 1/2	3 1/2	3 1/2	3 1/2	3 1/2
Standard interleave factor	1:1	1:1	1:1	1:1	1:1	1:1	1:1	1:1
Data transfer rate (K/second)	750	750	960	1170	780	1170	960	1170
Automatic head parking	No	No	Yes	Yes	Yes	Yes	Yes	Yes

Table 3.47   IBM-Installed ESDI Drives Used in the PS/2 Models 60 and 80

Drive form factor	5 1/4	5 1/4	5 1/4
Capacity	70MB	115MB	314MB
Physical/logical interface	ESDI	ESDI	ESDI
Average access rate (ms)	30	28	23
Read-ahead cache (K)	—	—	—
Encoding scheme	RLL	RLL	RLL
BIOS drive type number	—	—	—
Cylinders	583	915	1225

(continues)

Table 3.47   Continued

Drive form factor	5 1/4	5 1/4	5 1/4
Heads	7	7	15
Sectors/track	36	36	34
Rotational speed (RPM)	3600	3600	3283
Standard interleave factor	1:1	1:1	1:1
Data transfer rate (K/second)	1080	1080	930
Automatic head parking	Yes	Yes	Yes

Table 3.48   IBM-Installed SCSI DRives Used in the PS/2 Models 56, 57, 65, P75, 80, 90, and 95

Drive form factor	3 1/2	3 1/2	3 1/2	3 1/2	3 1/2	3 1/2
Capacity	60MB	80MB	120MB	160MB	320MB	400MB
Physical/logical interface	SCSI	SCSI	SCSI	SCSI	SCSI	SCS
Average access rate (ms)	23	17	23	16	12.5	11.5
Read-ahead cache (K)	32K	32K	32K	32K	64K	128K
SCSI transfer mode	Async	Async	Async	Async	Sync	Sync
Encoding scheme	RLL	RLL	RLL	RLL	RLL	RLL
BIOS drive type number	—	—	—	—	—	—
Cylinders	920	1021	920	1021	949	1201
Heads	4	4	8	8	14	14
Sectors/track	32	39	32	39	48	48
Rotational speed (RPM)	3600	3600	3600	3600	4318	4318
Standard interleave factor	1:1	1:1	1:1	1:1	1:1	1:1
Data transfer rate (K/second)	960	1170	960	1170	1727	1727
Automatic head parking	Yes	Yes	Yes	Yes	Yes	Yes

Table 3.49   PS/2 Video Displays and Adapters

Description	Part number	Notes
Analog displays		
8504 12-inch VGA Mono Display	8504001	640x480
8507 19-inch XGA Mono Display	8507001	1024x768
8604 16-inch XGA Mono Display	8604001	1024x768
PS/1 Color Display Upgrade	1057108	Upgrade for mono systems

Description	Part number	Notes
8512 14-inch Color Display	8512001	640x480, .41mm stripe
8513 12-inch VGA Color Display	8513001	640x480, .28mm dot, stand
Analog displays		
8514 16-inch XGA Color Display	8514001	1024x768, .31mm dot, stand
8515 14-inch XGA Color Display	8515021	024x768, 28mm dot, stand
8518 14-inch VGA Color Display	8518001	640x480, .28mm dot, stand
8516 14-inch XGA Touch Screen	8516001	1024,768, .28mm dot, stand
Analog display adapters		
XGA Adapter/A	75X5887	1024x768, For 55-95 (Not 60/P70)
Video Memory Expansion Option	75X5889	512K Video RAM for XGA
8514/A Display Adapter	1887972	1024x768x16, for 50-80 (Not P70)
8514/A Memory Expansion Kit	1887989	1024x768x256 colors
Miscellaneous display accessories		
Display Stand for 8512	1501215	Tilt-swivel stand
TouchSelect for 12-inch displays	91F7951	Adds Touch screen to 8513
Privacy Filter for 8512	1053405	Prevents side view of display
Privacy Filter for 8513	1053401	Prevents side view fo display
Privacy Filter for 8514	1053402	Prevents side view of display
Privacy Filter for 8515	1053403	Prevents side view of display

(continues)

Table 3.49 Continued

Description	Part number	Notes
ISA bus Token Ring NEtwork (TRN) adapters		
TRN Adapter II	2%F9858	$Mbps for 25-40 (not L40)
TRN 16/4 Adapter	25F7367	16/4Mbps for 25-40 (not L40)
TRN 16/4 Trace & Performance	74F5121	6/Mbps for 25-40 (not L40)
MCA bus Token Ring Network (TRN) adapters		
TRN ADapter/A (full-length)	69x8138	4mbps, for 50-95
TRN ADapter/A (half-length)	39F9598	4mbps for P70/75 (and 50-95)
TRN 16/4 Adapter/A	16F1133	16/4Mbps for 50-5
TRN 16/4 Adapter/A (half)	74F9410	16/Mbps, 50-95, 80 percent faster
TRN 16/4 Trace & Perf./A	74F5130	16/4Mbps for 50-95
TRN 16/4 Busmaster Server/A	74F4140	16/Mbps for 50-95 servers only
MCA bus EtherNet network adapters		
PS/2 EtherNet Adapter/A	6451091	0Mbps for 50-95 including boot ROM
Miscellaneous network adapter accessories		
TRN adapter cable	6339098	Connect card to LAN
TRN L-shaped connector cable	79F3229	For 74F9410 and P70/75
Miscellaneous network adapter accessories		
TRN 8230 Mbps media filter	53F5551	For unshielded twisted pair
TRN Adapter II boot ROM	83X7839	EPROM for 25F9858
TRN Adapter/A boot ROM	83X8881	EPROM for 69X8138/ 39F9598
TRN 16/4 Adapter/A boot ROM	25X8887	EPROM for 25F7367/ 16F1133

Chapter 4

System Communications Ports

This section shows the connector pinout specifications for a variety of connectors, from the ISA and MCA bus connectors to serial and parallel ports, as well as video display, keyboard, and even power-supply connectors. This information can be useful when you troubleshoot cables or connections between devices.

Keyboard/Mouse Information

Keyboard and Mouse Connectors

Table 4.1 and figure 4.1 show connector pinouts for each keyboard cable connectors.

Table 4.1 Keyboard Connector Signals			
Signal Name	5-pin DIN	6-pin mini-DIN	6-pin SDL
Keyboard data	2	1	B
Ground	4	3	C
+5v	5	4	E
Keyboard clock	1	5	D
Not connected	—	2	A
Not connected	—	6	F
Not connected	3	—	—

DIN = German Industrial Norm (Deutsche Industrie Norm), a committee that sets German dimensional standards

SDL = Shielded Data Link, a type of shielded connector created by AMP and used by IBM and others for keyboard cables.

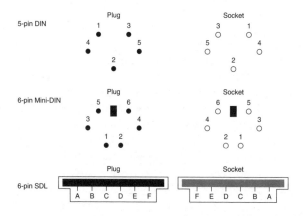

Fig. 4.1   IBM-Compatible keyboard connectors.

Keyboard Key Numbers and Scan Codes

When a keyswitch on the keyboard fails, the scan code of the failed keyswitch is reported by diagnostics software, such as the POST. The tables in this section list all the scan codes for every key on the 83-, 84-, and 101-key keyboards. By locating the reported scan code on these charts, you can determine which keyswitch is defective or needs to be cleaned. Notice that the 101-key enhanced keyboards are capable of three different scan code sets, with set 1 being the default.

Table 4.2 83-Key (PC/XT) Keyboard Key Numbers and Scan Codes

Key number	Scan code	Key
1	01	Escape
2	02	1
3	03	2
4	04	3
5	05	4
6	06	5
7	07	6
8	08	7
9	09	8
10	0A	9
11	0B	0
12	0C	-
13	0D	=
14	0E	Backspace
15	0F	Tab
16	10	q
17	11	w
18	12	e
19	13	r
20	14	t
21	15	y
22	16	u
23	17	i
24	18	o
25	19	p
26	1A	[
27	1B	]
28	1C	Enter
29	1D	Ctrl
30	1E	a
31	1F	s

(continues)

Table 4.2   Continued

Key number	Scan code	Key
32	20	d
33	21	f
34	22	g
35	23	h
36	24	j
37	25	k
38	26	l
39	27	;
40	28	'
41	29	`
42	2A	Left Shift
43	2B	\
44	2C	z
45	2D	x
46	2E	c
47	2F	v
48	30	b
49	31	n
50	32	m
51	33	,
52	34	.
53	35	/
54	36	Right Shift
55	37	*
56	38	Alt
57	39	Space bar
58	3A	Caps Lock
59	3B	F1
60	3C	F2
61	3D	F3
62	3E	F4
63	3F	F5
64	40	F6

Key number	Scan code	Key
65	41	F7
66	42	F8
67	43	F9
68	44	F10
69	45	Num Lock
70	46	Scroll Lock
71	47	Keypad 7 (Home)
72	48	Keypad 8 (Up arrow)
73	49	Keypad 9 (PgUp)
74	4A	Keypad -
75	4B	Keypad 4 (Left arrow)
76	4C	Keypad 5
77	4D	Keypad 6 (Right arrow)
78	4E	Keypad +
79	4F	Keypad 1 (End)
80	50	Keypad 2 (Down arrow)
81	51	Keypad 3 (PgDn)
82	52	Keypad 0 (Ins)
83	53	Keypad . (Del)

Table 4.3   84-Key (AT) Keyboard Key Numbers and Scan Codes

Key number	Scan code	Key
1	29	`
2	02	1
3	03	2
4	04	3
5	05	4
6	06	5
7	07	6
8	08	7
9	09	8
10	0A	9

(continues)

Table 4.3 Continued		
Key number	**Scan code**	**Key**
11	0B	0
12	0C	-
13	0D	=
14	2B	\
15	0E	Backspace
16	0F	Tab
17	10	q
18	11	w
19	12	e
20	13	r
21	14	t
22	15	y
23	16	u
24	17	i
25	18	o
26	19	p
27	1A	[
28	1B	]
30	1D	Ctrl
31	1E	a
32	1F	s
33	20	d
34	21	f
35	22	g
36	23	h
37	24	j
38	25	k
39	26	l
40	27	;
41	28	'
43	1C	Enter
44	2A	Left Shift

Key number	Scan code	Key
46	2C	z
47	2D	x
48	2E	c
49	2F	v
50	30	b
51	31	n
52	32	m
53	33	,
54	34	.
55	35	/
57	36	Right Shift
58	38	Alt
61	39	Space bar
64	3A	Caps Lock
65	3C	F2
66	3E	F4
67	40	F6
68	42	F8
69	44	F10
70	3B	F1
71	3D	F3
72	3F	F5
73	41	F7
74	43	F9
90	01	Escape
91	47	Keypad 7 (Home)
92	4B	Keypad 4 (Left arrow)
93	4F	Keypad 1 (End)
95	45	Num Lock
96	48	Keypad 8 (Up arrow)
97	4C	Keypad 5
98	50	Keypad 2 (Down arrow)

(continues)

Table 4.3 Continued

Key number	Scan code	Key
99	52	Keypad 0 (Ins)
100	46	Scroll Lock
101	49	Keypad 9 (PgUp)
102	4D	Keypad 6 (Right arrow)
103	51	Keypad 3 (PgDn)
104	53	Keypad . (Del)
105	54	SysRq
106	37	Keypad *
107	4A	Keypad –
108	4E	Keypad +

Table 4.4 101/102-Key (Enhanced) Keyboard Key Numbers and Scan Codes (Set 1)

Key number	Scan code	Key
1	29	`
2	02	1
3	03	2
4	04	3
5	05	4
6	06	5
7	07	6
8	08	7
9	09	8
10	0A	9
11	0B	0
12	0C	-
13	0D	=
15	0E	Backspace
16	0F	Tab
17	10	q

Key number	Scan code	Key
18	11	w
19	12	e
20	13	r
21	14	t
22	15	y
23	16	u
24	17	i
25	18	o
26	19	p
27	1A	[
28	1B	]
29	2B	\ (101-key only)
30	3A	Caps Lock
31	1E	a
32	1F	s
33	20	d
34	21	f
35	22	g
36	23	h
37	24	j
38	25	k
39	26	l
40	27	;
41	28	'
42	2B	# (102-key only)
43	1C	Enter
44	2A	Left Shift
45	56	\ (102-key only)
46	2C	z
47	2D	x
48	2E	c
49	2F	v
50	30	b

(continues)

Key number	Scan code	Key
		Table 4.4 Continued
51	31	n
52	32	m
53	33	,
54	34	.
55	35	/
57	36	Right Shift
58	1D	Left Ctrl
60	38	Left Alt
61	39	Space bar
62	E0,38	Right Alt
64	E0,1D	Right Ctrl
75	E0,52	Insert
76	E0,53	Delete
79	E0,4B	Left arrow
80	E0,47	Home
81	E0,4F	End
83	E0,48	Up arrow
84	E0,50	Down arrow
85	E0,49	Page Up
86	E0,51	Page Down
89	E0,4D	Right arrow
90	45	Num Lock
91	47	Keypad 7 (Home)
92	4B	Keypad 4 (Left arrow)
93	4F	Keypad 1 (End)
95	E0,35	Keypad /
96	48	Keypad 8 (Up arrow)
97	4C	Keypad 5
98	50	Keypad 2 (Down arrow)
99	52	Keypad 0 (Ins)
100	37	Keypad *
101	49	Keypad 9 (PgUp)

Key number	Scan code	Key
102	4D	Keypad 6 (Left arrow)
103	51	Keypad 3 (PgDn)
104	53	Keypad . (Del)
105	4A	Keypad -
106	4E	Keypad +
108	E0,1C	Keypad Enter
110	01	Escape
112	3B	F1
113	3C	F2
114	3D	F3
115	3E	F4
116	3F	F5
117	40	F6
118	41	F7
119	42	F8
120	43	F9
121	44	F10
122	57	F11
123	58	F12
124	E0,2A,E0,37	Print Screen
125	46	Scroll Lock
126	E1,1D,45,E1,9D, C5	Pause

Table 4.5 101/102-Key (Enhanced) Keyboard Key Numbers and Scan Codes (Set 2)

Key number	Scan Code	Key
1	0E	`
2	16	1
3	1E	2
4	26	3
5	25	4
6	2E	5

(continues)

Table 4.5   Continued

Key number	Scan Code	Key
7	36	6
8	3D	7
9	3E	8
10	46	9
11	45	0
12	4E	-
13	55	=
15	66	Backspace
16	0D	Tab
17	15	q
18	1D	w
19	24	e
20	2D	r
21	2C	t
22	35	y
23	3C	u
24	43	i
25	44	o
26	4D	p
27	54	[
28	5B	]
29	5D	\ (101-key only)
30	58	Caps Lock
31	1C	a
32	1B	s
33	23	d
34	2B	f
35	34	g
36	33	h
37	3B	j
38	42	k
39	4B	l
40	4C	;

Key number	Scan Code	Key
41	52	'
42	5D	# (102-key only)
43	5A	Enter
44	12	Left Shift
45	61	\ (102-key only)
46	1A	z
47	22	x
48	21	c
49	2A	v
50	32	b
51	31	n
52	3A	m
53	41	,
54	49	.
55	4A	/
57	59	Right Shift
58	14	Left Ctrl
60	11	Left Alt
61	29	Space bar
62	E0,11	Right Alt
64	E0,14	Right Ctrl
75	E0,70	Insert
76	E0,71	Delete
79	E0,6B	Left arrow
80	E0,6C	Home
81	E0,69	End
83	E0,75	Up arrow
84	E0,72	Down arrow
85	E0,7D	Page Up
86	E0,7A	Page Down
89	E0,74	Right arrow
90	77	Num Lock
91	6C	Keypad 7 (Home)
92	6B	Keypad 4 (Left arrow)

(continues)

Table 4.5 Continued

Key number	Scan Code	Key
93	69	Keypad 1 (End)
95	E0,4A	Keypad /
96	75	Keypad 8 (Up arrow)
97	73	Keypad 5
98	72	Keypad 2 (Down arrow)
99	70	Keypad 0 (Ins)
100	7C	Keypad *
101	7D	Keypad 9 (PgUp)
102	74	Keypad 6 (Left arrow)
103	7A	Keypad 3 (PgDn)
104	71	Keypad . (Del)
105	7B	Keypad -
106	E0,5A	Keypad +
108	E0,5A	Keypad Enter
110	76	Escape
112	05	F1
113	06	F2
114	04	F3
115	0C	F4
116	03	F5
117	0B	F6
118	83	F7
119	0A	F8
120	01	F9
121	09	F10
122	78	F11
123	07	F12
124	E0,12,E0,7C	Print Screen
125	7E	Scroll Lock
126	E1,14,77,E1,F0,14,F0,77	Pause

Table 4.6   101/102-Key (Enhanced) Keyboard Key Numbers and Scan Codes (Set 3)

Key number	Scan Code	Key
1	0E	`
2	16	1
3	1E	2
4	26	3
5	25	4
6	2E	5
7	36	6
8	3D	7
9	3E	8
10	46	9
11	45	0
12	4E	-
13	55	=
15	66	Backspace
16	0D	Tab
17	15	q
18	1D	w
19	24	e
20	2D	r
21	2C	t
22	35	y
23	3C	u
24	43	i
25	44	o
26	4D	p
27	54	[
28	5B	]
29	5C	\ (101-key only)
30	14	Caps Lock
31	1C	a
32	1B	s
33	23	d
34	2B	f

(continues)

Table 4.6   Continued

Key number	Scan Code	Key
35	34	g
36	33	h
37	3B	j
38	42	k
39	4B	l
40	4C	;
41	52	'
42	53	# (102-key only)
43	5A	Enter
44	12	Left Shift
45	13	\ (102-key only)
46	1A	z
47	22	x
48	21	c
49	2A	v
50	32	b
51	31	n
52	3A	m
53	41	,
54	49	.
55	4A	/
57	59	Right Shift
58	11	Left Ctrl
60	19	Left Alt
61	29	Space bar
62	39	Right Alt
64	58	Right Ctrl
75	67	Insert
76	64	Delete
79	61	Left arrow
80	6E	Home
81	65	End
83	63	Up arrow

Key number	Scan Code	Key
84	60	Down arrow
85	6F	Page Up
86	6D	Page Down
89	6A	Right arrow
90	76	Num Lock
91	6C	Keypad 7 (Home)
92	6B	Keypad 4 (Left arrow)
93	69	Keypad 1 (End)
95	77	Keypad /
96	75	Keypad 8 (Up arrow)
97	73	Keypad 5
98	72	Keypad 2 (Down arrow)
99	70	Keypad 0 (Ins)
100	7E	Keypad *
101	7D	Keypad 9 (PgUp)
102	74	Keypad 6 (Left arrow)
103	7A	Keypad 3 (PgDn)
104	71	Keypad . (Del)
105	84	Keypad -
106	7C	Keypad +
108	79	Keypad Enter
110	08	Escape
112	07	F1
113	0F	F2
114	17	F3
115	1F	F4
116	27	F5
117	2F	F6
118	37	F7
119	3F	F8
120	47	F9
121	4F	F10
122	56	F11

(continues)

Table 4.6 Continued		
Key number	Scan Code	Key
123	5E	F12
124	57	Print Screen
125	5F	Scroll Lock
126	62	Pause

Extended ASCII Keycodes for ANSI.SYS

Code	Keystroke	Code	Keystroke	Code	Keystroke
0;1	<Alt> Esc	0;66	F8	0;116	<Ctrl> RightArrow
0;3	Null Character	0;67	F9	0;117	<Ctrl> End
0;14	<Alt> Backspace	0;68	F10	0;118	<Ctrl> PgDn
0;15	<Shift> Tab	0;71	Home	0;119	<Ctrl> Home
0;16	<Alt> Q	0;72	UpArrow	0;120	<Alt> 1
0;17	<Alt> W	0;73	PgUp	0;121	<Alt> 2
0;18	<Alt> E	0;74	<Alt> Keypad -	0;122	<Alt> 3
0;19	<Alt> R	0;75	LeftArrow	0;123	<Alt> 4
0;20	<Alt> T	0;76	Keypad 5	0;124	<Alt> 5
0;21	<Alt> Y	0;77	RightArrow	0;125	<Alt> 6
0;22	<Alt> U	0;78	<Alt> Keypad +	0;126	<Alt> 7
0;23	<Alt> I	0;79	End	0;127	<Alt> 8
0;24	<Alt> O	0;80	DownArrow	0;128	<Alt> 9
0;25	<Alt> P	0;81	PgDn	0;129	<Alt> 0
0;26	<Alt> [	0;82	Ins	0;130	<Alt> -
0;27	<Alt>]	0;83	Del	0;131	<Alt> =
0;28	<Alt> Enter	0;84	<Shift> F1	0;132	<Ctrl> PgUp
0;30	<Alt> A	0;85	<Shift> F2	0;133	F11
0;31	<Alt> S	0;86	<Shift> F3	0;134	F12
0;32	<Alt> D	0;87	<Shift> F4	0;135	<Shift> F11
0;33	<Alt> F	0;88	<Shift> F5	0;136	<Shift> F12
0;34	<Alt> G	0;89	<Shift> F6	0;137	<Ctrl> F11
0;35	<Alt> H	0;90	<Shift> F7	0;138	<Ctrl> F12
0;36	<Alt> J	0;91	<Shift> F8	0;139	<Alt> F11
0;37	<Alt> K	0;92	<Shift> F9	0;140	<Alt> F12
0;38	<Alt> L	0;93	<Shift> F10	0;141	<Ctrl> UpArrow
0;39	<Alt> ;	0;94	<Ctrl> F1	0;142	<Ctrl> Keypad -
0;40	<Alt> '	0;95	<Ctrl> F2	0;143	<Ctrl> Keypad 5
0;41	<Alt> `	0;96	<Ctrl> F3	0;144	<Ctrl> Keypad +
0;43	<Alt> \	0;97	<Ctrl> F4	0;145	<Ctrl> DownArrow
0;44	<Alt> Z	0;98	<Ctrl> F5	0;146	<Ctrl> Ins
0;45	<Alt> X	0;99	<Ctrl> F6	0;147	<Ctrl> Del
0;46	<Alt> C	0;100	<Ctrl> F7	0;148	<Ctrl> Tab
0;47	<Alt> V	0;101	<Ctrl> F8	0;149	<Ctrl> Keypad
0;48	<Alt> B	0;102	<Ctrl> F9	0;150	<Ctrl> Keypad *
0;49	<Alt> N	0;103	<Ctrl> F10	0;151	<Alt> Home
0;50	<Alt> M	0;104	<Alt> F1	0;152	<Alt> UpArrow
0;51	<Alt> ,	0;105	<Alt> F2	0;153	<Alt> PgUp
0;52	<Alt> .	0;106	<Alt> F3	0;155	<Alt> LeftArrow
0;53	<Alt> /	0;107	<Alt> F4	0;157	<Alt> RightArrow
0;55	<Alt> Keypad *	0;108	<Alt> F5	0;159	<Alt> End
0;59	F1	0;109	<Alt> F6	0;160	<Alt> DownArrow
0;60	F2	0;110	<Alt> F7	0;161	<Alt> PgDn
0;61	F3	0;111	<Alt> F8	0;162	<Alt> Ins
0;62	F4	0;112	<Alt> F9	0;163	<Alt> Del
0;63	F5	0;113	<Alt> F10	0;164	<Alt> Keypad /
0;64	F6	0;114	<Ctrl> PrtScr	0;165	<Alt> Tab
0;65	F7	0;115	<Ctrl> LeftArrow	0;166	<Alt> Keypad Enter

Keyboard Typematic Repeat Rate and Delay

AT-style keyboards have a programmable typematic repeat rate and delay parameter. The DOS Mode command allows you to set the keyboard typematic (repeat) rate and delay before typematic action begins. The default value for the RATE parameter (r) is 20 for IBM AT-compatible systems and 21 for IBM PS/2 systems. The default value for the DELAY parameter (d) is 2. Use the MODE command as follows to set the keyboard typematic rate and delay:

MODE CON[:] [RATE=r DELAY=d]

The values for RATE and the resultant typematic rate in characters per second (cps) are shown in the following table:

RATE No.	Rate ± 20%
32	30.0cps
31	26.7cps
30	24.0cps
29	21.8cps
28	20.0cps
27	18.5cps
26	17.1cps
25	16.0cps
24	15.0cps
23	13.3cps
22	12.0cps
21	10.9cps
20	10.0cps
19	9.2cps
18	8.6cps
17	8.0cps
16	7.5cps
15	6.7cps
14	6.0cps
13	5.5cps
12	5.0cps
11	4.6cps
10	4.3cps
9	4.0cps
8	3.7cps
7	3.3cps
6	3.0cps
5	2.7cps
4	2.5cps
3	2.3cps
2	2.1cps
1	2.0cps

The values for DELAY and the resultant delay time in seconds are shown in the following table.

DELAY No.	Delay Time
1	.25sec
2	.50sec
3	.75sec
4	1.00sec

Serial Ports

Serial Port Connector Pinouts

The tables in this section show the pinouts for all the different types of serial and parallel port connectors.

Pin	Signal	Description	I/O
1	CD	Carrier detect	In
2	RD	Receive data	In
3	TD	Transmit data	Out
4	DTR	Data terminal ready	Out
5	SG	Signal ground	—
6	DSR	Data set ready	In
7	RTS	Request to send	Out
8	CTS	Clear to send	In
9	RI	Ring indicator	In

Pin	Signal	Description	I/O
1	—	Chassis Ground	—
2	TD	Transmit Data	Out
3	RD	Receive Data	In
4	RTS	Request to Send	Out
5	CTS	Clear to Send	In
6	DSR	Data Set Ready	In
7	SG	Signal Ground	—
8	CD	Carrier Detect	In
9	—	+Transmit Current Loop Return	Out
11	—	−Transmit Current Loop Data	Out
18	—	+Receive Current Loop Data	In
20	DTR	Data Terminal Ready	Out
22	RI	Ring Indicator	In
25	—	−Receive Current Loop Return	In

Pins 9, 11, 18, and 25 are used for a Current Loop interface only. Current Loop is not supported on the AT Serial/Parallel Adapter or PS/2 systems.

9-pin	25-pin	Signal	Description
1	8	CD	Carrier Detect
2	3	RD	Receive Data
3	2	TD	Transmit Data
4	20	DTR	Data Terminal Ready
5	7	SG	Signal Ground
6	6	DSR	Data Set Ready
7	4	RTS	Request to Send
8	5	CTS	Clear to Send
9	22	RI	Ring Indicator

Serial Port System Resources

System	COMx	Port	IRQ
All	COM1	3F8h	IRQ4
All	COM2	2F8h	IRQ3
ISA bus	COM3	3E8h	IRQ4
ISA bus	COM4	2E8h	IRQ3
ISA bus	COM3	3E0h	IRQ4
ISA bus	COM4	2E0h	IRQ3
ISA bus	COM3	338h	IRQ4
ISA bus	COM4	238h	IRQ3
MCA bus	COM3	3220h	IRQ3
MCA bus	COM4	3228h	IRQ3
MCA bus	COM5	4220h	IRQ3
MCA bus	COM6	4228h	IRQ3
MCA bus	COM7	5220h	IRQ3
MCA bus	COM8	5228h	IRQ3

Table 4.7	UART Chip Types
Chip	**Description**
8250	IBM used this original chip in the PC serial port card. The chip has several bugs, none of which is serious. The PC and XT ROM BIOS are written to anticipate at least one of the bugs. This chip was replaced by 8250B.
8250A	Do not use the second version of the 8250 in any system. This upgraded chip fixes several bugs in the 8250, including one in the interrupt enable register, but because the PC and XT ROM BIOS expect the bug, this chip does not work properly with those systems. The 8250A should work in an AT system that does not expect the bug, but does not work adequately at 9600 bps.
8250B	The last version of the 8250 fixes bugs from the previous two versions. The interrupt enable bug in the original 8250, expected by the PC and XT ROM BIOS software, has been put back into this chip, making the 8250B the most desirable chip for any non-AT serial port application. The 8250 chip may work in an AT under DOS, but does not run properly at 9600 bps.
16550	This newer UART improves on the 16450. This chip cannot be used in a FIFO (first in, first out) buffering mode, because of problems with the design, but it does enable a programmer to use multiple DMA channels and thus increase throughput on an AT or higher class computer sytem. I highly recommend replacing the 16550 UART with the 16550A.
16550A	This chip is a faster 16450 with a built-in 16-character Transmit and Receive FIFO (first in, first out) buffer that works. It also allows multiple DMA channel access. You should install this chip in your AT system serial port cards if you do any serious communications at 9600 bps or higher. If your communications program makes use of the FIFO, which most will today, it can greatly increase communications speed and eliminate lost characters and data at the higher speeds.

Wrap Plug (Loopback) Wiring

Many of the third-party diagnostics packages do not have correctly wired loopback connectors (also called wrap plugs). These plugs may pass their own tests, but will fail tests by other diagnostics, especially IBM's Advanced Diagnostics. The following diagrams show the wiring of IBM's Tri-Connector Wrap Plug P/N 72X8546. These plugs will pass IBM Advanced Diagnostics as well as virtually all compatible diagnostics software tests that check serial and parallel ports.

Table 4.8   IBM 25-Pin Serial (Female DB25S) Connector (Wrap Plug)

Schematic Diagram	Connected Pins
``` 1 - - - - -+ 2 - -+ ¦ 3 - -+ ¦ 4 - - - - -¦- -+ 5 - - - - -¦- -+ 6 - - - - -¦- -¦- -+ 7 - - - - -+ ¦ ¦ 8 - - - - - - - -+ ¦ 11 - - - - - - - - - - -+ 15 - - - - -+ ¦ 17 - - - - -+ ¦ 18 - -+ ¦ ¦ 20 - -¦- -¦- - - - -+ 22 - -¦- -¦- - - - -+ 23 - -¦- -+ 25 - -+ ```	1 to 7 2 to 3 4 to 5 to 8 6 to 11 to 20 to 22 15 to 17 to 23 18 to 25

Table 4.9 IBM 25-Pin Parallel (Male DB25P) Loopback Connector (Wrap Plug)

Schematic Diagram	Connected Pins
| ```
 1 ------+
 2 -----|--+
10 -----|--|--+
11 -----|--|--|--+
12 --+  |  |  |
13 --|--+  |  |
14 --+  |  |  |
15 --------+  |  |
16 -----------+  |
17 -------------+
``` | 1 to 13<br>2 to 15<br>10 to 16<br>11 to 17<br>12 to 14 |

Norton Diagnostics Loopback Connectors

The Norton Diagnostics program (NDIAGS.EXE) from the Norton Utilities 7.x and up by Symantec, uses nonstandard loopback connectors that are wired differently than other connectors. If you use standard loopback connectors that follow the IBM wiring specification, the serial and parallel port tests will fail. Symantec sells a set of wrap plugs wired to their specifications for about $30, but you can make your own by using the following wiring diagrams:

Table 4.10 SYMANTEC 25-Pin Serial (Female DB25S) Loopback Connector (Wrap Plug)

Schematic Diagram	Connected Pins
| ```
 2 --+
 3 --+
 4 --------+
 5 --------+
 6 ----------+
 8 ----------+
20 ----------+
22 ----------+
``` | 2 to 3<br><br>4 to 5<br><br>6 to 8 to 20 to 22 |

Table 4.11 SYMANTEC 9-Pin Serial (Female DB9S) Loopback Connector (Wrap Plug)

Schematic Diagram	Connected Pins
| ```
1 --------+
2 --+     ¦
3 --+     ¦
4 --------+
6 --------+
7 -----+  ¦
8 -----+  ¦
9 --------+
``` | 1 to 4 to 6 to 9<br>2 to 3<br><br><br>7 to 8 |

Table 4.12 SYMANTEC 25-Pin Parallel (Male DB25P) Loopback Connector (Wrap Plug)

Schematic Diagram	Connected Pins
| ```
 2 --------+
 3 -----+  ¦
 4 --+  ¦  ¦
 5 --¦--¦--¦--+
 6 --¦--¦--¦--¦--+
10 --¦--¦--¦--+  ¦
11 --¦--¦--¦------+
12 --+  ¦  ¦
13 -----+  ¦
15 --------+
``` | 2 to 15<br>3 to 13<br>4 to 12<br>5 to 10<br>6 to 11 |

Modem Control Codes

This section shows the command and control codes for popular modems. If you've ever had to work with these devices without the original documentation, you'll appreciate these tables. The following table shows the commands recognized by the popular Hayes and USRobotics modems. These modems have a standard command set that can get quite complicated in the higher-end models. This table comes in handy when you need to reconfigure a modem without the original manual. Even if your modem is not Hayes or USRobotics, it probably follows most of these commands because this command set has become somewhat of a standard.

Table 4.13 USRobotics and Hayes Modem Commands and Supported Features

Command	Modem Functions and Options	USR Dual	2400	Hayes 2400	1200
&	See Extended Command Set	X			
%	See Extended Command Set	X			
A	Force Answer mode when modem has not received an incoming call	X	X	X	X
A/	Re-execute last command once	X	X	X	X
A>	Repeat last command continuously	X			
Any key	Terminate current connection attempt; exit Repeat mode	X	X		
AT	Attention: must precede all other commands, except A/, A>, and +++	X	X	X	X
Bn	Handshake options	X		X	
	B0 CCITT answer sequence	x		x	

Command	Modem Functions and Options		USR Dual	2400	Hayes 2400	1200
	B1	Bell answer tone	x		x	
Cn	Transmitter On/Off		X	X	X	X
	C0	Transmitter Off	x	x	x	x
	C1	Transmitter On-Default	x	x	x	x
Dn	Dial number n and go into originate mode					
	Use any of these options:		X	X	X	X
	P	Pulse dial-Default	x	x	x	x
	T	Touch-Tone dial	x	x	x	x
	,	(Comma) Pause for 2 seconds	x	x	x	x
	;	Return to command state after dialing	x	x	x	x

(continues)

Table 4.13 Continued

Command	Modem Functions and Options	USR Dual	2400	Hayes 2400	1200
...	Dial the letters that follow	x	x		
!	Flash switch-hook to transfer call	x	x	x	
W	Wait for 2nd dial tone (if X3 or higher is set)	x	x	x	
@	Wait for an answer (if X3 or higher is set)	x	x	x	
R	Reverse frequencies	x	x	x	x
S	Dial stored number			x	
DL	Dial the last-dialed number	X			
DSn	Dial number stored in NVRAM at position n	X			
En	Command mode local echo; not applicable after a connection has been made	X	X	X	X

Command	Modem Functions and Options	USR Dual	Hayes 2400	2400	1200
	E0 Echo Off	x	x	x	x
	E1 Echo On	x	x	x	x
Fn	Local echo On/Off when a connection has been made	X	X	X	X
	F0 Echo On (Half duplex)	x	x	x	x
	F1 Echo Off	x	x	x	x
	(Full duplex)-Default				
Hn	On/Off hook control	X	X	X	X
	H0 Hang up	x	x	x	x
	(go on hook)-Default				
	H1 Go off hook	x	x	x	x

(continues)

Table 4.13 Continued

Command	Modem Functions and Options	USR Dual	Hayes 2400	2400	1200
In	Inquiry X	X	X	X	
	I0 Return product code	x	x	x	x
	I1 Return memory (ROM) checksum	x	x	x	x
	I2 Run memory (RAM) test	x	x	x	
	I3 Return call duration/real time	x	x		
	I4 Return current modem settings	x	x		
	I5 Return NVRAM settings	x			
	I6 Return link diagnostics	x			
	I7 Return product configuration	x			

Command	Modem Functions and Options	USR Dual	Hayes 2400	2400	1200
Kn	Modem clock operation	X			
	K0 ATI3 displays call	x			
	duration-Default				
	K1 ATI3 displays real x				
	time; set with				
	ATI3=HH:MM:SSK1				
Ln	Loudness of speaker volume:		X		
	L0 Low	x			
	L1 Low	x			
	L2 Medium	x			
	L3 High	x			

(continues)

Table 4.13 Continued

Command	Modem Functions and Options	USR Dual	Hayes 2400	2400	1200
Mn	Monitor (speaker) control	X	X	X	X
	M0 Speaker always Off	x	x	x	x
	M1 Speaker On until carrier is established-Default	x	x	x	x
	M2 Speaker always On	x	x	x	x
	M3 Speaker On after last digit dialed, Off at carrier detect	x	x	x	x
O	Return on-line after command execution	X	X	X	X
	O0 Return on-line, normal	x	x	x	x
	O1 Return on-line, retrain	x	x	x	x

Command	Modem Functions and Options	USR Dual	Hayes 2400	2400	1200
P	Pulse dial X	X	X	X	
Qn	Result codes display	X	X	X	X
	Q0 Result codes displayed	x	x	x	x
	Q1 Result codes suppressed (quiet mode)	x	x	x	x
	Q2 Quiet in answer mode only	x			
Sr=n	Set Register commands: r is any S-register; n must be a decimal number between 0 and 255.	X	X	X	X
Sr.b=n	Set bit .b of register r to n (0/Off or 1/On)	X			
Sr?	Query register r	X	X	X	X
T	Tone dial X	X	X	X	

(continues)

Table 4.13 Continued

Command	Modem Functions and Options	USR Dual	Hayes 2400	2400	1200
Vn	Verbal/Numeric result codes	X	X	X	X
	V0 Numeric mode	x	x	x	x
	V1 Verbal mode	x	x	x	x
Xn	Result code options	X	X	X	X
Yn	Long space disconnect			X	
	Y0 Disabled			x	
	Y1 Enabled; disconnects after 1.5-second break			x	
Z	Software reset	X	X	X	X
+++	Escape code sequence, preceded and followed by at least one second of no data transmission	X	X		

Command	Modem Functions and Options	USR Dual	Hayes 2400	2400	1200
/(Slash)	Pause for 125 msec	X			
>	Repeat command continuously or up to 10 dial attempts Cancel by pressing any key	X	X		
$	Online Help - Basic command summary	X	X		
&$	Online Help - Ampersand command summary	X			
%$	Online Help - Percent command summary	X			
D$	Online Help - Dial command summary	X	X		
S$	Online Help - S-register summary	X	X		
<Ctrl>-S	Stop/restart display of HELP screens		X		

(continues)

Table 4.13 Continued

Command	Modem Functions and Options	USR Dual	Hayes 2400	2400	1200
<Ctrl>-C	Cancel display HELP screens		X		
<Ctrl>-K	Cancel display HELP screens		X		
Extended command set					
&An	ARQ result codes 14-17, 19	X			
	&A0 Suppress ARQ result codes	x			
	&A1 Display ARQ result codes-Default	x			
	&A2 Display HST and V.32 result codes	x			
	&A3 Display protocol result codes	x			
&Bn	Data Rate, terminal-to-modem (DTE/DCE)	X			

Command	Modem Functions and Options		USR Dual	Hayes 2400	2400	1200
	&B0	DTE rate follows connection rate-Default	x			
	&B1	Fixed DTE rate	x			
	&B2	Fixed DTE rate in ARQ mode; variable DTE rate in non-ARQ mode	x			
&Cn		Carrier Detect (CD) operations	X		X	
	&C0	CD override	x		x	
	&C1	Normal CD operations	x		x	
&Dn		Data Terminal Ready (DTR) operations	X		X	
	&D0	DTR override	x		x	

(continues)

Table 4.13   Continued

Command	Modem Functions and Options		USR Dual	Hayes 2400	2400	1200
	&D1	DTR Off; goes to command state			x	
	&D2	DTR Off; goes to command state and on hook	x		x	
	&D3	DTR Off; resets modem			x	
&F	Load factory settings into RAM		X		X	
&Gn	Guard tone		X		X	
	&G0	No guard tone; U.S., Canada-Default	x		x	
	&G1	Guard tone; some European countries	x		x	
	&G2	Guard tone; U.K., requires B0	x		x	

Command	Modem Functions and Options		USR Dual	Hayes 2400	2400	1200
&Hn	Transmit Data flow control		X			
	&H0	Flow control disabled-Default	x			
	&H1	Hardware (CTS) flow control	x			
	&H2	Software (XON/XOFF) flow control	x			
	&H3	Hardware and software control	x			
&In	Received Data software flow control		X			
	&I0	Flow control disabled-Default	x			

(continues)

Table 4.13 Continued

Command	Modem Functions and Options	USR Dual	Hayes 2400	2400	1200
&I1	XON/XOFF to local modem and remote computer	X			
&I2	XON/XOFF to local modem only	X			
&I3	Host mode, Hewlett-Packard protocol	X			
&I4	Terminal mode, Hewlett-Packard protocol	X			
&I5	ARQ mode-same as &I2; non-ARQ mode; look for incoming XON/XOFF	X			
&Jn	Telephone jack selection			X	

Command	Modem Functions and Options		USR Dual	Hayes 2400	2400	1200
&Kn	Data compression		X			
	&J0	RJ-11/ RJ-41S/ RJ-45S			x	
	&J1	RJ-12/ RJ-13			x	
	&K0	Disabled	x			
	&K1	Auto enable/ disable-Default	x			
	&K2	Enabled	x			
	&K3	V.42bis only	x			
&Ln	Normal/Leased line operation		X		X	
	&L0	Normal phone line-Default	x		x	
	&L1	Leased line	x		x	

(continues)

Table 4.13 Continued

Command	Modem Functions and Options	USR Dual	Hayes 2400	2400	1200
&Mn	Error Control/Synchronous	X		X	
	Options				
	&M0 Normal mode, no error control	x		x	
	&M1 Synch mode	x		x	
	&M2 Synch mode 2 - stored number dialing			x	
	&M3 Synch mode 3 - manual dialing	x			
	&M4 Normal/ARQ mode-Normal if ARQ connection cannot be made-Default	x			
	&M5 ARQ mode-hang up if ARQ connection cannot be made	x			

Command	Modem Functions and Options	USR Dual	Hayes 2400	2400	1200
&Nn	Data Rate, data link (DCE/DCE)	X			
	&N0 Normal link operations-Default	×			
	&N1 300 bps	×			
	&N2 1200 bps	×			
	&N3 2400 bps	×			
	&N4 4800 bps	×			
	&N5 7200 bps	×			
	&N6 9600 bps	×			
	&N7 12K bps	×			
	&N8 14.4K bps	×			

(continues)

Table 4.13 Continued

Command	Modem Functions and Options	USR Dual	Hayes 2400	2400	1200
&Pn	Pulse dial make/break ratio	X		X	
	&P0 North America-Default	x		x	
	&P1 British Commonwealth	x		x	
&Rn	Received Data hardware (RTS) flow control	X		X	
	&R0 CTS tracks RTS	x		x	
	&R1 Ignore RTS-Default	x		x	
	&R2 Pass received data on RTS high; used Pass received data on RTS high; used	x			
&Sn	Data Set Ready (DSR) override	X		X	
	&S0 DSR override (always On-Default)	x		x	

Command		Modem Functions and Options	USR Dual	Hayes 2400	2400	1200
	&S1	Modem controls DSR	x		x	
	&S2	Pulsed DSR; CTS follows CD	x			
	&S3	Pulsed DSR	x			
&Tn		Modem Testing	X		X	
	&T0	End testing	x		x	
	&T1	Analog loopback	x		x	
	&T2	Reserved	x			
	&T3	Digital loopback	x		x	
	&T4	Grant remote digital loopback	x		x	
	&T5	Deny remote digital loopback	x		x	

(continues)

Table 4.13 Continued

Command	Modem Functions and Options	USR Dual	Hayes 2400	2400	1200
&T6	Initiate remote digital loopback	x		x	
&T7	Remote digital loopback with self test	x		x	
&T8	Analog loopback with self test	x		x	
&W	Write current settings to NVRAM	X		X	
&Xn	Synchronous timing source	X		X	
&X0	Modems transmit clock-Default	x		x	
&X1	Terminal equipment	x		x	
&X2	Modems receiver clock	x		x	

Command	Modem Functions and Options		USR Dual	Hayes 2400	2400	1200
&Yn	Break handling. Destructive breaks clear the buffer; expedited breaks are sent immediately to remote system.		X			
	&Y0	Destructive, but dont send break	x			
	&Y1	Destructive, expedited-Default	x			
	&Y2	Nondestructive, expedited	x			
	&Y3	Nondestructive, unexpedited	x			
&Zn=L	Store last-dialed phone number in NVRAM at position n		X			
&Zn=s	Write phone number(s) to NVRAM at position n (0-3); 36 characters maximum		X			

(continues)

Table 4.13   Continued

Command	Modem Functions and Options	USR Dual	Hayes 2400	2400	1200
&Zn?	Display phone number in NVRAM at position n (n=0-3)	X		X	
%Rn	Remote access to Rack	X			
	Controller Unit (RCU)				
	%R0 Disabled	x			
	%R1 Enabled	x			
%T	Enable Touch-Tone recognition	X			
	Modem S-Register Functions and Defaults				
S0	Number of rings before automatic answering when DIP switch 5 is UP. Default = 1. S0 = 0 disables Auto Answer, equivalent to DIP switch 5 Down	SW5	SW5	0	SW5

Command	Modem Functions and Options	USR Dual	Hayes 2400	2400	1200
S1	Counts and stores number of rings from incoming call	0	0	0	0
S2	Define escape code character. Default = +	43	43	43	43
S3	Define ASCII carriage return	13	13	13	13
S4	Define ASCII line feed	10	10	10	10
S5	Define ASCII Backspace	8	8	8	8
S6	Number of seconds modem waits before dialing	2	2	2	2
S7	Number of seconds modem waits for a carrier	60	30	30	30
S8	Duration (sec) for pause (,) option in Dial command and pause between command reexecutions for Repeat (>) command	2	2	2	2

(continues)

Table 4.13 Continued

Command	Modem Functions and Options	USR Dual	Hayes 2400	2400	1200
S9	Duration (.1 sec units) of remote carrier signal before recognition	6	6	6	6
S10	Duration (.1 sec units) modem waits after loss of carrier before hanging up	7	7	7	7
S11	Duration and spacing (ms) of dialed Touch-Tones	70	70	70	70
S12	Guard time (in .02 sec units) for escape code sequence	50	50	50	50
S13	Bit-mapped register:	0			
	1 Reset when DTR drops				
	2 Auto answer in originate mode				
	4 Disable result code pause				

Command	Modem Functions and Options	USR Dual	Hayes 2400	2400	1200
	8 DS0 on DTR low-to-high				
	16 DS0 on power up, ATZ				
	32 Disable HST modulation				
	64 Disable MNP Level 3				
	128 Watchdog hardware reset				
S15	Bit-mapped register:	0			
	1 Disable high-frequency equalization				
	2 Disable on-line fallback				
	4 Force 300-bps back channel				
	8 Set non-ARQ transmit buffer to 128 bytes				

(continues)

Table 4.13 Continued

Command	Modem Functions and Options	USR Dual	Hayes 2400	2400	1200
	16 Disable MNP Level 4				
	32 Set Del as Backspace key				
	64 Unusual MNP incompatibility				
	128 Custom applications only				
S16	Bit-mapped register:	0	0	0	
	1 Analog loopback				
	2 Dial test				
	4 Test pattern				
	8 Initiate remote digital loopback				
	16 Reserved				

Command	Modem Functions and Options	USR Dual	Hayes 2400	2400	1200
	32 Reserved				
	64 Reserved				
	128 Reserved				
S18	&Tn Test timer, disabled when set to 0	0		0	
S19	Set inactivity timer in minutes	0			
S21	Length of Break, DCE to DTE, in 10ms units	10		0	
S22	Define ASCII XON	17		17	
S23	Define ASCII XOFF	19		19	
S24	Duration (20ms units) of pulsed DSR when modem is set to &S2 or &S3	150			

(continues)

Table 4.13 Continued

Command	Modem Functions and Options	USR Dual	Hayes 2400	2400	1200
S25	Delay to DTR	5			
S26	Duration (10ms units) of delay between RTS and CTS, synchronous mode	1		1	
S27	Bit-mapped register:	0			
	1 Enable V.21 modulation, 300 bps				
	2 Enable unencoded V.32 modulation				

Command	Modem Functions and Options	USR Dual	Hayes 2400	2400	1200
4	Disable V.32 modulation				
	8 Disable 2100 Hz answer tone				
	16 Disable MNP handshake				
	32 Disable V.42 Detect phase				
	64 Reserved				
	128 Unusual software incompatibility				
S28	Duration (.1 sec units) of V.21/V.23 handshake delay	8			
S32	Voice/Data switch options: 1				
	0 Disabled				

(continues)

Table 4.13 Continued

Command	Modem Functions and Options	USR Dual	Hayes 2400	2400	1200
1	Go off hook in originate mode				
2	Go off hook in answer mode				
3	Redial last-dialed number				
4	Dial number stored at position 0				
5	Auto answer toggle On/Off				
6	Reset modem				
7	Initiate remote digital loopback				

Command	Modem Functions and Options	USR Dual	Hayes 2400	2400	1200
S34	Bit-mapped register:	0			
	1 Disable V.32bis				
	2 Disable enhanced V.32 mode				
	4 Disable quick V.32 retrain				
	8 Enable V.23 modulation				
	16 Change MR LED to DSR				
	32 Enable MI/MIC				
	64 Reserved				

(continues)

Table 4.13 Continued

Command	Modem Functions and Options	USR Dual	Hayes 2400	2400	1200
128	Reserved				
S38	Duration (sec) before disconnect when DTR drops during an ARQ call	0			

ARQ = Automatic repeat request
ASCII = American Standard Code for Information Interchange
BPS = Bits per second
CCITT = Consultative Committee for International Telephone and Telegraph
CD = Carrier detect
CRC = Cyclic redundancy check

DCE = Data communications equipment
DTE = Data terminal equipment
EIA = Electronic Industries Association
HDLC = High-level data lin k control
HST = High-speed technology
Hz = Hertz

LAPM = Link access procedure for modems
MI/MIC = Mode indicate/Mode indicate common
MNP = Microcom networking protocol
NVRAM = Nonvolatile memory
RAM = Random-access memory
ROM = Read-only memory

SDLC = Synchronous Data Link Control
MR = Modem ready
LED = Light-emitting diode
DTR = Data terminal ready
CTS = Clear to send
RTS = Ready to send
DSR = Data set ready

Parallel Port Connector Pinout

Table 4.14 25-Pin PC Compatible Parallel Port Connector		
Pin	Description	I/O
1	−Strobe	Out
2	+Data Bit 0	Out
3	+Data Bit 1	Out
4	+Data Bit 2	Out
5	+Data Bit 3	Out
6	+Data Bit 4	Out
7	+Data Bit 5	Out
8	+Data Bit 6	Out
9	+Data Bit 7	Out
10	−Acknowledge	In
11	+Busy	In
12	+Paper End	In
13	+Select	In
14	−Auto Feed	Out
15	−Error	In
16	−Initialize Printer	Out
17	−Select Input	Out
18	−Data Bit 0 Return (GND)	In
19	−Data Bit 1 Return (GND)	In
20	−Data Bit 2 Return (GND)	In
21	−Data Bit 3 Return (GND)	In
22	−Data Bit 4 Return (GND)	In
23	−Data Bit 5 Return (GND)	In
24	−Data Bit 6 Return (GND)	In
25	−Data Bit 7 Return (GND)	In

Printer Control Codes

Table 4.15 IBM Printer-Control Codes		
Function	**Codes in ASCII**	
Job-control commands:		
Escape (command start)	<ESC>	
Null (command end)	<NUL>	
Ring bell	<BELL>	
Cancel (clear printer buffer)	<CAN>	
Select printer	<DC1>	
Deselect printer *n*	<ESC>Q#	
Deselect printer	<DC3>	
Automatic ribbon band shift	<ESC>a	
Select ribbon band 1	<ESC>y	
Select ribbon band 2	<ESC>m	
Select ribbon band 3	<ESC>c	
Select ribbon band 4 (black)	<ESC>b	
Home print head	<ESC><	
Form feed	<FF>	
Horizontal tab	<HT>	
Backspace	<BS>	
Initialize function On	<ESC>?<SOH>	
Initialize function Off	<ESC>?<NUL>	
Unidirectional printing On	<ESC>U<SOH>	
Unidirectional printing Off	<ESC>U<NUL>	
Space #/120 fwd to next character	<ESC>d#	
Space #/120 bwd to next character	<ESC>e#	
Set aspect ratio to 1:1	<ESC>n<SOH>	
Set aspect ratio to 5:6	<ESC>n<NUL>	
Select control values = binary	<ESC> @ #<NUL>	
Select control values = ASCII	<ESC> @ <SOH>	

 # indicates a variable number in the code.

Codes in Hex	Pro-printer	Graphics-printer	Color-printer
1B	X	X	X
00	X	X	X
07	X	X	X
18	X	X	X
11	X		X
1B 51#	X		X
13	X		X
1B 61			X
1B 79			X
1B 6D			X
1B 63			X
1B 62			X
1B 3C		X	X
0C	X	X	X
09	X	X	X
08	X		X
1B 3F 01			X
1B 3F 00			X
1B 55 01	X	X	X
1B 55 00	X	X	X
1B 64 #			X
1B 65 #			X
1B 6E 01			X
1B 6E 00			X
1B 40 # 00			X
1B 40 01			X

(continues)

Table 4.15   Continued

Function	Codes in ASCII	
Printer-control commands:		
Ignore paper end On	<ESC>8	
Ignore paper end Off	<ESC>9	
Set length of page in lines (1-127)	<ESC>C#	
Set length of page in inches (1-22)	<ESC>C<SOH>#	
Automatic line justification On	<ESC>M<SOH>	
Automatic line justification Off	<ESC>M<NUL>	
Perforation skip On (1-127)	<ESC>N #	
Perforation skip Off	<ESC>O	
Set top of page (form)	<ESC>4	
Set left and right margins	<ESC>X #	
Clear tabs (set to power-on defaults)	<ESC>R	
Set horizontal tab stops	<ESC>D # <NUL>	
Set vertical tab stops	<ESC>B # <NUL>	
Carriage return	<CR>	
Line feed	<LF>	
Set n/72 lines per inch	<ESC>A #	
Set n/216 lines per inch	<ESC>3 #	
Set 8 lines per inch	<ESC>0	
Set 7/72nd line per inch	<ESC>1	
Start new line spacing	<ESC>2	
Vertical tab	<VT>	
Reverse line feed	<ESC>]	
Automatic line feed On	<ESC>5<SOH>	
Automatic line feed Off	<ESC>5<NUL>	

 # indicates a variable number in the code.

Codes in Hex	Pro-printer	Graphics-printer	Color-printer
1B 38		X	
1B 39		X	
1B 43 #	X	X	X
1B 43 01 #	X	X	X
1B 4D 01			X
1B 4D 00			X
1B 4E #	X	X	X
1B 4F	X	X	X
1B 34	X		X
1B 58 #			X
1B 52	X		X
1B 44 # 00	X	X	X
1B 42 # 00	X	X	X
0D	X	X	X
0A		X	X
1B 41 #	X	X	X
1B 33 #	X	X	#/144"
1B 30	X	X	X
1B 31	X	X	6/72"
1B 32	X	X	X
0B	X	X	X
1B 5D			X
1B 35 01	X		X
1B 35 00	X		X

(continues)

Table 4.15 Continued

Function	Codes in ASCII	
Font selection:		
Select character set 1	<ESC>7	
Select character set 2	<ESC>6	
10 cpi (compressed Off)	<DC2>	
17.1 cpi (compressed On)	<SI>	
Doublestrike On	<ESC>G	
Doublestrike Off	<ESC>H	
Doublewidth On (lines)	<ESC>W<SOH>	
Doublewidth Off (lines)	<ESC>W<NUL>	
Doublewidth by line On	<SO>	
Doublewidth by line Off	<DC4>	
Emphasized printing On	<ESC>E	
Emphasized printing Off	<ESC>F	
Subscript On	<ESC>S<SOH>	
Superscript On	<ESC>S<NUL>	
Subscript/superscript Off	<ESC>T	
Set draft quality	<ESC>I<SOH>	
Set text quality (near-letter quality)	<ESC>I<STX>	
Set letter quality	<ESC>I<ETX>	
Proportional spacing On	<ESC>P<SOH>	
Proportional spacing Off	<ESC>P<NUL>	
12-characters-per-inch spacing	<ESC>:	
Print all characters	<ESC>\ #	
Print next character	<ESC>^	
Underline On	<ESC>-<SOH>	
Underline Off	<ESC>-<NUL>	

 # indicates a variable number in the code.

Codes in Hex	Pro-printer	Graphics-printer	Color-printer
1B 37	X	X	X
1B 36	X	X	X
12	X	X	X
0F	X	X	X
1B 47	X	X	X
1B 48	X	X	X
1B 57 01	X	X	X
1B 57 00	X	X	X
0E	X	X	X
14	X	X	X
1B 45	X	X	X
1B 46	X	X	X
1B 53 01	X	X	X
1B 53 00	X	X	X
1B 54	X	X	X
1B 49 01			X
1B 49 02	X		X
1B 49 03			X
1B 50 01			X
1B 50 00			X
1B 3A	X		X
1B 5C #	X		X
1B 5E	X		X
1B 2D 01	X	X	X
1B 2D 00	X	X	X

(continues)

Table 4.15 Continued

Function	Codes in ASCII	
Graphics:		
Graphics, 60 dots per inch (DPI)	<ESC>K #	
Graphics, 70/84 DPI	<ESC>K #	
Graphics, 120 DPI half speed	<ESC>L #	
Graphics, 140/168 DPI half speed	<ESC>L #	
Graphics, 120 DPI normal speed	<ESC>Y #	
Graphics, 140/168 DPI normal speed	<ESC>Y #	
Graphics, 240 DPI half speed	<ESC>Z #	
Graphics, 280/336 DPI half speed	<ESC>Z #	

 # indicates a variable number in the code.

Table 4.16 Epson Printer-Control Codes

Function	Codes in ASCII	Codes in Hex
Job-control commands:		
Ring bell	<BELL>	07
Clear line	<CAN>	18
Select printer	<DC1>	11
Deselect printer	<DC3>	13
Set justification	<ESC>a	1B 61
Cut sheet-feeder control	<ESC>	EM1B 19

Codes in Hex	Pro-printer	Graphics-printer	Color-printer
1B 4B #	X	X	
1B 4B #			X
1B 4C #	X	X	
1B 4C #			X
1B 59 #	X	X	
1B 59 #			X
1B 5A #	X	X	
1B 5A #			X

Function	Codes in ASCII	Codes in Hex
Select character space	<ESC>	SP1B 20
Select mode combinations	<ESC>!	1B 21
Select active character set	<ESC>%	1B 25
Copies ROM to user RAM	<ESC>:	1B 3A
Defines user characters	<ESC>&	1B 26
Set MSB = 0	<ESC>>	1B 3E
Set MSB = 1	<ESC>=	1B 3D
Select international character set	<ESC>R#	1B 72#
Select 15 width	<ESC>g	1B 67
Select immediate print (typewriter mode)	<ESC>i	1B 69
Half-speed printing Off	<ESC>s<NUL>	1B 73 00
Half-speed printing On	<ESC>s<SOH>	1B 73 01
Set horizontal tab unit	<ESC>e<NUL>	1B 65 00
Set vertical tab unit	<ESC>e<SOH>	1B 6D 01

(continues)

Table 4.16 Continued

Function	Codes in ASCII	Codes in Hex
Special character-generator selection (control codes accepted)	<ESC>m<NUL>	1B 6D 00
Special character-generator selection (graphic characters accepted)	<ESC>m<SOH>	1B 6D 01
Unidirectional printing On	<ESC>U<SOH>	1B 55 01
Unidirectional printing Off	<ESC>U<NUL>	1B 55 00
Turn unidirectional (left to right) On	<ESC><	1B 3C
Form feed	<FF>	0C
Horizontal tab	<HT>	09
Initialize printer	<ESC>@	1B 40
Backspace	<BS>	08
Printer-control commands:		
Ignore paper end On	<ESC>8	1B 38
Ignore paper end Off	<ESC>9	1B 39
Set length of page in lines (1-127)	<ESC>C#	1B 43#
Set length of page in inches (1 - 22)	<ESC>C<NUL>#	1B 43 00#
Set absolute tab	<ESC>$	1B 24
Set vertical tab	<ESC>/	1B 2F
Set vertical tab	<ESC>b	1B 62
Set horizontal tab unit	<ESC>e<NUL>	1B 65 00
Set vertical tab unit	<ESC>e<SOH>	1B 65 01
Set horizontal skip position	<ESC>f<NUL>	1B 66 00
Set vertical skip position	<ESC>f<SOH>	1B 66 01
Perforation skip On (1-127)	<ESC>N#	1B 4E#
Perforation skip Off	<ESC>O	1B 4F
Set horizontal tab stop	<ESC>D	1B 44
Set vertical tab stop	<ESC>B	1B 42
Carriage return	<CR>	0D
Line feed	<LF>	0A

Function	Codes in ASCII	Codes in Hex
Set variable line feed to #/72 inch (1-85)	<ESC>A#	1B 41#
Set variable line feed to #/216 inch	<ESC>J#	1B 4A#
Set spacing at 1/8 inch	<ESC>0	1B 30
Set spacing at 7/72 inch	<ESC>1	1B 31
Set line spacing at 1/6 inch	<ESC>2	1B 32
Set #/216 inch line feed (0-225)	<ESC>3#	1B 33#
Vertical tab	<VT>	0B
Font selection:		
Deactivate high-order control codes	<ESC>6	1B 36
Turn alternate character (italics) On	<ESC>4	1B 34
10 CPI (compressed Off) spacing	<DC2>	12
17.1 CPI (compressed On) spacing	<SI>	0F
Doublestrike On	<ESC>G	1B 47
Doublestrike Off	<ESC>H	1B 48
Doublewidth On (lines)	<ESC>W<SOH>	1B 57 01
Doublewidth Off (lines)	<ESC>W<NUL>	1B 57 00
Enlarged print mode On	<SO>	0E
Enlarged print mode Off	<DC4>	14
Emphasized printing On	<ESC>E	1B 45
Emphasized printing Off	<ESC>F	1B 46
Turn alternate character (italics) On	<ESC>4	1B 34
Turn alternate character (italics) Off	<ESC>5	1B 35
Elite mode On (Pica mode off)	<ESC>M	1B 4D
Select family of type styles	<ESC>k	1B 6B
Proportional printing Off	<ESC>p<NUL>	1B 70 00

(continues)

Table 4.16 Continued		
Function	**Codes in ASCII**	**Codes in Hex**
Proportional printing Off	<ESC>p<NUL>	1B 70 00
Proportional printing On	<ESC>p<SOH>	1B 70 01
Select letter- or draft-quality printing	<ESC>z	1B 7A
Subscript On	<ESC>S<SOH>	1B 53 01
Superscript On	<ESC>S<NUL>	1B 53 00
Subscript/superscript Off	<ESC>T	1B 54
Control code select	<ESC>I	1B 49
Elite mode Off (Pica mode On)	<ESC>P	1B 50
Nine-pin graphics mode	<ESC>^	1B 5E
Underline On	<ESC>-<SOH>	1B 2D 01
Underline Off	<ESC>-<NUL>	1B 2D 00
Graphics:		
Normal-density bit image	<ESC>K	1B 4B##
Dual-density bit image	<ESC>L	1B 4C##
Double-speed, dual-density bit image	<ESC>Y	1B 59##
Quadruple-density bit image	<ESC>Z	1B 5A##

International character sets:
0 = U.S.   6 = Italy
1 = France   7 = Spain
2 = Germany   8 = Japan
3 = England   9 = Norway
4 = Denmark   10 = Denmark II
5 = Sweden

Characters in brackets are ASCII code names.
 # indicates a variable numeric value.

Table 4.17 HP LaserJet Printer-Control Codes

Function type	Function	Codes in ASCII	Codes in Hex
Job-control commands:			
Printer control	Reset printer	<ESC>E	1B 45
	Self test mode	<ESC>z	1B 7A
	Number of copies	<ESC>&l#X	1B 26 6C # 58
	Long-edge (left) offset	<ESC>&l#U	1B 26 6C # 55
	character set		
	Short-edge (top) offset	<ESC>&l#Z	1B 26 6C # 5A
	registration		
Printer-control commands:			
Paper source	Eject page	<ESC>&l0H	1B 26 6C 30 48
	Paper-tray auto feed	<ESC>&l1H	1B 26 6C 31 48

(continues)

Table 4.17 Continued

Function type	Function	Codes in ASCII	Codes in Hex
	Manual feed	<ESC>&l2H	1B 26 6C 32 48
	Manual envelope feed	<ESC>&l3H	1B 26 6C 33 48
	Feed from lower cassette	<ESC>&l4H	1B 26 6C 34 48
Page size	Executive	<ESC>&l1A	1B 26 6C 31 41
	Letter	<ESC>&l2A	1B 26 6C 32 41
	Legal	<ESC>&l3A	1B 26 6C 33 41
	A4	<ESC>&l26A	1B 26 6C 32 36 41
	Monarch (envelope)	<ESC>&l80A	1B 26 6C 38 30 41
	COM 10 (envelope)	<ESC>&l81A	1B 26 6C 38 31 41
	DL (envelope)	<ESC>&l90A	1B 26 6C 39 30 41
	C5 (envelope)	<ESC>&l91A	1B 26 6C 39 31 41

Function type	Function	Codes in ASCII	Codes in Hex
Orientation	Portrait mode	<ESC>&l0O	1B 26 6C 30 4F
	Landscape mode	<ESC>&l1O	1B 26 6C 31 4F
	Reverse portrait	<ESC>&l2O	1B 26 6C 32 4F
	Reverse landscape	<ESC>&l3O	1B 26 6C 33 4F
	Print direction	<ESC>&a#P	1B 26 61 # 50
Page settings	Page length	<ESC>&l#P	1B 26 6C # 50
	Top margin	<ESC>&l#E	1B 26 6C # 45
	Text length	<ESC>&l#F	1B 26 6C # 46
	Clear horizontal margins	<ESC>9	1B 39
	Set left margin	<ESC>&a#L	1B 26 61 # 4C
	Set right margin	<ESC>&a#M	1B 26 61 # 4D
	Perforation skip enable	<ESC>&l1L	1B 26 6C 31 4C

(continues)

Table 4.17 Continued

Function type	Function	Codes in ASCII	Codes in Hex
	Perforation skip disable	\<ESC>&l0L	1B 26 6C 30 4C
Line spacing	Vertical motion index	\<ESC>&l#C	1B 26 6C # 43
	Horizontal motion index	\<ESC>&k#H	1B 26 6B # 4B
	1 line/inch	\<ESC>&l1D	1B 26 6C 31 44
	2 lines/inch	\<ESC>&l2D	1B 26 6C 32 44
	3 lines/inch	\<ESC>&l3D	1B 26 6C 33 44
	4 lines/inch	\<ESC>&l4D	1B 26 6C 34 44
	6 lines/inch	\<ESC>&l6D	1B 26 6C 36 44
	8 lines/inch	\<ESC>&l8D	1B 26 6C 38 44
	12 lines/inch	\<ESC>&l12D	1B 26 6C 31 32 44
	16 lines/inch	\<ESC>&l16D	1B 26 6C 31 36 44

Function type	Function	Codes in ASCII	Codes in Hex
	24 lines/inch	<ESC>&l24D	1B 26 6C 32 34 44
	48 lines/inch	<ESC>&l48D	1B 26 6C 34 38 44
	Half line feed	<ESC>=	1B 3D
Stacking position	Default	<ESC>&l0T	1B 26 6C 30 54
	Toggle	<ESC>&l1T	1B 26 6C 31 54
Cursor positioning:			
Vertical position	Number of rows	<ESC>&a#R	1B 26 61 # 52
	Number of dots	<ESC>*p#Y	1B 2A 70 # 59
	Number of decipoints	<ESC>&a#V	1B 26 61 # 56
Horizontal position	Number of rows	<ESC>&a#C	1B 26 61 # 43
	Number of dots	<ESC>*p#X	1B 2A 70 # 58
	Number of decipoints	<ESC>&a#H	1B 26 61 # 48

(continues)

Table 4.17 Continued

Function type	Function	Codes in ASCII	Codes in Hex
End-of-line	CR=CR; LF=LF; FF=FF	<ESC>&k0G	1B 26 6B 30 47
	CR=CR+LF; LF=LF; FF=FF	<ESC>&k1G	1B 26 6B 31 47
	CR=CR; LF=CR+LF;	<ESC>&k2G	1B 26 6B 32 47
	FF=CR+FF		
	CR=CR+LF; LF=CR+LF;	<ESC>&k3G	1B 26 6B 33 47
	FF=CR+FF		
Push/Pop position	Push position	<ESC>&f0S	1B 26 66 30 53
	Pop position	<ESC>&f1S	1B 26 66 31 53
Font selection:			
Font symbol set	Roman-8	<ESC>(8U	1B 28 38 55
	USASCII	<ESC>(0U	1B 28 30 55

Function type	Function	Codes in ASCII	Codes in Hex
	Danish/Norwegian	<ESC>(0D	1B 28 30 44
	British (U.K.)	<ESC>(1E	1B 28 31 45
	French	<ESC>(1F	1B 28 31 46
	German	<ESC>(1G	1B 28 31 47
	Italian	<ESC>(0I	1B 28 30 49
	Swedish/Finnish	<ESC>(0S	1B 28 30 53
	Spanish	<ESC>(2S	1B 28 32 53
	Legal	<ESC>(1U	1B 28 31 55
	Linedraw	<ESC>(0B	1B 28 30 42
	Math8	<ESC>(8M	1B 28 38 4D
	Math7	<ESC>(0A	1B 28 30 41
	PiFont	<ESC>(15U	1B 28 31 35 55

(continues)

Table 4.17 Continued

Function type	Function	Codes in ASCII	Codes in Hex
	ECMA-94 Latin	<ESC>(0N	1B 28 30 4E
	PC-8	<ESC>(10U	1B 28 31 30 55
	PC-8 D/N	<ESC>(11U	1B 28 31 31 55
	PC 850	<ESC>(12U	1B 28 31 32 55
Primary spacing	Proportional	<ESC>(s1P	1B 28 73 31 50
	Fixed	<ESC>(s0P	1B 28 73 30 50
Character pitch	10 characters per inch	<ESC>(s10H	1B 28 73 31 30 48
	12 characters per inch	<ESC>(s12H	1B 28 73 31 32 48
	16.6 characters per inch	<ESC>(s16.6H	1B 28 73 31 36 2E 36 48
	Standard pitch (10 cpi)	<ESC>&k0S	1B 26 6B 30 53
	Compressed pitch (16.6 cpi)	<ESC>&k2S	1B 26 6B 32 53

Function type	Function	Codes in ASCII	Codes in Hex
Character point size	Elite (12.0)	<ESC>&k4s	1B 26 6B 34 53
	7 point	<ESC>(s7V	1B 28 73 37 56
	8 point	<ESC>(s8V	1B 28 73 38 56
	8.5 point	<ESC>(s8.5V	1B 28 73 38 2E 35 56
	10 point	<ESC>(s10V	1B 28 73 31 30 56
	12 point	<ESC>(s12V	1B 28 73 31 32 56
	14.4 point	<ESC>(s14.4V	1B 28 73 31 34 2E 34 56
Character style	Upright	<ESC>(s0S	1B 28 73 30 53
	Italic	<ESC>(s1S	1B 28 73 31 53
Character weight	Ultra thin	<ESC>(s-7B	1B 28 73 -37 42
	Extra thin	<ESC>(s-6B	1B 28 73 -36 42
	Thin	<ESC>(s-5B	1B 28 73 -35 42

(continues)

Table 4.17 Continued

Function type	Function	Codes in ASCII	Codes in Hex
	Extra light	<ESC>(s-4B	1B 28 73 -34 42
	Light	<ESC>(s-3B	1B 28 73 -33 42
	Demi light	<ESC>(s-2B	1B 28 73 -32 42
	Semi light	<ESC>(s-1B	1B 28 73 -31 42
	Medium (normal)	<ESC>(s0B	1B 28 73 30 42
	Semi bold	<ESC>(s1B	1B 28 73 31 42
	Demi bold	<ESC>(s2B	1B 28 73 32 42
	Bold	<ESC>(s3B	1B 28 73 33 42
	Extra bold	<ESC>(s4B	1B 28 73 34 42
	Black	<ESC>(s5B	1B 28 73 35 42
	Extra black	<ESC>(s6B	1B 28 73 36 42
	Ultra black	<ESC>(s7B	1B 28 73 37 42

Function type	Function	Codes in ASCII	Codes in Hex
Character typeface	Courier	<ESC>(s3T	1B 28 73 33 54
	Univers	<ESC>(s52T	1B 28 73 35 32 54
	Line printer	<ESC>(s0T	1B 28 73 30 54
	CG Times	<ESC>(s4101T	1B 28 73 34 31 30 31 54
	Helvetica	<ESC>(s4T	1B 28 73 34 54
	TMS RMN	<ESC>(s5T	1B 28 73 33 54
Font default	Primary font	<ESC>(3@	1B 28 33 40
	Secondary font	<ESC>)3@	1B 29 33 40
Underlining	Underline On	<ESC>&d#D	1B 26 64 30 44
	Underline floating	<ESC>&d3D	1B 26 64 33 44
	Underline Off	<ESC>&d@	1B 26 64 40
Transparent print	Number of bytes	<ESC>&p#X[Data]	1B 26 70 # 58

(continues)

Table 4.17 Continued

Function type	Function	Codes in ASCII	Codes in Hex
Font management:			
Assign font ID	Font ID number	<ESC>*c#D	1B 2A 63 # 44
Font and character control	Delete all fonts	<ESC>*c0F	1B 2A 63 30 46
	Delete all temporary fonts	<ESC>*c1F	1B 2A 63 31 46
	Delete last font ID specified	<ESC>*c2F	1B 2A 63 32 46
	Delete last font ID and char code	<ESC>*c3F	1B 2A 63 33 46
	Make temporary font	<ESC>*c4F	1B 2A 63 34 46
	Make permanent font	<ESC>*c5F	1B 2A 63 35 46
	Copy/assign font	<ESC>*c6F	1B 2A 63 36 46
Select font (ID)	Primary font ID number	<ESC>(#X	1B 28 # 58
	Secondary font ID number	<ESC>)#X	1B 29 # 58

Function type	Function	Codes in ASCII	Codes in Hex
Soft font creation:			
Font descriptor	Create font	<ESC>)s#W[Data]	1B 29 73 # 57
	Download character	<ESC>(s#W[Data]	1B 28 73 # 57
	ASCII character code number	<ESC>*c#E	1B 2A 63 # 45
Graphics:			
Vector graphics	Enter HP-GL/2 mode	<ESC>%0B	1B 25 30 42
	HP-GL/2 plot horizontal size	<ESC>%1B	1B 25 31 42
	HP-GL/2 plot vertical size	<ESC>*c#K	1B 2A 63 # 4B
	Set picture frame	<ESC>*0T	1B 2A 63 30 54
	Picture frame horizontal size	<ESC>*c#X	1B 2A 63 # 58
	Picture frame vertical size	<ESC>*c#Y	1B 2A 63 # 59

(continues)

Table 4.17 Continued

Function type	Function	Codes in ASCII	Codes in Hex
Raster resolution	75 dpi resolution	<ESC>*t75R	1B 2A 74 37 35 52
	100 dpi resolution	<ESC>*t100R	1B 2A 74 31 30 30 52
	150 dpi resolution	<ESC>*t150R	1B 2A 74 31 35 30 52
	300 dpi resolution	<ESC>*t300R	1B 2A 74 33 30 30 52
	Start at leftmost position	<ESC>*r0A	1B 2A 72 30 41
	Start at current cursor	<ESC>*r1A	1B 2A 72 31 41
Raster graphics presentation	Rotate image	<ESC>*r0F	1B 2A 72 30 46
	LaserJet landscape compatible	<ESC>*r3F	1B 2A 72 33 46
	Left raster graphics margin	<ESC>*r0A	1B 2A 72 30 41

Function type	Function	Codes in ASCII	Codes in Hex
	Current cursor	<ESC>*r1A	1B 2A 72 31 41
	Raster Y offset	<ESC>*b0M	1B 2A 62 # 59
Set raster compression	Uncoded	<ESC>*b0M	1B 2A 62 30 41
	Mode run-length encoded	<ESC>*b1M	1B 2A 62 31 41
	Tagged image file format	<ESC>*b2M	1B 2A 62 32 41
	Delta row	<ESC>*b3M	1B 2A 62 33 41
	Transfer graphic rows	<ESC>*b#W[Data]	1B 2A 62 # 57
	End graphics	<ESC>*rB	1B 2A 72 42
	Raster height	<ESC>*r#T	1B 2A 72 # 54
	Raster width	<ESC>*r#S	1B 2A 72 # 53

(continues)

Table 4.17 Continued

Function type	Function	Codes in ASCII	Codes in Hex
The print model:			
Select pattern	Solid black (default)	<ESC>*v0T	1B 2A 76 30 54
	Solid white	<ESC>*v1T	1B 2A 76 31 54
	HP-defined shading pattern	<ESC>*v2T	1B 2A 76 32 54
	HP-defined cross-hatched pattern	<ESC>*v3T	1B 2A 76 33 54
Select source	Transparent	<ESC>*v0N	1B 2A 76 30 42
Transparency	Opaque	<ESC>*v1N	1B 2A 76 31 42
Select pattern	Transparent	<ESC>*v0O	1B 2A 76 30 43
Transparency	Opaque	<ESC>*v1O	1B 2A 76 31 43
Rectangle width	Horizontal # dots in pattern	<ESC>*c#A	1B 2A 63 # 41

Function type	Function	Codes in ASCII	Codes in Hex
	Horizontal # decipoints in pattern	<ESC>*c#H	1B 2A 63 # 48
Rectangle height	Vertical # dots in pattern	<ESC>*c#B	1B 2A 63 # 42
	Vertical # decipoints in pattern	<ESC>*c#V	1B 2A 63 # 56
Fill rectangular	Solid black	<ESC>*c0P	1B 2A 63 30 50
Area	Erase (solid white area fill)	<ESC>*c1P	1B 2A 63 31 50
	Shade fill	<ESC>*c2P	1B 2A 63 32 50
	Cross-hatched fill	<ESC>*c3P	1B 2A 63 33 50
	User defined	<ESC>*c4P	1B 2A 63 34 50
	Current pattern	<ESC>*c5P	1B 2A 63 35 50
Pattern ID	Percent of shading or type of pattern	<ESC>*c#G	1B 2A 63 # 47

(continues)

Table 4.17 Continued

Function type	Function	Codes in ASCII	Codes in Hex
Shading	Print 2% gray scale	<ESC>*c2G	1B 2A 63 32 47
	Print 10% gray scale	<ESC>*c10G	1B 2A 63 31 30 47
	Print 15% gray scale	<ESC>*c15G	1B 2A 63 31 35 47
	Print 30% gray scale	<ESC>*c30G	1B 2A 63 33 30 47
	Print 45% gray scale	<ESC>*c45G	1B 2A 63 34 35 47
	Print 70% gray scale	<ESC>*c70G	1B 2A 63 37 30 47
	Print 90% gray scale	<ESC>*c90G	1B 2A 63 39 30 47
	Print 100% gray scale	<ESC>*c100G	1B 2A 63 31 30 30 47
Pattern	1 horizontal line	<ESC>*c1G	1B 2A 63 31 47
	2 vertical lines	<ESC>*c2G	1B 2A 63 32 47
	3 diagonal lines	<ESC>*c3G	1B 2A 63 33 47
	4 diagonal lines	<ESC>*c4G	1B 2A 63 34 47

Function type	Function	Codes in ASCII	Codes in Hex
	5 square grid	<ESC>*c5G	1B 2A 63 35 47
	6 diagonal grid	<ESC>*c6G	1B 2A 63 36 47
Macros:			
Macro ID	Macro ID number	<ESC>&f#Y	1B 26 66 # 59
Macro control	Start macro	<ESC>&f0X	1B 26 66 30 58
	Stop macro definition	<ESC>&f1X	1B 26 66 31 58
	Execute macro	<ESC>&f2X	1B 26 66 32 58
	Call macro	<ESC>&f3X	1B 26 66 33 58
	Enable overlay	<ESC>&f4X	1B 26 66 34 58
	Disable overlay	<ESC>&f5X	1B 26 66 35 58
	Delete macros	<ESC>&f6X	1B 26 66 36 58

(continues)

Table 4.17 Continued

Function type	Function	Codes in ASCII	Codes in Hex
	Delete all temporary macros	\<ESC>&f7X	1B 26 66 37 58
	Delete macro ID	\<ESC>&f8X	1B 26 66 38 58
	Make temporary	\<ESC>&f9X	1B 26 66 39 58
	Make permanent	\<ESC>&f10X	1B 26 66 31 30 58
Programming hints:			
Display functions	Display functions On	\<ESC>Y	1B 59
	Display functions Off	\<ESC>Z	1B 5A
End-of-line wrap	Enable	\<ESC>&s0C	1B 26 73 30 43
	Disable	\<ESC>&s1C	1B 26 73 31 43

 # indicates a variable numeric value.

[Data] indicates a bitstream of appropriate data.

Game (Joystick) Interface

The following table shows the interface connector specification for a PC-compatible Game Adapter. These adapters normally have a 15-pin D shell connector that is used to connect joysticks or paddles for controlling games. Because this adapter actually reads resistance and can easily be manipulated with standard programming languages, the game adapter serves as a poor man's data acquisition board or real-time interface card. With it, you can hook up sensors and easily read the data in the PC.

Pin	Signal	Function	I/O
Table 4.18 PC-Compatible Game Adapter Connector			
1	+5 Vdc		Out
2	Button 4	Paddle 1 button, joystick A button	In
3	Position 0	Paddle 1 position, joystick A x-coordinate	In
4	Ground		
5	Ground		
6	Position 1	Paddle 2 position, joystick a y-coordinate	In
7	Button 5	Paddle 2 button	In
8	+5 Vdc		Out
9	+5 Vdc		Out
10	Button 6	Paddle 3 button, joystick B button	In
11	Position 2	Paddle 3 position, joystick B x-coordinate	In
12	Ground		
13	Position 3	Paddle 4 position, joystick B y-coordinate	In
14	Button 7	Paddle 4 button	In
15	+5 Vdc		Out

Chapter 5

Disk Drives

This section has tables of information that pertain to disk drives. You can find a wealth of information here, including floppy and hard disk drive specifications and parameter data, information on the different disk interfaces from the ROM BIOS and DOS perspective, and even pinouts of the different hard disk interfaces.

Disk Software Interfaces

The following figure shows a representation of the relationship between the different disk software interfaces at work in an IBM-compatible system. This figure shows the chain of command from the hardware, which is the drive controller, to the ROM BIOS, DOS, and, finally, an application program.

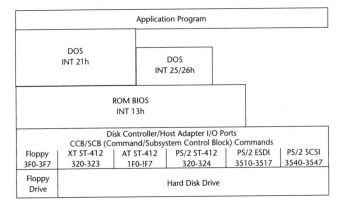

Fig. 5.1 Disk Software Interface levels and relationships.

The following table shows the different functions available at the Interrupt 13h BIOS interface. Some functions are available to floppy drives or hard drives only, while others are available to both types of drives.

Table 5.1	Int 13h BIOS Disk Functions		
Function	Floppy disk	Hard disk	Description
00h	X	X	Reset disk system
01h	X	X	Get status of last operation
02h	X	X	Read sectors
03h	X	X	Write sectors
04h	X	X	Verify sectors
05h	X	X	Format track
06h		X	Format bad track
07h		X	Format drive
08h	X	X	Read drive parameters
09h		X	Initialize drive characteristics
0Ah		X	Read long
0Bh		X	Write long
0Ch		X	Seek
0Dh		X	Alternate hard disk reset
0Eh		X	Read sector buffer
0Fh		X	Write sector buffer
10h		X	Test for drive ready
11h		X	Recalibrate drive
12h		X	Controller RAM diagnostic
13h		X	Controller drive diagnostic

Function	Floppy disk	Hard disk	Description
14h		X	Controller internal diagnostic
15h	X	X	Get disk type
16h	X		Get floppy disk change status
17h	X		Set floppy disk type for format
18h	X		Set media type for format
19h		X	Park hard disk heads
1Ah		X	ESDI—Low-level format
1Bh		X	ESDI—Get manufacturing header
1Ch		X	ESDI—Get configuration

The following table shows the error codes that may be returned by the BIOS INT 13h routines. In some cases you may see these codes referred to when running a Low-Level Format program, disk editor, or other program that can directly access a disk drive through the BIOS.

Table 5.2 IINT13h BIOS Error Codes	
Code	**Description**
00h	No error
01h	Bad command
02h	Address mark not found
03h	Write protect
04h	Request sector not found
05h	Reset failed
06h	Media change error

(continues)

Table 5.2 Continued	
Code	Description
07h	Initialization failed
09h	Cross 64K DMA boundary
0Ah	Bad sector flag detected
0Bh	Bad track flag detected
10h	Bad ECC on disk read
11h	ECC corrected data error
20h	Controller has failed
40h	Seek operation failed
80h	Drive failed to respond
AAh	Drive not ready
BBh	Undefined error
CCh	Write fault
0Eh	Register error
FFh	Sense operation failed

DOS Disk Formatting Information

With the DOS FORMAT command, you can perform low- and high-level formatting of floppy disks and high-level format of hard disks. The following syntax is used with the FORMAT command:

FORMAT d: [/V[:label]] [/Q] [/U] [/F:size] [/B | /S]

FORMAT d: [/V[:label]] [/Q] [/U] [/T:tracks /N:sectors] [/B | /S]

FORMAT d: [/V[:label]] [/Q] [/U] [/1] [/4] [/B | /S]

FORMAT d: [/Q] [/U] [/1] [/4] [/8] [/B | /S]

Table 5.3 is a concise and detailed list of all the parameters associated with the DOS FORMAT command, including parameters new to DOS 5. Also included are several undocumented parameters you may never have seen before.

Table 5.3   Format Command (Undocumented Features)

Standard parameters

/Q	Performs a Quick format
/U	Performs an Unconditional format
/S	Copies the DOS system files (IBMBIO.COM or IO.SYS and IBMDOS.COM or MSDOS.SYS) and COMMAND.COM from the boot drive to the new disk
/V[:label]	Creates a volume label on the new disk. The label can be as long as 11 characters.
/F:nnnn	Specifies the format of the floppy disk. For 5 1/4-inch drives, the size can be 160K, 180K, 320K, 360K, or 1.2M. For 3 1/2-inch drives, valid sizes are 720K, 1.44M, and 2.88M.
/4	Formats a 5 1/4-inch, 360K, double-sided, double-density floppy disk in a high-density 1.2M drive
/T:nnnn	Specifies the number of tracks (1 to 1,024) per side on the disk to format
/N:nn	Specifies the number of sectors (1 to 64) per track on the disk to format

Obsolete (but still functional) parameters

/1	Formats single-sided disks (5 1/4-inch only)
/8	Formats eight sectors per track (5 1/4-inch only)

(continues)

Table 5.3	**Continued**
/B	Creates dummy system files and reserves room for a DOS version SYS command to copy actual files later

Undocumented parameters (floppy disks only)

/H	Skips the message Insert new diskette for drive d: and strike ENTER when ready
/BACKUP	Skips the message Insert new diskette for drive d: and press ENTER when ready
/SELECT	Skips the message Insert new diskette for drive d: and press ENTER when ready. Also suppresses the disk space report, the Format another (Y/N)? message, and any error messages.
/AUTOTEST	Skips the Insert new diskette for drive d: and press ENTER when ready message. Also suppresses the disk space report, the Format another (Y/N)? message, any error messages, and the Volume label (11 characters, ENTER for none)? message.

Notes

/S	Looks for system files on the default drive in V3.3 or earlier versions; the boot drive is searched in V4.0 and later versions, and COMMAND.COM is copied in V5.0 and later versions
/V	Is assumed in 4.0 and later versions if /V:label is not specified; DOS 3.3 and earlier versions do not support the :label specification with /V
/F	Supported in 4.0 and later versions
/T and /N	/N defaults to 9 in DOS 3.3. No defaults are assumed in 4.0 and later versions; therefore, if one of the parameters is specified, the other must be specified as well
/H	Supported in V3.3 only
/BACKUP, /SELECT, AND /AUTOTEST	Supported in V4.0 and later versions

Table 5.4 shows the correct FORMAT command parameters to use when formatting low-density floppy disks in high-density drives. This table considers all possible permutations of floppy disk types, drive types, and DOS versions.

Typical Sector Format

The following table shows how the sectors on a typical disk are layed out. In this example, an MFM 17-Sector per track hard disk is used, but these structures are similar on all types of drives, including floppy drives. This table shows the true structure of a track on a disk, and demonstrates why the formatted capacity of a disk is lower than the unformatted capacity.

Table 5.4　Formatting Low-Density Floppy Disks in High-Density Drives

DOS version	Drive type	Floppy disk type	Format command
DOS 3.0+	5 1/4-inch, 1.2M	DD 360K	FORMAT d: /4
DOS 3.2+	5 1/4-inch, 1.2M	DD 360K	FORMAT d: /N:9 /T:40
DOS 4.0+	5 1/4-inch, 1.2M	DD 360K	FORMAT d: /F:360
DOS 3.3+	3 1/2-inch, 1.44M	DD 720K	FORMAT d: /N:9 /T:80
DOS 4.0+	3 1/2-inch, 1.44M	DD 720K	FORMAT d: /F:720
DOS 5.0+	3 1/2-inch, 2.88M	HD 1.44M	FORMAT d: /F:1.44
DOS 5.0+	3 1/2-inch, 2.88M	DD 720K	FORMAT d: /F:720

+ = Includes all higher versions
d: = Specifies the drive to format
DD = Double density
HD = High density

Table 5.5   Typical MFM Disk Sector Format

Bytes	Name	Description
16	POST INDEX GAP	All 4Eh, at the track beginning after the Index mark
13	ID VFO LOCK	Sector data; repeated 17 times for an MFM encoded track.
13	ID VFO LOCK	All 00h; synchronizes the VFO for the sector ID
1	SYNC BYTE	A1h; notifies the controller that data follows
1	ADDRESS MARK	FEh; defines that ID field data follows
2	CYLINDER NUMBER	A value that defines the actuator position
1	HEAD NUMBER	A value that defines the head selected
1	SECTOR NUMBER	A value that defines the sector
2	CRC	Cyclic Redundancy Check to verify ID data
3	WRITE TURN-ON GAP	00h written by format to isolate the ID from DATA
13	DATA SYNC VFO LOCK	All 00h; synchronizes the VFO for the DATA

(continues)

Table 5.5 Continued

Bytes	Name	Description
1	SYNC BYTE	A1h; notifies the controller that data follows
1	ADDRESS MARK	F8h; defines that user DATA field follows
512	DATA	The area for user DATA
2	CRC	Cyclic Redundancy Check to verify DATA
3	WRITE TURN-OFF GAP	00h; written by DATA update to isolate DATA
15	INTER-RECORD GAP	All 00h; a buffer for spindle speed variation
693	PRE-INDEX GAP	All 4Eh, at track end before Index mark

571 Total bytes per sector
512 Data bytes per sector
10416 Total bytes per track
8704 Data bytes per track

Default Allocation Unit (Cluster) Sizes

Table 5.6 shows the default cluster (allocation unit) size selected by DOS for all possible floppy disk formats and hard disk partition sizes.

Table 5.6   DOS Disk Default Cluster (Allocation Unit) Sizes

Floppy Disk

Disk or volume size	Cluster/allocation unit size	FAT type
5 1/4-inch 360K	2 sectors, or 1,024 bytes	12-bit
5 1/4-inch 1.2M	1 sectors, or 512 bytes	12-bit
3 1/2-inch 720K	2 sectors, or 1,024 bytes	12-bit
3 1/2-inch 1.44M	1 sectors, or 512 bytes	12-bit
3 1/2-inch 2.88M	2 sectors, or 1,024 bytes	12-bit

Hard Drive

Disk or volume size	Cluster/allocation unit size	FAT type
0M < Volume < 16M	8 sectors, or 4,096 bytes	12-bit
16M <= Volume <= 128M	4 sectors, or 2,048 bytes	16-bit
128M < Volume <= 256M	8 sectors, or 4,096 bytes	16-bit
256M < Volume <= 512M	16 sectors, or 8,192 bytes	16-bit
512M < Volume <= 1,024M	32 sectors, or 16,384 bytes	16-bit
1,024M < Volume <= 2,048M	64 sectors, or 32,768 bytes	16-bit

K = 1,024 bytes
M = 1,048,576 bytes

DOS Disk Structures and Layout

Table 5.7   Master Boot Record (Partition Table)

PARTITION TABLE ENTRY #1

Offset Hex	Dec	Length	Description
1BEh	446	1 byte	Boot Indicator Byte (80h = Active, else 00h)
1BFh	447	1 byte	Starting Head (or Side) of Partition
1C0h	448	16 bits	Starting Cylinder (10-bits) and Sector (6-bits)
1C2h	450	1 byte	System Indicator Byte (see table)
1C3h	451	1 byte	Ending Head (or Side) of Partition
1C4h	452	16 bits	Ending Cylinder (10-bits) and Sector (6-bits)
1C6h	454	1 dword	Relative Sector Offset of Partition
1CAh	458	1 dword	Total Number of Sectors in Partition

PARTITION TABLE ENTRY #2

Offset Hex	Dec	Length	Description
1CEh	462	1 byte	Boot Indicator Byte (80h = Active, else 00h)
1CFh	463	1 byte	Starting Head (or Side) of Partition
1D0h	464	16 bits	Starting Cylinder (10-bits) and Sector (6-bits)
1D2h	466	1 byte	System Indicator Byte (see table)

| Offset | | Length | Description |
Hex	Dec		
1D3h	467	1 byte	Ending Head (or Side) of Partition
1D4h	468	16 bits	Ending Cylinder (10-bits) and Sector (6-bits)
1D6h	470	1 dword	Relative Sector Offset of Partition
1DAh	474	1 dword	Total Number of Sectors in Partition

PARTITION TABLE ENTRY #3

| Offset | | Length | Description |
Hex	Dec		
1DEh	478	1 byte	Boot Indicator Byte (80h = Active, else 00h)
1DFh	479	1 byte	Starting Head (or Side) of Partition
1E0h	480	16 bits	Starting Cylinder (10-bits) and Sector (6-bits)
1E2h	482	1 byte	System Indicator Byte (see table)
1E3h	483	1 byte	Ending Head (or Side) of Partition
1E4h	484	16 bits	Ending Cylinder (10-bits) and Sector (6-bits)
1E6h	486	1 dword	Relative Sector Offset of Partition
1EAh	490	1 dword	Total Number of Sectors in Partition

PARTITION TABLE ENTRY #4

| Offset | | Length | Description |
Hex	Dec		
1EEh	494	1 byte	Boot Indicator Byte (80h = Active, else 00h)

(continues)

Table 5.7 Continued

Offset Hex	Dec	Length	Description
1EFh	495	1 byte	Starting Head (or Side) of Partition
1F0h	496	16 bits	Starting Cylinder (10-bits) and Sector (6-bits)
1F2h	498	1 byte	System Indicator Byte (see table)
1F3h	499	1 byte	Ending Head (or Side) of Partition
1F4h	500	16 bits	Ending Cylinder (10-bits) and Sector (6-bits)
1F6h	502	1 dword	Relative Sector Offset of Partition
1FAh	506	1 dword	Total Number of Sectors in Partition

SIGNATURE BYTES

Offset Hex	Dec	Length	Description
1FEh	510	2 bytes	Boot Sector Signature (55AAh)

NOTE: A WORD equals two bytes which are read in reverse order, and a DWORD equals two WORDS which are read in reverse order.

Table 5.8 Partition Table System Indicator Byte values

Value	Description
00h	No Partition allocated in this entry
01h	Primary DOS, 12-bit FAT (Partition < 16M)
04h	Primary DOS, 16-bit FAT (16M <= Partition <= 32M)
05h	Extended DOS (Points to next Primary Partition)
06h	Primary DOS, 16-bit FAT (Partition > 32M)

Value	Description
07h	OS/2 HPFS Partition
02h	MS-XENIX root Partition
03h	MS-XENIX usr Partition
08h	AIX File System Partition
09h	AIX Boot Partition
50h	Ontrack Disk Manager READ-ONLY Partition
51h	Ontrack Disk Manager READ/WRITE Partition
56h	Golden Bow Vfeature Partition
61h	Storage Dimensions Speedstor Partition
63h	IBM 386/ix or UNIX System V/386 Partition
64h	Novell Netware Partition
75h	IBM PCIX Partition
DBh	Digital Research Concurrent DOS/CPM-86 Partition
F2h	Some OEM's DOS 3.2+ second partition
FFh	UNIX Bad Block Table Partition

Table 5.9   DOS Boot Record

DOS Volume Boot Sector (DVB) format:

Offset			
Hex	**Dec**	**Field Length**	**Description**
00h	0	3 bytes	Jump Instruction to Boot Program Code
03h	3	8 bytes	OEM Name and DOS Version ("IBM 5.0")

(continues)

Table 5.9 Continued

DOS Volume Boot Sector (DVB) format:

Offset Hex	Dec	Field Length	Description
0Bh	11	1 word	Bytes / Sector (usually 512)
0Dh	13	1 byte	Sectors / Cluster (Must be a power of 2)
0Eh	14	1 word	Reserved Sectors (Boot Sectors, usually 1)
10h	16	1 byte	FAT Copies (usually 2)
11h	17	1 word	Maximum Root Directory Entries (usually 512)
13h	19	1 word	Total Sectors (If Partition <= 32M, else 0)
15h	21	1 byte	Media Descriptor Byte (F8h for Hard Disks)
16h	22	1 word	Sectors / FAT
18h	24	1 word	Sectors / Track
1Ah	26	1 word	Number of Heads
1Ch	28	1 dword	Hidden Sectors (If Partition <= 32M, 1 word only)

The following applies for DOS 4.0 or higher ONLY, else 00h:

Offset Hex	Dec	Field Length	Description
20h	32	1 dword	Total Sectors (If Partition > 32M, else 0)

Offset Hex	Dec	Field Length	Description
24h	36	1 byte	Physical Drive No. (00h=floppy, 80h=hard disk)
25h	37	1 byte	Reserved (00h)
26h	38	1 byte	Extended Boot Record Signature (29h)
27h	39	1 dword	Volume Serial Number (32-bit random number)
2Bh	43	11 bytes	Volume Label ("NO NAME " stored if no label)
36h	54	8 bytes	File System ID ("FAT12 " or "FAT16 ")

The following applies for all Versions of DOS:

Offset Hex	Dec	Field Length	Description
3Eh	62	450 bytes	Boot Program Code
1FEh	510	2 bytes	Signature Bytes (55AAh)

NOTE: A WORD is two bytes which are read in reverse order, and a DWORD is two WORDS which are read in reverse order.

Directory Structure

Table 5.10   DOS Directory Entries

Offset Hex	Dec	Field Length	Description
00h	0	8 bytes	Filename
08h	8	3 bytes	File Extension
0Bh	11	1 byte	File Attributes; (see table)
0Ch	12	10 bytes	Terserved; (00h)
16h	22	1 word	Time of Creation: (see table)
18h	24	1 word	Date of Creation: (see table)
1Ah	26	1 word	Starting Cluster
1Ch	28	1 dword	Size in Bytes

NOTE: Filenames ans Extensions are left-justified and padded with spaces (32h). The first byte of the filename indicates the file status as follows:

Hex	File Status
00h	Entry never used; Entries past this point not searched.
05h	Indicates first character of filename is actually E5h.
E5h	"_" (lowercase Sigma) indicates file has been erased.
2Eh	"." (period) indicates this entry is a directory. If the second byte is also 2Eh, the cluster field contains the cluster number of parent directory (0000h if the parent is the Root).

DOS Directory File Attribute Byte:

Bit Positions 7 6 5 4 3 2 1 0	Hex Value	Description
0 0 0 0 0 0 0 1	01h	Read Only file
0 0 0 0 0 0 1 0	02h	Hidden file
0 0 0 0 0 1 0 0	04h	System file
0 0 0 0 1 0 0 0	08h	Volume Label
0 0 0 1 0 0 0 0	10h	Subdirectory
0 0 1 0 0 0 0 0	20h	Archive (updated since Backup)
0 1 0 0 0 0 0 0	40h	Reserved
1 0 0 0 0 0 0 0	80h	Reserved
Examples		
0 0 1 0 0 0 0 1	21h	Read Only, Archive
0 0 1 1 0 0 1 0	32h	Hidden, Subdirectory, Archive
0 0 1 0 0 1 1 1	27h	Read Only, Hidden, System, Archive

Floppy Drives and Disks

This section provides information about the physical properties of floppy disks and drives. This information shows how one type of disk or drive differs from the others in operation and use. The tables in this section explain the difference between floppy disk formats, how data is written to a disk, and how one type of media differs from the others. Knowing this information helps you prevent improper use and formatting of floppy disks, thereby preventing unnecessary future data loss.

Floppy Disk Physical Layout

The following table indicates the physical geometry of each standard floppy disk format. From this information, you can see how the storage capacity of each type of disk is derived.

Table 5.11 5 1/4-inch Floppy Disk Drive Formats		
5.25-inch Diskettes	**Double Density 360K (DD)**	**High Density 1.2M (HD)**
Bytes per Sector	512	512
Sectors per Track	9	15
Tracks per Side	40	80
Sides	2	2
Capacity (KBytes)	360	1,200
Capacity (Megabytes)	0.352	1.172
Capacity (Million Bytes)	0.369	1.229

Table 5.12	3 1/2-inch Floppy Disk Drive Formats		
3.5-inch Diskettes	Double Density 720K (DD)	High Density 1.44M (HD)	Extra-High Density 2.88M (ED)
Bytes per Sector	512	512	512
Sectors per Track	9	18	36
Tracks per Side	80	80	80
Sides	2	2	2
Capacity (KBytes)	720	1,440	2,880
Capacity (Megabytes)	0.703	1.406	2.813
Capacity (Million Bytes)	0.737	1.475	2.949

The following table indicates the width of the magnetic track written by each of the standard floppy drives. Understanding this information helps you recognize when it's proper to exchange disks between two different drives.

Table 5.13	Floppy Disk Drive Track Width		
Drive type	No. of tracks	Track width	
5 1/4-inch 360K	40 per side	0.300 mm	0.0118 in.
5 1/4-inch 1.2M	80 per side	0.155 mm	0.0061 in.
3 1/2-inch 720K	80 per side	0.115 mm	0.0045 in.
3 1/2-inch 1.44M	80 per side	0.115 mm	0.0045 in.
3 1/2-inch 2.88M	80 per side	0.115 mm	0.0045 in.

For example, this table shows that because the 360K drive writes a track .330 millimeters wide, overwriting such a track with a 1.2M drive probably would result in a problem: when a wider track is overwritten by a narrower one, the overwrite will not be complete. Usually, the 360K drive cannot further read a disk written this way. You also should be able to derive that full read-and-write interchangeability occurs between *all* the 3 1/2-inch drives. In other words, a 2.88M drive can write perfectly on 720K or 1.44M formatted floppy disks with no problems because the written track widths are the same between all of the standard 3 1/2-inch drives.

Floppy Disk Media Specifications

The following table shows the physical differences between the various standard floppy disk media. A common misconception seems to exist among some users that double-density (DD) and high-density (HD) floppy disks are the same, especially in the 3 1/2-inch media. This is untrue. Many users who believe this myth are improperly formatting DD floppy disks as HD disks. These floppy disks are in fact very different physically and magnetically, as outlined here.

This information should be used to discourage the use of "hole punchers" or other devices designed to allow someone to "fool" a drive into believing that a DD floppy disk is really a HD floppy disk. Improper formatting and use of such floppy disks causes data loss after the disk has been stored a while (usually six months to a year later) because of the inability of the lower-coercivity media to hold the magnetic patterns stable. Using devices or techniques to improperly format floppy disks in this fashion should be discouraged.

Table 5.14 Floppy Disk Media Specifications

Media Parameters	5 1/4-inch			3 1/2-inch		
	Double Density (DD)	Quad Density (QD)	High Density (HD)	Double Density (DD)	High Density (HD)	Extra-High Density (ED)
Tracks Per Inch (TPI)	48	96	96	135	135	135
Bits Per Inch (BPI)	5,876	5,876	9,646	8,717	17,434	34,868
Media Formulation	Ferrite	Ferrite	Cobalt	Cobalt	Cobalt	Barium
Coercivity (Oersteds)	300	300	600	600	720	750
Thickness (Micro-In.)	100	100	50	70	40	100
Recording Polarity	Horiz.	Horiz.	Horiz.	Horiz.	Horiz.	Vert.

Floppy Controller Interface Pinout

The following table shows the pinout of the standard 34-pin floppy controller interface connector.

Table 5.15   IBM Compatible Floppy Controller Interface Connector pinout

Signal Name	Pin	Pin	Signal Name
GROUND	1	2	-Reduced Write
GROUND	3	4	Not Connected
KEY (no pin)	5	6	Not Connected
GROUND	7	8	-Index
GROUND	9	10	-Motor Enable 0
GROUND	11	12	-Drive Select 0
GROUND	13	14	-Drive Select 1
GROUND	15	16	-Motor Enable 1
GROUND	17	18	-Direction Select
GROUND	19	20	-Step
GROUND	21	22	-Write Data
GROUND	23	24	-Write Enable
GROUND	25	26	-Track 0
GROUND	27	28	-Write Protect
GROUND	29	30	-Read Data
GROUND	31	32	-Head 1 Select
GROUND	33	34	-Diskette Change

Floppy Disk Parameters and Format Maps

The following table shows the logical parameters and structure for each of the possible floppy drive formats. DOS uses and writes this information when it formats a floppy disk.

Table 5.16 Floppy Disk Logical (DOS) Parameters

Disk Size (in.) Disk Capacity (KB)	Current Formats				Obsolete Formats			
	3 1/2" 2,880	3 1/2" 1,440	3 1/2" 720	5 1/4" 1,200	5 1/4" 360	5 1/4" 320	5 1/4" 180	5 1/4" 160
Media Descriptor Byte	F0h	F0h	F9h	F9h	FDh	FFh	FCh	FEh
Sides (Heads)	2	2	2	2	2	2	1	1
Tracks per Side	80	80	80	80	40	40	40	40
Sectors per Track	36	18	9	15	9	8	9	8
Bytes per Sector	512	512	512	512	512	512	512	512
Sectors per Cluster	2	1	2	1	2	2	1	1

Disk Size (in.) Disk Capacity (KB)	Current Formats					Obsolete Formats		
	3 1/2" 2,880	3 1/2" 1,440	3 1/2" 720	5 1/4" 1,200	5 1/4" 360	5 1/4" 320	5 1/4" 180	5 1/4" 160
FAT Length (Sectors)	9	9	3	7	2	1	2	1
Number of FATs	2	2	2	2	2	2	2	2
Root Dir. Length (Sectors)	15	14	7	14	7	7	4	4
Maximum Root Entries	240	224	112	224	112	112	64	64
Total Sectors per Disk	5,760	2,880	1,440	2,400	720	640	360	320
Total Available Sectors	5,726	2,847	1,426	2,371	708	630	351	313
Total Available Clusters	2,863	2,847	713	2,371	354	315	351	313

Figure 5.2 shows the drive map for floppy disks of type 01 (360K) formatted under MS-DOS as follows:

Drive type:	5 1\4-inch double-density 360K floppy
Drive geometry:	40 cylinders, 2 heads, 9 sectors/tracks
DOS version:	IBM or MS-DOS 2.0 or later
DVB:	Cylinder 0, head 0, sector 1; DOS sector 0
FAT #1:	Sectors 1-2; 2 sectors long
FAT #2:	Sectors 3-4; 2 sectors long
Root directory:	Sectors 5-11; 7 sectors long (112 entries)
Data area:	Sectors 12-719; clusters 2-355
Cluster size:	2 sectors (1,024 bytes)

Notes:

DVB = DOS volume boot sector
FAT = file allocation table

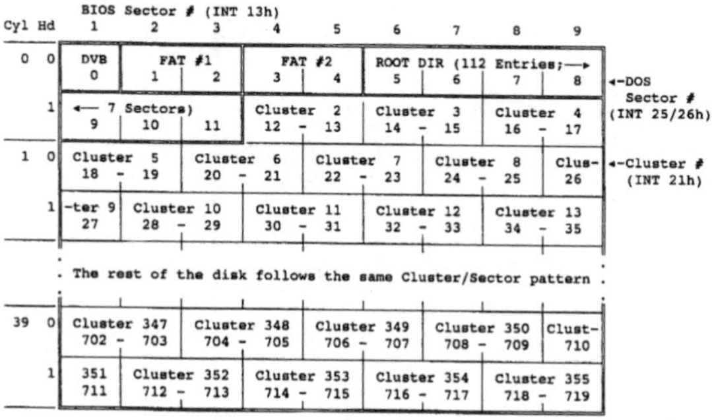

Fig. 5.2 Disk map for 5 1/4-inch 360K floppy disk.

Figure 5.3 shows the drive map for floppy disks of type 02 (1.2M) formatted under MS-DOS as follows:

Drive type:	5 1/4-inch high-density 1.2M floppy
Drive geometry:	80 cylinders, 2 heads, 15 sectors/track

DOS version:	IBM or MS-DOS 3.0 or later (through 5.x)
DVB:	cylinder 0, head 0, sector 1; DOS sector 0
FAT #1:	Sectors 1-7; 7 sectors long
FAT #2:	Sectors 8-14; 7 sectors long
Root directory:	Sectors 15-28; 14 sectors long (224 entries)
Data area:	Sectors 29-2399; clusters 2-2372
Cluster size:	1 sector (512 bytes)

Notes:

DVB = DOS volume boot sector

FAT = file allocation table

BIOS Sector # (INT 13h)

Cyl	Hd	1	2	3	4	5	6	7	8	9	10	11	12	13	14	15	
0	0	DVB 0	← FAT #1 (7 Sectors, 1-7) → 1	2	3	4	5	6	7	← FAT #2 (7 Sectors, 8-14) → 8	9	10	11	12	13	14	←DOS Sector # (INT 25/26h)
	1	← ROOT DIRECTORY (224 Entries; 14 Sectors, 15-28) → 15	16	17	18	19	20	21	22	23	24	25	26	27	28	2 29	
1	0	3 30	4 31	5 32	6 33	7 34	8 35	9 36	10 37	11 38	12 39	13 40	14 41	15 42	16 43	17 44	←Cluster # (INT 21h)
	1	18 45	19 46	20 47	21 48	22 49	23 50	24 51	25 52	26 53	27 54	28 55	29 56	30 57	31 58	32 59	
		The remainder of the disk follows the same Cluster/Sector pattern.															
79	0	2343 2370	2344 2371	2345 2372	2346 2373	2347 2374	2348 2375	2349 2376	2350 2377	2351 2378	2352 2379	2353 2380	2354 2381	2355 2382	2356 2383	2357 2384	
	1	2358 2385	2359 2386	2360 2387	2361 2388	2362 2389	2363 2390	2364 2391	2365 2392	2366 2393	2367 2394	2368 2395	2369 2396	2370 2397	2371 2398	2372 2399	

Fig. 5.3 Disk map for 5 1/4-inch 1.2M floppy disk.

Figure 5.4 shows the drive map for floppy disks of type 03 (720K) fromatted under MS-DOS as follows:

Drive type:	3 1/2-inch double-density 720K floppy
Drive geometry:	80 cylinders, 2 heads, 9 sectors/ track

DOS version:	IBm or MS-DOS 3.2 or later
DVB:	Cylinder 0, head 0 sector 1; DOS sector 0
FAT #1:	Sectors 1-3; 3 sectors long
FAT #2:	Sectors 4-6; 3 sectors long
Root directory:	Sectors 7-13; 7 sectors long (112 entries)
Data area:	Sectors 14-1439; clusters 2-714
Cluster size:	2 sectors (1,024 bytes)

Notes:

DVB = DOS volume boot sector

FAT = file allocation table

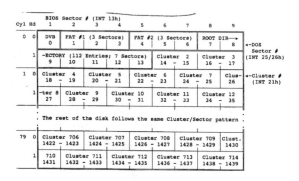

Fig. 5.4   Disk map for 3 1/2-inch 720K floppy disk.

Figure 5.5 shows the drive map for floppy disks of type 04 (1.44M) formatted under MS-DOS as follows:

Drive type:	3 1/2-inch high-density 1.44M floppy
Drive geometry:	80 cylinders, 2 heads, 18 sectors/track
DOS version:	IBM or MS-DOS 3.3 or later
DVB:	Cylinder 0, head0, sector 1; DOS sector 0
FAT #1:	Sectors 1-9; 9 sectors long
FAT #2:	Sectors 10-18; 9 sectors long

Root directory:	Sectors 19-32; 14 sectors long (224 entries)
Data area:	Sectors 33-2879; clusters 2-2848
Cluster Size:	1 Sector (512 Bytes)

Notes:

DVB = DOS volume boot sector

FAT = file allocation table

Fig. 5.5 Disk map for 3 1/2-inch 1.44M floppy disk.

Hard Disk Drives

This section has a great deal of information concerning all aspects of hard disk drives, including a table that lists a large number of different drive parameters, organized by manufacturer. Because Seagate is the largest supplier of hard disks in the world, and its product line is so extensive, a separate table references Seagate's hard disk product line, which shows the parameters of all its drives. This section also shows BIOS hard drive parameter tables for a number of different ROM BIOS versions, including those from IBM, COMPAQ, AMI, Award, Phoenix, and Zenith. Finally, this section includes the pinouts of popular hard disk interfaces such as ST-506/412, ESDI, IDE, and SCSI.

The following table shows parameters and specifications for a large number of different hard disk drives. This table can be very helpful when you are trying to install one of these drives in a system with no documentation for the drive.

Table 5.17 Hard Disk Drive Specifications			
Make/Model	Capacity (MB)	Cyls	
Atasi			
502	46.0	755	
504	46.0	755	
514	117.2	1,224	
519MFM	159.8	1,224	
519RLL	244.4	1,224	
617	149.0	1,223	
628	234.2	1,223	
638	319.3	1,223	
3046	39.3	645	
3051	42.9	704	
3051+	44.7	733	
3085	71.3	1,024	
V130	25.8	987	
V150	43.0	987	
V170	60.1	987	
V185	71.0	1,166	
Brand Technology			
BT8085	71.3	1,024	
BT8128	109.1	1,024	
BT8170E	142.5	1,023	
Conner Peripherals			
CP-342	42.7	981	
CP-344	42.9	805	
CP-3024	21.4	634	
CP-3044	43.1	526	
CP-3102-A	104.9	776	
CP-3102-B	104.3	772	
CP-3104	104.9	776	
CP-3184	84.3	832	

Hds	Sectors per Track	Write Pre-comp	Park Cyl
7	17	—	—
7	17	—	—
11	17	—	—
15	17	—	—
15	26	—	—
7	34	—	—
11	34	—	—
15	34	—	—
7	17	323	644
7	17	352	703
7	17	368	732
8	17	0	—
3	17	128	—
5	17	128	—
7	17	128	—
7	17	128	—
8	17	512	—
8	26	—	—
8	34	—	—
5	17	—	—
4	26	—	—
2	33	—	—
4	40	—	—
8	33	—	—
8	33	—	—
8	33	—	—
6	33	—	—

(continues)

Table 5.17 Continued			
Make/Model	Capacity (MB)	Cyls	
CP-3204	209.8	1,348	
CP-3204F	212.9	684	
CP-30104	121.6	1,522	
CMI			
CM-6626	22.3	640	
CM-6640	33.4	640	
Data-Tech Memories			
DTM-553	44.6	1,024	
DTM-853	44.6	640	
DTM-885	71.3	1,024	
Fujitsu			
M2225D	21.4	615	
M2227D	42.8	615	
M2241AS	26.3	754	
M2242AS	45.9	754	
M2243AS	72.2	754	
M2244E	71.5	822	
M2245E	100.2	822	
M2246E	143.1	822	
M2247E	151.3	1,242	
M2248E	237.8	1,242	
M2249E	324.3	1,242	
M2261E	359.7	1,657	
M2263E	674.5	1,657	
M2611T	45.1	1,334	
M2612T	90.2	1,334	
M2613T	135.2	1,334	
M2614T	180.3	1,334	

	Hds	Sectors per Track	Write Pre-comp	Park Cyl
	8	38	—	—
	16	38	—	—
	4	39	—	—
	4	17	256	615
	6	17	256	615
	5	17	850	—
	8	17	256	—
	8	17	850	—
	4	17	—	615
	8	17	—	615
	4	17	128	—
	7	17	128	—
	11	17	128	—
	5	34	—	—
	7	34	—	—
	10	34	—	—
	7	34	—	—
	11	34	—	—
	15	34	—	—
	8	53	—	—
	15	53	—	—
	2	33	—	—
	4	33	—	—
	6	33	—	—
	8	33	—	—

(continues)

Table 5.17 Continued			
Make/Model	Capacity (MB)	Cyls	
Hewlett-Packard			
97544EF	339.9	1,456	
97548EF	679.9	1,456	
Hitachi			
DK511-3	30.4	699	
DK511-5	42.6	699	
DK511-8	71.6	823	
DK512-8	71.5	822	
DK512-10	85.9	822	
DK512-12	100.2	822	
DK512-17	143.1	822	
DK514-38	329.7	902	
DK522-10	85.9	822	
Imprimis (CDC)			
9415-519	18.2	697	
9415-536	30.3	697	
9415-538	31.9	733	
94155-48	40.3	925	
94155-57	48.3	925	
94155-67	56.4	925	
94155-77	64.4	925	
94155-85	71.3	1,024	
94155-85P	71.3	1,024	
94155-86	72.5	925	
94155-96	80.2	1,024	
94155-96P	80.2	1,024	

	Hds	Sectors per Track	Write Pre-comp	Park Cyl
	8	57	128	—
	16	57	128	—
	5	17	300	699
	7	17	300	699
	10	17	256	—
	5	34	—	—
	6	34	—	—
	7	34	—	—
	10	34	—	—
	14	51	—	—
	6	34	—	—
	3	17	128	—
	5	17	128	—
	5	17	128	—
	5	17	128	—
	6	17	128	—
	7	17	128	—
	8	17	128	—
	8	17	—	—
	8	17	128	—
	9	17	128	—
	9	17	—	—
	9	17	128	—

(continues)

Table 5.17 Continued

Make/Model	Capacity (MB)	Cyls
94155-120	102.2	960
94155-120P	102.2	960
94155-135	115.0	960
94155-135P	115.0	960
94156-48	40.3	925
94156-67	56.4	925
94156-86	72.5	925
94166-101	84.3	968
94166-141	118.0	968
94166-182	151.7	968
94186-383	319.3	1,411
94186-383H	319.3	1,223
94186-442H	368.4	1,411
94196-766	663.9	1,631
94204-65	65.5	941
94204-71	71.3	1,024
94205-51	43.0	989
94205-77	65.8	989
94211-106	89.0	1,023
94244-383	338.1	1,747
94246-383	331.7	1,746
94354-160	143.3	1,072
94354-200	177.8	1,072
94354-230	211.0	1,272
94355-100	84.0	1,072
94355-150	128.4	1,072
94356-111	93.2	1,071
94356-155	130.5	1,071
94356-200	167.8	1,071

	Hds	Sectors per Track	Write Pre-comp	Park Cyl
	8	26	—	—
	8	26	128	—
	9	26	—	—
	9	26	128	—
	5	17	128	—
	7	17	128	—
	9	17	128	—
	5	34	—	—
	7	34	—	—
	9	34	—	—
	13	34	—	—
	15	34	—	—
	15	34	—	—
	15	53	—	—
	8	17	128	—
	8	17	128	—
	5	17	128	—
	5	26	128	—
	5	34	—	—
	7	54	—	—
	7	53	—	—
	9	29	128	—
	9	36	—	—
	9	36	—	—
	9	17	128	—
	9	26	128	—
	5	34	—	—
	7	34	—	—
	9	34	—	—

(continues)

Table 5.17 Continued		
Make/Model	**Capacity (MB)**	**Cyls**
Kalok		
KL320	21.4	615
KL330	32.7	615
KL343	42.5	670
Kyocera		
KC20A	21.4	616
KC20B	21.4	615
KC30A	32.8	616
KC30B	32.7	615
KC40GA	42.5	977
Lapine		
TITAN20	21.4	615
Maxtor		
LXT50S	48.0	733
LXT100S	96.1	733
LXT200A	200.5	816
LXT200S	212.9	1,320
LXT213A	212.6	683
LXT340S	352.2	1,560
LXT340AT	352.2	1,560
XT1050	39.3	902
XT1065	55.9	918
XT1085	71.3	1,024
XT1105	87.9	918
XT1120R	109.1	1,024
XT1140	119.9	918
XT1160	133.7	1,024
XT1240R	204.5	1,024
XT2085	74.6	1,224
XT2140	117.2	1,224

		Sectors per Track	Write Pre-comp	Park Cyl
	4	17	—	660
	4	26	—	660
	4	31	—	669
	4	17	0	—
	4	17	0	664
	4	26	0	—
	4	26	0	664
	5	17	0	980
	4	17	0	615
	4	32	—	—
	8	32	—	—
	15	32	—	—
	7	45	—	—
	16	38	—	—
	7	63	—	—
	7	63	—	—
	5	17	—	—
	7	17	—	—
	8	17	—	—
	11	17	—	—
	8	26	—	—
	15	17	—	—
	15	17	—	—
	15	26	—	—
	7	17	—	—
	11	17	—	—

(continues)

Table 5.17   Continued

Make/Model	Capacity (MB)	Cyls	
XT2190	159.8	1,224	
XT4170E	149.2	1,224	
XT4170S	149.2	1,224	
XT4175	149.2	1,224	
XT4230E	203.0	1,224	
XT4280	234.4	1,224	
XT4380E	338.4	1,224	
XT4380S	338.4	1,224	
XT8380E	361.0	1,632	
XT8380S	361.0	1,632	
XT8610E	541.5	1,632	
XT8760E	676.8	1,632	
XT8760S	676.8	1,632	
XT8702S	617.9	1,490	
XT8800E	694.7	1,274	
Micropolis			
1323	35.7	1,024	
1323A	44.6	1,024	
1324	53.5	1,024	
1324A	62.4	1,024	
1325	71.3	1,024	
1333	35.7	1,024	
1333A	44.6	1,024	
1334	53.5	1,024	
1334A	62.4	1,024	
1335	71.3	1,024	
1353	71.2	1,023	
1353A	89.0	1,023	
1354	106.9	1,023	

	Hds	Sectors per Track	Write Pre-comp	Park Cyl
	15	17	—	—
	7	34	—	—
	7	34	—	—
	7	34	—	—
	9	36	—	—
	11	34	—	—
	15	36	—	—
	15	36	—	—
	8	54	—	—
	8	54	—	—
	12	54	—	—
	15	54	—	—
	15	54	—	—
	15	54	—	—
	15	71	—	—
	4	17	—	—
	5	17	—	—
	6	17	—	—
	7	17	—	—
	8	17	—	—
	4	17	—	—
	5	17	—	—
	6	17	—	—
	7	17	—	—
	8	17	—	—
	4	34	—	—
	5	34	—	—
	6	34	—	—

(continues)

Table 5.17 Continued

Make/Model	Capacity (MB)	Cyls
1354A	124.7	1,023
1355	142.5	1,023
1551	149.0	1,223
1554	234.2	1,223
1555	255.5	1,223
1556	276.8	1,223
1557	298.1	1,223
1558	319.3	1,223
1568-15	663.9	1,631
1653-4	86.9	1,248
1653-5	108.6	1,248
1654-6	130.4	1,248
1654-7	152.1	1,248
1664-7	337.9	1,779
1743-5	110.9	1,140
Microscience		
HH-325	21.4	615
HH-725	21.4	615
HH-1050	44.6	1,024
HH-1060	68.2	1,024
HH-1075	62.4	1,024
HH-1090	80.1	1,314
HH-1095	95.4	1,024
HH-1120	122.4	1,314
HH-2120	124.7	1,023
HH-2160	155.4	1,275
4050	44.6	1,024
4060	68.2	1,024
4070	62.4	1,024

	Hds	Sectors per Track	Write Pre-comp	Park Cyl
	7	34	—	—
	8	34	—	—
	7	34	—	—
	11	34	—	—
	12	34	—	—
	13	34	—	—
	14	34	—	—
	15	34	—	—
	15	53	—	—
	4	34	—	—
	5	34	—	—
	6	34	—	—
	7	34	—	—
	7	53	—	—
	5	38	—	—
	4	17	—	615
	4	17	—	615
	5	17	—	—
	5	26	—	—
	7	17	—	—
	7	17	—	—
	7	26	—	—
	7	26	—	—
	7	34	—	—
	7	34	—	—
	5	17	768	—
	5	26	768	—
	7	17	768	—

(continues)

Table 5.17 Continued			
Make/Model	Capacity (MB)	Cyls	
4090	95.4	1,024	
5040-00	45.9	854	
5070-00	76.5	854	
5070-20	85.9	959	
5100-00	107.1	854	
5100-20	120.3	959	
5160-00	159.3	1,270	
7040-00	46.0	855	
7070-00	76.6	855	
7070-20	86.0	960	
7100-00	107.3	855	
7100-20	120.4	960	
Miniscribe			
1006	5.3	306	
1012	10.7	306	
2006	5.3	306	
2012	10.7	306	
3012	10.7	612	
3053	44.6	1,024	
3085	71.3	1,170	
3130E	112.0	1,250	
3180E	156.8	1,250	
3180S	161.9	1,255	
3212	10.7	612	
3412	10.7	306	
3425	21.4	615	
3425P	21.4	615	
3438	32.7	615	
3438P	32.7	615	
3650	42.2	809	

	Hds	Sectors per Track	Write Pre-comp	Park Cyl
	7	26	768	—
	3	35	—	—
	5	35	—	—
	5	35	—	—
	7	35	—	—
	7	35	—	—
	7	35	—	—
	3	35	—	—
	5	35	—	—
	5	35	—	—
	7	35	—	—
	7	35	—	—
	2	17	128	336
	4	17	128	336
	2	17	128	336
	4	17	128	336
	2	17	128	656
	5	17	512	—
	7	17	512	—
	5	35	—	—
	7	35	—	—
	7	36	—	—
	2	17	128	656
	4	17	128	336
	4	17	128	656
	4	17	128	656
	4	26	128	656
	4	26	128	656
	6	17	128	852

(continues)

Table 5.17 Continued			
Make/Model	**Capacity (MB)**	**Cyls**	
3650R	64.6	809	
3675	64.6	809	
4010	8.4	480	
4020	16.7	480	
6032	26.7	1,024	
6053	44.6	1,024	
6079	68.2	1,024	
6085	71.3	1,024	
6128	109.1	1,024	
7040A	42.7	981	
7080A	85.4	981	
8051A	42.7	745	
8051S	42.7	745	
8212	10.7	615	
8225	20.5	771	
8225A	21.4	615	
8225XT	21.4	805	
8412	10.7	306	
8425	21.4	615	
8425F	21.4	615	
8425S	21.4	615	
8425XT	21.4	615	
8438	32.7	615	
8438F	32.7	615	
8450	41.1	771	
8450A	42.7	745	
8450XT	42.9	805	
9380E	329.0	1,224	
9380S	336.8	1,218	

	Hds	Sectors per Track	Write Pre-comp	Park Cyl
	6	26	128	852
	6	26	128	852
	2	17	128	522
	4	17	128	522
	3	17	512	—
	5	17	512	—
	5	26	512	—
	8	17	512	—
	8	26	512	—
	5	17	—	—
	10	17	—	—
	4	28	—	—
	4	28	—	—
	2	17	128	656
	2	26	128	810
	4	17	—	810
	2	26	—	820
	4	17	128	336
	4	17	128	664
	4	17	128	664
	4	17	—	664
	4	17	—	664
	4	26	128	664
	4	26	128	664
	4	26	128	810
	4	28	—	810
	4	26	—	820
	15	35	—	—
	15	36	—	—

(continues)

Table 5.17 Continued			
Make/Model	Capacity (MB)	Cyls	
9780E	676.1	1,661	
Mitsubishi			
MR522	21.3	612	
MR535	42.5	977	
MR535RLL	65.0	977	
MR5310E	85.0	976	
NEC			
D3126	21.4	615	
D3142	44.7	642	
D3146H	42.8	615	
D3661	111.4	914	
D3741	45.0	423	
D5126	21.4	615	
D5126H	21.4	615	
D5127H	32.7	615	
D5128	21.4	615	
D5146H	42.8	615	
D5147H	65.5	615	
D5452	71.6	823	
D5652	143.1	822	
D5655	149.0	1,223	
D5662	319.3	1,223	
D5682	664.3	1,632	
Newbury			
NDR320	21.4	615	
NDR340	42.8	615	
NDR360	65.5	615	
NDR1065	55.9	918	
NDR1085	71.3	1,024	

		Sectors per Track	Write Pre-comp	Park Cyl
	15	53	—	—
	4	17	300	612
	5	17	0	—
	5	26	0	—
	5	34	—	—
	4	17	256	664
	8	17	128	664
	8	17	256	664
	7	34	—	—
	8	26	—	423
	4	17	128	664
	4	17	128	664
	4	26	128	664
	4	17	128	664
	8	17	128	664
	8	26	128	664
	10	17	512	—
	10	34	—	—
	7	34	—	—
	15	34	—	—
	15	53	—	—
	4	17	—	615
	8	17	—	615
	8	26	—	615
	7	17	—	—
	8	17	—	—

(continues)

Table 5.17 Continued		
Make/Model	**Capacity (MB)**	**Cyls**
NDR1105	87.9	918
NDR1140	119.9	918
NDR2190	159.8	1,224
NDR4170	149.0	1,223
NDR4380	319.3	1,223
Pacific Magtron		
4115E	114.6	1,599
4140E	143.3	1,599
4170E	171.9	1,599
Plus Development		
40AT	42.0	965
80AT	84.0	965
120AT	120.0	814
170AT	168.5	968
210AT	209.2	873
52AT/LP	52.3	751
80AT/LP	85.8	616
105AT/LP	105.1	755
Priam		
502	46.0	755
504	46.0	755
514	117.2	1,224
519	159.8	1,224
617	143.8	751
623	196.1	751
638	319.3	1,223
V130	25.8	987
V150	43.0	987
V170	60.1	987

	Hds	Sectors per Track	Write Pre-comp	Park Cyl
	11	17	—	—
	15	17	—	—
	15	17	—	—
	7	34	—	—
	15	34	—	—
	4	35	—	—
	5	35	—	—
	6	35	—	—
	5	17	—	—
	10	17	—	—
	9	32	—	—
	10	34	—	—
	13	36	—	—
	8	17	—	—
	16	17	—	—
	16	17	—	—
	7	17	—	—
	7	17	—	—
	11	17	—	—
	15	17	—	—
	11	34	—	—
	15	34	—	—
	15	34	—	—
	3	17	128	—
	5	17	128	—
	7	17	128	—

(continues)

Table 5.17 Continued

Make/Model	Capacity (MB)	Cyls	
V185	71.0	1,166	
PTI			
PT225	21.4	615	
PT234	28.5	820	
PT338	32.1	615	
PT351	42.8	820	
PT238R	32.7	615	
PT251R	43.7	820	
PT357R	49.1	615	
PT376R	65.5	820	
Quantum			
40AT	42.0	965	
80AT	84.0	965	
120AT	120.0	814	
170AT	168.5	968	
210AT	209.2	873	
LPS52	52.3	751	
LPS80	85.8	616	
LPS105	105.1	755	
Q520	17.8	512	
Q530	26.7	512	
Q540	35.7	512	
Rodime			
203	16.8	321	
204	22.4	321	
202E	22.3	640	
203E	33.4	640	
204E	44.6	640	
3099A	80.2	373	

	Hds	Sectors per Track	Write Pre-comp	Park Cyl
	7	17	128	—
	4	17	410	—
	4	17	547	—
	6	17	410	—
	6	17	547	—
	4	26	410	—
	4	26	547	—
	6	26	410	—
	6	26	547	—
	5	17	—	—
	10	17	—	—
	9	32	—	—
	10	34	—	—
	13	36	—	—
	8	17	—	—
	16	17	—	—
	16	17	—	—
	4	17	256	512
	6	17	256	512
	8	17	256	512
	6	17	132	321
	8	17	132	321
	4	17	0	640
	6	17	0	640
	8	17	0	640
	15	28	—	—

(continues)

Table 5.17 Continued

Make/Model	Capacity (MB)	Cyls	
3139A	112.5	523	
3259A	212.9	990	
3000A-NAT	43.2	625	
3000A-XLAT	43.2	992	
3060R	49.9	750	
3075R	59.9	750	
3085R	69.9	750	
5040	32.0	1,224	
5065	53.3	1,224	
5090	74.6	1,224	
Samsung			
SHD2020	21.8	820	
SHD2021	23.5	820	
SHD2030	28.5	820	
SHD2040	43.7	820	
SHD2041	47.0	820	
Siemens			
MF-1200	169.2	1,215	
MF-1300	253.8	1,215	
MF-4410	321.9	1,099	
Syquest			
SQ312RD	10.7	612	
SQ315F	21.3	612	
SQ338F	32.0	612	
Tandon			
TN262	21.4	615	
TN362	21.4	615	
TN703	25.2	578	
TN703AT	31.9	733	

Hds	Sectors per Track	Write Pre-comp	Park Cyl
15	28	—	—
15	28	—	—
5	27	0	—
5	17	0	—
5	26	0	—
6	26	0	—
7	26	0	—
3	17	0	—
5	17	0	—
7	17	0	—
2	26	—	—
2	28	—	—
4	17	—	—
4	26	—	—
4	28	—	—
8	34	—	—
12	34	—	—
11	52	—	—
2	17	0	615
4	17	0	615
6	17	0	615
4	17	0	615
4	17	0	615
5	17	0	615
5	17	0	733

(continues)

Table 5.17 Continued

Make/Model	Capacity (MB)	Cyls
TN705	41.9	962
TN755	42.7	981
Toshiba		
MK-53F	36.1	830
MK-53FRLL	55.2	830
MK-54F	50.6	830
MK-54FRLL	77.3	830
MK-56F	72.2	830
MK-56FRLL	110.5	830
MK-72PCMFM	72.2	830
MK-72PCRLL	110.5	830
MK-134FAMFM	44.7	733
MK-134FARLL	68.3	733
MK-153FA	72.2	829
MK-154FA	101.0	829
MK-156FA	144.3	829
MK-232FC	45.4	845
MK-234FC-I	106.0	845
MK-355FA	398.3	1,631
MK-358FA	663.9	1,631
MK-538FB	1229.0	1,980
Tulin		
TL226	22.3	640
TL240	33.4	640
Vertex		
V130	25.8	987
V150	43.0	987
V170	60.1	987
V185	71.0	1,166

	Hds	Sectors per Track	Write Pre-comp	Park Cyl
	5	17	0	962
	5	17	128	981
	5	17	—	—
	5	26	—	—
	7	17	—	—
	7	26	—	—
	10	17	—	—
	10	26	—	—
	10	17	—	—
	10	26	512	—
	7	17	—	—
	7	26	512	—
	5	34	—	—
	7	34	—	—
	10	34	—	—
	3	35	—	—
	7	35	—	—
	9	53	—	—
	15	53	—	—
	15	80	—	—
	4	17	—	640
	6	17	—	640
	3	17	128	—
	5	17	128	—
	7	17	128	—
	7	17	128	—

(continues)

Table 5.17   Continued

Make/Model	Capacity (MB)	Cyls
Western Digital		
WD-93024A	21.6	782
WD-93028A	21.6	782
WD-93044A	43.2	782
WD-93048A	43.2	782
WD-95028A	21.6	782
WD-95044A	43.2	782
WD-95048A	43.2	782
WD-AC140	42.6	980
WD-AC280	85.3	980
WD-AP4200	212.2	987
WD-SP4200	209.7	1,280
WD-SC8320	326.5	949
WD-SC8400	413.2	1,201

—*No write precompensation required, or no parking cylinder required (autopark).*

	Hds	Sectors per Track	Write Pre-comp	Park Cyl
	2	27	—	—
	2	27	—	—
	4	27	—	—
	4	27	—	—
	2	27	—	—
	4	27	—	—
	4	27	—	—
	5	17	—	—
	10	17	—	—
	12	35	—	—
	8	40	—	—
	14	48	—	—
	14	48	—	—

Table 5.18 Seagate Hard Disk Drive Specifications

	Imprimis Model #	Cyls	Hds	
ST1057a		1024	6	
ST1090a	94354-90	1072	5	
Opt. CMOS Values:		335	16	
ST1090n	94351-90	1068	5	
ST1096n		906	7	
ST1100	94355-100	1072	9	
ST1102a		1024	10	
ST1106r		977	7	
ST1111a	94354-111	1072	5	
Opt. CMOS Values:		402	10	
ST1111e	94356-111	1072	5	
ST1111n	94351-111	1068	5	
ST11200n		1872	15	
ST1126a	94354-126	1072	7	
Opt. CMOS Values:		469	16	
ST1126n	94351-125	1068	7	
ST1133a	94354-133	1272	5	
Opt. CMOS Values:		477	8	
ST1133n	94351-133s	1268	5	
ST1144a		1001	15	
ST1150r	94355-150	1072	9	
ST1156a	94354-156	1072	7	
Opt. CMOS Values:		536	9	
ST1156e	94356-156	1072	7	
ST1156n	94351-155	1068	7	
ST1156r	94355-156	1072	7	
ST1162a	94354-162	1072	9	
Opt. CMOS Values:		603	16	
ST1162n	94351-160	1068	9	
ST1182e		972	9	
ST1186a	94354-186	1272	7	
Opt. CMOS Values:		636	9	
ST1186n	94351-186	1268	7	
ST11950n		2706	15	
ST1201a	94354-201	1072	9	
Opt. CMOS Values:		804	9	
ST1201e	94356-201	1072	9	
ST1201n	94351-200	1068	9	

WPC	Park Cyl.	Sectors per Track	Capacity (MB)	Total Sectors
-1	1024	17*	53.5	104448
-1	1072	29	79.6	155440
335	335	29	79.6	155440
-1	1068	29	79.3	154860
-1	906	26	84.4	164892
-1	1072	17	84.0	164016
-1	1024	17*	89.1	174080
-1	977	26	91.0	177814
-1	1072	36	98.8	192960
402	402	48	98.8	192960
-1	1072	36	98.8	192960
-1	1068	36	98.4	192240
-1	1872	73*	1049.5	2049840
-1	1072	29	111.4	217616
469	469	29	111.4	217616
-1	1068	29	111.0	216804
-1	1272	36	117.2	228960
477	477	60	117.2	228960
-1	1268	36	116.9	228240
-1	1001	17*	130.7	255255
300	1072	26	128.4	250848
-1	1072	36	138.3	270144
536	536	56	138.3	270144
-1	1072	36	138.3	270144
-1	1068	36	137.8	269136
300	1072	36	138.3	270144
-1	1072	29	143.3	279792
603	603	29	143.3	279792
-1	1068	29	142.7	278748
-1	972	36	161.2	314928
-1	1272	36	164.1	320544
636	636	56	164.1	320544
-1	1268	36	163.6	319536
-1	2706	99*	2057.4	4018410
-1	1072	36	177.8	347328
804	804	48	177.8	347328
-1	1072	36	177.8	347328
-1	1068	36	177.2	346032

(continues)

Table 5.18 Continued

	Imprimis Model #	Cyls	Hds	
ST1239a	94354-239	1272	9	
Opt. CMOS Values:		848	9	
ST1239n	94351-230	1268	9	
ST124		615	4	
ST12400n		2626	19	
ST125		615	4	
ST125-1		615	4	
ST12550N		2707	19	
ST12551N		2707	19	
ST12550ND		2707	19	
ST12551ND		2707	19	
ST125a		404	4	
Opt. CMOS Values:		615	4	
ST125n		407	4	
ST137r		615	6	
ST138		615	6	
ST138a		604	4	
Opt. CMOS Values:		615	6	
ST138n		615	4	
ST138r		615	4	
ST1400a		1018	12	
ST1400n		1476	7	
ST1400ns		1476	7	
ST1401a		726	15	
ST1401n		1100	9	
ST1401ns		1100	9	
ST1480a		1474	9	
Opt. CMOS Values:		1015	15	
ST1480n		1476	9	
ST1480ns		1476	9	
ST1481n		1476	9	
ST151		977	5	
ST157a		560	6	
Opt. CMOS Values:		733	7	
ST157n		615	6	
ST157r		615	6	

WPC	Park Cyl.	Sectors per Track	Capacity (MB)	Total Sectors
-1	1272	36	211.0	412128
848	848	54	211.0	412128
-1	1268	36	210.3	410832
-1	670	17	21.4	41820
-1	2626	82*	2094.7	4091308
-1	615	17	21.4	41820
-1	615	17	21.4	41820
—	2707	81*	2133.0	4166073
—	2707	81*	2133.0	4166073
—	2707	81*	2133.0	4166073
—	2707	81*	2133.0	4166073
-1	404	26	21.5	42016
615	615	17	21.4	41820
-1	408	26	21.7	42328
-1	670	26	49.1	95940
-1	615	17	32.1	62730
-1	604	26	32.2	62816
615	615	17	32.1	62730
-1	615	26	32.7	63960
-1	615	26	32.7	63960
-1	1018	53*	331.5	647448
-1	1476	62*	328.0	640584
-1	1476	62*	328.0	640584
-1	726	61*	340.1	664290
-1	1100	66*	334.5	653400
-1	1100	66*	334.5	653400
-1	1474	62*	421.1	822492
1015	1015	54*	420.9	822150
-1	1476	62*	421.7	823608
-1	1476	62*	421.7	823608
-1	1476	62*	421.7	823608
-1	977	17	42.5	83045
-1	560	26	44.7	87360
733	733	17	44.7	87227
-1	615	26	49.1	95940
-1	615	26	49.1	95940

(continues)

Table 5.18 Continued

	Imprimis Model #	Cyls	Hds	
ST1581n		1476	9	
ST177n		921	5	
ST1980n		1730	13	
ST2106e	94216-106	1024	5	
ST2106n	94211-091	1024	5	
ST2106n	94211-106	1024	5	
ST2106nm	94211-106	1024	5	
ST212		306	4	
ST2125n	94221-125	1544	3	
ST2125nm	94221-125	1544	3	
ST2125nv	94221-125	1544	3	
ST213		615	2	
ST2182e	94246-182	1453	4	
ST2209n	94221-209	1544	5	
ST2209nm	94221-209m	1544	5	
ST2209nv	94221-209	1544	5	
ST224n		615	2	
ST225		615	4	
ST225n		615	4	
ST225r		667	2	
ST2274a	94244-274	1747	5	
Opt. CMOS Values:		536	16	
ST238		615	4	
ST2383a	94244-383	1747	7	
Opt. CMOS Values:		737	16	
ST2383e	94246-383	1747	7	
ST2383n	94241-383	1260	7	
ST2383nm	94241-383	1260	7	
ST238r		615	4	
ST2502n	94241-502	1756	7	
ST2502nm	94241-502	1756	7	
ST2502nv	94241-502	1756	7	
ST250n		667	4	
ST250r		667	4	
ST251		820	6	
ST251n-0		820	4	
ST251n-1		630	4	
ST252		820	6	

WPC	Park Cyl.	Sectors per Track	Capacity (MB)	Total Sectors
-1	1476	77*	523.7	1022868
-1	921	26	61.3	119730
-1	1730	74*	852.1	1664260
-1	1024	36	94.4	184320
-1	1024	36	94.4	184320
-1	1024	36	94.4	184320
-1	1024	36	94.4	184320
128	319	17	10.7	20808
-1	1544	45*	106.7	208440
-1	1544	45*	106.7	208440
-1	1544	45*	106.7	208440
300	670	17	10.7	20910
-1	1453	54	160.7	313848
-1	1544	45*	177.9	347400
-1	1544	45*	177.9	347400
-1	1544	45*	177.9	347400
-1	615	17	10.7	20910
300	670	17	21.4	41820
-1	615	17	21.4	41820
-1	670	31	21.2	41354
-1	1747	54	241.5	471690
536	536	55	241.5	471680
-1	670	26	32.7	63960
-1	1747	54	338.1	660366
737	737	56	338.1	660352
-1	1747	54	338.1	660366
-1	1260	74*	334.2	652680
-1	1260	74*	334.2	652680
-1	670	26	32.7	63960
-1	1755	69*	434.3	848148
-1	1755	69*	434.3	848148
-1	1755	69*	434.3	848148
-1	670	31	42.3	82708
-1	670	31	42.3	82708
-1	820	17	42.8	83640
-1	820	26	43.7	85280
-1	630	34	43.9	85680
-1	820	17	42.8	83640

(continues)

Table 5.18 Continued			
	Imprimis Model #	Cyls	Hds
ST253	94205-51	989	5
ST274a	94204-74	948	5
ST277n-0		820	6
ST277n-1		628	6
ST277r		820	6
ST278r		820	6
ST279r	94205-77	989	5
ST280a	94204-71	1032	5
Opt. CMOS Values:		1024	8
ST280a	94204-81	1032	5
Opt. CMOS Values:		1024	8
ST296n		820	6
ST3051a		820	6
ST3096a		1024	10
ST31200n		2626	9
ST3120a		1024	12
ST3123a		1024	12
ST3144a		1001	15
ST3145a		1001	15
ST3195a		981	10
ST3243a		1024	12
ST325a		615	4
ST325a/x		615	4
ST325n		654	2
ST325x		615	4
ST3283a		978	14
ST3283n		1689	5
ST3290a		1001	15
ST3385a		767	14
ST3390a		768	14
ST3390n		2676	3
ST3500a		895	15
ST351a		820	6
ST351a/x		820	6
ST351x		820	6
ST3550a		1018	14
ST3550n		2126	5

WPC	Park Cyl.	Sectors per Track	Capacity (MB)	Total Sectors
128	989	17	43.0	84065
-1	948	27	65.5	127980
-1	820	26	65.5	127920
-1	628	34	65.6	128112
-1	820	26	65.5	127920
-1	820	26	65.5	127920
-1	989	26	65.8	128570
-1	1032	27	71.3	139320
1024	1024	17	71.3	139264
-1	1032	27	71.3	139320
1024	1024	17	71.3	139264
-1	820	34	85.6	167280
-1	820	17	42.8	83640
-1	1024	17	89.1	174080
-1	2626	79*	955.9	1867086
-1	1024	17*	107.0	208896
-1	1024	17*	107.0	208896
-1	1001	17*	130.7	255255
-1	1001	17*	130.7	255255
-1	981	34*	170.8	333540
-1	1024	34*	213.9	417792
-1	615	17	21.4	41820
-1	615	17	21.4	41820
-1	654	32	21.4	41856
-1	615	17	21.4	41820
-1	978	35*	245.4	479220
-1	1689	57*	246.5	481365
-1	1001	34*	261.4	510510
-1	767	62*	340.9	665756
-1	768	62*	341.3	666624
-1	2676	83*	341.2	666324
-1	895	62*	426.2	832350
-1	820	17	42.8	83640
-1	820	17	42.8	83640
-1	820	17	42.8	83640
-1	1018	62*	452.4	883624
-1	2126	83*	451.7	882290

(continues)

Table 5.18   Continued

	Imprimis Model #	Cyls	Hds	
ST3600n		1872	7	
ST3610n		1872	7	
ST3655a		1024	16	
ST3655n		2676	5	
ST4026		615	4	
ST4038		733	5	
ST4038m		733	5	
ST4051		977	5	
ST4053		1024	5	
ST406		306	2	
ST4085		1024	8	
ST4086	94155-86	925	9	
ST4086p	94155-86p	925	9	
ST4096		1024	9	
ST4097	94155-96	1024	9	
ST4097p	94155-96p	1024	9	
ST412		306	4	
ST41200n	94601-12g	1931	15	
ST41200nm	94601-12g	1931	15	
ST41200nv	94601-12g	1931	15	
ST4135r	94155-135	960	9	
ST4144r		1024	9	
ST41520n		2101	17	
ST41600n		2098	17	
ST41650n		2110	15	
ST41651n		2107	15	
ST4182e	94166-155	969	9	

WPC	Park Cyl.	Sectors per Track	Capacity (MB)	Total Sectors
-1	1872	79*	530.0	1035216
-1	1872	52*	348.9	681408
-1	1024	63*	528.5	1032192
-1	2676	79*	541.2	1057020
-1	670	17	21.4	41820
-1	733	17	31.9	62305
-1	733	17	31.9	62305
-1	977	17	42.5	83045
-1	1024	17	44.6	87040
128	319	17	5.3	10404
-1	1024	17	71.3	39264
-1	925	17	72.5	141525
128	925	17	72.5	141525
-1	1024	17	80.2	156672
-1	1024	17	80.2	156672
128	1024	17	80.2	156672
128	319	17	10.7	20808
-1	1931	71*	1052.9	2056515
-1	1931	71*	1052.9	2056515
-1	1931	71*	1052.9	2056515
-1	960	26	115.0	224640
-1	1024	26	122.7	239616
-1	2101	77*	1408.1	2750209
-1	2098	74*	1351.3	2639284
-1	2110	88*	1426.0	2785200
-1	2107	87*	1407.8	2749635
-1	969	36	160.7	313956

(continues)

Table 5.18   Continued

	Imprimis Model #	Cyls	Hds	
ST4182e	94166-182	969	9	
ST4182n	94161-182	967	9	
ST4182nm	94161-182	967	9	
ST419		306	6	
ST42000n		2624	16	
ST42100n		2573	15	
ST42400n		2624	19	
ST425		306	8	
ST43400n		2735	21	
ST4350n	94171-300	1412	9	
ST4350n	94171-307	1412	9	
ST4350n	94171-327	1412	9	
ST4350n	94171-350	1412	9	
ST4350nm	94171-327	1412	9	
ST4376n	94171-344	1549	9	
ST4376n	94171-376	1549	9	
ST4376nm	94171-344	1549	9	
ST4376nv	94171-344	1549	9	
ST4383e	94186-383	1412	13	
ST4384e	94186-383h	1224	15	
ST4385n	94181-385h	791	15	
ST4385nm	94181-385h	791	15	
ST4385nv	94181-385h	791	15	
ST4442e	94186-442	1412	15	
ST4702n	94181-702	1546	15	
ST4702nm	94181-702	1546	15	
ST4766e	94196-766	1632	15	
ST4766n	94191-766	1632	15	
ST4766nm	94191-766	1632	15	
ST4766nv	94191-766	1632	15	
ST4767e		1399	15	
ST4767n	94601-767h	1356	15	
ST4767nm	94601-767h	1356	15	
ST4767nv	94601-767h	1356	15	
ST4769e		1552	15	
ST506		153	4	
ST9025a		1024	4	

WPC	Park Cyl.	Sectors per Track	Capacity (MB)	Total Sectors
-1	969	36	160.7	313956
-1	967	36	160.4	313308
-1	967	36	160.4	313308
128	319	17	16.0	31212
-1	2624	83*	1784.2	3484672
-1	2573	96*	1897.0	3705120
-1	2624	83*	2118.7	4138048
128	319	17	21.3	41616
-1	2735	99*	2911.3	5686065
-1	1412	46*	299.3	584568
-1	1412	46*	299.3	584568
-1	1412	46*	299.3	584568
-1	1412	46*	299.3	584568
-1	1412	46*	299.3	584568
-1	1549	45*	321.2	627345
-1	1549	45*	321.2	627345
-1	1549	45*	321.2	627345
-1	1549	45*	321.2	627345
-1	1412	36	338.3	660816
-1	1224	36	338.4	660960
-1	791	55*	334.1	652575
-1	791	55*	334.1	652575
-1	791	55*	334.1	652575
-1	1412	36	390.4	762480
-1	1546	50*	593.7	1159500
-1	1546	50*	593.7	1159500
-1	1632	54	676.8	1321920
-1	1632	54	676.8	1321920
-1	1632	54	676.8	1321920
-1	1632	54	676.8	1321920
-1	1399	63	676.9	1322055
-1	1356	64*	666.5	1301760
-1	1356	64*	666.5	1301760
-1	1356	64*	666.5	1301760
-1	1552	58	691.3	1350240
128	157	17	5.3	10404
-1	1024	17	35.7	69632

(continues)

Table 5.18 Continued			
	Imprimis Model #	Cyls	Hds
ST9051a		1024	6
ST9052a		980	5
ST9077a		669	11
ST9080a		823	4
ST9096a		980	10
ST9100a		748	14
ST9140a		980	15
ST9144a		980	15
ST9145a		980	15
ST9190a		873	16
ST9235a		985	13
ST9235n		985	13
ST----	9415-521	697	3
ST----	9415-525	697	4
ST----	9415-536	697	5
ST----	9415-538	733	5
ST----	94151-42	921	5
ST----	94151-62	921	7
ST----	94151-80	921	9
ST----	94155-48	925	5
ST----	94155-48p	925	5
ST----	94155-57	925	6
ST----	94155-57p	925	6
ST----	94155-67	925	7
ST----	94155-67p	925	7
ST----	94155-92	989	9
ST----	94155-92p	989	9

	WPC	Park Cyl.	Sectors per Track	Capacity (MB)	Total Sectors
	-1	1024	17	53.5	104448
	-1	980	17*	42.6	83300
	-1	669	17	64.1	125103
	-1	823	38*	64.0	125096
	-1	980	17*	85.3	166600
	-1	748	16*	85.8	167552
	-1	980	17*	127.9	249900
	-1	980	17*	127.9	249900
	-1	980	17*	127.9	249900
	-1	873	24*	171.6	335232
	-1	985	32*	209.8	409760
	-1	985	32*	209.8	409760
	0	697	17	18.2	35547
	0	697	17	24.3	47396
	0	697	17	30.3	59245
	0	733	17	31.9	62305
	-1	921	17	40.1	78285
	-1	921	17	56.1	109599
	-1	921	17	72.1	140913
	-1	925	17	40.3	78625
	128	925	17	40.3	78625
	-1	925	17	48.3	94350
	128	925	17	48.3	94350
	-1	925	17	56.4	110075
	128	925	17	56.4	110075
	-1	989	17	77.5	151317
	128	989	17	77.5	151317

(continues)

Table 5.18 Continued

	Imprimis Model #	Cyls	Hds	
ST----	94155-92p	989	9	
ST----	94155-130	024	9	
ST----	94156-48	925	9	
ST----	94156-67	925	7	
ST----	94156-86	925	7	
ST----	94161-86	969	5	
ST----	94161-103	969	6	
ST----	94161-121	969	7	
ST----	94161-138	969	8	
ST----	94166-86	969	5	
ST----	94166-103	969	6	
ST----	94166-121	969	7	
ST----	94166-138	969	8	
ST----	94244-219	1747	4	
Opt. CMOS Values:		536	16	

Because these drives use zoned recording, the sectors-per-track value is an average, rounded down to the next-lower integer.

Notice that "Opt. CMOS Values" indicates optional translated values for the preceeding drive in the table, which can be entered if the CMOS Setup program will not accept the actual values for the drive.

Seagate Model designations follow a specific format shown as follows:

ST-FXXXI PR-A

The various parts of each model number designation have meanings according to the following tables.

Code	Description
ST	Seagate Technologies
F	Form Factor (see following table)
XXX	Unformatted Capacity in MB
I	Interface Type (see following table)
PR	Paired Solution (shipped with controller and installation software)
A	Access time; 0 = Standard, 1= Fast

WPC	Park Cyl.	Sectors per Track	Capacity (MB)	Total Sectors
128	989	17	77.5	151317
128	1024	26	122.7	239616
-1	925	17	72.5	141525
-1	925	17	56.4	110075
-1	925	17	56.4	110075
-1	969	35	86.8	169575
-1	969	35	104.2	203490
-1	969	35	121.6	237405
-1	969	35	138.9	271320
-1	969	35	86.8	169575
-1	969	35	104.2	203490
-1	969	35	121.6	237405
-1	969	35	138.9	271320
-1	1747	54	193.2	377352
536	536	44	193.2	377344

F-Code	Description
1	3.5-inch Half Height (41mm)
2	5.25-inch Half Height (41mm)
3	3.5-inch 1-inch High (25mm)
4	5.25-inch Full Height (82mm)
6	9-inch
8	8-inch
9	2.5-inch .75-inch High (19mm)

I Code	Description
None	ST-412 MFM interface
R	ST-412 (RLL certified) interface
E	ESDI interface
A	ATA (AT Attachment) IDE interface
X	XT-Bus (8-bit) IDE interface
A/X	Switchable ATA IDE or XT-Bus interface
M or P	Modified Precompensation
N	SCSI Single Ended (SE) interface
NM	SCSI SE interface (Macintosh Plus)
NV	SCSI SE interface (Novell NetWare)
NS	SCSI SE interface (Synchronized Spindle)
ND	SCSI Differential interface

For example, the model designation ST112550N equates to a 3.5-inch Half Height drive with an unformatted capacity of approximately 2550MB, and a SCSI Single Ended interface.

Hard Disk Parameter Tables

When a hard disk drive is installed in a system, the system BIOS must be informed about the physical geometry of the drive in order for the Int 13h BIOS functions to work. Usually, the BIOS is informed through a table contained in the motherboard or controller BIOS that has entries defining various drive geometries. The disk installer then selects the entry that matches the drive being installed and normally informs the BIOS through the system's SETUP utility. After entering the drive type through SETUP, the type information usually is maintained in CMOS RAM by virtue of a long-life lithium battery. With XT-class systems, the Int 13h BIOS support usually is found directly on the hard disk controller in a built-in BIOS. In this case, selection of a specific drive type usually is done by moving jumpers on the controller card.

In the case of the battery-maintained CMOS memory, this Setup procedure usually is performed only during these conditions:

- The system is new and has not yet been set up.

- A new peripheral is installed. CMOS normally stores information about these items only:

    Floppy drive types
    Hard drive types
    Base and extended memory amount
    Video Display Adapter and mode
    Math coprocessor—installed or not
    Date and time

- The battery is dead or dying.

The Setup program comes on a disk for systems made by IBM or COMPAQ; most compatibles made after 1987, however, have the Setup program built directly into the BIOS. As a feature of some of the newer PS/2 systems (Models 57, 90, and 95), the Setup program, as well as the entire ROM BIOS, is stored on the hard disk in a special hidden, 3M partition—the system partition. Having the Setup built into the motherboard BIOS or loaded from a system partition, as in the newer PS/2 systems, is very convenient, and eliminates the need for a separate floppy disk containing the Setup program. Most of the time these BIOS-based Setup programs are activated by a particular keystroke sequence either at any time or only during the Power-On Self Test. The four popular compatible BIOS manufacturers use these keystrokes to activate Setup:

Phoenix BIOS	Ctrl-Alt-Esc or Ctrl-Alt-S
AMI BIOS	Del key during the POST
Award BIOS	Ctrl-Alt-Esc
IBM PS/2 BIOS	Ctrl-Alt-Ins after Ctrl-Alt-Del

With the Phoenix, Award, or IBM BIOS, you must hold the three keys down simultaneously to invoke Setup. With AMI, you just press the Del key during the POST. Notice that only certain PS/2 models support Initial Microcode Load (IML) from the hard disk, which means that the BIOS and Reference disk (Setup) can be invoked with the indicated keystrokes.

To select the correct hard disk type for most ST-506/412, IDE, or ESDI type drives, you first must know your drive's physical characteristics. With most IDE drives, you need to know just the total number of sectors on the drive. SCSI drives almost always automatically configure to the system by entering a disk type of "0."

This step enables the SCSI BIOS to execute a SCSI Read Capacity command and supply the parameters to the system "on the fly."

Drive parameter information can be found in the technical-reference documentation that came with your drive or system. If you did not get this documentation, call your vendor and demand it. After knowing the parameters for your drive, you need to find a table entry in your specific BIOS that matches the drive parameters. If none is an exact match, in some cases you can use an entry that is close as long as the entries for cylinders, heads, or sectors per track are not more than the drive is capable of. You also should match as close as possible the Write Precompensation starting cylinder value for reliable operation on the drive's inner cylinders.

Because a variety of BIOS manufacturers are available in the marketplace, your systems may contain different tables. Each BIOS manufacturer has defined its own drive tables, usually starting with entries that are the same as IBM's. Most BIOS drive tables are similar to IBM for the first 15 or 23 entries, but from there they vary from manufacturer to manufacturer. For this reason, a drive manufacturer cannot simply stamp the drive type on the drive itself. For example, the correct drive type used for a Seagate ST-251 drive varies according to the BIOS manufacturer:

IBM BIOS	Type 8
COMPAQ BIOS	Type 5
AMI BIOS	Type 40
Award BIOS	Type 40
Phoenix BIOS	Type 44

Notice that because of the lack of a user-definable type in the IBM and COMPAQ BIOS, this drive is not used to full capacity in those systems (especially in the IBM). So, if Seagate were to put the drive type on the drive, which number should it use? Obviously, it cannot do so, and the installer or data-recovery specialist must make the correct selection.

The tables in this section show the contents of the disk tables for a variety of BIOS manufacturers including IBM, COMPAQ, Phoenix, AMI, and Award. This information is helpful in determining the correct drive type for a particular drive and system combination. Notice that some BIOS vendors now provide user-definable entries in their tables, which means that the values in the table can be typed directly from the keyboard, thereby allowing for virtually infinite customization without having to modify the BIOS itself.

Also included are tables for IBM's XT controllers, whose table format differs slightly from the tables in AT-class systems.

Table 5.19   IBM 10M XT Hard Disk Controller (Xebec 1210) Drive

Entry	Type	Cyls	Heads	WPC
0	–	306	2	0
1	–	375	8	0
2	–	306	6	256
3	–	306	4	0

Table 5.20   IBM 20M Hard Disk Controller (Xebec 1210) Drive Parameter Tables

Entry	Type	Cyls	Heads	WPC
0	1	306	4	0
1	16	612	4	0
2	2	615	4	300
3	13	306	8	128

Entry = Controller table position
Type = Drive type number
Cyls = Total number of cylinders
Heads = Total number of heads
WPC = Write precompensation starting cylinder
Ctrl = Control byte, values as follows:

Bit 0	01h, drive step rate
Bit 1	02h, drive step rate
Bit 2	04h, drive step rate
Bit 3	08h, more than eight heads
Bit 4	10h, embedded servo drive
Bit 5	20h, OEM defect map at (Cyls + 1)
Bit 6	40h, disable ECC retries
Bit 7	80h, disable disk access retries

Xebec 1210 Drive Step Rate Coding (Control Byte bits 0-3)

00h, 3-millisecond step rate
04h, 200-microsecond buffered step
05h, 70-microsecond buffered step
06h, 30-microsecond buffered step
07h, 15-microsecond buffered step

LZ = Landing zone cylinder for head parking
S/T = Number of sectors per track
Meg = Drive capacity in megabytes
MB = Drive capacity in millions of bytes
The Landing Zone field and Sectors per Track fields are not used in the 10M (original) controller and contain 00h values for each entry.

Ctrl	LZ	S/T	Meg	MB
00h	00h	00h	5.08	5.33
05h	00h	00h	24.90	26.11
05h	00h	00h	15.24	15.98
05h	00h	00h	10.16	10.65

Ctrl	LZ	S/T	Meg	MB
05h	305	17	10.16	10.65
05h	663	17	20.32	21.31
05h	615	17	20.42	21.41
05h	319	17	20.32	21.31

Note

MB and *Meg* sometimes are used interchangeably, but this is not exactly correct. MB is one Million Bytes, or 1,000,000 bytes. Meg (or M) is one Megabyte, which is equal to 1,048,576 bytes. (1 megabyte = 1 kilobyte times 1 kilobyte, and 1 kilobyte = 1,024 bytes. Thus, 1 megabyte = 1,024 times 1,024 = 1,048,576.)

To select one of the drive table entries in the IBM XT controllers (Xebec 1210), you would set the drive table selection jumper (Jumper W5). The following table shows how these jumpers should be set to select a particular table entry. For example, to select table entry 2 for drive 0 (C:), you would set the jumper Off at position 1 and On at position 2.

Table 5.21 IBM XT controller (Xebec 1210) drive table jumper (W5) settings)

Drive 0 Table Entry	1	2	3	4
Jumper 1	On	On	Off	Off
Jumper 2	On	Off	On	Off
Drive 1 Table Entry	**1**	**2**	**3**	**4**
Jumper 3	On	On	Off	Off
Jumper 4	On	Off	On	Off

Table 5.22 IBM AT and PS/2 BIOS Hard Disk Table

Type	Cylinders	Heads	WPC	Ctrl	
1	306	4	128	00h	
2	615	4	300	00h	
3	615	6	300	00h	
4	940	8	512	00h	
5	940	6	512	00h	
6	615	4	65535	00h	
7	462	8	256	00h	
8	733	5	65535	00h	
9	900	15	65535	08h	
10	820	3	65535	00h	
11	855	5	65535	00h	
12	855	7	65535	00h	
13	306	8	128	00h	
14	733	7	65535	00h	
15	0	0	0	00h	
16	612	4	0	00h	
17	977	5	300	00h	
18	977	7	65535	00h	
19	1024	7	512	00h	
20	733	5	300	00h	
21	733	7	300	00h	
22	733	5	300	00h	
23	306	4	0	00h	
24	612	4	305	00h	

AT Motherboard BIOS Hard Drive Tables

Table 5.22 shows the IBM motherboard ROM BIOS hard disk parameters for AT or PS/2 systems using ST-506/412 (standard or IDE) controllers.

	LZ	S/T	Meg	MB
	305	17	10.16	10.65
	615	17	20.42	21.41
	615	17	30.63	32.12
	940	17	62.42	65.45
	940	17	46.82	49.09
	615	17	20.42	21.41
	511	17	30.68	32.17
	733	17	30.42	31.90
	901	17	112.06	117.50
	820	17	20.42	21.41
	855	17	35.49	37.21
	855	17	49.68	52.09
	319	17	20.32	21.31
	733	17	42.59	44.66
	0	0	0	0
	663	17	20.32	21.31
	977	17	40.55	42.52
	977	17	56.77	59.53
	1023	17	59.50	62.39
	732	17	30.42	31.90
	732	17	42.59	44.66
	733	17	30.42	31.90
	336	17	10.16	10.65
	663	17	20.32	21.31

(continues)

Type	Cylinders	Heads	WPC	Ctrl	
25	306	4	65535	00h	
26	612	4	65535	00h	
27	698	7	300	20h	
28	976	5	488	20h	
29	306	4	0	00h	
30	611	4	306	20h	
31	732	7	300	20h	
32	1023	5	65535	20h	
33	614	4	65535	20h	
34	775	2	65535	20h	
35	921	2	65535	20h	
36	402	4	65535	20h	
37	580	6	65535	20h	
38	845	2	65535	20h	
39	769	3	65535	20h	
40	531	4	65535	20h	
41	577	2	65535	20h	
42	654	2	65535	20h	
43	923	5	65535	20h	
44	531	8	65535	20h	
45	0	0	0	00h	
46	0	0	0	00h	
47	0	0	0	00h	

Table 5.22 Continued

LZ = Landing zone cylinder for head parking

S/T = Number of sectors per track

Meg = Drive capacity in megabytes

MB = Drive capacity in millions of bytes

The Landing zone and Sectors per Track fields are not used in the 10MB (original) controller and contain 00h values for each entry.

	LZ	S/T	Meg	MB
	340	17	10.16	10.65
	670	17	20.32	21.31
	732	17	40.56	42.53
	977	17	40.51	42.48
	340	17	10.16	10.65
	663	17	20.29	21.27
	732	17	42.53	44.60
	1023	17	42.46	44.52
	663	25	29.98	31.44
	900	27	20.43	21.43
	1000	33	29.68	31.12
	460	26	20.41	21.41
	640	26	44.18	46.33
	1023	36	29.71	31.15
	1023	36	40.55	42.52
	532	39	40.45	42.41
	1023	36	20.29	21.27
	674	32	20.44	21.43
	1023	36	81.12	85.06
	532	39	80.89	84.82
	0	0	0.00	0.00
	0	0	0.00	0.00
	0	0	0.00	0.00

Table entry 15 is reserved to act as a pointer to indicate that the type is greater than 15. Most IBM systems do not have every entry in this table. The maximum usable type number varies for each particular ROM version. The maximum usable type for each IBM ROM is indicated in the table on IBM ROM versions, earlier in this chapter. If you have a compatible, this table may be inaccurate for many of the entries past type 15. Instead, you should see whether one of the other tables listed here applies to your specific compatible ROM.

Most compatibles follow the IBM table for at least the first 15 entries.

Most IBM PS/2 systems now are supplied with hard disk drives that have the defect map written as data on the cylinder one cylinder beyond the highest reported cylinder. This special data is read by the IBM PS/2 Advanced Diagnostics low-level format program. This process automates the entry of the defect list and eliminates the chance of human error, as long as you use only the IBM PS/2 Advanced Diagnostics for hard disk low-level formatting.

Table 5.23   Compaq Deskpro 386 Hard Disk Table

Type	Cylinders	Heads	WPC	Ctrl
1	306	4	128	00h
2	615	4	128	00h
3	615	6	128	00h
4	1024	8	512	00h
5	940	6	512	00h
6	697	5	128	00h
7	462	8	256	00h
8	925	5	128	00h
9	900	15	65535	08h
10	980	5	65535	00h
11	925	7	128	00h
12	925	9	128	08h
13	612	8	256	00h
14	980	4	128	00h
15	0	0	0	00h
16	612	4	0	00h
17	980	5	128	00h
18	966	6	128	00h
19	1023	8	65535	00h

This type of table does not apply to IBM ESDI or SCSI hard disk controllers, host adapters, and drives. Because the ESDI and SCSI controllers or host adapters query the drive directly for the required parameters, no table-entry selection is necessary. Notice, however, that the table for the ST-506/412 drives can still be found currently in the ROM BIOS of most of the PS/2 systems, even if the model came standard with an ESDI or SCSI disk subsystem.

Table 5.23 shows the COMPAQ motherboard ROM BIOS hard disk parameters for the COMPAQ Deskpro 386.

LZ	S/T	Meg	MB
305	17	10.16	10.65
638	17	20.42	21.41
615	17	30.63	32.12
1023	17	68.00	71.30
939	17	46.82	49.09
696	17	28.93	30.33
511	17	30.68	32.17
924	17	38.39	40.26
899	17	112.06	117.50
980	17	40.67	42.65
924	17	53.75	56.36
924	17	69.10	72.46
611	17	40.64	42.61
980	17	32.54	34.12
0	0	0	0
612	17	20.32	21.31
980	17	40.67	42.65
966	17	48.11	50.45
1023	17	67.93	71.23

(continues)

Type	Cylinders	Heads	WPC	Ctrl	
20	733	5	256	00h	
21	733	7	256	00h	
22	805	6	65535	00h	
23	924	8	65535	00h	
24	966	14	65535	08h	
25	966	16	65535	08h	
26	1023	14	65535	08h	
27	966	10	65535	08h	
28	748	16	65535	08h	
29	805	6	65535	00h	
30	615	4	128	00h	
31	615	8	128	00h	
32	905	9	128	08h	
33	748	8	65535	00h	
34	966	7	65535	00h	
35	966	8	65535	00h	
36	966	9	65535	08h	
37	966	5	65535	00h	
38	611	16	65535	08h	
39	1023	11	65535	08h	
40	1023	15	65535	08h	
41	1023	15	65535	08h	
42	1023	16	65535	08h	
43	805	4	65535	00h	
44	805	2	65535	00h	
45	748	8	65535	00h	
46	748	6	65535	00h	
47	966	5	128	00h	

Table 5.23 Continued

Table entry 15 is reserved to act as a pointer to indicate that the type is greater than 15.

	LZ	S/T	Meg	MB
	732	17	30.42	31.90
	732	17	42.59	44.66
	805	17	40.09	42.04
	924	17	61.36	64.34
	966	17	112.26	117.71
	966	17	128.30	134.53
	1023	17	118.88	124.66
	966	17	80.19	84.08
	748	17	99.34	104.17
	805	26	61.32	64.30
	615	25	30.03	31.49
	615	25	60.06	62.98
	905	25	99.43	104.26
	748	34	99.34	104.17
	966	34	112.26	117.71
	966	34	128.30	134.53
	966	34	144.33	151.35
	966	34	80.19	84.08
	611	63	300.73	315.33
	1023	33	181.32	190.13
	1023	34	254.75	267.13
	1023	33	247.26	259.27
	1023	63	503.51	527.97
	805	26	40.88	42.86
	805	26	20.44	21.43
	748	33	96.42	101.11
	748	33	72.32	75.83
	966	25	58.96	61.82

Table 5.24 shows the COMPAQ motherboard ROM BIOS hard disk parameters for the COMPAQ Deskpro 286 Revision F.

Type	Cylinders	Heads	WPC	Ctrl	
	Table 5.24 Compaq Deskpro 286 Revision F Hard Disk Tabl				
Type	Cylinders	Heads	WPC	Ctrl	
1	306	4	128	00h	
2	615	4	128	00h	
3	615	6	128	00h	
4	1024	8	512	00h	
5	940	6	512	00h	
6	697	5	128	00h	
7	462	8	256	00h	
8	925	5	128	00h	
9	900	15	65535	08h	
10	980	5	65535	00h	
11	925	7	128	00h	
12	925	9	128	08h	
13	612	8	256	00h	
14	980	4	128	00h	
15	0	0	0	00h	
16	612	4	0	00h	
17	980	5	128	00h	
18	966	6	128	00h	
19	1023	8	65535	00h	
20	733	5	256	00h	
21	733	7	256	00h	
22	768	6	65535	00h	
23	771	6	65535	00h	
24	966	14	65535	08h	
25	966	16	65535	08h	
26	1023	14	65535	08h	
27	966	10	65535	08h	
28	771	3	65535	00h	
29	578	4	65535	00h	
30	615	4	128	00h	
31	615	8	128	00h	
32	966	3	65535	00h	
33	966	5	65535	00h	

LZ	S/T	Meg	MB
305	17	10.16	10.65
638	17	20.42	21.41
615	17	30.63	32.12
1023	17	68.00	71.30
939	17	46.82	49.09
696	17	28.93	30.33
511	17	30.68	32.17
924	17	38.39	40.26
899	17	112.06	117.50
980	17	40.67	42.65
924	17	53.75	56.36
924	17	69.10	72.46
611	17	40.64	42.61
980	17	32.54	34.12
0	0	0	0
612	17	20.32	21.31
980	17	40.67	42.65
966	17	48.11	50.45
1023	17	67.93	71.23
732	17	30.42	31.90
732	17	42.59	44.66
768	17	38.25	40.11
771	17	38.40	40.26
966	17	112.26	117.71
966	17	128.30	134.53
1023	17	118.88	124.66
966	17	80.19	84.08
771	17	19.20	20.13
578	17	19.19	20.12
615	25	30.03	31.49
615	25	60.06	62.98
966	34	48.11	50.45
966	34	80.19	84.08

(continues)

Table 5.24	Continued				
Type	Cylinders	Heads	WPC	Ctrl	
34	966	7	65535	00h	
35	966	8	65535	00h	
36	966	9	65535	08h	
37	966	5	65535	00h	
38	1023	9	65535	08h	
39	1023	11	65535	08h	
40	1023	13	65535	08h	
41	1023	15	65535	08h	
42	1023	16	65535	08h	
43	756	4	65535	00h	
44	756	2	65535	00h	
45	768	4	65535	00h	
46	768	2	65535	00h	
47	966	5	128	00h	

Table entry 15 is reserved to act as a pointer to indicate that
the type is greater than 15.

Table 5.25	Compaq Deskpro 286 Revision B Hard Disk Tabl				
Type	Cylinders	Heads	WPC	Ctrl	
1	306	4	128	00h	
2	615	4	128	00h	
3	615	6	128	00h	
4	1024	8	512	00h	
5	805	6	65535	00h	
6	697	5	128	00h	
7	462	8	256	00h	
8	925	5	128	00h	
9	900	15	65535	08h	
10	980	5	65535	00h	

LZ	S/T	Meg	MB
966	34	112.26	117.71
966	34	128.30	134.53
966	34	144.33	151.35
966	34	80.19	84.08
1023	33	148.35	155.56
1023	33	181.32	190.13
1023	33	214.29	224.70
1023	33	247.26	259.27
1023	34	271.73	284.93
756	26	38.39	40.26
756	26	19.20	20.13
768	26	39.00	40.89
768	26	19.50	20.45
966	25	58.96	61.82

Table 5.25 shows the COMPAQ motherboard ROM BIOS
hard disk parameters for the COMPAQ Deskpro 286e
Revision B (03/22/89).

LZ	S/T	Meg	MB
305	17	10.16	10.65
638	17	20.42	21.41
615	17	30.63	32.12
1023	17	68.00	71.30
805	17	40.09	42.04
696	17	28.93	30.33
511	17	30.68	32.17
924	17	38.39	40.26
899	17	112.06	117.50
980	17	40.67	42.65

(continues)

Table 5.25   Continued

Type	Cylinders	Heads	WPC	Ctrl
11	925	7	128	00h
12	925	9	128	08h
13	612	8	256	00h
14	980	4	128	00h
15	0	0	0	00h
16	612	4	0	00h
17	980	5	128	00h
18	966	5	128	00h
19	754	11	65535	08h
20	733	5	256	00h
21	733	7	256	00h
22	524	4	65535	00h
23	924	8	65535	00h
24	966	14	65535	08h
25	966	16	65535	08h
26	1023	14	65535	08h
27	832	6	65535	00h
28	1222	15	65535	08h
29	1240	7	65535	00h
30	615	4	128	00h
31	615	8	128	00h
32	905	9	128	08h
33	832	8	65535	00h
34	966	7	65535	00h
35	966	8	65535	00h
36	966	9	65535	08h
37	966	5	65535	00h
38	611	16	65535	08h
39	1023	11	65535	08h
40	1023	15	65535	08h
41	1630	15	65535	08h
42	1023	16	65535	08h

		LZ	S/T	Meg	MB
		924	17	53.75	56.36
		924	17	69.10	72.46
		611	17	40.64	42.61
		980	17	32.54	34.12
		0	0	0	0
		612	17	20.32	21.31
		980	17	40.67	42.65
		966	17	40.09	42.04
		753	17	68.85	72.19
		732	17	30.42	31.90
		732	17	42.59	44.66
		524	40	40.94	42.93
		924	17	61.36	64.34
		966	17	112.26	117.71
		966	17	128.30	134.53
		1023	17	118.88	124.66
		832	33	80.44	84.34
		1222	34	304.31	319.09
		1240	34	144.10	151.10
		615	25	30.03	31.49
		615	25	60.06	62.98
		905	25	99.43	104.26
		832	33	107.25	112.46
		966	34	112.26	117.71
		966	34	128.30	134.53
		966	34	144.33	151.35
		966	34	80.19	84.08
		611	63	300.73	315.33
		1023	33	181.32	190.13
		1023	34	254.75	267.13
		1630	52	620.80	650.96
		1023	63	503.51	527.97

(continues)

Table 5.25   Continued

Type	Cylinders	Heads	WPC	Ctrl	
43	805	4	65535	00h	
44	805	2	65535	00h	
45	748	8	65535	00h	
46	748	6	65535	00h	
47	966	5	128	00h	

Table entry 15 is reserved to act as a pointer to indicate that the type is greater than 15.

Table 5.26   AMI ROM BIOS (286 BIOS Version 04/30/89) Hard Disk

Type	Cylinders	Heads	WPC	Ctrl	
1	306	4	128	00h	
2	615	4	300	00h	
3	615	6	300	00h	
4	940	8	512	00h	
5	940	6	512	00h	
6	615	4	65535	00h	
7	462	8	256	00h	
8	733	5	65535	00h	
9	900	15	65535	08h	
10	820	3	65535	00h	
11	855	5	65535	00h	
12	855	7	65535	00h	
13	306	8	128	00h	
14	733	7	65535	00h	
15	0	0	0	00h	
16	612	4	0	00h	
17	977	5	300	00h	
18	977	7	65535	00h	
19	1024	7	512	00h	
20	733	5	300	00h	

	LZ	S/T	Meg	MB
	805	26	40.88	42.86
	805	26	20.44	21.43
	748	33	96.42	101.11
	748	33	72.32	75.83
	966	25	58.96	61.82

Table 5.26 shows the AMI ROM BIOS (286 BIOS Version 04/30/89) hard disk parameters.

	LZ	S/T	Meg	MB
	305	17	10.16	10.65
	615	17	20.42	21.41
	615	17	30.63	32.12
	940	17	62.42	65.45
	940	17	46.82	49.09
	615	17	20.42	21.41
	511	17	30.68	32.17
	733	17	30.42	31.90
	901	17	112.06	117.50
	820	17	20.42	21.41
	855	17	35.49	37.21
	855	17	49.68	52.09
	319	17	20.32	21.31
	733	17	42.59	44.66
	0	0	0	0
	663	17	20.32	21.31
	977	17	40.55	42.52
	977	17	56.77	59.53
	1023	17	59.50	62.39
	732	17	30.42	31.90

(continues)

Type	Cylinders	Heads	WPC	Ctrl	
21	733	7	300	00h	
22	733	5	300	00h	
23	306	4	0	00h	
24	925	7	0	00h	
25	925	9	65535	08h	
26	754	7	526	00h	
27	754	11	65535	08h	
28	699	7	256	00h	
29	823	10	65535	08h	
30	918	7	874	00h	
31	1024	11	65535	08h	
32	1024	15	65535	08h	
33	1024	5	1024	00h	
34	612	2	128	00h	
35	1024	9	65535	08h	
36	1024	8	512	00h	
37	615	8	128	00h	
38	987	3	805	00h	
39	987	7	805	00h	
40	820	6	820	00h	
41	977	5	815	00h	
42	981	5	811	00h	
43	830	7	512	00h	
44	830	10	65535	08h	
45	917	15	65535	08h	
46	1224	15	65535	08h	
47	0	0	0	00h	

Table 5.26   Continued

Table entry 15 is reserved to act as a pointer to indicate that the type is greater than 15.

This BIOS uses type 47 as a user-definable entry.

	LZ	S/T	Meg	MB
	732	17	42.59	44.66
	733	17	30.42	31.90
	336	17	10.16	10.65
	925	17	53.75	56.36
	925	17	69.10	72.46
	754	17	43.81	45.94
	754	17	68.85	72.19
	699	17	40.62	42.59
	823	17	68.32	71.63
	918	17	53.34	55.93
	1024	17	93.50	98.04
	1024	17	127.50	133.69
	1024	17	42.50	44.56
	612	17	10.16	10.65
	1024	17	76.50	80.22
	1024	17	68.00	71.30
	615	17	40.84	42.82
	987	17	24.58	25.77
	987	17	57.35	60.14
	820	17	40.84	42.82
	977	17	40.55	42.52
	981	17	40.72	42.69
	830	17	48.23	50.57
	830	17	68.90	72.24
	918	17	114.18	119.72
	1223	17	152.40	159.81
	0	0	0.00	0.00

Table 5.27 shows the Award ROM BIOS (286 BIOS Version 04/30/89) (Modular 286, 386SX, and 386 BIOS Version 3.05) hard disk parameters.

Table entry 15 is reserved to act as a pointer to indicate that the type is greater than 15.

Type	Cylinders	Heads	WPC	Ctrl	
1	306	4	128	00h	
2	615	4	300	00h	
3	615	6	300	00h	
4	940	8	512	00h	
5	940	6	512	00h	
6	615	4	65535	00h	
7	462	8	256	00h	
8	733	5	65535	00h	
9	900	15	65535	08h	
10	820	3	65535	00h	
11	855	5	65535	00h	
12	855	7	65535	00h	
13	306	8	128	00h	
14	733	7	65535	00h	
15	0	0	0	00h	
16	612	4	0	00h	
17	977	5	300	00h	
18	977	7	65535	00h	
19	1024	7	512	00h	
20	733	5	300	00h	
21	733	7	300	00h	
22	733	5	300	00h	
23	306	4	0	00h	
24	977	5	65535	00h	
25	1024	9	65535	08h	
26	1224	7	65535	00h	
27	1224	11	65535	08h	
28	1224	15	65535	08h	
29	1024	8	65535	00h	
30	1024	11	65535	08h	
31	918	11	65535	08h	
32	925	9	65535	08h	
33	1024	10	65535	08h	

Table header: **Table 5.27 Award ROM BIOS Version 3.05 Hard Disk Table**

	LZ	S/T	Meg	MB
	305	17	10.16	10.65
	615	17	20.42	21.41
	615	17	30.63	32.12
	940	17	62.42	65.45
	940	17	46.82	49.09
	615	17	20.42	21.41
	511	17	30.68	32.17
	733	17	30.42	31.90
	901	17	112.06	117.50
	820	17	20.42	21.41
	855	17	35.49	37.21
	855	17	49.68	52.09
	319	17	20.32	21.31
	733	17	42.59	44.66
	0	0	0	0
	663	17	20.32	21.31
	977	17	40.55	42.52
	977	17	56.77	59.53
	1023	17	59.50	62.39
	732	17	30.42	31.90
	732	17	42.59	44.66
	733	17	30.42	31.90
	336	17	10.16	10.65
	976	17	40.55	42.52
	1023	17	76.50	80.22
	1223	17	71.12	74.58
	1223	17	111.76	117.19
	1223	17	152.40	159.81
	1023	17	68.00	71.30
	1023	17	93.50	98.04
	1023	17	83.82	87.89
	926	17	69.10	72.46
	1023	17	85.00	89.13

(continues)

Table 5.27 Continued					
Type	Cylinders	Heads	WPC	Ctrl	
34	1024	12	65535	08h	
35	1024	13	65535	08h	
36	1024	14	65535	08h	
37	1024	2	65535	00h	
38	1024	16	65535	08h	
39	918	15	65535	08h	
40	820	6	65535	00h	
41	1024	5	65535	00h	
42	1024	5	65535	00h	
43	809	6	65535	00h	
44	820	6	65535	00h	
45	776	8	65535	00h	
46	0	0	0	00h	
47	0	0	0	00h	

This BIOS uses types 46 and 47 as user-definable entries.

Table 5.28 shows the Award ROM BIOS hard disk parameters (modular 286, 386SX, and 386 BIOS Version 3.1).

Table 5.28 Award ROM BIOS Version 3.1 Hard Disk Table					
Type	Cylinders	Heads	WPC	Ctrl	
1	306	4	128	00h	
2	615	4	300	00h	
3	615	6	300	00h	
4	940	8	512	00h	
5	940	6	512	00h	
6	615	4	65535	00h	
7	462	8	256	00h	
8	733	5	65535	00h	
9	900	15	65535	08h	
10	820	3	65535	00h	

LZ	S/T	Meg	MB
1023	17	102.00	106.95
1023	17	110.50	115.87
1023	17	119.00	124.78
1023	17	17.00	17.83
1023	17	136.00	142.61
1023	17	114.30	119.85
820	17	40.84	42.82
1023	17	42.50	44.56
1023	26	65.00	68.16
808	17	40.29	42.25
819	26	62.46	65.50
775	33	100.03	104.89
0	0	0.00	0.00
0	0	0.00	0.00

LZ	S/T	Meg	MB
305	17	10.16	10.65
615	17	20.42	21.41
615	17	30.63	32.12
940	17	62.42	65.45
940	17	46.82	49.09
615	17	20.42	21.41
511	17	30.68	32.17
733	17	30.42	31.90
901	17	112.06	117.50
820	17	20.42	21.41

(continues)

Type	Cylinders	Heads	WPC	Ctrl
Table 5.28 Continued				
11	855	5	65535	00h
12	855	7	65535	00h
13	306	8	128	00h
14	733	7	65535	00h
15	0	0	0	00h
16	612	4	0	00h
17	977	5	300	00h
18	977	7	65535	00h
19	1024	7	512	00h
20	733	5	300	00h
21	733	7	300	00h
22	733	5	300	00h
23	306	4	0	00h
24	977	5	65535	00h
25	1024	9	65535	08h
26	1224	7	65535	00h
27	1224	11	65535	08h
28	1224	15	65535	08h
29	1024	8	65535	00h
30	1024	11	65535	08h
31	918	11	65535	08h
32	925	9	65535	08h
33	1024	10	65535	08h
34	1024	12	65535	08h
35	1024	13	65535	08h
36	1024	14	65535	08h
37	1024	2	65535	00h
38	1024	16	65535	08h
39	918	15	65535	08h
40	820	6	65535	00h
41	1024	5	65535	00h
42	1024	5	65535	00h
43	809	6	65535	00h

	LZ	S/T	Meg	MB
	855	17	35.49	37.21
	855	17	49.68	52.09
	319	17	20.32	21.31
	733	17	42.59	44.66
	0	0	0	0
	663	17	20.32	21.31
	977	17	40.55	42.52
	977	17	56.77	59.53
	1023	17	59.50	62.39
	732	17	30.42	31.90
	732	17	42.59	44.66
	733	17	30.42	31.90
	336	17	10.16	10.65
	976	17	40.55	42.52
	1023	17	76.50	80.22
	1223	17	71.12	74.58
	1223	17	111.76	117.19
	1223	17	152.40	159.81
	1023	17	68.00	71.30
	1023	17	93.50	98.04
	1023	17	83.82	87.89
	926	17	69.10	72.46
	1023	17	85.00	89.13
	1023	17	102.00	106.95
	1023	17	110.50	115.87
	1023	17	119.00	124.78
	1023	17	17.00	17.83
	1023	17	136.00	142.61
	1023	17	114.30	119.85
	820	17	40.84	42.82
	1023	17	42.50	44.56
	1023	26	65.00	68.16
	852	17	40.29	42.25

(continues)

Table 5.28   Continued

Type	Cylinders	Heads	WPC	Ctrl	
44	809	6	65535	00h	
45	776	8	65535	00h	
46	684	16	65535	08h	
47	615	6	65535	00h	

Table entry 15 is reserved to act as a pointer to indicate that the type is greater than 15.

This BIOS uses types 48 and 49 as user-definable entries.

Table 5.29   Phoenix 286 (80286 ROM BIOS Version 3.01) Hard Disk Table

Type	Cylinders	Heads	WPC	Ctrl	
1	306	4	128	00h	
2	615	4	300	00h	
3	615	6	300	00h	
4	940	8	512	00h	
5	940	6	512	00h	
6	615	4	65535	00h	
7	462	8	256	00h	
8	733	5	65535	00h	
9	900	15	65535	08h	
10	820	3	65535	00h	
11	855	5	65535	00h	
12	855	7	65535	00h	
13	306	8	128	00h	
14	733	7	65535	00h	
15	0	0	0	00h	
16	612	4	0	00h	
17	977	5	300	00h	
18	977	7	65535	00h	
19	1024	7	512	00h	

		LZ	S/T	Meg	MB
		852	26	61.62	64.62
		775	33	100.03	104.89
		685	38	203.06	212.93
		615	17	30.63	32.12

Table 5.29 shows the Phoenix 286 ROM BIOS (80286 ROM BIOS version 3.01, dated 11/01/86) hard disk parameters.

		LZ	S/T	Meg	MB
		305	17	10.16	10.65
		638	17	20.42	21.41
		615	17	30.63	32.12
		940	17	62.42	65.45
		940	17	46.82	49.09
		615	17	20.42	21.41
		511	17	30.68	32.17
		733	17	30.42	31.90
		901	17	112.06	117.50
		820	17	20.42	21.41
		855	17	35.49	37.21
		855	17	49.68	52.09
		319	17	20.32	21.31
		733	17	42.59	44.66
		0	0	0.00	0.00
		633	17	20.32	21.31
		977	17	40.55	42.52
		977	17	56.77	59.53
		1023	17	59.50	62.39

(continues)

Type	Cylinders	Heads	WPC	Ctrl	
20	733	5	300	00h	
21	733	7	300	00h	
22	733	5	300	00h	
23	0	0	0	00h	
24	0	0	0	00h	
25	0	0	0	00h	
26	0	0	0	00h	
27	0	0	0	00h	
28	0	0	0	00h	
29	0	0	0	00h	
30	0	0	0	00h	
31	0	0	0	00h	
32	0	0	0	00h	
33	0	0	0	00h	
34	0	0	0	00h	
35	0	0	0	00h	
36	1024	5	512	00h	
37	830	10	65535	08h	
38	823	10	256	08h	
39	615	4	128	00h	
40	615	8	128	00h	
41	917	15	65535	08h	
42	1023	15	65535	08h	
43	823	10	512	08h	
44	820	6	65535	00h	
45	1024	8	65535	00h	
46	925	9	65535	08h	
47	1024	5	65535	00h	

Table 5.29   Continued

Table entry 15 is reserved to act as a pointer to indicate that
the type is greater than 15.

LZ	S/T	Meg	MB
732	17	30.42	31.90
733	17	42.59	44.66
733	17	30.42	31.90
0	0	0.00	0.00
0	0	0.00	0.00
0	0	0.00	0.00
0	0	0.00	0.00
0	0	0.00	0.00
0	0	0.00	0.00
0	0	0.00	0.00
0	0	0.00	0.00
0	0	0.00	0.00
0	0	0.00	0.00
0	0	0.00	0.00
0	0	0.00	0.00
0	0	0.00	0.00
1024	17	42.50	44.56
830	17	68.90	72.24
824	17	68.32	71.63
664	17	20.42	21.41
664	17	40.84	42.82
918	17	114.18	119.72
1024	17	127.38	133.56
823	17	68.32	71.63
820	17	40.84	42.82
1024	17	68.00	71.30
925	17	69.10	72.46
1024	17	42.50	44.56

Table 5.30 shows the Phoenix 286 ROM BIOS (286 BIOS Plus, version 3.10) hard disk parameters.

Table 5.30   Phoenix 286 ROM BIOS (286 BIOS Plus Version 3.10) Hard Disk Table

Type	Cylinders	Heads	WPC	Ctrl
1	306	4	128	00h
2	615	4	300	00h
3	615	6	300	00h
4	940	8	512	00h
5	940	6	512	00h
6	615	4	65535	00h
7	462	8	256	00h
8	733	5	65535	00h
9	900	15	65535	08h
10	820	3	65535	00h
11	855	5	65535	00h
12	855	7	65535	00h
13	306	8	128	00h
14	733	7	65535	00h
15	0	0	0	00h
16	612	4	0	00h
17	977	5	300	00h
18	977	7	65535	00h
19	1024	7	512	00h
20	733	5	300	00h
21	733	7	300	00h
22	733	5	300	00h
23	306	4	0	00h
24	0	0	0	00h
25	615	4	0	00h
26	1024	4	65535	00h
27	1024	5	65535	00h
28	1024	8	65535	00h
29	512	8	256	00h
30	615	2	615	00h
31	989	5	0	00h

LZ	S/T	Meg	MB
305	17	10.16	10.65
615	17	20.42	21.41
615	17	30.63	32.12
940	17	62.42	65.45
940	17	46.82	49.09
615	17	20.42	21.41
511	17	30.68	32.17
733	17	30.42	31.90
901	17	112.06	117.50
820	17	20.42	21.41
855	17	35.49	37.21
855	17	49.68	52.09
319	17	20.32	21.31
733	17	42.59	44.66
0	0	0	0
663	17	20.32	21.31
977	17	40.55	42.52
977	17	56.77	59.53
1023	17	59.50	62.39
732	17	30.42	31.90
732	17	42.59	44.66
733	17	30.42	31.90
336	17	10.16	10.65
0	0	0.00	0.00
615	17	20.42	21.41
1023	17	34.00	35.65
1023	17	42.50	44.56
1023	17	68.00	71.30
512	17	34.00	35.65
615	17	10.21	10.71
989	17	41.05	43.04

(continues)

Table 5.30 Continued					
Type	Cylinders	Heads	WPC	Ctrl	
32	1020	15	65535	08h	
33	0	0	0	00h	
34	0	0	0	00h	
35	1024	9	1024	08h	
36	1024	5	512	00h	
37	830	10	65535	08h	
38	823	10	256	08h	
39	615	4	128	00h	
40	615	8	128	00h	
41	917	15	65535	08h	
42	1023	15	65535	08h	
43	823	10	512	08h	
44	820	6	65535	00h	
45	1024	8	65535	00h	
46	925	9	65535	08h	
47	699	7	256	00h	

Table entry 15 is reserved to act as a pointer to indicate that the type is greater than 15.

This BIOS uses types 48 and 49 as user-definable entries.

Table 5.31 Phoenix 386 ROM BIOS (A386 BIOS 1.01) Hard Disk Table					
Type	Cylinders	Heads	WPC	Ctrl	
1	306	4	128	00h	
2	615	4	300	00h	
3	615	6	300	00h	
4	940	8	512	00h	
5	940	6	512	00h	
6	615	4	65535	00h	
7	462	8	256	00h	

	LZ	S/T	Meg	MB
	1024	17	127.00	133.17
	0	0	0.00	0.00
	0	0	0.00	0.00
	1024	17	76.50	80.22
	1024	17	42.50	44.56
	830	17	68.90	72.24
	824	17	68.32	71.63
	664	17	20.42	21.41
	664	17	40.84	42.82
	918	17	114.18	119.72
	1024	17	127.38	133.56
	823	17	68.32	71.63
	820	17	40.84	42.82
	1024	17	68.00	71.30
	925	17	69.10	72.46
	700	17	40.62	42.59

Table 5.31 shows the Pheonix 386 ROM BIOS (A386 BIOS 1.01 Reference ID 08, dated 04/19/90) hard disk parameters.

	LZ	S/T	Meg	MB
	305	17	10.16	10.65
	615	17	20.42	21.41
	615	17	30.63	32.12
	940	17	62.42	65.45
	940	17	46.82	49.09
	615	17	20.42	21.41
	511	17	30.68	32.17

(continues)

Table 5.31 Continued				
Type	Cylinders	Heads	WPC	Ctrl
8	733	5	65535	00h
9	900	15	65535	08h
10	820	3	65535	00h
11	855	5	65535	00h
12	855	7	65535	00h
13	306	8	128	00h
14	733	7	65535	00h
15	0	0	0	00h
16	987	12	65535	08h
17	977	5	300	00h
18	977	7	65535	00h
19	1024	7	512	00h
20	733	5	300	00h
21	733	7	300	00h
22	1024	16	0	08h
23	914	14	0	08h
24	1001	15	0	08h
25	977	7	815	00h
26	1024	4	65535	00h
27	1024	5	65535	00h
28	1024	8	65535	00h
29	980	10	812	08h
30	1024	10	0	08h
31	832	6	832	00h
32	1020	15	65535	08h
33	776	8	0	00h
34	782	4	0	00h
35	1024	9	1024	08h
36	1024	5	512	00h
37	830	10	65535	08h
38	823	10	256	08h
39	980	14	65535	08h
40	615	8	128	00h

LZ	S/T	Meg	MB
733	17	30.42	31.90
901	17	112.06	117.50
820	17	20.42	21.41
855	17	35.49	37.21
855	17	49.68	52.09
319	17	20.32	21.31
733	17	42.59	44.66
0	0	0	0
988	35	202.41	212.24
977	17	40.55	42.52
977	17	56.77	59.53
1023	17	59.50	62.39
732	17	30.42	31.90
732	17	42.59	44.66
0	17	136.00	142.61
0	17	106.22	111.38
0	17	124.64	130.69
977	26	86.82	91.04
1023	17	34.00	35.65
1023	17	42.50	44.56
1023	17	68.00	71.30
990	17	81.35	85.30
0	17	85.00	89.13
832	33	80.44	84.34
1024	17	127.00	133.17
0	33	100.03	104.89
862	27	41.24	43.24
1024	17	76.50	80.22
1024	17	42.50	44.56
830	17	68.90	72.24
824	17	68.32	71.63
990	30	200.98	210.74
664	17	40.84	42.82

(continues)

Table 5.31 Continued					
Type	Cylinders	Heads	WPC	Ctrl	
41	917	15	65535	08h	
42	1023	15	65535	08h	
43	823	10	512	08h	
44	820	6	65535	00h	
45	1024	8	65535	00h	
46	0	0	0	00h	
47	0	0	0	00h	

Table entry 15 is reserved to act as a pointer to indicate that the type is greater than 15.

This BIOS uses types 46 and 47 as user-definable entries.

Table 5.32 Zenith BIOS Hard Disk Table					
Type	Cylinders	Heads	WPC	Ctrl	
1	306	4	128	00h	
2	615	4	300	00h	
3	699	5	256	00h	
4	940	8	512	00h	
5	940	6	512	00h	
6	615	4	65535	00h	
7	699	7	256	00h	
8	733	5	65535	00h	
9	900	15	65535	08h	
10	925	5	0	00h	
11	855	5	65535	00h	
12	855	7	65535	00h	
13	306	8	128	00h	
14	733	7	65535	00h	
15	0	0	0	00h	
16	612	4	0	00h	
17	977	5	300	00h	

	LZ	S/T	Meg	MB
	918	17	114.18	119.72
	1024	17	127.38	133.56
	823	17	68.32	71.63
	820	17	40.84	42.82
	1024	17	68.00	71.30
	0	0	0.00	0.00
	0	0	0.00	0.00

Table 5.32 shows the Zenith motherboard BIOS (80286
Technical Reference 1988) hard disk parameters.

	LZ	S/T	Meg	MB
	305	17	10.16	10.65
	615	17	20.42	21.41
	710	17	29.01	30.42
	940	17	62.42	65.45
	940	17	46.82	49.09
	615	17	20.42	21.41
	710	17	40.62	42.59
	733	17	30.42	31.90
	901	17	112.06	117.50
	926	17	38.39	40.26
	855	17	35.49	37.21
	855	17	49.68	52.09
	319	17	20.32	21.31
	733	17	42.59	44.66
	0	0	0	0
	663	17	20.32	21.31
	977	17	40.55	42.52

(continues)

Table 5.32 Continued

Type	Cylinders	Heads	WPC	Ctrl	
18	977	7	65535	00h	
19	1024	7	512	00h	
20	733	5	300	00h	
21	733	7	300	00h	
22	733	5	300	00h	
23	306	4	0	00h	
24	612	2	65535	00h	
25	615	6	300	00h	
26	462	8	256	00h	
27	820	3	65535	00h	
28	981	7	65535	00h	
29	754	11	65535	08h	
30	918	15	65535	08h	
31	987	5	65535	00h	
32	830	6	400	00h	
33	697	4	0	00h	
34	615	4	65535	00h	
35	615	4	128	00h	
36	1024	9	65535	08h	
37	1024	5	512	00h	
38	820	6	65535	00h	
39	615	4	306	00h	
40	925	9	0	08h	
41	1024	8	512	00h	
42	1024	5	1024	00h	
43	615	8	300	00h	
44	989	5	0	00h	
45	0	0	0	00h	
46	0	0	0	00h	
47	0	0	0	00h	

LZ	S/T	Meg	MB
977	17	56.77	59.53
1023	17	59.50	62.39
732	17	30.42	31.90
732	17	42.59	44.66
733	17	30.42	31.90
336	17	10.16	10.65
611	17	10.16	10.65
615	17	30.63	32.12
511	17	30.68	32.17
820	17	20.42	21.41
986	17	57.00	59.77
754	17	68.85	72.19
918	17	114.30	119.85
987	17	40.96	42.95
830	17	41.34	43.35
696	17	23.14	24.27
615	17	20.42	21.41
663	17	20.42	21.41
1024	17	76.50	80.22
1024	17	42.50	44.56
910	17	40.84	42.82
684	17	20.42	21.41
924	17	69.10	72.46
1023	17	68.00	71.30
1023	17	42.50	44.56
615	17	40.84	42.82
988	17	41.05	43.04
0	0	0.00	0.00
0	0	0.00	0.00
0	0	0.00	0.00

Table entry 15 is reserved to act as a pointer to indicate that the type is greater than 15.

Type = Drive type number

Cyls = Total number of cylinders

Heads = Total number of heads

WPC = Write precompensation starting cylinder

65535 = No Write precompensation

0 = Write precompensation on all cylinders

Ctrl = Control byte, with values according to the following table:

Bit number	Hex	Meaning
Bit 0	01h	Not used (XT = drive step rate)
Bit 1	02h	Not used (XT = drive step rate)
Bit 2	04h	Not used (XT = drive step rate)
Bit 3	08h	More than eight heads
Bit 4	10h	Not used (XT = embedded servo drive)
Bit 5	20h	OEM defect map at (cyls + 1)
Bit 6	40h	Disable ECC retries
Bit 7	80h	Disable disk access retries

LZ = Landing-zone cylinder for head parking

S/T = Number of sectors per track

Meg = Drive capacity in megabytes

MB = Drive capacity in millions of bytes

Hard Disk Interface Connector Pinouts

This section details the interface connector pinouts of each of the popular hard disk drive interfaces, including ST-506/412, ESDI, IDE, and SCSI.

ST-506/412 Interface Connectors

The ST-506/412 Interface uses two connections, a 34-pin Control connector and a 20-pin Data connector. The following tables show the pinouts for these connectors.

Table 5.33 ST-506/412 Hard Disk Interface 34-pin Control Connector Pinout			
Signal Name	Pin	Pin	Signal Name
GROUND	1	2	-HD SLCT 3
GROUND	3	4	-HD SLCT 2
GROUND	5	6	-WRITE GATE
GROUND	7	8	-SEEK CMPLT
GROUND	9	10	-TRACK 0
GROUND	11	12	-WRITE FAULT
GROUND	13	14	-HD SLCT 0
KEY (no pin)	15	16	Not Connected
GROUND	17	18	-HD SLCT 1
GROUND	19	20	-INDEX
GROUND	21	22	-READY
GROUND	23	24	-STEP
GROUND	25	26	-DRV SLCT 0
GROUND	27	28	-DRV SLCT 1
GROUND	29	30	Not Connected
GROUND	31	32	Not Connected
GROUND	33	34	-DIRECTION IN

Table 5.34   ST-506/412 Hard Disk Interface 20-pin Data Connector Pinout

Signal Name	Pin	Pin	Signal Name
-DRV SLCTD	1	2	GROUND
Not Connected	3	4	GROUND
Not Connected	5	6	GROUND
Not Connected	7	8	KEY (no pin)
Not Connected	9	10	Not Connected
GROUND	11	12	GROUND
+MFM WRITE	13	14	-MFM WRITE
GROUND	15	16	GROUND
+MFM READ	17	18	-MFM READ
GROUND	19	20	GROUND

ESDI Interface Connectors

ESDI (Enhanced Small Device Interface) uses two connections, a 34-pin Control connector and a 20-pin Data connector. The following tables show the pinouts for these connectors.

Table 5.35   ESDI (Enhanced Small Device Interface) 34-pin Control Connector Pinout***

Signal Name	Pin	Pin	Signal Name
GROUND	1	2	-HD SLCT 3
GROUND	3	4	-HD SLCT 2
GROUND	5	6	-WRITE GATE
GROUND	7	8	-CNFG/STATUS
GROUND	9	10	-XFER ACK
GROUND	11	12	-ATTENTION
GROUND	13	14	-HD SLCT 0
KEY (no pin)	15	16	-SECTOR
GROUND	17	18	-HD SLCT 1
GROUND	19	20	-INDEX
GROUND	21	22	-READY
GROUND	23	24	-XFER REQ
GROUND	25	26	-DRV SLCT 0
GROUND	27	28	-DRV SLCT 1

Signal Name	Pin	Pin	Signal Name
GROUND	29	30	Reserved
GROUND	31	32	-READ GATE
GROUND	33	34	-CMD DATA

Table 5.36   ESDI (Enhanced Small Device interface) 20-pin Data Connector Pinout

Signal Name	Pin	Pin	Signal Name
-DRV SLCTD	1	2	-SECTOR
-CMD COMPL	3	4	-ADDR MK EN
GROUND	5	6	GROUND
+WRITE CLK	7	8	-WRITE CLK
GROUND	9	10	+RD/REF CLK
-RD/REF CLK	11	12	GROUND
+NRZ WRITE	13	14	-NRZ WRITE
GROUND	15	16	GROUND
+NRZ READ	17	18	-NRZ READ
GROUND	19	20	-INDEX

IDE (Integrated Drive Electronics) Connectors

A number of different IDE (Integrated Drive Electronics) interfaces have been used in PC systems. The following have been most widely used:

- ATA (AT Attachment) IDE
- XT-Bus IDE
- IBM XT-Bus IDE
- IBM MCA (Micro Channel Architecture) IDE

The most common would be the ATA (AT Attachment) version, which is an ANSI standard interface that is by far the most popular IDE interface, and the only one of these still being used in new systems today. When the term "IDE" is used, you can usually assume it means ATA IDE. Because the ATA IDE interface is a 16-bit design, it could not be used in 8-bit (XT type) systems, so some of the drive manufacturers standardized on an XT-Bus (8-bit) IDE interface for XT class systems. These drives were never very popular, and were usually only available in capacities from 20M to 40M. IBM used a custom version of the XT-Bus IDE interface in the PS/2 Model 25 and Model 30 systems. IBM also developed an MCA (Micro Channel Architecture) IDE interface for use in the Micro Channel based PS/2 systems. MCA IDE was used in many of the desktop PS/2s, including the Model 50Z, 55, 70, and P70 systems, and were available in capacities ranging from 30M to 160M.

The following tables show each of the the IDE interface connector pinouts.

ATA IDE

Table 5.37 ATA (AT Attachment) IDE (Integrated Drive Electronics) Connector Pinout			
Signal Name	**Pin**	**Pin**	**Signal Name**
-RESET	1	2	GROUND
Data Bit 7	3	4	Data Bit 8
Data Bit 6	5	6	Data Bit 9
Data Bit 5	7	8	Data Bit 10
Data Bit 4	9	10	Data Bit 11
Data Bit 3	11	12	Data Bit 12
Data Bit 2	13	14	Data Bit 13
Data Bit 1	15	16	Data Bit 14
Data Bit 0	17	18	Data Bit 15
GROUND	19	20	KEY (pin missing)
DRQ 3	21	22	GROUND
-IOW	23	24	GROUND
-IOR	25	26	GROUND
I/O CH RDY	27	28	SPSYNC:CSEL
-DACK 3	29	30	GROUND
IRQ 14	31	32	-IOCS16
Address Bit 1	33	34	-PDIAG

Signal Name	Pin	Pin	Signal Name
-CS1FX	37	38	-CS3FX
-DA/SP	39	40	GROUND
+5 Vdc (Logic)	41	42	+5 Vdc (Motor)
GROUND	43	44	-TYPE (0=ATA)

XT-Bus IDE

Table 5.38   XT-Bus IDE (Integrated Drive Electronics Connector Pinout

Signal Name	Pin	Pin	Signal Name
-RESET	1	2	GROUND
Data Bit 7	3	4	GROUND
Data Bit 6	5	6	GROUND
Data Bit 5	7	8	GROUND
Data Bit 4	9	10	GROUND
Data Bit 3	11	12	GROUND
Data Bit 2	13	14	GROUND
Data Bit 1	15	16	GROUND
Data Bit 0	17	18	GROUND
GROUND	19	20	KEY (pin missing)
AEN	21	22	GROUND
-IOW	23	24	GROUND
-IOR	25	26	GROUND
-DACK 3	27	28	GROUND
DRQ 3	29	30	GROUND
IRQ 5	31	32	GROUND
Address Bit 1	33	34	GROUND
Address Bit 0	35	36	GROUND
-CS1FX	37	38	GROUND
-Drive Active	39	40	GROUND

IBM XT-Bus IDE

Table 5.39   IBM Unique XT-Bus (PS/2 Model 25 and 30) IDE Connector Pinout

Signal Name	Pin	Pin	Signal Name
-RESET	1	2	-Disk Installed
Data Bit 0	3	4	GROUND
Data Bit 1	5	6	GROUND
Data Bit 2	7	8	GROUND
Data Bit 3	9	10	GROUND
Data Bit 4	11	12	GROUND
Data Bit 5	13	14	GROUND
Data Bit 6	15	16	GROUND
Data Bit 7	17	18	GROUND
-IOR	19	20	GROUND
-IOW	21	22	GROUND
-CS1FX	23	24	GROUND
Address Bit 0	25	26	GROUND
Address Bit 1	27	28	GROUND
Address Bit 2	29	30	+5 Vdc
RESERVED	31	32	+5 Vdc
-DACK 3	33	34	GROUND
DRQ 3	35	36	GROUND
IRQ 5	37	38	GROUND
I/O CH RDY	39	40	+ 12 Vdc
Spare	41	42	+ 12 Vdc
Spare	39	44	+ 12 Vdc

MCA IDE

Table 5.40   MCA (Micro Channel Architecture) IDE Connector Pinout

Signal Name	Pin	Pin	Signal Name
-CD SETUP	A1	B1	Address Bit 15
Address Bit 13	A2	B2	Address Bit 14

Signal Name	Pin	Pin	Signal Name
GROUND	A3	B3	GROUND
Address Bit 11	A4	B4	OSC (14.3MHz)
Address Bit 10	A5	B5	GROUND
Address Bit 9	A6	B6	Address Bit 12
+5 Vdc	A7	B7	-CMD
Address Bit 8	A8	B8	-CD SFDBK
Address Bit 7	A9	B9	GROUND
Address Bit 6	A10	B10	Data Bit 1
+5 Vdc	A11	B11	Data Bit 3
Address Bit 5	A12	B12	Data Bit 4
Address Bit 4	A13	B13	GROUND
Address Bit 3	A14	B14	CHRESET
+5 Vdc	A15	B15	Data Bit 8
Address Bit 2	A16	B16	Data Bit 9
Address Bit 1	A17	B17	GROUND
Address Bit 0	A18	B18	Data Bit 12
+12 Vdc	A19	B19	Data Bit 14
-ADL	A20	B20	Data Bit 15
-PREEMPT	A21	B21	GROUND
-BURST	A22	B22	Data Bit 0
+5 Vdc	A23	B23	Data Bit 2
ARB 0	A24	B24	Data Bit 5
ARB 1	A25	B25	GROUND
ARB 2	A26	B26	Data Bit 6
+12 Vdc	A27	B27	Data Bit 7
ARB 3	A28	B28	Data Bit 10
+ARB/-GRANT	A29	B29	GROUND
-TC	A30	B30	Data Bit 11
+5 Vdc	A31	B31	Data Bit 13
-S0	A32	B32	-SBHE
-S1	A33	B33	GROUND
+M/-IO	A34	B34	-CD DS 16
GROUND	A35	B35	-IRQ 14
CD CHRDY	A36	B36	GROUND

SCSI (Small Computer System Interface)

The following section details the pinouts of the various SCSI cables and connectors. There are two electrically different versions of SCSI: Single Ended and Differential. These two versions are electrically incompatible, and must not be interconnected or damage will result. Fortunately, very few Differential SCSI applications are available in the PC industry, so you will rarely (if ever) encounter it. Within each electrical type (Single Ended or Differential), there are basically three SCSI cable types:

- A-Cable (Standard SCSI)

- P-Cable (Wide SCSI)

- Q-Cable (32-bit Wide SCSI)

The A-Cable is used in most SCSI-1 and SCSI-2 installations, and is the standard one you will encounter. SCSI-2 Wide (16-bit) applications use a P-Cable instead, which completely replaces the A-Cable. You can intermix standard and wide SCSI devices on a single SCSI bus by interconnecting A- and P-Cables with special adapters. 32-bit wide SCSI-3 applications use both the P- and Q-Cables in parallel to each 32-bit device. Today there are virtually no PC applications for 32-bit Wide SCSI-3, and because of the two cable requirement, it is not likely to catch on.

The A-Cables can have Pin Header (Internal) type connectors or External Shielded connectors, each with a different pinout. The P- and Q-Cables feature the same connector pinout on either Internal or External cable connections.

The following tables show all of the possible interface, cable, and connector pinout specifications. A hyphen preceding a signal name indicates the signal is Active Low. The RESERVED lines have continuity from one end of the SCSI bus to the other. In an A-Cable bus, the RESERVED lines should be left open in SCSI devices (but may be connected to ground), and are connected to ground in the bus terminator assemblies. In the P- and Q-Cables, the RESERVED lines are left open in SCSI devices as well as in the bus terminator assemblies.

Single Ended SCSI Signals
A-Cable (Single-Ended) Connectors

Table 5.41 A-Cable (Single Ended) Internal Unshielded Header Connector Pinout

Signal Name	Pin	Pin	Signal Name
GROUND	1	2	-DB(0)
GROUND	3	4	-DB(1)
GROUND	5	6	-DB(2)
GROUND	7	8	-DB(3)
GROUND	9	10	-DB(4)
GROUND	11	12	-DB(5)
GROUND	13	14	-DB(6)
GROUND	15	16	-DB(7)
GROUND	17	18	-DB(Parity)
GROUND	19	20	GROUND
GROUND	21	22	GROUND
RESERVED	23	24	RESERVED
Open	25	26	TERMPWR
RESERVED	27	28	RESERVED
GROUND	29	30	GROUND
GROUND	31	32	-ATN
GROUND	33	34	GROUND
GROUND	35	36	-BSY
GROUND	37	38	-ACK
GROUND	39	40	-RST
GROUND	41	42	-MSG
GROUND	43	44	-SEL
GROUND	45	46	-C/D
GROUND	47	48	-REQ
GROUND	49	50	-I/O

Table 5.42   A-Cable (Single Ended) External Shielded Connector Pinout

Signal Name	Pin	Pin	Signal Name
GROUND	1	26	-DB(0)
GROUND	2	27	-DB(1)
GROUND	3	28	-DB(2)
GROUND	4	29	-DB(3)
GROUND	5	30	-DB(4)
GROUND	6	31	-DB(5)
GROUND	7	32	-DB(6)
GROUND	8	33	-DB(7)
GROUND	9	34	-DB(Parity)
GROUND	10	35	GROUND
GROUND	11	36	GROUND
RESERVED	12	37	RESERVED
Open	13	38	TERMPWR
RESERVED	14	39	RESERVED
GROUND	15	40	GROUND
GROUND	16	41	-ATN
GROUND	17	42	GROUND
GROUND	18	43	-BSY
GROUND	19	44	-ACK
GROUND	20	45	-RST
GROUND	21	46	-MSG
GROUND	22	47	-SEL
GROUND	23	48	-C/D
GROUND	24	49	-REQ
GROUND	25	50	-I/O

IBM has standardized on the SCSI interface for virtually all PS/2 systems introduced since 1990. These systems use a Micro Channel SCSI adapter or have the SCSI Host Adapter built into the motherboard. In either case, IBM's SCSI interface uses a special 60-pin mini-Centronics type external shielded connector that is unique in the industry. A special

IBM cable is required to adapt this connector to the standard 50-pin Centronics style connector used on most external SCSI devices. The pinout of the IBM 60-pin mini-Centronics style External Shielded connector is shown in the following table. Note that although the pin arrangement is unique, the pin number to signal designations corresponds with the standard unshielded internal pin header type of SCSI connector.

Table 5.43 IBM PS/2 SCSI External Shielded 60-pin Connector Pinout			
Signal Name	Pin	Pin	Signal Name
GROUND	1	60	Not Connected
-DB(0)	2	59	Not Connected
GROUND	3	58	Not Connected
-DB(1)	4	57	Not Connected
GROUND	5	56	Not Connected
-DB(2)	6	55	Not Connected
GROUND	7	54	Not Connected
-DB(3)	8	53	Not Connected
GROUND	9	52	Not Connected
-DB(4)	10	51	GROUND
GROUND	11	50	-I/O
-DB(5)	12	49	GROUND
GROUND	13	48	-REQ
-DB(6)	14	47	GROUND
GROUND	15	46	-C/D
-DB(7)	16	45	GROUND
GROUND	17	44	-SEL
-DB(Parity)	18	43	GROUND
GROUND	19	42	-MSG
GROUND	20	41	GROUND
GROUND	21	40	-RST
GROUND	22	39	GROUND
RESERVED	23	38	-ACK

(continues)

Table 5.43 Continued			
Signal Name	Pin	Pin	Signal Name
RESERVED	24	37	GROUND
Open	25	36	-BSY
TERMPWR	26	35	GROUND
RESERVED	27	34	GROUND
RESERVED	28	33	GROUND
GROUND	29	32	-ATN
GROUND	30	31	GROUND

P-Cable (Single-Ended) Connector

Table 5.44 P-Cable (Single Ended) Internal or External Shielded Connector Pinout			
Signal Name	Pin	Pin	Signal Name
GROUND	1	35	-DB(12)
GROUND	2	36	-DB(13)
GROUND	3	37	-DB(14)
GROUND	4	38	-DB(15)
GROUND	5	39	-DB(Parity 1)
GROUND	6	40	-DB(0)
GROUND	7	41	-DB(1)
GROUND	8	42	-DB(2)
GROUND	9	43	-DB(3)
GROUND	10	44	-DB(4)
GROUND	11	45	-DB(5)
GROUND	12	46	-DB(6)
GROUND	13	47	-DB(7)
GROUND	14	48	-DB(Parity 0)
GROUND	15	49	GROUND
GROUND	16	50	GROUND
TERMPWR	17	51	TERMPWR
TERMPWR	18	52	TERMPWR
RESERVED	19	53	RESERVED
GROUND	20	54	GROUND

Signal Name	Pin	Pin	Signal Name
GROUND	21	55	-ATN
GROUND	22	56	GROUND
GROUND	23	57	-BSY
GROUND	24	58	-ACK
GROUND	25	59	-RST
GROUND	26	60	-MSG
GROUND	27	61	-SEL
GROUND	28	62	-C/D
GROUND	29	63	-REQ
GROUND	30	64	-I/O
GROUND	31	65	-DB(8)
GROUND	32	66	-DB(9)
GROUND	33	67	-DB(10)
GROUND	34	68	-DB(11)

Q-Cable (Single Ended) Connector

Table 5.45 Q-Cable (Single Ended) Internal or External Shielded Connector Pinout			
Signal Name	Pin	Pin	Signal Name
GROUND	1	35	-DB(28)
GROUND	2	36	-DB(29)
GROUND	3	37	-DB(30)
GROUND	4	38	-DB(31)
GROUND	5	39	-DB(Parity 3)
GROUND	6	40	-DB(16)
GROUND	7	41	-DB(17)
GROUND	8	42	-DB(18)
GROUND	9	43	-DB(19)
GROUND	10	44	-DB(20)
GROUND	11	45	-DB(21)
GROUND	12	46	-DB(22)

(continues)

Table 5.45 Continued			
Signal Name	Pin	Pin	Signal Name
GROUND	13	47	-DB(23)
GROUND	14	48	-DB(Parity 2)
GROUND	15	49	GROUND
GROUND	16	50	GROUND
TERMPWRQ	17	51	TERMPWRQ
TERMPWRQ	18	52	TERMPWRQ
RESERVED	19	53	RESERVED
GROUND	20	54	GROUND
GROUND	21	55	TERMINATED
GROUND	22	56	GROUND
GROUND	23	57	TERMINATED
GROUND	24	58	-ACKQ
GROUND	25	59	TERMINATED
GROUND	26	60	TERMINATED
GROUND	27	61	TERMINATED
GROUND	28	62	TERMINATED
GROUND	29	63	-REQQ
GROUND	30	64	TERMINATED
GROUND	31	65	-DB(24)
GROUND	32	66	-DB(25)
GROUND	33	67	-DB(26)
GROUND	34	68	-DB(27)

Differential SCSI Signals

Differential SCSI is not normally used in a PC environment, howver the interface connector specifications are show here for reference.

A-Cable (Differential) Connectors

Table 5.46 A-Cable (Differential) Internal Unshielded Header Connector Pinout			
Signal Name	Pin	Pin	Signal Name
GROUND	1	2	GROUND
+DB(0)	3	4	-DB(0)
+DB(1)	5	6	-DB(1)
+DB(2)	7	8	-DB(2)
+DB(3)	9	10	-DB(3)
+DB(4)	11	12	-DB(4)
+DB(5)	13	14	-DB(5)
+DB(6)	15	16	-DB(6)
+DB(7)	17	18	-DB(7)
+DB(Parity)	19	20	-DP(Parity)
DIFFSENS	21	22	GROUND
RESERVED	23	24	RESERVED
TERMPWR	25	26	TERMPWR
RESERVED	27	28	RESERVED
+ATN	29	30	-ATN
GROUND	31	32	GROUND
+BSY	33	34	-BSY
+ACK	35	36	-ACK
+RST	37	38	-RST
+MSG	39	40	-MSG
+SEL	41	42	-SEL
+C/D	43	44	-C/D
+REQ	45	46	-REQ
+I/O	47	48	-I/O
GROUND	49	50	GROUND

Table 5.47   A-Cable (Differential) External Shielded Connector Pinout

Signal Name	Pin	Pin	Signal Name
GROUND	1	26	GROUND
+DB(0)	2	27	-DB(0)
+DB(1)	3	28	-DB(1)
+DB(2)	4	29	-DB(2)
+DB(3)	5	30	-DB(3)
+DB(4)	6	31	-DB(4)
+DB(5)	7	32	-DB(5)
+DB(6)	8	33	-DB(6)
+DB(7)	9	34	-DB(7)
+DB(Parity)	10	35	-DP(Parity)
DIFFSENS	11	36	GROUND
RESERVED	12	37	RESERVED
TERMPWR	13	38	TERMPWR
RESERVED	14	39	RESERVED
+ATN	15	40	-ATN
GROUND	16	41	GROUND
+BSY	17	42	-BSY
+ACK	18	43	-ACK
+RST	18	44	-RST
+MSG	20	45	-MSG
+SEL	21	46	-SEL
+C/D	22	47	-C/D
+REQ	23	48	-REQ
+I/O	24	49	-I/O
GROUND	25	50	GROUND

P-Cable (Differential) Connector

Table 5.48 P-Cable (Differential) Internal or External Shielded Connector Pinout			
Signal Name	**Pin**	**Pin**	**Signal Name**
+DB(12)	1	35	-DB(12)
+DB(13)	2	36	-DB(13)
+DB(14)	3	37	-DB(14)
+DB(15)	4	38	-DB(15)
+DB(Parity 1)	5	39	-DB(Parity 1)
GROUND	6	40	GROUND
+DB(0)	7	41	-DB(0)
+DB(1)	8	42	-DB(1)
+DB(2)	9	43	-DB(2)
+DB(3)	10	44	-DP(3)
+DB(4)	11	45	-DB(4)
+DB(5)	12	46	-DB(5)
+DB(6)	13	47	-DB(6)
+DB(7)	14	48	-DB(7)
+DB(Parity 0)	15	49	-DB(Parity 0)
DIFFSENS	16	50	GROUND
TERMPWR	17	51	TERMPWR
TERMPWR	18	52	TERMPWR
RESERVED	19	53	RESERVED
+ATN	20	54	-ATN
GROUND	21	55	GROUND
+BSY	22	56	-BSY
+ACK	23	57	-ACK
+RST	24	58	-RST
+MSG	25	59	-MSG
+SEL	26	60	-SEL
+C/D	27	61	-C/D
+REQ	28	62	-REQ

(continues)

Table 5.48 Continued			
Signal Name	Pin	Pin	Signal Name
+I/O	29	63	-I/O
GROUND	30	64	GROUND
+DB(8)	31	65	-DB(8)
+DB(9)	32	66	-DB(9)
+DB(10)	33	67	-DB(10)
+DB(11)	34	68	-DB(11)

Q Cable (Differential) Connector

Table 5.49 Q-Cable (Differential) Internal or External Shielded Connector Pinout			
Signal Name	Pin	Pin	Signal Name
+DB(28)	1	35	-DB(28)
+DB(29)	2	36	-DB(29)
+DB(30)	3	37	-DB(30)
+DB(31)	4	38	-DB(31)
+DB(Parity 3)	5	39	-DB(Parity 3)
GROUND	6	40	GROUND
+DB(16)	7	41	-DB(16)
+DB(17)	8	42	-DB(17)
+DB(18)	9	43	-DB(18)
+DB(19)	10	44	-DP(19)
+DB(20)	11	45	-DB(20)
+DB(21)	12	46	-DB(21)
+DB(22)	13	47	-DB(22)
+DB(23)	14	48	-DB(23)
+DB(Parity 2)	15	49	-DB(Parity 2)
DIFFSENS	16	50	GROUND
TERMPWRQ	17	51	TERMPWRQ

Signal Name	Pin	Pin	Signal Name
TERMPWRQ	18	52	TERMPWRQ
RESERVED	19	53	RESERVED
TERMINATED	20	54	TERMINATED
GROUND	21	55	GROUND
TERMINATED	22	56	TERMINATED
+ACKQ	23	57	-ACKQ
TERMINATED	24	58	TERMINATED
TERMINATED	25	59	TERMINATED
TERMINATED	26	60	TERMINATED
TERMINATED	27	61	TERMINATED
+REQQ	28	62	-REQQ
TERMINATED	29	63	TERMINATED
GROUND	30	64	GROUND
+DB(24)	31	65	-DB(24)
+DB(25)	32	66	-DB(25)
+DB(26)	33	67	-DB(26)
+DB(27)	34	68	-DB(27)

Chapter 6

Troubleshooting Error Codes

The following sections show a variety of system error codes. Included are manufacturer test POST codes, display POST error codes, and advanced diagnostics error codes. This section also includes a detailed list of SCSI interface error codes, which can be helpful when you troubleshoot SCSI devices.

ROM BIOS Port 80h Power-On Self Test (POST) Codes

When the ROM BIOS is performing the Power-On Self Test, in most systems the results of these tests are sent to I/O Port 80h so that they can be monitored by a special diagnostics card. These tests sometimes are called *manufacturing tests* because they were designed into the system for testing systems on the assembly line without a video display attached. The POST-code cards have a two-digit hexadecimal display used to report the number of the currently executing test routines. Before executing each test, a hexadecimal numeric code is sent to the port, and then the test is run. If the test fails and locks up the machine, the hexadecimal code of the last test being executed remains on the card's display.

Many tests are executed in a system before the video display card is enabled, especially if the display is EGA or VGA. Therefore, many errors can occur that would lock up the system before it could possibly display an error code through the video system. To most normal troubleshooting procedures, a system with this type of problem (such as a memory failure in Bank 0) would appear completely "dead." By using one of the commercially available POST-code cards, however, you can correctly diagnose the problem.

These codes are completely BIOS dependent because the card does nothing but display the codes sent to it. Some BIOSes have better Power-On Self Test procedures and, therefore, send more informative codes. Some BIOS versions also send audio codes that can be used to help diagnose such problems. The Phoenix BIOS, for example, sends the most informative set of audio codes, which eliminates the need for a Port 80h POST card. Tables 6.1, 6.2, and 6.3 list the Port 80h codes and audio codes sent by a number of different BIOS manufacturers and versions.

AMI BIOS Audio and Port 80h Error Codes

Table 6.1 AMI BIOS Audio POST Codes

Beep code	Fatal errors
1 short	DRAM refresh failure
2 short	Parity circuit failure
3 short	Base 64K RAM failure
4 short	System timer failure
5 short	Processor failure
6 short	Keyboard controller Gate A20 error
7 short	Virtual mode exception error
8 short	Display memory R/W test failure
9 short	ROM BIOS checksum failure
Beep code	**Nonfatal errors**
1 long, 3 short	Conventional/extended memory failure
1 long, 8 short	Display/retrace test failed

Table 6.2 AMI 286 BIOS Plus Port 80h POST Codes

Checkpoint	Meaning
01h	NMI disabled and 286 register test about to start
02h	286 register test over
03h	ROM checksum OK
04h	8259 initialization OK
05h	CMOS pending interrupt disabled
06h	Video disabled and system timer counting OK
07h	CH-2 of 8253 test OK
08h	CH-2 of delta count test OK
09h	CH-1 delta count test OK
0Ah	CH-0 delta count test OK
0Bh	Parity status cleared
0Ch	Refresh and system timer OK
0Dh	Refresh link toggling OK
0Eh	Refresh period On/Off 50% OK
10h	Confirmed refresh On and about to start 64K memory
11h	Address line test OK
12h	64K base memory test OK
13h	Interrupt vectors initialized
14h	8042 keyboard controller test OK
15h	CMOS read/write test OK
16h	CMOS checksum/battery check OK
17h	Monochrome mode set OK
18h	Color mode set OK
19h	About to look for optional video ROM
1Ah	Optional video ROM control OK
1Bh	Display memory R/W test OK
1Ch	Display memory R/W test for alternate display OK
1Dh	Video retrace check OK
1Eh	Global equipment byte set for video OK

(continues)

Table 6.2 Continued

Checkpoint	Meaning
1Fh	Mode set call for Mono/Color OK
20h	Video test OK
21h	Video display OK
22h	Power-on message display OK
30h	Virtual mode memory test about to begin
31h	Virtual mode memory test started
32h	Processor in virtual mode
33h	Memory address line test in progress
34h	Memory address line test in progress
35h	Memory below IMB calculated
36h	Memory size computation OK
37h	Memory test in progress
38h	Memory initialization over below IMB
39h	Memory initialization over above IMB
3Ah	Display memory size
3Bh	About to start below 1M memory test
3Ch	Memory test below 1M OK
3Dh	Memory test above 1M OK
3Eh	About to go to real mode (shutdown)
3Fh	Shutdown successful and entered in real mode
40h	About to disable gate A-20 address line
41h	Gate A-20 line disabled successfully
42h	About to start DMA controller test
4Eh	Address line test OK
4Fh	Processor in real mode after shutdown
50h	DMA page register test OK
51h	DMA unit-1 base register test about to start
52h	DMA unit-1 channel OK, about to begin CH-2
53h	DMA CH-2 base register test OK
54h	About to test f/f latch for unit-1
55h	f/f latch test both unit OK

Checkpoint	Meaning
56h	DMA unit 1 and 2 programmed OK
57h	8259 initialization over
58h	8259 mask register check OK
59h	Master 8259 mask register OK, about to start slave
5Ah	About to check timer and keyboard interrupt level
5Bh	Timer interrupt OK
5Ch	About to test keyboard interrupt
5Dh	ERROR! timer/keyboard interrupt not in proper level
5Eh	8259 interrupt controller error
5Fh	8259 interrupt controller test OK
70h	Start of keyboard test
71h	Keyboard BAT test OK
72h	Keyboard test OK
73h	Keyboard global data initialization OK
74h	Floppy setup about to start
75h	Floppy setup OK
76h	Hard disk setup about to start
77h	Hard disk setup OK
79h	About to initialize timer data area
7Ah	Verify CMOS battery power
7Bh	CMOS battery verification done
7Dh	About to analyze diagnostics test result for memory
7Eh	CMOS memory size update OK
7Fh	About to check optional ROM C000:0.
80h	Keyboard sensed to enable SETUP
81h	Optional ROM control OK
82h	Printer global data initialization OK
83h	RS-232 global data initialization OK
84h	80287 check/test OK

(continues)

Table 6.2 Continued

Checkpoint	Meaning
85h	About to display soft error message
86h	About to give control to system ROM E000.0
87h	System ROM E000.0 check over
00h	Control given to Int 19, boot loader

Table 6.3 AMI Color BIOS Port 80h POST Codes

Port 80h code	Test description
01h	Processor register test about to start, and NMI to be disabled
02h	NMI is disabled; power-on delay starting
03h	Power-on delay complete; any initialization before keyboard BAT is in progress
04h	Any initialization before keyboard BAT is complete; reading keyboard SYS bit to check soft reset/power-on
05h	Soft reset/power-on determined; going to enable ROM (that is, disable shadow RAM/cache if any)
06h	ROM enabled; calculating ROM BIOS checksum and waiting for KB controller input buffer to be free
07h	ROM BIOS checksum passed, KB controller I/B free; going to issue BAT command to keyboard controller
08h	BAT command to keyboard controller issued; going to verify BAT command
09h	Keyboard controller BAT result verified; keyboard command byte to be written next
0Ah	Keyboard-command byte code issued; going to write command byte data
0Bh	Keyboard controller command byte written; going to issue Pin-23,24 blocking/unblocking command
0Ch	Pin-23,24 of keyboard controller blocked/unblocked; NOP command of keyboard controller to be issued next

Port 80h code	Test description
0Dh	NOP command processing done; CMOS shutdown register test to be done next
0Eh	CMOS shutdown register R/W test passed; going to calculate CMOS checksum and update DIAG byte
0Fh	CMOS checksum calculation done and DIAG byte written; CMOS initialization to begin (If INIT CMOS IN EVERY BOOT is set)
10h	CMOS initialization done (if any); CMOS status register about to initialize for date and time
11h	CMOS status register initialized; going to disable DMA and interrupt controllers
12h	DMA controller #1,#2, interrupt controller #1,#2 disabled; about to disable video display and init port-B
13h	Video display is disabled and port-B initialized; chipset init/auto memory detection to begin
14h	Chipset initialization/auto memory detection over; 8254 timer test about to start
15h	CH-2 timer test halfway; 8254 CH-2 timer test to be complete
16h	Ch-2 timer test over; 8254 CH-1 timer test to be complete
17h	CH-1 timer test over; 8254 CH-0 timer test to be complete
18h	CH-0 timer test over; about to start memory refresh
19h	Memory refresh started; memory refresh test to be done next
1Ah	Memory refresh line is toggling; going to check 15 micro-second On/Off time
1Bh	Memory refresh period 30 micro-second test complete; base 64K memory test about to start
20h	Base 64K memory test started; address line test to be done next
21h	Address line test passed; going to do toggle parity

(continues)

Table 6.3 Continued	
Port 80h code	**Test description**
22h	Toggle parity over; going for sequential data R/W test
23h	Base 64K sequential data R/W test passed; any setup before interrupt vector initialization about to start
24h	Setup required before vector initialization complete; interrupt vector initialization about to begin
25h	Interrupt vector initialization done; going to read I/O port of 8042 for turbo switch (if any)
26h	I/O port of 8042 is read; going to initialize global data for turbo switch
27h	Global data initialization is over; any initialization after interrupt vector to be done next
28h	Initialization after interrupt vector is complete; going for monochrome mode setting
29h	Monochrome mode setting is done; going for color mode setting
2Ah	Color mode setting is done; about to go for toggle parity before optional ROM test
2Bh	Toggle parity over; about to give control for any setup required before optional video ROM check
2Ch	Processing before video ROM control is done; about to look for optional video ROM and give control
2Dh	Optional video ROM control is done; about to give control to do any processing after video ROM returns control
2Eh	Return from processing after the video ROM control; if EGA/VGA not found, then do display memory R/W test
2Fh	EGA/VGA not found; display memory R/W test about to begin
30h	Display memory R/W test passed; about to look for the retrace checking
31h	Display memory R/W test or retrace checking failed; about to do alternate display memory R/W test

Port 80h code	Test description
32h	Alternate display memory R/W test passed; about to look for the alternate display retrace checking
33h	Video display checking over; verification of display type with switch setting and actual card to begin
34h	Verification of display adapter done; display mode to be set next
35h	Display mode set complete; BIOS ROM data area about to be checked
36h	BIOS ROM data area check over; going to set cursor for power-on message
37h	Cursor setting for power-on message ID complete; going to display the power-on message
38h	Power-on message display complete; going to read new cursor position
39h	New cursor position read and saved; going to display the reference string
3Ah	Reference string display is over; going to display the Hit <Esc> message
3Bh	Hit <Esc> message displayed; virtual mode memory test about to start
40h	Preparation for virtual mode test started; going to verify from video memory
41h	Returned after verifying from display memory; going to prepare the descriptor tables
42h	Descriptor tables prepared; going to enter virtual mode for memory test
43h	Entered in virtual mode; going to enable interrupts for diagnostics mode
44h	Interrupts enabled (if diagnostics switch is on); going to initialize data to check memory wrap-around at 0:0
45h	Data initialized; going to check for memory wrap-around at 0:0 and find total system memory size

(continues)

Table 6.3 Continued

Port 80h code	Test description
46h	Memory wrap-around test done; memory-size calculation over; about to go for writing patterns to test memory
47h	Pattern to be test-written in extended memory; going to write patterns in base 640K memory
48h	Patterns written in base memory; going to determine amount of memory below 1M memory
49h	Amount of memory below 1M found and verified; going to determine amount of memory above 1M memory
4Ah	Amount of memory above 1M found and verified; going for BIOS ROM data area check
4Bh	BIOS ROM data area check over; going to check <Esc> and clear memory below 1M for soft reset
4Ch	Memory below 1M cleared (Soft Reset); going to clear memory above 1M
4Dh	Memory above 1M cleared (Soft Reset); going to save the memory size
4Eh	Memory test started (No Soft Reset); about to display the first 64K memory test
4Fh	Memory size display started; will be updated during memory test; going for sequential and random memory test
50h	Memory test below 1M complete; going to adjust memory size for relocation and shadow
51h	Memory size adjusted due to relocation/shadow; memory test above 1M to follow
52h	Memory test above 1M complete; going to prepare to go back to real mode
53h	CPU registers are saved including memory size; going to enter in real mode
54h	Shutdown successful, CPU in real mode; going to restore registers saved during preparation for shutdown

Port 80h code	Test description
55h	Registers restored; going to disable Gate A20 address line
56h	A20 address line disable successful; BIOS ROM data area about to be checked
57h	BIOS ROM data area check halfway; BIOS ROM data area check to be complete
58h	BIOS ROM data area check over; going to clear Hit <ESC> message
59h	Hit <ESC> message cleared; <WAIT...> message displayed; about to start DMA and interrupt controller test
60h	DMA page-register test passed; about to verify from display memory
61h	Display memory verification over; about to go for DMA #1 base register test
62h	DMA #1 base register test passed; about to go for DMA #2 base register test
63h	DMA #2 base register test passed; about to go for BIOS ROM data area check
64h	BIOS ROM data area check halfway; BIOS ROM data area check to be complete
65h	BIOS ROM data area check over; about to program DMA unit 1 and 2
66h	DMA unit 1 and 2 programming over; about to initialize 8259 interrupt controller
67h	8259 initialization over; about to start keyboard test
80h	Keyboard test started, clearing output buffer, checking for stuck key; about to issue keyboard reset command
81h	Keyboard reset error/stuck key found; about to issue keyboard controller interface test command
82h	Keyboard controller interface test over; about to write command byte and initialize circular buffer
83h	Command byte written, global data initialization done; about to check for lock-key

(continues)

Table 6.3   Continued

Port 80h code	Test description
84h	Lock-key checking over; about to check for memory-size mismatch with CMOS
85h	Memory size check done; about to display soft error and check for password or bypass setup
86h	Password checked; about to do programming before setup
87h	Programming before setup complete; going to CMOS setup program
88h	Returned from CMOS setup program and screen is cleared; about to do programming after setup
89h	Programming after setup complete; going to display power-on screen message
8Ah	First screen message displayed; about to display <WAIT...> message
8Bh	<WAIT...> message displayed; about to do main and video BIOS shadow
8Ch	Main and video BIOS shadow successful; Setup options programming after CMOS setup about to start
8Dh	Setup options are programmed, mouse check and initialization to be done next
8Eh	Mouse check and initialization complete; going for hard disk, floppy reset
8Fh	Floppy check returns that floppy is to be initialized; floppy setup to follow
90h	Floppy setup is over; test for hard disk presence to be done
91h	Hard disk presence test over; hard disk setup to follow
92h	Hard disk setup complete; about to go for BIOS ROM data area check
93h	BIOS ROM data area check halfway; BIOS ROM data area check to be complete
94h	BIOS ROM data area check over; going to set base and extended memory size

Port 80h code	Test description
95h	Memory size adjusted due to mouse and hard disk type 47 support; going to verify display memory
96h	Returned after verifying display memory; going to do initialization before C800 optional ROM control
97h	Any initialization before C800 optional ROM control is over; optional ROM check and control to be done next
98h	Optional ROM control is done; about to give control to do any required processing after optional ROM returns control
99h	Any initialization required after optional ROM test over; going to set up timer data area and printer base address
9Ah	Return after setting timer and printer base address; going to set the RS-232 base address
9Bh	Returned after RS-232 base address; going to do any initialization before coprocessor test
9Ch	Required initialization before coprocessor is over; going to initialize the coprocessor next
9Dh	Coprocessor initialized; going to do any initialization after coprocessor test
9Eh	Initialization after coprocessor test is complete; going to check extended keyboard, keyboard ID, and Num Lock
9Fh	Extended keyboard check is done, ID flag set, Num Lock on/off; keyboard ID command to be issued
A0h	Keyboard ID command issued; keyboard ID flag to be reset
A1h	Keyboard ID flag reset; cache memory test to follow
A2h	Cache memory test over; going to display any soft errors
A3h	Soft error display complete; going to set the keyboard typematic rate

(continues)

Table 6.3 Continued	
Port 80h code	**Test description**
A4h	Keyboard typematic rate set; going to program memory wait states
A5h	Memory wait states programming over; screen to be cleared next
A6h	Screen cleared; going to enable parity and NMI
A7h	NMI and parity enabled; going to do any initialization required before giving control to optional ROM at E000
A8h	Initialization before E000 ROM control over; E000 ROM to get control next
A9h	Returned from E000 ROM control; going to do any initialization required after E000 optional ROM control
AAh	Initialization after E000 optional ROM control is over; going to display the system configuration
00h	System configuration is displayed; going to give control to Int 19h boot loader

Award BIOS Port 80h POST Codes

Table 6.4 provides information on the majority of Award POST codes displayed during the POST sequence. These POST codes are output to I/O port address 80h. Although this chart specifically lists all the POST codes output by the Award Modular BIOS, Version 3.1, the codes are valid also for these Award Modular BIOS types:

- PC/XT Version 3.0 and greater

- AT Version 3.02 and greater

Not all these POST codes apply to all of the BIOS types. Note that the POST tests do not necessarily execute in the numeric order shown:

The POST sequence may vary depending on the BIOS.

Table 6.4 Award BIOS Port 80h POST Codes	
Port 80h code	**Code meaning**
01h	Processor Test 1. Processor status verification. Tests the following processor-status flags; carry, zero, sign, and overflow. The BIOS sets each flag, verifies that they are set, and turns each flag off and verifies that it is off. Failure of a flag causes a fatal error.
02h	Determine POST Type. This test determines whether the status of the system is manufacturing or normal. The status can be set by a physical jumper on some motherboards. If the status is normal, the POST continues through and, assuming no errors, boot is attempted. If manufacturing POST is installed, POST is run in a continuous loop, and boot is not attempted.
03h	8042 Keyboard Controller. Tests controller by sending TEST_KBRD command (AAh) and verifying that controller reads command.
04h	8042 Keyboard Controller. Verifies that keyboard controller returned AAh, sent in test 3.
05h	Get Manufacturing Status. The last test in the manufacturing cycle. If test 2 found the status to be manufacturing, this POST triggers a reset and POSTs 1 through 5 are repeated continuously.
06h	Initialize Chips. POST 06h performs these functions: disables color and mono video, disables parity circuits, disables DMA (8237) chips, resets math co-processor, initializes timer 1 (8255), clears DMA chip, clears all page registers, and clears CMOS shutdown byte.

(continues)

Table 6.4 Continued	
Port 80h code	**Code meaning**
07h	Processor Test 2. Reads, writes, and verifies all CPU registers except SS, SP, and BP with data pattern FF and 00.
08h	Initialize CMOS Timer. Updates timer cycle normally.
09h	EPROM Checksum. Checksums EPROM; test failed if sum not equal to 0. Also checksums sign-on message.
0Ah	Initialize Video Interface. Initializes video controller register 6845 to the following: 80 characters per row 25 rows per screen 8/14 scan lines per row for mono/color First scan line of cursor 6/11 Last scan line of cursor 7/12 Reset display offset to 0
0Bh	Test Timer (8254) Channel 0. These three timer tests verify that the 8254 timer chip is functioning properly.
0Ch	Test Timer (8254) Channel 1.
0Dh	Test Timer (8254) Channel 2.
0Eh	Test CMOS Shutdown Byte. Uses a walking bit algorithm to check interface to CMOS circuit.
0Fh	Test Extended CMOS. On motherboards with chipsets that support extended CMOS configurations, such as Chips & Technologies, the BIOS tables of CMOS information are used to configure the chip set. These chip sets have an extended storage mechanism that enables the user to save a desired system configuration after the power is turned off. A checksum is used to verify the validity of the extended storage and, if valid, permit the information to be loaded into extended CMOS RAM.

Port 80h code	Code meaning
10h	Test DMA Channel 0. These three functions initialize the DMA (direct memory access) chip and then test the chip using an AA, 55, FF, 00 pattern. Port addresses are used to check the address circuit to DMA page registers.
11h	DMA Channel 1.
12h	DMA Page Registers.
13h	Keyboard Controller. Tests keyboard controller interface.
14h	Test Memory Refresh. RAM must be refreshed periodically to keep the memory from decaying. This function ensures that the memory-refresh function is working properly.
15h	First 64K of System Memory. An extensive parity test is performed on the first 64K of system memory. This memory is used by the BIOS.
16h	Interrupt Vector Table. Sets up and loads interrupt vector tables in memory for use by the 8259 PIC chip.
17h	Video I/O Operations. This function initializes the video, either CGA, MDA, EGA, or VGA. If a CGA or MDA adapter is installed, the video is initialized by the system BIOS. If the system BIOS detects an EGA or VGA adapter, the option ROM BIOS installed on the video adapter is used to initialize and set up the video.
18h	Video Memory. Tests memory for CGA and MDA video boards. This test is not performed by the system BIOS on EGA or VGA video adapters—the board's own EGA or VGA BIOS ensures that it is functioning properly.

(continues)

Table 6.4 Continued	
Port 80h code	Code meaning
19h	Test 8259 Mask Bits - Channel 1. These two tests verify 8259 masked interrupts by alternately turning the interrupt lines off and on. Unsuccessful completion generates a fatal error.
1Ah	8259 Mask Bits - Channel 2.
1Bh	CMOS Battery Level. Verifies that the battery status bit is set to 1. A 0 value can indicate a bad battery or some other problem, such as bad CMOS.
1Ch	CMOS Checksum. This function tests the CMOS checksum data (located at 2Eh, and 2Fh) and extended CMOS checksum, if present, to be sure that they are valid.
1Dh	Configuration from CMOS. If the CMOS checksum is good, the values are used to configure the system.
1Eh	System Memory. The system memory size is determined by writing to addresses from 0K to 640K, starting at 0 and continuing until an address does not respond. Memory size value then is compared to the CMOS value to ensure that they are the same. If they are different, a flag is set, and, at the end of POST an error message is displayed.
1Fh	Found System Memory. Tests memory from 64K to the top of the memory found by writing the pattern FFAA and 5500, and then reading the pattern back, byte by byte, and verifying that it is correct.
20h	Stuck 8259 Interrupt Bits. These three tests verify the functionality of the 8259 interrupt controller.

Port 80h code	Code meaning
21h	Stuck NMI Bits (Parity or I/O Channel Check).
22h	8259 Function.
23h	Protected Mode. Verifies protected mode: 8086 virtual mode as well as 8086 page mode. Protected mode ensures that any data about to be written to extended memory (above 1M) is checked to ensure that it is suitable for storage there.
24h	Extended Memory. This function sizes memory above 1M by writing to addresses starting at 1M and continuing to 16M on 286 and 386SX systems, and to 64M on 386 systems until there is no response. This process determines the total extended memory, which is compared with CMOS to ensure that the values are the same. If the values are different, a flag is set and at the end of POST an error message is displayed.
25h	Found Extended Memory. This function tests extended memory using virtual 8086 paging mode and writing an FFFF, AA55, 0000 pattern.
26h	Protected Mode Exceptions. This function tests other aspects of protected mode operations.
27h	Cache Control or Shadow RAM. Tests for shadow RAM and cache controller (386 and 486 only) functionality. Systems with CGA and MDA adapters indicate that video shadow RAM is enabled, even though there is no BIOS ROM to shadow (this is normal).
28h	8242. Optional Intel 8242/8248 keyboard controller detection and support.
29h	Reserved.

(continues)

Table 6.4	Continued
Port 80h code	Code meaning
2Ah	Initialize Keyboard. Initialize keyboard controller.
2Bh	Floppy Drive and Controller. Initializes floppy disk drive controller and any drives present.
2Ch	Detect and Initialize Serial Ports. Initializes any serial ports present.
2Dh	Detect and Initialize Parallel Ports. Initializes any parallel ports present.
2Eh	Initialize Hard Drive and Controller. Initializes hard drive controller and any drives present.
2Fh	Detect and Initialize Math Coprocessor. Initializes math coprocessor.
30h	Reserved.
31h	Detect and Initialize Option ROMs. Initializes any option ROMs present from C800h to EFFFh.
3Bh	Initialize Secondary Cache with OPTi chipset. Initializes secondary cache controller for systems based on the OPTi chipset (486 only).
CAh	Micronics Cache Initialization. Detects and initializes Micronics cache controller if present.
CCh	NMI Handler Shutdown. Detects untrapped Non-Maskable Interrupts during boot.
EEh	Unexpected Processor Exception.
FFh	Boot Attempt. When the POST is complete, if all the system components and peripherals are initialized, and if no error flags were set (such as memory size error), then the system attempts to boot.

Phoenix BIOS Audio and Port 80h POST Codes

Table 6.5 is a list of POST fatal errors that may be reported by the Phoenix BIOS. Table 6.6 is a list of nonfatal errors. Fatal errors halt the system and prevent any further processing from occurring; nonfatal errors are less severe.

Table 6.5 Phoenix BIOS Fatal System-Board Errors		
Beep code	Code at Port 80h	Description
None	01h	CPU register test in progress
1-1-3	02h	CMOS write/read failure
1-1-4	03h	ROM BIOS checksum failure
1-2-1	04h	Programmable interval timer failure
1-2-2	05h	DMA initialization failure
1-2-3	06h	DMA page register write/read failure
1-3-1	08h	RAM refresh verification failure
None	09h	First 64K RAM test in progress
1-3-3	0Ah	First 64K RAM chip or data line failure, multibit
1-3-4	0Bh	First 64K RAM odd/even logic failure
1-4-1	0Ch	Address line failure first 64K RAM
1-4-2	0Dh	Parity failure first 64K RAM
2-1-1	10h	Bit 0 first 64K RAM failure
2-1-2	11h	Bit 1 first 64K RAM failure
2-1-3	12h	Bit 2 first 64K RAM failure
2-1-4	13h	Bit 3 first 64K RAM failure
2-2-1	14h	Bit 4 first 64K RAM failure
2-2-2	15h	Bit 5 first 64K RAM failure
2-2-3	16h	Bit 6 first 64K RAM failure

(continues)

Table 6.5 Continued

Beep code	Code at Port 80h	Description
2-2-4	17h	Bit 7 first 64K RAM failure
2-3-1	18h	Bit 8 first 64K RAM failure
2-3-2	19h	Bit 9 first 64K RAM failure
2-3-3	1Ah	Bit 10 first 64K RAM failure
2-3-4	1Bh	Bit 11 first 64K RAM failure
2-4-1	1Ch	Bit 12 first 64K RAM failure
2-4-2	1Dh	Bit 13 first 64K RAM failure
2-4-3	1Eh	Bit 14 first 64K RAM failure
2-4-4	1Fh	Bit 15 first 64K RAM failure
3-1-1	20h	Slave DMA register failure
3-1-2	21h	Master DMA register failure
3-1-3	22h	Master interrupt mask register failure
3-1-4	23h	Slave interrupt mask register failure
None	25h	Interrupt vector loading in progress
3-2-4	27h	Keyboard controller test failure
None	28h	CMOS power failure/checksum calculation in progress
None	29h	Screen configuration validation in progress
3-3-4	2Bh	Screen initialization failure
3-4-1	2Ch	Screen retrace failure
3-4-2	2Dh	Search for video ROM in progress
None	2Eh	Screen running with video ROM
None	30h	Screen operable
None	31h	Monochrome monitor operable

Beep code	Code at Port 80h	Description
None	32h	Color monitor (40 column) operable
None	33h	Color monitor (80 column) operable

Table 6.6 Nonfatal System-Board Errors

Beep code	Code at Port 80h	Description
4-2-1	34h	Timer tick interrupt test in progress or failure
4-2-2	35h	Shutdown test in progress or failure
4-2-3	36h	Gate A20 failure
4-2-4	37h	Unexpected interrupt in protected mode
4-3-1	38h	RAM test in progress or address failure > FFFFh
4-3-3	3Ah	Interval timer Channel 2 test or failure
4-3-4	3Bh	Time-of-day clock test or failure
4-4-1	3Ch	Serial port test or failure
4-4-2	3Dh	Parallel port test or failure
4-4-3	3Eh	Math coprocessor test or failure
low 1-1-2	41h	System-board select failure
low 1-1-3	42h	Extended CMOS RAM failure

low *means that a lower-pitched beep precedes the other tones.*

Hewlett-Packard POST and Diagnostics Error Codes

Table 6.7 Hewlett-Packard 386/N & 486N POST Error Codes	
Code	**Description**
000F	Microprocessor test error. Check CPU and system board.
001x	ROM BIOS memory error. Check ROM BIOS and system board.
008x	Memory error in address range C000-C7FF. Check system board video ROM and/or video adapter.
009x, 00Ax, 00Bx	Memory error in address range C800-DFFF. Check Adapter ROMs.
00C0	Memory error in address range E000-EFFF. Check Adapters or System Board LAN Boot ROM.
011x	CMOS register test error. Real Time Clock (RTC) is not working correctly.
0120, 0130	CMOS Real Time Clock (RTC) failed or corrupted. Check Battery.
0240	CMOS system configuration information corrupted by power failure. Check Battery.
0250	CMOS system configuration information does not match system. Run Setup, Check Battery.
0241, 0280	CMOS power failure, check Battery.
02C0, 02C1	EEPROM master configuration information corrupted or not set correctly. Check system board configuration switches. If the fifth switch (Clear EEPROM) is ON, set it to the OFF position, reset the system, and run Setup to reenter the system configuration.
030x, 0311, 0312, 03E0, 03E1, 03E2, 03E3, 03E4, 03EC	Keyboard/mouse controller failed to respond to a command. Check system board.

Code	Description
034x, 035x	Keyboard failed to respond during keyboard test. Check Keyboard cable, Keyboard, system board.
03E5, 03E6, 03E7, 03E8, 03E9, 03EA, 03EB	Mouse test failure, check mouse and cable.
0401	Protected Mode switch failure, check system board.
0503, 0505	Serial Port failure or Configuration error. Check setup and system board.
0543, 0545	Parallel port failure or Configuration error. Check setup and system board.
0506, 0546	Serial or Parallel port conflict, check configuration.
06xx	Stuck Key failure, xx = the Scan Code of the stuck key.
0800	System board LAN Boot ROM conflict. Check memory address configurations.
0801	Cannot find LAN Boot ROM declared in Setup, check configuration, Boot ROM.
110x, 1200, 1201	System timer failure, check the system board.

20xA	SIMM size mismatch, interleaved memory disabled, check SIMM installation in the affected bank or banks as identified below:
	
	 201A = A 205A = A,C 209A = A,D
	      20DA = A,C,D
	 202A = B 206A = B,C 20AA = B,D
	      20EA = B,C,D
	 203A = A,B 207A = A,B,C 20BA = A,B,D
	      20FA = A,B,C,D
	 204A = C 208A = D 20CA = C,D

21xx, 22xx	DMA channel failure, check system board.
4F01, 4F02, 4F03, 4F04, 4F05, 4F06, 4F07, 4F08	SIMM memory error, check the defective SIMM as identified below: 4F01 = Bank A, slot 1 4F05 = Bank C, slot 1 4F02 = Bank A, slot 2 4F06 = Bank C, slot 2 4F03 = Bank B, slot 1 4F07 = Bank D, slot 1 4F04 = Bank B, slot 2 4F08 = Bank D, slot 2
61xx	Memory Address Line failure, check SIMMs and system board.
63xx	Memory Parity Error, check Memory and system board.

(continues)

Table 6.7   Continued

Code	Description
6500	ROM BIOS shadowing error, check system memory, ROM BIOS
6510	Video ROM Shadowing error, check system memory, Video ROM BIOS.
6520	LAN Option ROM Shadowing error, check system memory, LAN Option ROM.
65A0, 65B0, 65C0, 65D0, 65E0, 65F0	ROM BIOS Shadowing error, memory segment failure, check system memory in the segment indicated by the third digit, A = A000, B = B000, C = C000, D = D000, E = E000, F = F000.
66xx	ROM BIOS Shadowing error, check configuration or ROM checksum.
7xxx	Interrupt failure, check system board.
8003, 8006	Hard drive configuration error, parameters do not match drive, check configuration and cabling.
8004, 8007	CMOS hard disk configuration error, check drive and battery.
800D, 8010, 8012, 8020, 8021, 8038, 803C, 8040, 8045	Hard Disk Controller timeout (12 seconds without responding), check drive and controller.
800E	Hard Disk Boot failure, check cables, disk drive failure.
800F	Hard Disk CMOS configuration does not match drive.
8011, 8013, 8030, 8039, 803A, 803B, 8041, 8042, 8043, 8044, 8049, 804B, 8310, 8311, 8313	Hard Drive does not respond to commands, check drive, controller and cables.
8048, 804A	System failed to identify installed hard disk drive, check setup and cables.

Code	Description
8050	System failed to identify installed hard disk controller, check configuration.
8400	Hard disk drive boot sector was corrupted or could not be loaded, check drive partitions.
9x00, 9x01, 9x02, 9x03, 9x04, 9x05, 9x06, 9x07, 9x08, 9x09	Floppy drive error, check drives and cables. Drive "x" not responding, where: X = 0 for drive 0 X = 1 for drive 1 X = 2 for drive 2 X = 3 for drive 3 Check cables and drives.
9x10, 9x0A	CMOS floppy configuration error, where: X = 0 for drive 0 X = 1 for drive 1 X = 2 for drive 2 X = 3 for drive 3
A00x	Math Coprocessor error, check coprocessor and system board.
B300	Memory cache controller error.
Exxx	Memory adapter error, check adapters or SIMMs.

IBM POST and Diagnostics Display Error Codes

When an IBM or compatible system is first powered on, the system runs a Power-On Self Test (POST). If errors are encountered during the POST, the errors are displayed in the form of a code number and possibly some additional text. When you are running the IBM Advanced Diagnostics, which you can purchase from IBM or which is included on many of the PS/2 Reference Diskettes, similar codes are displayed if errors are encountered during the tests. IBM has developed a system in which the first part of the error code indicates the device the error involves, and the last part indicates the exact error meaning. One of the biggest problems with these error codes is that IBM does not publish a complete list of the errors in any single publication; instead, it details specific error codes in many different publications. I have researched these codes for many years; tables 6.8 and 6.9 represent all the codes I have found meanings for. These codes have been selected from a number of sources, including all of IBM's technical-reference and hardware-maintenance and service manuals.

When diagnostics are run, any code ending in 00 indicates that the particular test has passed. For example, an error code of 1700 indicates that the hard disk diagnostics tests have passed.

After completing the Power-On Self Test (POST), an audio code indicates either a normal condition or that one of several errors has occurred. Table 6.8 lists the audio codes for IBM systems, and table 6.9 lists the IBM POST and diagnostics error codes.

Table 6.8   IBM POST Audio Error Codes

Audio code	Sound graph	Fault domain
1 short beep	•	Normal POST - system OK
2 short beeps	••	POST error - error code on CRT
No beep		Power supply, system board
Continuous beep	———	Power supply, system board
Repeating short beeps	••••••	Power supply, system board
1 long, 1 short beep	—•	System board
1 long, 2 short beeps	—••	Display adapter (MDA, CGA)
1 long, 3 short beeps	—•••	Enhanced Graphics Adapter (EGA)
3 long beeps	– – –	3270 keyboard card

Table 6.9	IBM POST and Diagnostics Error-Code List
Code	**Description**
1xx	**System-Board errors**
101	System-board interrupt failure (Unexpected interrupt)
102	System-board timer failure
102	PS/2; real-time clock (RTC)/64 byte CMOS RAM test failure
103	System-board timer interrupt failure
103	PS/2; 2K CMOS RAM extension test failure
104	System-board protected mode failure
105	System-board 8042 Keyboard Controller command failure
106	System-board converting logic test failure
107	System-board Non-Maskable Interrupt (NMI) test failure, Hot NMI
108	System-board timer bus test failure
109	System-board memory select error, Low MB chip select test failed
110	PS/2 system-board parity check error (PARITY CHECK 1)
111	PS/2 I/O channel (bus) parity check error (PARITY CHECK 2)
112	PS/2 Micro Channel Arbitration error; watchdog time-out (NMI error)
113	PS/2 Micro Channel Arbitration error; DMA arbitration time-out (NMI error)
114	PS/2 external ROM checksum error
115	Cache parity error, ROM checksum error or DMA error
116	System board port read/write failure
118	System board parity or L2-cache error during previous power-on
119	"E" Step level 82077 (floppy controller) and 2.88M drive installed (not supported)

(continues)

Table 6.9 Continued

Code	Description
120	Microprocessor self-test error
121	256K ROM checksum error (second 128KB bank)
121	Unexpected hardware interrupts occurred
131	PC system-board Cassette port wrap test failure
131	Direct memory access (DMA) compatibility registers error
132	Direct memory access (DMA) extended registers error
133	Direct memory access (DMA) verify logic error
134	Direct memory access (DMA) arbitration logic error
151	Battery or CMOS RAM failure
152	Real-time clock or CMOS RAM failure
160	PS/2 system-board ID not recognized
161	CMOS configuration empty (dead battery)
162	CMOS checksum error or adapter ID mismatch
163	CMOS error; date and time not set (Clock not updating)
164	Memory size error; CMOS setting does not match memory
165	PS/2 Micro Channel adapter ID and CMOS mismatch
166	PS/2 Micro Channel adapter time-out error, Card busy
167	PS/2 CMOS clock not updating
168	CMOS configuration error; math coprocessor
169	System board and processor card configuration mismatch, run Setup
170	ASCII setup conflict error
170	PC Convertible; LCD not in use when suspended

Code	Description
171	Rolling-bit-test failure on CMOS shutdown address byte
171	PC Convertible; base 128K checksum failure
172	Rolling-bit-test failure on NVRAM diagnostic byte
172	PC Convertible; diskette active when suspended
173	Bad CMOS/NVRAM checksum
173	PC Convertible; real-time clock RAM verification error
174	Bad configuration
174	PC Convertible; LCD configuration changed
175	Bad EEPROM CRC #1
175	PC Convertible; LCD alternate mode failed
176	Tamper evident
177	Bad PAP (Privileged-Access Password) CRC
177	Bad EEPROM
178	Bad EEPROM
179	NVRAM error log full
180x	Sub Address data error, x = Slot number, which caused the error
181	Unsupported configurations
182	Privileged-access switch (JMP2) is not in the write-enable position
183	PAP is needed to boot from the system programs
183	Privileged-access password required
184	Bad Power On Password checksum - Erase it
184	Bad power-on password
185	Bad startup sequence
186	Password protection hardware error
187	Serial number error
188	Bad EEPROM checksum CRC #2
189	Excessive incorrect password attempts
191	82385 cache controller test failure
194	System-board memory error

(continues)

Code	Description
Table 6.9	**Continued**
199	User indicated INSTALLED DEVICES list is not correct
2xx	**Memory (RAM) errors**
20x	Memory error
201	Memory test failure, error location may be displayed
202	Memory address error; lines 00-15
203	Memory address error; lines 16-23 (ISA) or 16-31 (MCA)
204	Memory remapped due to error (run diagnostics again)
205	Base 128K memory error; memory remapped
207	ROM failure
210	System board memory Parity error
211	PS/2 memory; base 64K on system-board failed
212	Watchdog timeout error (reported by NMI interrupt handler)
213	DMA bus arbitration timeout (reported by NMI interrupt handler)
215	PS/2 memory; base 64K on daughter/SIP 2 failed
216	PS/2 memory; base 64K on daughter/SIP 1 failed
221	PS/2 memory; ROM to RAM copy failed (ROM shadowing)
225	PS/2 memory; wrong-speed memory on system board, unsupported SIMM
230	Overlapping adapter and planar memory (Family 1)
231	Non-contiguous adapter memory installed (Family 1)
231	2/4-16MB Enhanced 386 memory adapter; memory module 1 failed
235	Stuck data line on memory module, microprocessor or system board
241	2/4-16MB Enhanced 386 memory adapter; memory module 2 failed
251	2/4-16MB Enhanced 386 memory adapter; memory module 3 failed

Code	Description
3xx	**Keyboard errors**
301	Keyboard reset or stuck key failure (SS 301, SS = Scan Code in hex)
302	System unit keylock is locked
303	Keyboard-to-system board interface error, keyboard controller failure
304	Keyboard or system-board error; keyboard clock high
305	Keyboard +5v dc error; PS/2 keyboard fuse (on system board) error
306	Unsupported keyboard attached
341	Keyboard error
342	Keyboard cable error
343	Keyboard LED card or cable failure
365	Keyboard LED card or cable failure
366	Keyboard interface cable failure
367	Keyboard LED card or cable failure
4xx	**Monochrome Display Adapter (MDA) errors**
4xx	**PS/2 System-Board Parallel Port errors**
401	Monochrome memory, horizontal sync frequency, or video test failure
401	PS/2 system-board parallel port failure
408	User indicated display attributes failure
416	User indicated character set failure
424	User indicated 80525 mode failure
432	Parallel port test failure; Monochrome Display Adapter
5xx	**Color Graphics Adapter (CGA) errors**
501	CGA memory, horizontal sync frequency, or video test failure
503	CGA adapter controller failed
508	User indicated display attribute failure

(continues)

Table 6.9 Continued

Code	Description
516	User indicated character set failure
524	User indicated 80x25 mode failure
532	User indicated 40x25 mode failure
540	User indicated 320x200 graphics mode failure
548	User indicated 640x200 graphics mode failure
556	User indicated light-pen test failed
564	User indicated paging test failure
6xx	**Floppy Drive/Controller errors**
601	Floppy drive/controller Power-On Self Test failure, Disk drive or controller error
602	Diskette boot sector is not valid
603	. Diskette size error
604	Non-media sense
605	Diskette drive locked
606	Diskette verify test failure
607	Write protect error
608	Drive command error
610	Diskette initialization failure; track 0 bad
611	Drive time-out error
612	Controller chip (NEC) error
613	Direct memory access (DMA) error
614	Direct memory access (DMA) boundary overrun error
615	Drive index timing error
616	Drive speed error
621	Drive seek error
622	Drive cyclic redundancy check (CRC) error
623	Sector not found error
624	Address mark error
625	Controller chip (NEC) seek error
626	Diskette data compare error
627	Diskette change error

Code	Description
628	Diskette removed
630	Index stuck high; Drive A:
631	Index stuck low; Drive A:
632	Track 0 stuck off; Drive A:
633	Track 0 stuck on; Drive A:
640	Index stuck high; Drive B:
641	Index stuck low; Drive B:
642	Track 0 stuck off; Drive B:
643	Track 0 stuck on; Drive B:
645	No index pulse
646	Drive track 0 detection failed
647	No transitions on read data line
648	Format test failed
649	Incorrect media type in drive
650	Drive speed error
651	Format failure
652	Verify failure
653	Read failure
654	Write failure
655	Controller error
656	Drive failure
657	Write protect stuck protected
658	Changeline stuck changed
659	Write protect stuck unprotected
660	Changeline stuck unchanged
7xx	**Math Coprocessor errors**
701	Math coprocessor presence/initialization error
702	Exception errors test failure
703	Rounding test failure
704	Arithmetic test 1 failure
705	Arithmetic test 2 failure
706	Arithmetic test 3 (80387 only) failure
707	Combination test failure

(continues)

Table 6.9 Continued

Code	Description
708	Integer load/store test failure
709	Equivalent expressions errors
710	Exception (interrupt) errors
711	Save state (FSAVE) errors
712	Protected mode test failure
713	Special test (voltage/temperature sensitivity) failure
9xx	**Parallel Printer Adapter errors**
901	Printer adapter data register latch error
902	Printer adapter control register latch error
903	Printer adapter register address decode error
904	Printer adapter address decode error
910	Status line(s) wrap connector error
911	Status line bit 8 wrap error
912	Status line bit 7 wrap error
913	Status line bit 6 wrap error
914	Status line bit 5 wrap error
915	Status line bit 4 wrap error
916	Printer adapter interrupt wrap error
917	Unexpected printer adapter interrupt
92x	Feature register error
10xx	**Alternate Parallel Printer Adapter errors**
1001	Printer adapter data register latch error
1002	Printer adapter control register latch error
1003	Printer adapter register address decode error
1004	Printer adapter address decode error
1010	Status line(s) wrap connector error
1011	Status line bit 8 wrap error
1012	Status line bit 7 wrap error
1013	Status line bit 6 wrap error

Code	Description
1014	Status line bit 5 wrap error
1015	Status line bit 4 wrap error
1016	Printer adapter interrupt wrap error
1017	Unexpected printer adapter interrupt
102x	Feature register error
11xx	**Primary Async Communications (serial COM1:) errors**
1101	16450/16550 chip error, Serial port A error
1102	Card selected feedback error
1102	PC Convertible internal modem test failed
1103	Port 102h register test failure
1103	PC Convertible internal modem dial tone test 1 failed
1104	PC Convertible internal modem dial tone test 2 failed
1106	Serial option cannot be put to sleep
1107	Cable error
1108	Interrupt request (IRQ) 3 error
1109	Interrupt request (IRQ) 4 error
1110	16450/16550 chip register failure
1111	Internal wrap test of 16450/16550 chip modem control line failure
1112	External wrap test of 16450/16550 chip modem control line failure
1113	16450/16550 chip transmit error
1114	16450/16550 chip receive error
1115	16450/16550 chip receive error; data not equal to transmit data
1116	16450/16550 chip interrupt function error
1117	16450/16550 chip baud rate test failure

(continues)

Table 6.9	Continued
Code	**Description**
1118	16450/16550 chip receive external data wrap test failure
1119	16550 chip first-in first-out (FIFO) buffer failure
1120	Interrupt enable register error; all bits cannot be set
1121	Interrupt enable register error; all bits cannot be reset
1122	Interrupt pending; stuck on
1123	Interrupt ID register; stuck on
1124	Modem control register error; all bits cannot be set
1125	Modem control register error; all bits cannot be reset
1126	Modem status register error; all bits cannot be set
1127	Modem status register error; all bits cannot be reset
1128	Interrupt ID error
1129	Cannot force overrun error
1130	No modem status interrupt
1131	Invalid interrupt pending
1132	No data ready
1133	No data available interrupt
1134	No transmit holding interrupt
1135	No interrupts
1136	No received sine status interrupt
1137	No receive data available
1138	Transmit holding register not empty
1139	No modem status interrupt
1140	Transmit holding register not empty
1141	No interrupts
1142	No interrupt 4
1143	No interrupt 3
1144	No data transferred
1145	Maximum baud rate error
1146	Minimum baud rate error
1148	Time-out error
1149	Invalid data returned
1150	Modem status register error

Code	Description
1151	No data set ready and delta data set ready
1152	No data set ready
1153	No delta data set ready
1154	Modem status register not clear
1155	No clear to send and delta clear to send
1156	No clear to send
1157	No delta clear to send
12xx	**Alternate Async Communications (Serial COM2:, COM3:, and COM4:) errors**
1201	16450/16550 chip error
1202	Card selected feedback error
1203	Port 102h register test failure
1206	Serial option cannot be put to sleep
1207	Cable error
1208	Interrupt request (IRQ) 3 error
1209	Interrupt request (IRQ) 4 error
1210	16450/16550 chip register failure
1211	Internal wrap test of 16450/16550 chip modem control line failure
1212	External wrap test of 16450/16550 chip modem control line failure
1213	16450/16550 chip transmit error
1214	16450/16550 chip receive error
1215	16450/16550 chip receive error; data not equal to transmit data
1216	16450/16550 chip interrupt function error
1217	16450/16550 chip baud rate test failure
1218	16450/16550 chip receive external data wrap test failure
1219	16550 chip first-in first-out (FIFO) buffer failure
1220	Interrupt enable register error; all bits cannot be set

(continues)

Table 6.9	Continued
Code	**Description**
1221	Interrupt enable register error; all bits cannot be reset
1222	Interrupt pending; stuck on
1223	Interrupt ID register; stuck on
1224	Modem control register error; all bits cannot be set
1225	Modem control register error; all bits cannot be reset
1226	Modem status register error; all bits cannot be set
1227	Modem Status Register error; all bits cannot be reset
1228	Interrupt ID error
1229	Cannot force overrun error
1230	No modem status interrupt
1231	Invalid interrupt pending
1232	No data ready
1233	No data available interrupt
1234	No transmit holding interrupt
1235	No interrupts
1236	No received sine status interrupt
1237	No receive data available
1238	Transmit holding register not empty
1239	No modem status interrupt
1240	Transmit holding register not empty
1241	No interrupts
1242	No interrupt 4
1243	No interrupt 3
1244	No data transferred
1245	Maximum baud rate error
1246	Minimum baud rate error
1248	Time-out error
1249	Invalid data returned
1250	Modem status register error
1251	No data set ready and delta data set ready
1252	No data set ready

Code	Description
1253	No delta data set ready
1254	Modem status register not clear
1255	No clear to send and delta clear to send
1256	No clear to send
1257	No delta clear to send
13xx	**Game Control Adapter errors**
1301	Game control adapter test failure
1302	Joystick test failure
14xx	**Matrix Printer errors**
1401	Printer test failure
1402	Printer not ready error
1403	Printer no-paper error
1404	System-board time-out
1405	Parallel adapter failure
1406	Printer presence test failed
15xx	**Synchronous Data Link Control (SDLC) communications adapter errors**
1501	SDLC adapter test failure
1510	8255 Port B failure
1511	8255 Port A failure
1512	8255 Port C failure
1513	8253 Timer #1 did not reach terminal count
1514	8253 Timer #1 stuck on
1515	8253 Timer #0 did not reach terminal count
1516	8253 Timer #0 stuck on
1517	8253 Timer #2 did not reach terminal count
1518	8253 Timer #2 stuck on
1519	8273 Port B error
1520	8273 Port A error
1521	8273 command/read time-out
1522	Interrupt Level 4 failure
1523	Ring Indicate stuck on

(continues)

Table 6.9 Continued

Code	Description
1524	Receive Clock stuck on
1525	Transmit Clock stuck on
1526	Test Indicate stuck on
1527	Ring Indicate not on
1528	Receive Clock not on
1529	Transmit Clock not on
1530	Test Indicate not on
1531	Data Set Ready not on
1532	Carrier Detect not on
1533	Clear to Send not on
1534	Data Set Ready stuck on
1535	Carrier Detect stuck on
1536	Clear to Send stuck on
1537	Interrupt level 3 failure
1538	Receive interrupt results error
1539	Wrap data compare error
1540	Direct memory access channel 1 error
1541	Direct memory access channel 1 error
1542	8273 error checking or status reporting error
1547	Stray Interrupt level 4
1548	Stray Interrupt level 3
1549	Interrupt presentation sequence time-out
16xx	**Display Station Emulation Adapter (DSEA) errors (5520, 525x)**
1604	DSEA or Twinaxial network error
1608	DSEA or Twinaxial network error
1624	DSEA error
1634	DSEA error
1644	DSEA error
1652	DSEA error
1654	DSEA error
1658	DSEA error

Code	Description
1662	DSEA interrupt level error
1664	DSEA error
1668	DSEA interrupt level error
1669	DSEA diagnostics error; use 3.0 or higher
1674	DSEA diagnostics error; use 3.0 or higher
1674	DSEA station address error
1684	DSEA device address error
1688	DSEA device address error
17xx	**ST-506/412 Fixed Disk and Controller errors**
1701	Fixed disk general POST error
1702	Drive/controller time-out error
1703	Drive seek error
1704	Controller failed
1705	Drive sector not found error
1706	Write fault error
1707	Drive track 0 error
1708	Head select error
1709	Error-correction code (ECC) error
1710	Sector buffer overrun
1711	Bad address mark
1712	Internal controller diagnostics failure
1713	Data compare error
1714	Drive not ready
1715	Track 0 indicator failure
1716	Diagnostics cylinder errors
1717	Surface read errors
1718	Hard drive type error
1720	Bad diagnostics cylinder
1726	Data compare error
1730	Controller error
1731	Controller error
1732	Controller error
1733	BIOS Undefined error return

(continues)

Table 6.9	Continued
Code	**Description**
1735	Bad command error
1736	Data corrected error
1737	Bad track error
1738	Bad sector error
1739	Bad initialization error
1740	Bad sense error
1750	Drive verify failure
1751	Drive read failure
1752	Drive write failure
1753	Drive random read test failure
1754	Drive seek test failure
1755	Controller failure
1756	Controller error-correction code (ECC) test failure
1757	Controller head select failure
1780	Seek failure; drive 0
1781	Seek failure; drive 1
1782	Controller test failure
1790	Diagnostic cylinder read error; drive 0
1791	Diagnostic cylinder read error; drive 1
18xx	**I/O Expansion Unit errors**
1801	I/O expansion unit POST failure
1810	Enable/disable failure
1811	Extender card wrap test failure; disabled
1812	High-order address lines failure; disabled
1813	Wait state failure; disabled
1814	Enable/disable could not be set on
1815	Wait state failure; disabled
1816	Extender card wrap test failure; enabled
1817	High-order address lines failure; enabled
1818	Disable not functioning
1819	Wait request switch not set correctly

Code	Description
1820	Receiver card wrap test failure
1821	Receiver high order address lines failure
19xx	**3270 PC Attachment Card errors**
20xx	**Binary Synchronous Communications (BSC) Adapter errors**
2001	BSC adapter test failure
2010	8255 Port A failure
2011	8255 Port B failure
2012	8255 Port C failure
2013	8253 Timer #1 did not reach terminal count
2014	8253 Timer #1 stuck on
2015	8253 Timer #2 did not reach terminal count
2016	8253 Timer #2 output stuck on
2017	8251 data set ready failed to come on
2018	8251 clear to send not sensed
2019	8251 data SET ready stuck on
2020	8251 clear to send stuck on
2021	8251 hardware reset failure
2022	8251 software reset failure
2023	8251 software "error reset" failure
2024	8251 transmit ready did not come on
2025	8251 receive ready did not come on
2026	8251 could not force "overrun" error status
2027	Interrupt failure; no timer interrupt
2028	Interrupt failure; transmit, replace card or planar
2029	Interrupt failure; transmit, replace card
2030	Interrupt failure; receive, replace card or planar
2031	Interrupt failure; receive, replace card
2033	Ring indicate stuck on
2034	Receive clock stuck on
2035	Transmit clock stuck on
2036	Test indicate stuck on

(continues)

Table 6.9   Continued

Code	Description
2037	Ring indicate stuck on
2038	Receive clock not on
2039	Transmit clock not on
2040	Test indicate not on
2041	Data set ready not on
2042	Carrier detect not on
2043	Clear to send not on
2044	Data set ready stuck on
2045	Carrier detect stuck on
2046	Clear to send stuck on
2047	Unexpected transmit interrupt
2048	Unexpected receive interrupt
2049	Transmit data did not equal receive data
2050	8251 detected overrun error
2051	Lost data set ready during data wrap
2052	Receive time-out during data wrap
21xx	**Alternate Binary Synchronous Communications (BSC) Adapter errors**
2101	BSC adapter test failure
2110	8255 Port A failure
2111	8255 Port B failure
2112	8255 Port C failure
2113	8253 Timer #1 did not reach terminal count
2114	8253 Timer #1 stuck on
2115	8253 Timer 2 did not reach terminal count
2116	8253 Timer #2 output stuck on
2117	8251 Data set ready failed to come on
2118	8251 Clear to send not sensed
2119	8251 Data set ready stuck on
2120	8251 Clear to send stuck on
2121	8251 Hardware reset failure
2122	8251 Software reset failure

Code	Description
2123	8251 Software "error reset" failure
2124	8251 Transmit ready did not come on
2125	8251 Receive ready did not come on
2126	8251 could not force "overrun" error status
2127	Interrupt failure; no timer interrupt
2128	Interrupt failure; transmit, replace card or planar
2129	Interrupt failure; transmit, replace card
2130	Interrupt failure; receive, replace card or planar
2131	Interrupt failure; receive, replace card
2133	Ring indicate stuck on
2134	Receive clock stuck on
2135	Transmit clock stuck on
2136	Test indicate stuck on
2137	Ring indicate stuck on
2138	Receive clock not on
2139	Transmit clock not on
2140	Test indicate not on
2141	Data set ready not on
2142	Carrier detect not on
2143	Clear to send not on
2144	Data set ready stuck on
2145	Carrier detect stuck on
2146	Clear to send stuck on
2147	Unexpected transmit interrupt
2148	Unexpected receive interrupt
2149	Transmit data did not equal receive data
2150	8251 detected overrun error
2151	Lost data set ready during data wrap
2152	Receive time-out during data wrap

(continues)

Table 6.9	Continued
Code	Description
22xx	Cluster Adapter errors
23xx	Plasma Monitor Adapter errors
24xx	Enhanced Graphics Adapter (EGA) or Video Graphics Array (VGA) errors
2401	Video adapter test failure
2402	Video display error
2408	User indicated display attribute test failed
2409	Video display error
2410	Video adapter error; video port error
2416	User indicated character set test failed
2424	User indicated 80525 mode failure
2432	User indicated 40525 mode failure
2440	User indicated 3205200 graphics mode failure
2448	User indicated 6405200 graphics mode failure
2456	User indicated light-pen test failure
2464	User indicated paging test failure
25xx	Alternate Enhanced Graphics Adapter (EGA) errors
2501	Video adapter test failure
2502	Video display error
2508	User indicated display attribute test failed
2509	Video display error
2510	Video adapter error
2516	User indicated character set test failed
2524	User indicated 80525 mode failure
2532	User indicated 40525 mode failure
2540	User indicated 3205200 graphics mode failure
2548	User indicated 6405200 graphics mode failure
2556	User indicated light-pen test failure
2564	User indicated paging test failure

Code	Description
26xx	**XT or AT/370 370-M (Memory) and 370-P (Processor) Adapter errors**
2601	370-M (memory) adapter error
2655	370-M (memory) adapter error
2657	370-M (memory) adapter error
2668	370-M (memory) adapter error
2672	370-M (memory) adapter error
2673	370-P (processor) adapter error
2674	370-P (processor) adapter error
2677	370-P (processor) adapter error
2680	370-P (processor) adapter error
2681	370-M (memory) adapter error
2682	370-P (processor) adapter error
2694	370-P (processor) adapter error
2697	370-P (processor) adapter error
2698	XT or AT/370 diagnostic diskette error
27xx	**XT or AT/370 3277-EM (Emulation) Adapter errors**
2701	3277-EM adapter error
2702	3277-EM adapter error
2703	3277-EM adapter error
28xx	**3278/79 Emulation Adapter or 3270 Connection Adapter errors**
29xx	**Color/Graphics Printer errors**
30xx	**Primary PC Network Adapter errors**
3001	Processor test failure
3002	ROM checksum test failure
3003	Unit ID PROM test failure
3004	RAM test failure
3005	Host interface controller test failure
3006	±12v test failure
3007	Digital loopback test failure
3008	Host detected host interface controller failure

(continues)

Table 6.9 · Continued

Code	Description
3009	Sync failure and no Go bit
3010	Host interface controller test OK and no Go bit
3011	Go bit and no command 41
3012	Card not present
3013	Digital failure; fall through
3015	Analog failure
3041	Hot carrier; not this card
3042	Hot carrier; this card!
31xx	**Secondary PC Network Adapter errors**
3101	Processor test failure
3102	ROM checksum test failure
3103	Unit ID PROM test failure
3104	RAM test failure
3105	Host interface controller test failure
3106	± 12v test failure
3107	Digital loopback test failure
3108	Host detected host interface controller failure
3109	Sync failure and no Go bit
3110	Host interface controller test OK and no Go bit
3111	Go bit and no command 41
3112	Card not present
3113	Digital failure; fall through
3115	Analog failure
3141	Hot carrier; not this card
3142	Hot carrier; this card!
32xx	**3270 PC or AT Display and Programmed Symbols Adapter errors**
33xx	**Compact Printer errors**
35xx	**Enhanced Display Station Emulation Adapter (EDSEA) errors**
3504	Adapter connected to Twinaxial cable during off-line test
3508	Workstation address error

Code	Description
3509	Diagnostic program failure
3540	Workstation address invalid
3588	Adapter address switch error
3599	Diagnostic program failure
36xx	**General-Purpose Interface Bus (GPIB) adapter errors**
3601	Adapter test failure
3602	Serial poll mode register write error
3603	Adapter address error
3610	Adapter listen error
3611	Adapter talk error
3612	Adapter control error
3613	Adapter standby error
3614	Adapter Asynchronous control error
3615	Adapter Asynchronous control error
3616	Adapter error; cannot pass control
3617	Adapter error; cannot address to listen
3618	Adapter error; cannot un-address to listen
3619	Adapter error; cannot address to talk
3620	Adapter error; cannot un-address to talk
3621	Adapter error; cannot address to listen with extended addressing
3622	Adapter error; cannot un-address to listen with extended addressing
3623	Adapter error; cannot address to talk with extended addressing
3624	Adapter error; cannot un-address to talk with extended addressing
3625	Write to self error
3626	Generate handshake error
3627	Cannot detect "Device Clear" message error
3628	Cannot detect "Selected Device Clear" message error

(continues)

Table 6.9 Continued

Code	Description
3629	Cannot detect end with end of identify
3630	Cannot detect end of transmission with end of identify
3631	Cannot detect end with 0-bit end of string
3632	Cannot detect end with 7-bit end of string
3633	Cannot detect group execute trigger
3634	Mode 3 addressing error
3635	Cannot recognize undefined command
3636	Cannot detect remote, remote changed, lockout, or lockout changed
3637	Cannot clear remote or lockout
3638	Cannot detect service request
3639	Cannot conduct serial poll
3640	Cannot conduct parallel poll
3650	Adapter error; direct memory access (DMA) to 7210
3651	Data error; error on direct memory access (DMA) to 7210
3652	Adapter error; direct memory access (DMA) from 7210
3653	Data error on direct memory access (DMA) from 7210
3658	Uninvoked interrupt received
3659	Cannot interrupt on address status changed
3660	Cannot interrupt on address status changed
3661	Cannot interrupt on command output
3662	Cannot interrupt on data out
3663	Cannot interrupt on data in
3664	Cannot interrupt on error
3665	Cannot interrupt on device clear
3666	Cannot interrupt on end
3667	Cannot interrupt on device execute trigger
3668	Cannot interrupt on address pass through
3669	Cannot interrupt on command pass through

Code	Description
3670	Cannot interrupt on remote changed
3671	Cannot interrupt on lockout changed
3672	Cannot interrupt on service request In
3673	Cannot interrupt on terminal count on direct memory access to 7210
3674	Cannot interrupt on terminal count on direct memory access from 7210
3675	Spurious direct memory access terminal-count interrupt
3697	Illegal direct memory access configuration setting detected
3698	Illegal interrupt level setting detected
37xx	**System board SCSI controller error**
38xx	**Data acquisition adapter errors**
3801	Adapter test failure
3810	Timer read test failure
3811	Timer interrupt test failure
3812	Delay, binary input 13 test failure
3813	Rate, binary input 13 test failure
3814	Binary output 14, interrupt status - interrupt request test failure
3815	Binary output 0, count-in test failure
3816	Binary input strobe, count-out test failure
3817	Binary output 0, binary output clear to send test failure
3818	Binary output 1, binary input 0 test failure
3819	Binary output 2, binary input 1 test failure
3820	Binary output 3, binary input 2 test failure
3821	Binary output 4, binary input 3 test failure
3822	Binary output 5, binary input 4 test failure
3823	Binary output 6, binary input 5 test failure
3824	Binary output 7, binary input 6 test failure
3825	Binary output 8, binary input 7 test failure

(continues)

Table 6.9	Continued
Code	**Description**
3826	Binary output 9, binary input 8 test failure
3827	Binary output 10, binary input 9 test failure
3828	Binary output 11, binary input 10 test failure
3829	Binary output 12, binary input 11 test failure
3830	Binary output 13, binary input 12 test failure
3831	Binary output 15, analog input CE test failure
3832	Binary output strobe, binary output GATE test failure
3833	Binary input clear to send, binary input HOLD test failure
3834	Analog input command output, binary input 15 test failure
3835	Counter interrupt test failure
3836	Counter read test failure
3837	Analog output 0 ranges test failure
3838	Analog output 1 ranges test failure
3839	Analog input 0 values test failure
3840	Analog input 1 values test failure
3841	Analog input 2 values test failure
3842	Analog input 3 values test failure
3843	Analog input interrupt test failure
3844	Analog input 23 address or value test failure
39xx	**Professional Graphics Adapter (PGA) errors**
3901	PGA test failure
3902	ROM1 self-test failure
3903	ROM2 self-test failure
3904	RAM self-test failure
3905	Cold start cycle power error
3906	Data error in communications RAM
3907	Address error in communications RAM
3908	Bad data reading/writing 6845-like register
3909	Bad data in lower E0h bytes reading/writing 6845-like registers
3910	Graphics controller display bank output latches error

Code	Description
3911	Basic clock error
3912	Command control error
3913	Vertical sync scanner error
3914	Horizontal sync scanner error
3915	Intech error
3916	Look-up table address error
3917	Look-up table red RAM chip error
3918	Look-up table green RAM chip error
3919	Look-up table blue RAM chip error
3920	Look-up table data latch error
3921	Horizontal display error
3922	Vertical display error
3923	Light-pen error
3924	Unexpected error
3925	Emulator addressing error
3926	Emulator data latch error
3927	Base for error codes 3928-3930 (Emulator RAM)
3928	Emulator RAM error
3929	Emulator RAM error
3930	Emulator RAM error
3931	Emulator horizontal/vertical display problem
3932	Emulator cursor position error
3933	Emulator attribute display problem
3934	Emulator cursor display error
3935	Fundamental emulation RAM problem
3936	Emulation character set problem
3937	Emulation graphics display error
3938	Emulation character display problem
3939	Emulation bank select error
3940	Adapter RAM U2 error
3941	Adapter RAM U4 error
3942	Adapter RAM U6 error
3943	Adapter RAM U8 error

(continues)

Table 6.9	Continued
Code	**Description**
3944	Adapter RAM U10 error
3945	Adapter RAM U1 error
3946	Adapter RAM U3 error
3947	Adapter RAM U5 error
3948	Adapter RAM U7 error
3949	Adapter RAM U9 error
3950	Adapter RAM U12 error
3951	Adapter RAM U14 error
3952	Adapter RAM U16 error
3953	Adapter RAM U18 error
3954	Adapter RAM U20 error
3955	Adapter RAM U11 error
3956	Adapter RAM U13 error
3957	Adapter RAM U15 error
3958	Adapter RAM U17 error
3959	Adapter RAM U19 error
3960	Adapter RAM U22 error
3961	Adapter RAM U24 error
3962	Adapter RAM U26 error
3963	Adapter RAM U28 error
3964	Adapter RAM U30 error
3965	Adapter RAM U21 error
3966	Adapter RAM U23 error
3967	Adapter RAM U25 error
3968	Adapter RAM U27 error
3969	Adapter RAM U29 error
3970	Adapter RAM U32 error
3971	Adapter RAM U34 error
3972	Adapter RAM U36 error
3973	Adapter RAM U38 error
3974	Adapter RAM U40 error
3975	Adapter RAM U31 error
3976	Adapter RAM U33 error

Code	Description
3977	Adapter RAM U35 error
3978	Adapter RAM U37 error
3979	Adapter RAM U39 error
3980	Graphics controller RAM timing error
3981	Graphics controller read/write latch error
3982	Shift register bus output latches error
3983	Addressing error (vertical column of memory; U2 at top)
3984	Addressing error (vertical column of memory; U4 at top)
3985	Addressing error (vertical column of memory; U6 at top)
3986	Addressing error (vertical column of memory; U8 at top)
3987	Addressing error (vertical column of memory; U10 at top)
3988	Base for error codes 3989-3991 (horizontal bank latch errors)
3989	Horizontal bank latch errors
3990	Horizontal bank latch errors
3991	Horizontal bank latch errors
3992	RAG/CAG graphics controller error
3993	Multiple write modes, nibble mask errors
3994	Row nibble (display RAM) error
3995	Graphics controller addressing error
44xx	**5278 Display Attachment Unit and 5279 Display errors**
45xx	**IEEE Interface Adapter (IEEE-488) errors**
46xx	**A Real-Time Interface Coprocessor (ARTIC) Multiport/2 adapter errors**
4611	ARTIC adapter error
4612	Memory module error
4613	Memory module error

(continues)

Table 6.9	Continued
Code	**Description**
4630	ARTIC adapter error
4640	Memory module error
4641	Memory module error
4650	ARTIC interface cable error
48xx	**Internal Modem errors**
49xx	**Alternate Internal Modem errors**
50xx	**PC Convertible LCD errors**
5001	LCD display buffer failure
5002	LCD font buffer failure
5003	LCD controller failure
5004	User indicated PEL/drive test failed
5008	User indicated display attribute test failed
5016	User indicated character set test failed
5020	User indicated alternate character set test failure
5024	User indicated 80x25 mode test failure
5032	User indicated 40x25 mode test failure
5040	User indicated 320x200 graphics test failure
5048	User indicated 640x200 graphics test failure
5064	User indicated paging test failure
51xx	**PC Convertible Portable Printer errors**
5101	Portable printer interface failure
5102	Portable printer busy error
5103	Portable printer paper or ribbon error
5104	Portable printer time-out
5105	User indicated print-pattern test error
56xx	**Financial communication system errors**
70xx	**Phoenix BIOS/chipset unique error codes**
7000	Chipset CMOS failure
7001	Chipset shadow RAM failure
7002	Chipset CMOS configuration error
71xx	**Voice Communications Adapter (VCA) errors**
7101	Adapter test failure
7102	Instruction or external data memory error

Code	Description
7103	PC to VCA interrupt error
7104	Internal data memory error
7105	Direct memory access (DMA) error
7106	Internal registers error
7107	Interactive shared memory error
7108	VCA to PC interrupt error
7109	DC wrap error
7111	External analog wrap and tone-output error
7112	Microphone to speaker wrap error
7114	Telephone attachment test failure
73xx	**3 1/2-inch External Diskette Drive errors**
7301	Diskette drive/adapter test failure
7306	Disk Changeline failure
7307	Diskette is write protected
7308	Drive command error
7310	Diskette initialization failure; track 0 bad
7311	Drive time-out error
7312	Controller chip (NEC) error
7313	Direct memory access (DMA) error
7314	Direct memory access (DMA) boundary overrun
7315	Drive index timing error
7316	Drive speed error
7321	Drive seek error
7322	Drive cyclic redundancy check (CRC) error
7323	Sector not found error
7324	Address mark error
7325	Controller chip (NEC) seek error
74xx	**IBM PS/2 Display Adapter (VGA card) errors**
74xx	**8514/A Display Adapter errors**
7426	8514 display error
7440	8514/A memory module 31 error
7441	8514/A memory module 30 error
7442	8514/A memory module 29 error

(continues)

Table 6.9	Continued
Code	**Description**
7443	8514/A memory module 28 error
7444	8514/A memory module 22 error
7445	8514/A memory module 21 error
7446	8514/A memory module 18 error
7447	8514/A memory module 17 error
7448	8514/A memory module 32 error
7449	8514/A memory module 14 error
7450	8514/A memory module 13 error
7451	8514/A memory module 12 error
7452	8514/A memory module 06 error
7453	8514/A memory module 05 error
7454	8514/A memory module 02 error
7455	8514/A memory module 01 error
7460	8514/A memory module 16 error
7461	8514/A memory module 27 error
7462	8514/A memory module 26 error
7463	8514/A memory module 25 error
7464	8514/A memory module 24 error
7465	8514/A memory module 23 error
7466	8514/A memory module 20 error
7467	8514/A memory module 19 error
7468	8514/A memory module 15 error
7469	8514/A memory module 11 error
7470	8514/A memory module 10 error
7471	8514/A memory module 09 error
7472	8514/A memory module 08 error
7473	8514/A memory module 07 error
7474	8514/A memory module 04 error
7475	8514/A memory module 03 error
76xx	**4216 PagePrinter Adapter errors**
7601	Adapter test failure
7602	Adapter error

Code	Description
7603	Printer error
7604	Printer cable error
84xx	**PS/2 Speech Adapter errors**
85xx	**2MB XMA Memory Adapter or XMA Adapter/A errors**
850x	Adapter error
851x	Adapter error
852x	Memory module error
8599	Unusable memory segment found
86xx	**PS/2 Pointing Device (Mouse) errors**
8601	Pointing device error; mouse time-out
8602	Pointing device error; mouse interface
8603	Pointing device or system-bus failure; mouse interrupt
8604	Pointing device or system-board error
8611	System bus error - I/F between 8042 and TrackPoint II
8612	TrackPoint II error
8613	System bus error or TrackPoint II error
89xx	**Musical Instrument Digital Interface (MIDI) Adapter errors**
91xx	**IBM 3363 Write-Once Read Multiple (WORM) Optical Drive/Adapter errors**
96xx	**SCSI Adapter with Cache (32-bit) errors**
100xx	**Multiprotocol Adapter/A errors**
10001	Presence test failure
10002	Card selected feedback error
10003	Port 102h register rest failure
10004	Port 103h register rest failure
10006	Serial option cannot be put to sleep
10007	Cable error
10008	Interrupt request (IRQ) 3 error
10009	Interrupt request (IRQ) 4 error

(continues)

Table 6.9 Continued	
Code	**Description**
10010	16550 chip register failure
10011	Internal wrap test of 16550 chip modem control line failure
10012	External wrap test of 16550 chip modem control line failure
10012	External wrap test of 16550 chip modem control line failure
10013	16550 chip transmit error
10014	16550 chip receive error
10015	16550 chip receive error; data not equal to transmit data
10016	16550 chip interrupt function error
10017	16550 chip baud rate test failure
10018	16550 chip receive external data wrap test failure
10019	16550 chip first-in first-out (FIFO) buffer failure
10026	8255 Port A error
10027	8255 Port B error
10028	8255 Port C error
10029	8254 timer 0 error
10030	8254 timer 1 error
10031	8254 timer 2 error
10032	Binary sync data set ready response to data terminal ready error
10033	Binary sync clear to send response to ready to send error
10034	8251 hardware reset test failed
10035	8251 function error
10036	8251 status error
10037	Binary sync timer interrupt error
10038	Binary sync transmit interrupt error
10039	Binary sync receive interrupt error
10040	Stray interrupt request (IRQ) 3 error
10041	Stray interrupt request (IRQ) 4 error
10042	Binary sync external wrap error

Code	Description
10044	Binary sync data wrap error
10045	Binary sync line status/condition error
10046	Binary sync time-out error during data wrap test
10050	8273 command acceptance or results ready time-out error
10051	8273 Port A error
10052	8273 Port B error
10053	SDLC modem status change logic error
10054	SDLC timer interrupt request (IRQ) 4 error
10055	SDLC modem status change interrupt request (IRQ) 4 error
10056	SDLC external wrap error
10057	SDLC interrupt results error
10058	SDLC data wrap error
10059	SDLC transmit interrupt error
10060	SDLC receive interrupt error
10061	Direct memory access (DMA) channel 1 transmit error
10062	Direct memory access (DMA) channel 1 receive error
10063	8273 status detect failure
10064	8273 error detect failure
101xx	**300/1200bps Internal Modem/A**
10101	Presence test failure
10102	Card selected feedback error
10103	Port 102h register test failure
10106	Serial option cannot be put to sleep
10108	Interrupt request (IRQ) 3 error
10109	Interrupt request (IRQ) 4 error
10110	16450 chip register failure
10111	Internal wrap test of 16450 modem control line failure

(continues)

Table 6.9	Continued
Code	Description
10113	16450 transmit error
10114	16450 receive error
10115	16450 receive error data not equal transmit data
10116	16450 interrupt function error
10117	16450 baud rate test failure
10118	16450 receive external data wrap test failure
10125	Modem reset result code error
10126	Modem general result code error
10127	Modem S registers write/read error
10128	Modem turn echo on/off error
10129	Modem enable/disable result codes error
10130	Modem enable number/word result codes error
10133	Connect results for 300 baud not received
10134	Connect results for 1200 baud not received
10135	Modem fails local analog loopback test at 300 baud
10136	Modem fails local analog loopback test at 1200 baud
10137	Modem does not respond to escape/reset sequence
10138	S-Register 13 does not show correct parity or number of data bits
10139	S-Register 15 does not reflect correct bit rate
104xx	**ESDI or MCA IDE Fixed Disk or Adapter errors**
10450	Read/write test failed
10451	Read verify test failed
10452	Seek test failed
10453	Wrong drive type indicated
10454	Controller sector buffer test failure
10455	Controller invalid failure
10456	Controller diagnostic command failure

Code	Description
10461	Drive format error
10462	Controller head select error
10463	Drive read/write sector error
10464	Drive primary defect map unreadable
10465	Controller; error-correction code (ECC) 8-bit error
10466	Controller; error-correction code (ECC) 9-bit error
10467	Drive soft seek error
10468	Drive hard seek error
10469	Drive soft error count exceeded
10470	Controller attachment diagnostic error
10471	Controller wrap mode interface error
10472	Controller wrap mode drive select error
10473	Read verify test errors
10480	Seek failure; drive 0
10481	Seek failure; drive 1
10482	Controller transfer acknowledge error
10483	Controller reset failure
10484	Controller; head select 3 error
10485	Controller; head select 2 error
10486	Controller; head select 1 error
10487	Controller; head select 0 error
10488	Controller; read gate - command complete 2 error
10489	Controller; write gate - command complete 1 error
10490	Diagnostic area read error; drive 0
10491	Diagnostic area read error; drive 1
10492	Controller error, drive 1
10493	Reset error, drive 1
10499	Controller failure

(continues)

Table 6.9	Continued
Code	**Description**
107xx	5 1/4-inch External Diskette Drive or Adapter errors
112xx	SCSI Adapter (16-bit without Cache) errors
113xx	System Board SCSI Adapter (16-bit) errors
129xx	Processor Complex (CPU Board) errors
129005	DMA error
12901	Processor board; processor test failed
12902	Processor board; cache test failed
12904	Second level cache failure
12905	Cache enable/disable errors
12907	Cache fatal error
12908	Cache POST program error
12912x	Hardware failure
12913x	Micro channel bus timeout
12914x	Software failure
12915x	Processor complex error
12916x	Processor complex error
12917x	Processor complex error
12918x	Processor complex error
12919x	Processor complex error
12940x	Processor complex failure
12950x	Processor complex failure
129900	Processor complex serial-number mismatch
149xx	P70/P75 Plasma Display and Adapter errors
14901	Plasma Display Adapter failure
14902	Plasma Display Adapter failure
14922	Plasma display failure
14932	External display failure

Code	Description
152xx	**XGA Display Adapter/A errors**
164xx	**120MB Internal Tape Drive errors**
165xx	**6157 Streaming Tape Drive or Tape Attachment Adapter errors**
16520	Streaming tape drive failure
16540	Tape attachment adapter failure
166xx	**Primary Token Ring Network Adapter errors**
167xx	**Alternate Token Ring Network Adapter errors**
180xx	**PS/2 Wizard Adapter errors**
18001	Interrupt controller failure
18002	Incorrect timer count
18003	Timer interrupt failure
18004	Sync check interrupt failure
18005	Parity check interrupt failure
18006	Access error interrupt failure
18012	Bad checksum error
18013	Micro Channel interface error
18021	Wizard memory compare or parity error
18022	Wizard memory address line error
18023	Dynamic RAM controller failure
18029	Wizard memory byte enable error
18031	Wizard memory-expansion module memory compare or parity error
18032	Wizard memory-expansion module address line error
18039	Wizard memory-expansion module byte enable error

(continues)

Table 6.9   Continued

Code	Description
185xx	DBCS Japanese Display Adapter/A errors
194xx	80286 Memory-Expansion Option Memory-Module errors
200xx	Image Adapter/A errors
208xx	Unknown SCSI Device errors
209xx	SCSI Removable Disk errors
210xx	SCSI Fixed Disk errors
210PLSC	"PLSC" codes indicate errors
	P = SCSI ID number (Physical Unit Number or PUN)
	L = Logical unit number (LUN, usually 0)
	S = Host Adapter slot number
	C = SCSI Drive capacity:
	A = 60M
	B = 80M
	C = 120M
	D = 160M
	E = 320M
	F = 400M
	H = 1,024M (1GB)
	I = 104M
	J = 212M
	U = Undetermined or Non IBM OEM Drive
211xx	SCSI Tape Drive errors
212xx	SCSI Printer errors
213xx	SCSI Processor errors
214xx	SCSI Write-Once Read Multiple (WORM) Drive errors
215xx	SCSI CD-ROM Drive errors
216xx	SCSI Scanner errors
217xx	SCSI Magneto Optical Drive errors
218xx	SCSI Jukebox Changer errors
219xx	SCSI Communications errors
243xxxx	XGA-2 Adapter/A errors

Code	Description
I998xxxx	**Dynamic Configuration Select (DCS) information codes**
I998001x	Bad integrity of DCS master boot record
I988002x	Read failure of DCS master boot record
I988003x	DCS master boot record is not compatible with the planar ID
I988004x	DCS master boot record is not compatible with the model/submodel byte
I988005x	Bad integrity of CMOS/NVRAM (or internal process error)
I988006x	Read failure of header/mask/configuration record
I988007x	Bad integrity of header/mask/configuration record
I988008x	Hard disk does not support the command to set the maximum RBA
I988009x	DCS master boot record is older than system ROM
I9880402	Copyright notice in E000 segment does not match the one in DCS MBR
I9880403	DCS MBR is not compatible with the system board ID or model/submodel byte
I99900xx	**Initial Microcode Load (IML) error**
I999001x	Invalid disk IML record
I999002x	Disk IML record load error
I999003x	Disk IML record incompatible with system board
I999004x	Disk IML record incompatible with processor/processor card
I999005x	Disk IML not attempted
I999006x	Disk stage II System Image load error
I999007x	Disk stage II image checksum error

(continues)

Code	Description
Table 6.9	**Continued**
I999008x	IML not supported on primary disk drive
I999009x	Disk IML record is older than ROM
I99900x1	Invalid diskette IML record
I99900x2	Diskette IML record load error
I99900x3	Diskette IML record incompatible with system board
I99900x4	Diskette IML record incompatible with processor card
I99900x5	Diskette IML recovery prevented (valid password and CE override not set)
I99900x6	Diskette stage II image loade error
I99900x7	Diskette stage II image checksum error
I99900x9	Diskette IML record older than ROM
I99903xx	**No bootable device, Initial Program Load (IPL) errors**
I9990302	Invalid disk boot record, unable to read IPL boot record from disk.
I9990303	IML System Partition boot failure
I9990304	No bootable device with ASCII console
I9990305	No bootable media found
I9990306	Invalid SCSI Device boot record
I99904xx	**IML-to-System mismatch**
I9990401	Unauthorized access (manufacturing boot request with valid password)
I9990402	Missing ROM IBM Copyright notice
I9990403	IML Boot Record incompatible with system board/processor card.
I99906xx	**IML errors**

IBM SCSI Error Codes

With the new IBM SCSI adapter and SCSI devices comes a new set of error codes. This section contains tables describing all the known IBM SCSI Power-On Self Test (POST) and advanced diagnostics error codes. These codes can be used to determine the meaning of errors that occur on the IBM SCSI adapters and any attached SCSI devices. The error codes that occur during POST and diagnostics tests have the format shown in figure 6.1.

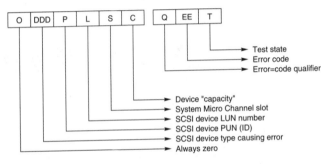

Fig. 6.1   IBM SCSI POST and diagnostics error code format.

This section shows what each part of the error code indicates.

The DDD field in figure 6.1 indicates the SCSI device causing the error. Table 6.10 shows the device codes.

The P field indicates the SCSI device physical unit number (PUN) or SCSI ID. This value is between 0 and 7, with the host adapter normally set to 7 and the first (bootable) SCSI hard disk set to 6.

The L field indicates the SCSI device logical unit number (LUN). For most SCSI devices it is 0 because normally there is only a single LUN per physical unit or SCSI ID.

The S field indicates the system Micro Channel Architecture (MCA) slot number containing the SCSI host adapter to which the device in error is connected. If S equals 0, the error is an adapter initialization error (there is no MCA slot 0). In this case, the DDD number is 096, 112, or 113, and you must use the following adapter initialization error chart to determine the error. The specific errors in this chart are indicated by the value in the L field, which immediately precedes the S field. In this case, the L does *not* represent the logical unit number (as it normally does), but instead shows a specific initialization error for the adapter. If S is not equal to 0, no error is on the adapter (or device attached to the adapter) in slot S. You can determine these standard errors by using the rest of the tables in this section.

Table 6.10   SCSI Device Error Codes

DDDxxxx xxxx	Error
096xxxx xxxx	32-bit cached SCSI host adapter
112xxxx xxxx	16-bit non-cached SCSI host adapter
113xxxx xxxx	System board SCSI host adapter
208xxxx xxxx	Unknown SCSI device type
209xxxx xxxx	Direct access (disk) device with removable media and/or other than 512 byte blocks
210xxxx xxxx	Direct access (disk) device with nonremovable media and 512 byte blocks (hard disk)
211xxxx xxxx	Sequential access device (magnetic tape)
212xxxx xxxx	Printer device
213xxxx xxxx	Processor device (host to host)
214xxxx xxxx	Write-Once, Read Multiple device (optical WORM drive)
215xxxx xxxx	Read-only device (CD-ROM drive)
216xxxx xxxx	Scanner device
217xxxx xxxx	Optical memory device (optical drive)
218xxxx xxxx	Media changer device (multiple tray CD-ROM or jukebox)
219xxxx xxxx	Communications device (LAN bridge)

DDD0LS0 0000	SCSI adapter initialization errors, where S = 0
DDD0100 0000	No extended CMOS setup data available. On systems with Non-Volatile RAM (NVRAM), this means that SCSI setup data was not located or the checksum did not verify. On systems without NVRAM (Model 50, for example), the setup data must be on the first non-SCSI fixed disk
DDD0200 0000	No hard disk at PUN 6, LUN 0. (Also expect to see 161, 162, or 165 errors)
DDD0300 0000	No space available in extended BIOS data area for SCSI data table
DDD0400 0000	ROM modules not found on SCSI adapter
DDD0500 0000	ROM checksum error in the second 16K portion of 32K SCSI adapter ROM space

A value of *x* indicates any number or character.

The C field indicates the capacity of the device originating the error code. The capacity codes for each of the available IBM SCSI hard disk drives are listed in table 6.11. In the case of error codes from a device with no capacity (such as a SCSI adapter or printer), this field is 0.

Table 6.11   SCSI Device Capacity Codes

DDDxxxC xxxx	SCSI device capacity
DDDxxx0 xxxx	Not a storage device
DDDxxxA xxxx	60M
DDDxxxB xxxx	80M
DDDxxxC xxxx	120M
DDDxxxD xxxx	160M
DDDxxxE xxxx	320M
DDDxxxF xxxx	400M

(continues)

Table 6.11 Continued	
DDDxxxC xxxx	**SCSI device capacity**
DDDxxxH xxxx	1,024M (1GB)
DDDxxxI xxxx	104M
DDDxxxJ xxxx	212M
DDDxxxU xxxx	Undetermined Device Capacity or Non-IBM OEM Drive

The Q field is the error code (EE field) qualifier. Q can have a value from 0 through 7. Depending on the value of Q, the error codes take on different meanings, because Q indicates what class of error occurred or what part of the SCSI system the error is coming from. To determine the error code meaning, use one of the following tables that correspond to the value of Q you have.

The Q value defines the origin of the EE code reported. Error codes with Q = 0 or 1 are generated by the SCSI host adapter, and all error codes with Q greater than 1 are developed using information returned by the adapter or a SCSI device. If Q = 2, the EE code indicates the value returned in the Command Error field (word 8, bits 15-8) of the SCSI Command Complete Status Block (CCSB) for values indicating hardware problems (codes of 20h or greater). If Q = 3, then EE also indicates the value returned in the Command Error field (word 8, bits 15-8) of the Command Complete Status Block (CCSB), but for values indicating software problems (codes less than 20h). If Q = 4, then EE indicates the value returned in the Sense Key field (byte 2, bits 3-0) of a Sense Data Block returned to the SCSI host adapter by a device following a SCSI Request Sense command. If Q = 5, then EE indicates the value returned in the Additional Sense Code field (byte 12) of a Sense Data Block returned by a Direct Access (Disk) device following a SCSI Request Sense command. If Q = 6, then EE indicates the value returned in the Device Error Code field (word 8, bits 7-0) of the Command Complete Status Block (CCSB). If Q = 7, a device error has occurred that normally would not be considered an error, but is now considered an error based on when the code was returned—for example, a Medium Corrupted error from a device with nonremovable media.

Although IBM has a unique format for displaying SCSI error codes, almost all except the adapter-specific errors are part of the SCSI specification. Because many of these codes come from the devices attached to the SCSI bus and not the host adapter, a new code not listed here possibly could appear because some errors can be dependent on the particular device, and some devices send manufacturer-specific errors. You then can look up the error code in the manufacturer's documentation for the device to determine the meaning. The tables in this section are standard as defined in the SCSI Common Command Set (CCS) of the ANSI SCSI-1 specification. Further information is in the IBM hardware-maintenance and service manual for the IBM SCSI adapter and the various SCSI devices.

Table 6.12   SCSI Host Adapter Error Codes with Q = 0

DDDxxxx QEEx	Error code
96xxxx 001x	80188 ROM test failure
96xxxx 002x	Local RAM test failure
96xxxx 003x	Power protection error (terminator or fuse)
96xxxx 004x	80188 internal peripheral test failure
96xxxx 005x	Buffer control chip test failure
96xxxx 006x	Buffer RAM test failure
96xxxx 007x	System interface control chip test failure
96xxxx 008x	SCSI interface test failure
112xxxx 001x	8032 ROM test failure
112xxxx 002x	Local RAM test failure
112xxxx 003x	Power protection device error (terminator or fuse)
112xxxx 004x	8032 internal peripheral test failure
112xxxx 005x	Buffer control chip test failure
112xxxx 006x	Undefined error condition

(continues)

Table 6.12   Continued

DDDxxxx QEEx	Error code
112xxxx 006x	Undefined error condition
112xxxx 007x	System interface control chip test failure
112xxxx 008x	SCSI interface test failure
113xxxx 001x	Microprocessor ROM test failure
113xxxx 002x	Local RAM test failure
113xxxx 003x	Power protection device error (terminator or fuse)
113xxxx 004x	Microprocessor internal peripheral test failure
113xxxx 005x	Buffer control chip test failure
113xxxx 006x	Undefined error condition
113xxxx 007x	System interface control chip test failure
113xxxx 008x	SCSI interface test failure

Table 6.13   SCSI Adapter Error Codes with Q = 1

DDDxxxx QEEx	Error code
DDDxxxx 107x	Adapter hardware failure
DDDxxxx 10Cx	Command completed with failure
DDDxxxx 10Ex	Command error (invalid command or parameter)
DDDxxxx 10Fx	Software sequencing error
DDDxxxx 180x	Time out
DDDxxxx 181x	Adapter busy error
DDDxxxx 182x	Unexpected interrupt presented by adapter
DDDxxxx 183x	Adapter register test failure
DDDxxxx 184x	Adapter reset (via basic control register) failure
DDDxxxx 185x	Adapter buffer test failure (cached adapter only)
DDDxxxx 186x	Adapter reset count expired
DDDxxxx 187x	Adapter registers not cleared on reset (power-on or channel reset)
DDDxxxx 188x	Card ID in adapter microcode did not match ID in POS registers

DDDxxxx QEEx	Error code
DDDxxxx 190x	Expected device did not respond (target device not powered on)
DDDxxxx 190x	DMA arbitration level conflict (if device number is 096, 112, or 113)

Table 6.14 SCSI Hardware Error Codes with Q = 2

DDDxxxx QEEx	Error code
DDDxxxx 220x	Adapter hardware error
DDDxxxx 221x	Global command time-out on adapter (device did not respond)
DDDxxxx 222x	Adapter DMA error
DDDxxxx 223x	Adapter buffer defective
DDDxxxx 224x	Command aborted by adapter
DDDxxxx 280x	Adapter microprocessor detected error

Table 6.15 SCSI Software Error Codes with A = 3

DDDxxxx QEEx	Error code
DDDxxxx 301x	Invalid parameter in subsystem control block
DDDxxxx 302x	Reserved
DDDxxxx 303x	Command not supported
DDDxxxx 304x	Command aborted by system
DDDxxxx 305x	Command rejected (buffer not disabled)
DDDxxxx 306x	Command rejected (adapter diagnostic failure)
DDDxxxx 307x	Format rejected (sequence error)
DDDxxxx 308x	Assign rejected (command in progress on device)
DDDxxxx 309x	Assign rejected (device already assigned)
DDDxxxx 30Ax	Command rejected (device not assigned)
DDDxxxx 30Bx	Maximum logical block address exceeded
DDDxxxx 30Cx	16-bit card slot address range exceeded
DDDxxxx 313x	Invalid device for command
DDDxxxx 3FFx	Status not returned by adapter

Table 6.16 SCSI Device Sense Key Error Codes with Q = 4

DDDxxxx QEEx	Error code
DDDxxxx 401x	Recovered error (not considered an error condition)
DDDxxxx 402x	Device not ready
DDDxxxx 403x	Device media error
DDDxxxx 404x	Device hardware error
DDDxxxx 405x	Illegal request for device
DDDxxxx 406x	Device unit attention would not clear
DDDxxxx 407x	Device data protect error
DDDxxxx 408x	Device blank check error
DDDxxxx 409x	Device vendor unique error
DDDxxxx 40Ax	Device copy aborted
DDDxxxx 40Bx	Command aborted by device
DDDxxxx 40Cx	Device search data command satisfied
DDDxxxx 40Dx	Device volume overflow (residual data still in buffer)
DDDxxxx 40Ex	Device miscompare (source and medium data don't match)
DDDxxxx 40Fx	Reserved

Table 6.17 SCSI Device Extended Sense Error Codes with Q=5

DDDxxxx QEEx	Error code
DDDxxxx 501x	No index or sector signal
DDDxxxx 502x	Seek incomplete
DDDxxxx 503x	Write fault
DDDxxxx 504x	Drive not ready
DDDxxxx 505x	Drive not selected
DDDxxxx 506x	No track 0 found
DDDxxxx 507x	Multiple drives selected
DDDxxxx 508x	Logical unit communication failure
DDDxxxx 509x	Head positioning error (track following error)
DDDxxxx 50Ax	Error log overflow

DDDxxxx QEEx	Error code
DDDxxxx 50Cx	Write error
DDDxxxx 510x	CRC or ECC error on ID field
DDDxxxx 511x	Unrecoverable read error
DDDxxxx 512x	Address mark not found for ID field
DDDxxxx 513x	Address mark not found for data field
DDDxxxx 514x	Record not found
DDDxxxx 515x	Seek error
DDDxxxx 516x	Data synchronization mark error
DDDxxxx 517x	Recovered read data with retries (without ECC)
DDDxxxx 518x	Recovered read data with ECC correction
DDDxxxx 519x	Defect list error
DDDxxxx 51Ax	Parameter list length overrun
DDDxxxx 51Bx	Synchronous data transfer error
DDDxxxx 51Cx	Primary defect list not found
DDDxxxx 51Dx	Data miscompare during verify
DDDxxxx 51Ex	Recovered ID read with ECC correction
DDDxxxx 520x	Invalid command operation code
DDDxxxx 521x	Illegal logical block address (out of range)
DDDxxxx 522x	Illegal function for device type
DDDxxxx 524x	Invalid field in command descriptor block
DDDxxxx 525x	Invalid logical unit number (LUN not supported)
DDDxxxx 526x	Invalid field in parameter list
DDDxxxx 527x	Media write protected
DDDxxxx 528x	Media changed error (ready went true)
DDDxxxx 529x	Power-on or bus device reset occurred (not an error)
DDDxxxx 52Ax	Mode select parameters changed (not an error)
DDDxxxx 52Bx	Copy command can't execute because host can't disconnect
DDDxxxx 52Cx	Command sequence error
DDDxxxx 52Fx	Tagged commands cleared by another initiator

(continues)

Table 6.17   Continued

DDDxxxx QEEx	Error code
DDDxxxx 530x	Incompatible media (unknown or incompatible format)
DDDxxxx 531x	Medium format corrupted
DDDxxxx 532x	Defect spare location unavailable
DDDxxxx 537x	Rounded parameter error
DDDxxxx 539x	Saving parameters not supported
DDDxxxx 53Ax	Media not present
DDDxxxx 53Cx	Link flag bit not supported
DDDxxxx 53Dx	Invalid bits in identify message
DDDxxxx 53Ex	Logical unit has not self-configured
DDDxxxx 53Fx	Target operating conditions have changed
DDDxxxx 540x	Device RAM failure
DDDxxxx 541x	Data path diagnostic failure
DDDxxxx 542x	Device power-on diagnostic failure
DDDxxxx 543x	Device message rejected
DDDxxxx 544x	Target device internal controller error
DDDxxxx 545x	Select/reselect failure (device unable to reconnect)
DDDxxxx 546x	Device soft reset unsuccessful
DDDxxxx 547x	SCSI interface parity error
DDDxxxx 548x	Initiator detected error
DDDxxxx 549x	Illegal command or command out of sequence error
DDDxxxx 54Ax	SCSI command phase error
DDDxxxx 54Bx	SCSI data phase error
DDDxxxx 54Cx	Logical unit failed self-configuration
DDDxxxx 54Ex	Overlapped commands attempted
DDDxxxx 560x	Status error from second-party copy command
DDDxxxx 588x	Not digital audio track
DDDxxxx 589x	Not CD-ROM data track
DDDxxxx 58Ax	Drive not in play audio state
DDDxxxx 5F0x	Format in progress (not an error)
DDDxxxx 5F1x	Spinup in progress

Table 6.18   SCSI Device Condition Error Codes with Q=7

DDDxxxx QEEx	Error
DDDxxxx 601x	SCSI bus reset occurred
DDDxxxx 602x	SCSI interface fault
DDDxxxx 610x	SCSI selection time-out (device not available)
DDDxxxx 611x	Unexpected SCSI bus free
DDDxxxx 612x	Mandatory SCSI message rejected
DDDxxxx 613x	Invalid SCSI phase sequence
DDDxxxx 620x	Short length record error

Table 6.19 shows the diagnostics test state codes used when a failure occurs. Position *T* indicates the POST *or* diagnostics test state in which the failure occurred.

Table 6.19   SCSI Diagnostics Test State Codes

DDDxxxx xxxT	Test state code
DDDxxxx xxx0	Not applicable for error code
DDDxxxx xxxA	Adapter initialization
DDDxxxx xxxB	Adapter reset
DDDxxxx xxxC	Adapter register test
DDDxxxx xxxD	Adapter buffer test Phase 1 (cached adapter only)
DDDxxxx xxxE	Adapter buffer test Phase 2 (cached adapter only)
DDDxxxx xxxF	Adapter buffer test Phase 3 (cached adapter only)
DDDxxxx xxxG	Adapter buffer test Phase 4 (cached adapter only)
DDDxxxx xxxH	Adapter information test state (buffer enable/size, retry enable, etc.)
DDDxxxx xxxI	Device assignment sequence

(continues)

Table 6.19 Continued	
DDDxxxx xxxT	**Test state code**
DDDxxxx xxxJ	Device not ready (also initial unit attention clearing)
DDDxxxx xxxK	Device reset
DDDxxxx xxxL	Device starting phase (appropriate devices only)
DDDxxxx xxxM	Device in process of starting (wait for device to become ready)
DDDxxxx xxxN	Device block size determination
DDDxxxx xxxO	Device self test
DDDxxxx xxxP	Device single block (logical block address) read
DDDxxxx xxxQ	Device double block (logical block address) read
DDDxxxx xxxS	Error occurred after device testing had completed

DOS Error Messages

Table 6.20 DOS Extended Error Codes		
Hex Code	**Dec Code**	**Description**
01h	1	Invalid function number
02h	2	File not found
03h	3	Path not found
04h	4	Too many open files (no handles left)
05h	5	Access denied
06h	6	Invalid handle
07h	7	Memory control blocks destroyed
08h	8	Insufficient memory
09h	9	Invalid memory block address
0Ah	10	Invalid environment
0Bh	11	Invalid format
0Ch	12	Invalid access code
0Dh	13	Invalid data
0Eh	14	Reserved
0Fh	15	Invalid drive was specified

Hex Code	Dec Code	Description
10h	16	Attempt to write on write-protected diskette
11h	17	Not same devise
12h	18	No more files
13h	19	Attempt to write-protect diskette
14h	20	Unknown unit
15h	21	Drive not ready
16h	22	Unkown command
17h	23	Cyclic Redundancy Check (CRC) error
18h	24	Bad request structure length
19h	25	Seek error
1Ah	26	Unknown media type
1Bh	27	Sector not found
1Ch	28	Printer out of paper
1Dh	29	Write fault
1Eh	30	Read fault
1Fh	31	General failure
20h	32	Sharing violation
21h	33	Lock violation
22h	34	Invalid disk change
23h	35	FCB unavailable
24h	36	Sharing buffer overflow
25h	37	Reserved by DOS 5.0
26h	38	Unable to complete file operation
27h - 31h	39 - 49	Reserved by DOS 5.0
32h	50	Network request not supported
33h	51	Remote computer not listening
34h	52	Duplicate name on network
35h	53	Network path not found
36h	54	Network busy
37h	55	Network device no longer exists
38h	56	NETBIOS command limit exceeded
39h	57	System error; NETBIOS error
3Ah	58	Incorrect response from network
3Bh	59	Unexpected network error
3Ch	60	Incompatible remote adapter
3Dh	61	Print queue full
3Eh	62	Note enough space for print file
3Fh	63	Print file was cancelled
40h	64	Network name was deleted

(continues)

Table 6.20   Continued

Hex Code	Dec Code	Description
41h	65	Access denied
42h	66	Network device type incorrect
43h	67	Network name not found
44h	68	Network name limit exceeded
45h	69	NETBIOS session limit exceeded
46h	70	Sharing temporarily paused
47h	71	Network request not accepted
48h	72	Print or disk redirection is paused
49h - 4Fh	73 - 79	Reserved
50h	80	File exists
51h	81	Reserved
52h	82	Cannot make directory entry
53h	83	Fail on Interrupt 24
54h	84	Too many redirections
55h	85	Duplicate redirection
56h	86	Invalid password
57h	87	Invalid parameter
58h	88	Network data fault
59h	89	Function not supported by network
5Ah	90	Required system component not installed

Table 6.21   DOS Parse Error Codes

Code	Description
1	Too many paramters
2	Required parameter missing
3	Invalid switch
4	Invalid keyword
6	Parameter value not in allowed range
7	Parameter value not allowed
8	Parameter value not allowed
9	Parameter format not correct
10	Invalid parameter
11	Invalid parameter combination

Chapter 7

IBM Technical Manuals and Updates

IBM has an extensive array of documentation available to help a system troubleshooter responsible for upgrading and repairing any system. These manuals are primarily in three categories: Guide to Operations or Quick Reference Manuals, Hardware Maintenance Manuals, and Technical Reference Manuals. You purchase these manuals in basic form and then buy updates that reflect changes in newer systems as they are introduced. All of the manuals together with the updates present a bewildering—and expensive—array of documentation. If you are interested in obtaining any of this documentation, this section is very useful.

This section explains each manual type and gives information needed for ordering this documentation, and tables describe all the available manuals and updates, including part numbers and prices.

Guide to Operations and Quick-Reference Manuals

These publications contain instructions for system operation, testing, relocation, and option installation. A diagnostics floppy disk is included, which includes the Advanced Diagnostics for most PS/2 Model 50 and higher systems.

Table 7.1 Guide to Operations and Quick Reference Manual Part Numbers and Prices

Description	Part number	Price
Model 25	75X1051	$29.75
Model 25 286	15F2179	37.75
Model 30	68X2230	56.25
Model 30 286	15F2143	44.00
Model 35 SX	84F9844	35.75
Model 40 SX	84F7765	42.50
Model L40 SX	84F7577	81.50
Model 50	68X2321	56.25
Model N51 SX	04G5107	70.75
Model 55 SX	91F8575	49.50
Model 56 SX and 56 SLC	10G6001	66.25
Model 57 SX and 57 SLC	04G3382	64.75
Model 60	68X2213	56.25
Model 65 SX	91F8622	28.75
Model 70	91F8577	50.50
Model 70 486	91F8619	57.75
Model P70 386	68X2380	17.00
Model P75 486	84F7590	39.25
Model 80	91F8580	50.50
Model 90 48	92F2685	90.25
Model 90 (Models 0H5 and 0H9 only)	41G8561	85.25
Model 90 (Models 0L9 and 0LF only)	41G8330	65.00
Model 95 486	92F2684	103.00
Model 95 (Models 0H9 and 0HF only)	41G8562	111.00
Model 95 (Model 0LF only)	41G8331	68.00
External Storage Enclosure for SCSI Devices	15F2159	15.25
FAX Concentrator Adapter/A	15F2260	31.50
Remote Program Load for Ethernet Networks	15F2292	29.00

Description	Part number	Price
PC Systems:		
AT	6280066	$49.50
AT Model 339	6280102	80.00
PC	6322510	50.00
PC Convertible	6280629	71.50
PC*jr*	1502292	23.25
Portable PC	6936571	66.75
XT	6322511	50.00
XT Models 089 268 278	6280085	88.00
XT Model 286	6280147	65.00

Hardware-Maintenance Library

The Hardware-Maintenance Library consists of a two-part set of manuals, including a Service manual, a Reference manual, as well as possible supplements or updates.

The Hardware-Maintenance Service manuals contain all the information necessary to diagnose a failure. Maintenance-analysis procedures (MAPs), the parts catalog, and Reference Disks containing the advanced diagnostics tests are included with these manuals. The Hardware-Maintenance Reference contains product descriptions, field-replaceable unit (FRU) locations and removal procedures, and information about the diagnostics programs. To maintain an accurate library, you should add all available supplements.

Table 7.2 PS/2 Hardware-Maintenance Service Manual Part Numbers and Prices		
Description	**Part number**	**Price**
PS/2 Hardware-Maintenance Service Library:	SBOF-3988	N/A
(includes all of the following pamphlets)		
General Information	15F2189	$3.70
Model 25/30	15F2191	3.70

(continues)

Table 7.2 Continued

Description	Part number	Price
Model 25 SX	10G6609	2.95
Model 25 286	15F2181	5.75
Model 30 286	91F9231	2.30
Model 35 SX	10G6621	2.05
Model 40 SX	84F7767	1.80
Model L40 SX	15F2266	1.65
Model 50	15F2193	1.60
Model N51 SX	04G5112	4.55
Model 55 SX	91F8637	2.40
Model 56 SX and 56 SLC	10G6003	3.40
Model 57 SX, 57 SLC, & M57 SLC	04G3383	2.70
Model 60	84F9825	3.55
Model 65 SX	84F8549	1.70
Model 70 (includes Model 70 486)	91F8635	2.40
Model P70 386	15F2198	1.60
Model P75 486	84F7593	5.55
Model 80	84F8547	1.70
Model 90 XP 486	04G3389	2.20
Model 95 XP 486	04G3394	2.20
Option pamphlets		
Communications Cartridge (for L40 SX)	10G5993	$1.95
External Devices Parts Catalog	64F4022	3.55
External SCSI Devices	92F1656	4.65
300/1200/2400 Internal Modem/A	68X2384	10.75
Adapter/A for Ethernet Networks	84F9863	19.50
8504 Monochrome display	15F2241	11.00
Host Connected keyboard errata sheet	92F1682	6.55

Table 7.3   PS/2 Hardware-Maintenance Reference Manual Part Numbers and Prices

Description	Part number	Price
PS/2 Hardware-Maintenance Reference Library:	SBOF-3989	N/A
(includes all of the following manuals)		
General Information Manual	64F3983	$5.95
Diagnostics for Micro Channel Systems	15F2245	6.00
Diagnostics for Non-Micro Channel Systems	64F3985	5.95
Model 25	64F3986	2.65
Model 25 SX	10G6610	2.80
Model 25 286	64F3811	2.65
Model 30	64F3987	2.65
Model 30 286	64F3988	2.65
Model 35 SX	10G6620	2.45
Model 40 SX	84F7768	5.10
Model L40 SX	15F2267	2.85
Model 50	64F3989	2.65
Model N51 SX	04G5111	5.25
Model 55 SX	15F2250	2.15
Model 56 SX	04G3295	3.55
Model 56 SX and 56 SLC	10G6002	3.55
Model 57 SX, 57 SLC, & M57 SLC	04G3384	2.95
Model 60	64F3991	2.65
Model 65 SX	64F3992	2.65
Model 70	64F3993	2.65
Model P70 386	64F3994	2.65
Model P75 486	84F8525	8.80
Model 80	84F8548	2.85
Model 90 XP 486	04G3388	2.50
Model 95 XP 486	04G3393	5.25
Options and Adapter Information	64F3996	2.65

(continues)

Table 7.3 Continued

Option manuals		
Communications Cartridge (for L40 SX)	10G5992	$1.95
Adapter/A for Ethernet Networks	15F2290	2.20
5.25-inch Slim High Diskette Drive	15F2274	1.55
1-8MB 286 Memory	85F1672	15.75
2.88MB Diskette Drive	85F1648	6.35
FAX Concentrator Adapter/A	15F2262	3.50
External Storage Enclosure for SCSI Devices	91F9233	2.20

Table 7.4 PS/2 Hardware-Maintenance Library Part Numbers and Prices

Description	Part Number	Price
PS/2 Hardware-Maintenance Library Supplements:		
(includes HMS and HMR update and Diskette)		
Model 25 SX	10G6616	$36.00
Model 25 286	15F2180	17.00
Model 35 SX	92F2735	28.50
Model 40 SX	85F1645	13.75
Model L40 SX	15F2271	38.00
Model N51 SX and N51 SLC	04G5108	33.25
Model 56 SX and 56 SLC	10G6005	28.75
Model M57 SLC	10G3340	23.00
Model 57 SX and 57 SLC	04G3385	11.25
Model P70 386	15F2149	44.00
Model 90 486	04G3391	14.50
Model 95 486	04G3396	14.50
Communications Cartridge (for L40 SX)	10G5994	27.95
400MB Hard Disk Drive	15F2233	2.00

Description	Part Number	Price
Image Adapter/A	15F2240	36.25
2.3GB Full Height SCSI Tape Drive	91F9250	20.00
Rewritable Optical Drive	91F9234	13.25
8517 Color Display	92F2676	11.75
8518 Color Display	85F1692	25.50
Cached Processor Option	04G5106	13.00
Manual Binders and Inserts		
Empty HMS (Service) Binder	85F8542	$41.00
HMS Vinyl Insert (pkg. of 6)	84F8543	11.75
Empty HMR (Reference) Binder	01F0200	17.00

Table 7.5 PC Family Hardware-Maintenance Service Manual Part Numbers and Prices		
Description	Part number	Price
PC Hardware-Maintenance Service (PC, XT, AT, PPC):	6280087	$244.00
Supplements to 6280087:		
AT Model 339	6280139	$12.00
XT Model 286	68X2211	12.00
XT Models 089, 268, 278	6280109	12.00
PS/2 Display Adapter (VGA Card)	68X2216	37.00
PC Music Feature	75X1049	52.00
2MB Expanded Memory Adapter	74X9923	67.25
3 1/2-inch internal Floppy Disk Drive	6280159	7.05
3 1/2-inch external Floppy Disk Drive	6280111	12.25
5 1/4-inch external Floppy Disk Drive	68X2273	12.25
20MB Hard Disk Drive Model 25	01F0246	9.45
Empty supplement binder	1502561	9.45

(continues)

Table 7.5 Continued

Description	Part number	Price
Color Printer Model 5182	68X2237	$63.75
Graphics and Compact Printer	6280079	43.00
PCjr	1502294	96.75
PC Convertible	6280641	101.00
Supplement to 6280641:		
Speech Adapter	59X9964	$23.00

Table 7.6 PC Family Hardware-Maintenance Reference Manual Part Numbers and Prices

Description	Part number	Price
PC Hardware-Maintenance Reference (PC, XT, AT, PPC):	6280088	$187.00
Supplements to 6280088:		
AT Model 339	6280138	$7.40
XT Model 286	68X2212	12.00
XT Models 089, 268, and 278	6280108	7.40
PS/2 Display Adapter (VGA Card)	68X2238	7.50
Color Display 8514	68X2218	7.50
3 1/2-inch internal Floppy Disk Drive	6280160	7.40
20MB Hard Disk Drive Model 25	01F0244	4.30
Empty supplement binder	01F0200	21.00

Technical-Reference Library

The publications listed in the following table provide system-specific hardware and software interface information for the IBM PC and PS/2 products. The publications are intended for developers who provide hardware and software products to operate with these systems. The library is divided into system, options and adapters, and BIOS interface publications.

Table 7.7   PC and AT-Bus System Technical-Reference Manual Part Numbers and Prices

Description	Part number	Price
Hardware Interface Technical-Reference AT-Bus Systems:	85F1646	$63.00
Updates to 85F1646:		
PS/2 Model 25 SX	10G6457	10.60
PS/2 Models 35 and 40	41G2950	10.60
Keyboard/Auxiliary Device and AT-Bus Architecture	41G5096	10.75
PS/2 Model L40 SX (Laptop)	15F2270	59.00
PS/2 Model 25	75X1055	35.75
Supplement to 75X1055:		
20MB Hard Disk Drive	01F0245	4.20
PS/2 Model 30	68X2201	94.25
PS/2 Model 30 286	01F0237	30.25
Supplements to 01F0237:		
PS/2 Model 25 286	15F2182	20.00
PC	6322507	37.50
PC AT	6280070	131.00
Supplements to 6280070:		
PC AT Model 339	6280099	62.00
PC XT Model 286	68X2210	62.75
PC XT and Portable PC	6280089	62.00
PC Convertible	6280648	94.25
Supplements to 6280648:		
Speech Adapter	59X9965	23.00
256KB Memory and Enhanced Modem	75X1035	5.20
PC*jr*	1502293	51.25

Hardware Interface Technical Reference

These publications provide interface and design information for the system units. Information is included for the system board, math coprocessor, power supply, video subsystem, keyboard, instruction sets, and other features of the system.

Table 7.8 MCA-Bus Hardware Interface Technical Reference Manual Part Numbers and Prices

Description	Part number	Price
PS/2 Hardware Interface Technical Reference Manuals:		
System Specific Information Technical Reference	84F9807	$75.00
Updates to 84F9807:		
Models 90, 95 and Model 57	04G3280	20.75
Models 56 SX and 56 SLC	41G2912	10.00
Supplements to 84F9807:		
Model N51 SX	04G5120	16.75
Model P75 486	84F7592	35.50
Architectures Technical Reference	84F9808	55.00
Update to 84F9808:		
Micro Channel Architecture and Setup	04G3282	16.00
Supplements to 84F9808:		
Subsystem Control Block Architecture	85F1678	15.00
Common Interfaces Technical Reference	84F9808	75.00
Update to 84F9809:		
Floppy Controller, Keyboard, Keyboard/Auxiliary Device Controller, Serial Port Controller, Video Subsystem, and SCSI	04G3281	21.75
Supplement to 84F9809:		
Model P70 386	68X2377	15.50

BIOS Interface Technical Reference

This publication provides basic input-output system (BIOS) interface information. It is intended for developers of hardware or software products that operate with the IBM PC and PS/2 products.

Table 7.9   BIOS Interface Technical Reference Manual Part Numbers and Prices

Description	Part number	Price
BIOS Interface Technical Reference (4th edition)	04G3283	$55.00

Options and Adapters Technical Reference

These publications provide interface and design information for the options and adapters available for various systems. This information includes a hardware description, programming considerations, interface specifications, and BIOS information (where applicable).

Table 7.10   Options and Adapters Technical Reference Manual Part Numbers and Prices

Description	Part number	Price
Options and Adapters Technical Reference includes:	6322509	$156.00
Asynchronous Communications Adapter		
Bisynchronous Communications Adapter		
Cluster Adapter		
Color Display		
Color/Graphics Monitor Adapter		

(continues)

Table 7.10   Continued

Description	Part number	Price
Color, Compact, and Graphics Printers		
Expansion Unit		
Hard Disk Drive Adapter		
Game Control Adapter		
Monochrome Display		
Monochrome/Printer Adapter		
Printer Adapter		
SDLC Adapter		
Slimline Floppy Disk Drive		
10M Hard Disk Drive		
5.25-Inch Floppy Disk Drive and Adapter		
64/256K Memory Option		
Engineering/Scientific Adapters, Includes:	6280133	42.25
Data Acquisition and Control Adapter (DAC)		
DAC Distribution Panel		
General Purpose Interface Bus Adapter		
Professional Graphics Controller		
Professional Graphics Display		
Personal Computer AT, Includes:	6280134	16.00
Double-Sided Floppy Disk Drive		
Hard Disk and Floppy Disk Drive Adapter		
High-Capacity Floppy Disk Drive		
Serial/Parallel Adapter		
128K Memory Expansion Option		
20MB Hard Disk Drive		
512K Memory Expansion Option		

Description	Part number	Price
Communications		
Dual Async Adapter/A (Second Edition)	68X2315	$7.50
Multiprotocol Adapter/A (Second Edition)	68X2316	14.75
300/1200 Internal Modem/A	68X2275	7.50
300/1200/2400 Internal Modem/A	68X2378	6.40
Displays		
PS/2 Color Display 8514	68X2214	$7.50
PS/2 Display Adapter (VGA Card)	68X2251	12.25
PS/2 Display Adapter 8514/A	68X2248	12.25
PS/2 Displays 8503, 8512, and 8513	68X2206	7.50
EGA, EGA Display and EGA Memory Expansion Card	6280131	12.00
Floppy Disk Drives and Adapters		
3 1/2-Inch External Drive	59X9945	$6.50
3 1/2-Inch External Drive Adapter	59X9946	6.50
3 1/2-Inch 720K/1.44M/2.88M Drive	15F2258	11.50
5 1/4-Inch External Drive (360K)	68X2272	12.25
5 1/4-Inch External Drive (1.2MB)	68X2348	11.75
5 1/4-Inch Internal Drive (1.2MB)	68X2350	11.75
5 1/4-Inch Drive Adapter (1.2MB)	68X2349	11.75
Floppy Disk Drive Half Height (XT,AT)	6280093	7.40
Hard Disk Drive and Adapters		
Hard Disk Drive Adapter/A	68X2226	$14.75
Hard Disk Drive Adapter/A, ESDI	68X2234	14.75
Hard Disk/Floppy Disk Adapter (for XT Model 286)	68X2215	7.50
20MB Drive (XT-089, -278, -286)	68X2208	8.75
20MB Adapter (XT-089, -268, -278)	6280092	7.40
20MB Drive and Adapter (Model 25)	01F0247	3.45
3 1/2-Inch 20MB Drive (Model 30)	68X2205	7.50
3 1/2-Inch 20MB Drive (Model 50)	68X2219	12.25
30MB Drive (AT)	68X2310	23.00

(continues)

Table 7.10 Continued

Description	Part number	Price
30MB Drive (Model 50-031)	68X2324	12.25
20/30/45MB Drive (Model 25 and 30)	92F1655	13.00
40MB/80MB Drive	91F9230	17.25
44MB Drive (Second Edition)	68X2317	7.50
60MB Adapter (50-021 and 50-031)	68X2343	4.95
60/120MB Drives (Models 50 and 70)	68X2314	11.00
70/115/314MB Drives	68X2236	7.50
Other Storage Devices and Adapters		
CD-ROM Drive	15F2134	$13.00
Rewritable Optical Drive	64F1513	17.50
2.3GB SCSI Tape Drive	84F9801	19.75
Micro Channel SCSI Adapter	68X2397	16.25
Micro Channel SCSI Adapter w/Cache	68X2365	17.25
FAX Concentrator Adapter/A Device Driver Reference	15F2263	18.00
FAX Concentrator Adapter/A Extended Device Driver Ref.	15F2276	30.00
Internal Data/FAX Modem for the L40 SX	15F2268	14.00
Memory		
128/640K Memory Adapter	1502544	$7.40
256K Memory Expansion	6280132	12.00
512KB/2MB Memory Adapter	6183075	7.40
2MB Expanded Memory Adapter	75X1086	10.75
Expanded Memory Adapter/A (0-8MB)	01F0228	7.80
80286 Memory Expansion Option	68X2227	7.50
80286 Memory Expansion Option 2-8MB	68X2356	7.60
80386 Memory Expansion Option 2-6MB	68X2257	12.25
80386 Memory Expansion Option 2-8MB	68X2339	14.75

Description	Part number	Price
Other		
PS/2 Speech Adapter	68X2207	$15.75
Voice Communications Adapter	55X8864	7.40
PS/2 Mouse	68X2229	7.50
PC Music Feature	75X1048	21.75
Empty Options and Adapters Binder	6280115	9.30
Software Reference Manuals		
Basic Reference Version 3.30	6280189	$56.00
DOS Technical Reference Version 5.02	53G1686	85.00

Ordering Information

IBM technical and service publications can be ordered by calling toll-free 1-800-IBM-PCTB (1-800-426-7282), Monday through Friday, 8 a.m. to 8 p.m. Eastern time. In Canada, call toll-free 1-800-465-1234, Monday through Friday, from 8:30 a.m. to 4:30 p.m. Eastern time. In British Columbia, call toll-free 112-800-465-1234. In Alaska, call 1-414-633-8108.

When you order by telephone, you can use a credit card. You also may call to request additional copies of the Technical Directory (catalog) or to inquire about the availability of technical information on newly announced products that may not be listed here.

Chapter 8

Vendor Contact Information

Industry and Worldwide Standards Information

The following list shows official sources for documentation on industry and worldwide standards that relate to the computer industry.

FIPS or CCITT Recommendations:
National Technical Information Service
Springfield, VA 22161
(703) 487-4650

Standard Reference Materials (SRMs):
Office of Standards Reference Materials
National Bureau of Standards
Room B311, Chemistry Building
Gaithersburg, MD 20899
(301) 975-6776

ANSI or ISO Standards:
National Standards Institute
1430 Broadway, New York, NY 10018
(212) 642-4900

X3 Standards:
X3 Secretariat
CBEMA
311 First Street, N.W., Suite 500
Washington, DC 20001
(202)737-8888

or

Global Engineering Documents
15 Inverness Way East
Englewood, CO 80112-5704
(303)792-2181
(800)854-7179
(303)792-2192 FAX

EIA Standards:
Electronic Industries Association
Engineering Department
2001 Eye Street N.W.
Washington, DC 20006
(202)457-4500

MIL Standards:
Navy Publication Center
Philadelphia, PA
(215)697-2667 orders
(215)697-2191 publications
(215)697-4834 customer services

IEEE Standards:
IEEE Service Center
445 Hoes Lane
Piscataway, NJ 08854
(201)981-0060

or

IEEE Computer Society Press
Worldway Postal Center
Los Angeles, CA 90080
(714)821-8380

Federal Telecommunications Standards (FED-STD):
General Services Administration
Specifications Sales (WFRI)
7th and D Streets, S.W.
Washington, DC 20407
(202)472-2205

ECMA standards:
European Computer Manufacturers Association
114 Rue de Rhone
CH-1204 Geneva, Switzerland

Commonly Used IBM Phone Numbers

Most frequently used IBM Phone Numbers for PC Support:

IBM General Information	(800)426-3333
IBM Authorized Dealer Locator	(800)447-4700
IBM PS/1 Dealer Locator	(800)IBM-3377
IBM PC Direct (Mail Order Sales)	(800)IBM-2YOU
IBM OS/2 Products Order Line	(800)3IBM-OS2
IBM Technical Manuals	(800)IBM-PCTB
IBM Personal Systems Help Center	(800)PS2-2227
IBM Parts Order Center	(303)924-4100
IBM Part Number ID and Lookup	(303)924-4015
IBM NSD Hardware Service (PC Repair)	(800)IBM-SERV
IBM NSD Software Support	(800)237-5511
IBM Multi-Media Marketing Assistance	(800)426-9402
IBM Multi-Media Technical Assistance	(800)241-1620
IBM PC Company Bulletin Board System (BBS)	(919)517-0001
IBM PS/1 Bulletin Board System (BBS)	(404)835-8230
IBM PC Company Product Information FAXback System	(800)IBM-4FAX
IBM PC Company Technical Support FAXback System	(800)IBM-3395

Other frequently used IBM Numbers:

IBM Educational Fulfillment (Students, Schools)	(800)222-7257
IBM CAD Assistance	(303)924-7262
IBM Credit Card	(800)426-4856
IBM Customer Relations	(201)930-3443
IBM Employee Sales	(800)426-3675
IBM Industrial PC Support	(800)526-6602
IBM Industrial PC Technical Support	(800)241-1620
IBM Maintenance Department (Maintenance Agreements)	(800)624-6875
IBM Manufacturing Systems Information	(800)526-6602
IBM Product Information Center	(800)426-7699
IBM Software Services and Support	(800)336-5430
IBM Special Needs or Disabilities Information Center	(800)426-2133
IBM Independent Developer Information/ Registration	(800)982-6408

Vendor Phone List and BBS Directory

One of the most frustrating things about supporting PCs is finding a specific adapter board, part, driver program, or whatever you need to make a system work. If you are supporting or installing products, you will often need access to technical support or documentation for products that you may not have purchased yourself. Over the years I have compiled a list of companies whose products are popular or whose products I have found to work exceptionally well. I use these contacts regularly to provide information and components that enable me to support PC systems effectively.

Many of these companies have been mentioned previously in this book, but others not specifically mentioned have been added here. These companies carry many computer products that you often will have contact with, or that I simply recommend. I have tried to list as many vendors as possible that are important in day-to-day work with PC systems. These vendors can supply documentation for components you have, provide parts and service, and be used as a source for new equipment and even software. This list is as up-to-date as possible, but companies move or go out of business all the time. If you find any information in this list that no longer is accurate, please call me or leave me a message on CompuServe. My address, phone number, and CIS ID are under the listing for Mueller Technical Research.

Many of the companies listed also provide support via electronic Bulletin Board Systems (BBSs). Ward Christensen (creator of the XModem protocol) and Randy Seuss created the first Computerized Bulletin Board System (CBBS) system which went on-line on February 16, 1978, and which is still running today using the original software! You can call Ward & Randy's CBBS at (312)545-8086. Since that first BBS came on-line, BBS systems have proliferated throughout the world. While originally exclusively the domain of computer enthusiasts, today many companies use BBS systems to provide a high level of technical support. Through a company-run BBS you can often receive detailed technical support on that company's products, as well as download product literature and reference materials. I usually find that the level of support I can obtain through a BBS is superior to traditional phone support, especially since I don't have to wait on hold!

Many of these companies also provide on-line support and services through the CompuServe Information System (CIS). You will find many major hardware and software companies on CIS, however, most of these same companies also run standard BBS systems as well. Access to CIS is charged by the hour based on the connect speed (up to 9600 bps), but the phone call itself is usually a local one. If you wish to access CIS, you can contact them via a voice line (see the vendor list) and request a startup kit.

With each company listing, I have included both standard phone numbers as well as 800 numbers where possible, so that U.S. and international readers can easily contact these companies. Also included are FAX and Bulletin Board System (BBS) numbers, when available. I have not included any communications parameter settings, but virtually all BBS systems will work with at least 2400 bps (v.22bis), 8 data bits, no parity, and 1 stop bit. Many of these systems also will support faster communications rates up to 14,400 bps (v.32bis), or even 28,800 bps (v.32fast). Some companies run a FAXback system, which is an automated system through which you can request product and technical information to be sent directly to your own FAX machine. FAXback systems are an excellent way to get immediate documentation or technical support to solve tough problems.

Finally, each listing also includes a short description of the products or services that the company provides. I use this vendor list constantly myself; I hope that you find this list as useful as I do!

3M Data Storage Products Division
3M Center Building #223-5N-01
St. Paul, MN 55144
(612)736-1866

Manufactures magnetic disk and tape media. DC-600 and DC-2000 media are standards for tape-backup data cartridges.

Accurite Technologies, Inc.
231 Charcot Ave.
San Jose, CA 95131
(408)433-1980

Manufactures Accurite Drive Probe floppy disk diagnostics program, as well as HRD, DDD, and ADD industry-standard test disks.

Acer Technologies Corporation
401 Charcot Avenue
San Jose, CA 95131
(408)922-0333
(800)538-1542
(800)833-8241 BBS

Manufactures PC-compatible systems, monitors, and printers.

Acme Electric/Safe Power
20 Water Street
Cuba, NY 14727
(716)968-2400
(800)325-5848

Manufactures uninterruptible power supply (UPS) systems and power conditioners.

Adaptec
691 S. Milpitas Boulevard
Milpitas, CA 95035
(408)945-8600
(408)945-2550 Technical Support
(800)959-7274 Technical Support
(800)934-2766 Literature
(408)945-7727 BBS

Manufactures a variety of excellent hard disk controllers and SCSI host adapters. Their SCSI Host Adapters have become a de facto standard and have an enormous amount of third-party support.

Adaptive Technologies

127 N. Ventura Blvd.
Port Hueneme, CA 93041
(805)488-8832
(805)488-4890 FAX

Manufactures and sells the PROMPAQ automobile ECM chip selector. This is a device that installs EPROMS in General Motors automobiles and allows for switching between as many as four EPROMS with different vehicle operating programs. The selected PROM is enabled as if it were plugged into the ECM. The switch can be changed even while the vehicle is running, instantly enabling the new PROM program! I used this device to install four custom EPROMS in one of my vehicles.

Addison-Wesley Publishing Co, Inc.

Route 128
Reading, MA 01867
(617)944-3700

Publishes technical publications and books.

Adobe Systems, Inc.

1585 Charleston Road
Box 7900
Mountain View, CA 94039
(415)961-0911
(800)447-3577

Created and manufactures the PostScript language and a variety of graphics software.

Advanced Digital Information Corporation

14737 NE 87th Street
Box 2996
Redmond, WA 98073-2966
(206)881-8004
(800)336-1233
(206)881-2296 FAX
(714)894-0893 BBS

Manufactures high-capacity, tape-backup subsystems.

Advanced Logic Research (ALR)

9401 Jeronimo Street
Irvine, CA 92718
(714)581-6770
(800)444-4257
(714)581-9240 FAX
(714)458-1952 Technical Support
(714)458-6834 BBS

Manufactures PC compatibles featuring ISA, EISA, and MCA buses.

Advanced Micro Devices (AMD)

901 Thompson Place
Box 3453
Sunnyvale, CA 94088
(408)732-2400

Manufactures 386-compatible chips and math coprocessors.

Aeronics, Inc.

12741 Research Blvd.
Suite #500
Austin, TX 78759
(512)258-2303
(512)258-4392 FAX

Manufactures the highest quality Active and Forced Perfect
Terminators for use in SCSI bus systems. They are known for
solving problems with longer distances or multiple SCSI devices.

Aldus Corporation

411 1st Avenue South
Seattle, WA 98104
(206)622-5500
(800)333-2538

Manufactures PageMaker desktop publishing software and a variety of other
graphical programs.

ALL Computers, Inc.

1220 Yonge Street
Second Floor
Toronto, ONT M4T1W1
(416)960-0111
(800)387-2744
(416)960-0111 Technical Support
(416)960-5426 FAX
(416)960-8679 BBS

Manufactures the ALL Chargecard memory coprocessor.

Allied Computer Services, Inc.

3417 Center Point Road N.E.
Cedar Rapids, IA 52402
(319)378-1383
(319)378-1489 FAX

Manufactures and sells the Trapcard II IRQ and DMA diagnostic board.

AllMicro, Inc.

1250 Rogers Street
Suite D
Clearwater, FL 34616
(813)446-6660

Manufacturer and distributor of the Rescue data recovery software and various other hardware and software diagnostics and troubleshooting tools.

Alloy Computer Products

165 Forest Street
Marlborough, MA 01752
(508)481-8500
(800)544-7551
(508)486-0001 Technical Support
(508)481-7711 FAX
(508)460-8140 BBS

Manufactures tape-backup subsystems.

Alpha Research Corporation

8200 Mopac Expressway North
Park North Building, #120
Austin, TX 78759
(512)345-6465
(512)345-6496 FAX

Manufactures a complete line of caching and noncaching disk controllers, local bus motherboards, and video cards. Specializes in IDE and SCSI adapters that are fast and flexible.

ALPS America

3553 N. First Street
San Jose, CA 95134
(408)432-6000

Supplies 5 1/4-inch and 3 1/2-inch floppy drives to IBM for use in the original XT, AT, and now the PS/2 systems. Also manufactures a line of printers and scanners.

Altex Electronics, Inc.

300 Breesport
San Antonio, TX 78216
(512)349-8795
(800)531-5369

Supplies mail-order electronics parts.

Ambra Computer Corporation

3200 Beechleaf Court
Raleigh, NC 27604-1063
(919)713-1550
(800)25-AMBRA
(919)713-1599 FAX

An IBM company that manufactures and sells low-cost high-performance compatible systems featuring Pentium and IBM Blue Lightning processors as well as other unique features.

Amdek Corporation

3471 N. First Street
San Jose, CA 95134
(408)473-1200
(800)722-6335
(408)435-2770 Technical Support
(408)922-5729 FAX
(408)922-4400 BBS

Division of Wyse Technology that manufactures monitors.

American Megatrends, Inc. (AMI)

6145-F Northbelt Parkway
Norcross, GA 30071
(404)263-8181
(800)828-9264
(404)246-8780 BBS

Manufactures the most popular IBM-compatible BIOS, excellent ISA, EISA, VL-Bus, and PCI Local bus motherboards, and diagnostics software such as AMIDIAG, SCSI DIAG, and Remote.

American National Standards Institute

11 West 42nd Street
13th Floor
New York, NY 10036
(212)642-4900

ANSI committees set standards throughout the computer industry. Copies of any ANSI-approved standard can be ordered here.

AMP, Inc.

AMP Building
Harrisburg, PA 17105
(717)564-0100
(800)522-6752

Manufactures a variety of computer connectors, sockets, and cables used by many OEMs, including IBM.

Andromeda Research

P.O. Box 222
Milford, OH 45150
(513)831-9708
(513)831-7562

Manufactures an excellent EPROM programmer that runs from a
PC parallel port. The device can program up to 4M EPROMS and includes
software for menu-driven operation on IBM-compatible systems.

Annabooks

11848 Bernardo Plaza Court
Suite 110
San Diego, CA 92128-2417
(619) 673-0870
(800) 462-1042
(619)673-1432 FAX

Publishes and sells an excellent line of technical publications and books
especially for those in PC hardware and software design.

Anthem Technology Systems (ATS)

1160 Ridder Park Drive
San Jose, CA 95131
(408)441-7177
(800)359-3580
(800)359-9877 FAX

A large distributor of Hewlett-Packard DAT tape and hard disk drives. They also
distribute other hard disk and storage products.

Anvil Cases

15650 Salt Lake Avenue
Industry, CA 91745
(818)968-4100
(800)359-2684

Manufactures heavy-duty equipment cases.

AOX, Inc.

486 Totten Pond Road
Waltham, MA 02154
(617)890-4402
(800)726-0269

Manufactures PS/2 MCA bus master 386 and 486 processor upgrade boards.

Apple Computer, Inc.
20525 Mariani Avenue
Cupertino, CA 95014
(408)996-1010
(800)538-9696

Manufactures a line of Apple-compatible systems, peripherals, and software.

Archive Technology/Ardat, Inc.
1650 Sunflower Avenue
Costa Mesa, CA 92626
(714)641-1230
(800)537-2724

Manufactures high-capacity tape drives.

Arco Electronics, Inc.
2750 N. 29th Ave.
Suite 316
Hollywood, CA 33020
(305)925-2688
(305)925-2889 FAX
(305)925-2791 BBS

Manufactures a complete line of Micro Channel ATA IDE adapters which can be used to upgrade IBM PS/2 systems.

Areal Technology, Inc.
2075 Zanker Road
San Jose, CA 95131
(408)436-6800

Manufactures high-capacity 3 1/2-inch hard disk drives.

Arrow Electronics, Inc.
25 Hub Drive
Melville, NY 11747
(516)391-1300
(800)447-5270

System and peripheral distributor.

Arrowfield International, Inc.
2822-C Walnut Ave.
Tustin, CA 92680
(714)669-0101
(714)669-0526 FAX

Manufactures an incredible array of disk drive brackets, rails, slides, cable adapters, bezels, cabinets, and complete drive upgrade and repair assemblies for IBM, Compaq, and IBM-compatible systems.

AST Research, Inc.

16215 Alton Parkway
Irvine, CA 92713-9658
(714)727-4141
(800)876-4278
(714)727-4723 BBS

Manufactures an extensive line of adapter boards and peripherals for IBM and compatible computers, as well as a line of IBM-compatible systems.

Astec Standard Power

Division of Astec America, Inc.
401 Jones Road
Oceanside, CA 92054-1216
(619)757-1880
(619)439-4243 FAX

Manufactures high-end power supplies for PC systems as well as many other applications. Astec power supplies are used as OEM equipment in many of the top manufacturer's systems, including IBM and others.

AT&T

55 Corporate Drive
Bridgewater, NJ 08807
(404)446-4734
(800)247-1212
(201)769-6397 BBS

Manufactures a line of IBM-compatible computer systems.

AT&T National Parts Sales Center

2551 E. 40th Avenue
Denver, CO 80205
(800)222-7278

Supplies parts and components for AT&T computer systems.
Call and ask for the free AT&T parts catalog.

ATI Technologies, Inc.

33 Commerce Valley Drive East
Thornhill, ONT L3T7N6
(416)882-2600
(416)882-2626 Technical Support
(416)882-2620 FAX
(416)764-9404 BBS

Manufactures an excellent line of high-performance standard and local bus video cards and chipsets.

Autodesk, Inc.
2320 Marinship Way
Sausalito, CA 94965
(415)332-2344
(800)445-5415

Manufactures AutoCAD software.

Award Software, Inc.
130 Knowles Drive
Los Gatos, CA 95030-1832
(408)370-7979
(408)370-3399 FAX
(408)370-3139 BBS

Manufactures a line of IBM-compatible ROM BIOS software.

Beckman Industrial
3883 Ruffin Road
San Diego, CA 92123
(619)495-3200
(800)854-2708

Manufactures diagnostics and test equipment.

Belden Wire and Cable
P.O. Box 1980
Richmond, IN 47375
(317)983-5200
(800)235-3361

Manufactures cable and wire products.

Berkshire Products, Inc.
2180 Pleasant Hill Road
Suite A-5185
Duluth, GA 30136-4663
(404)271-0088
(404)932-0082 FAX

Manufactures a diagnostics monitoring product called System
Sentry, which continuously monitors power supply performance
and system internal temperature as well as CMOS battery voltage and BIOS
POST codes. It is designed for diagnostics applications as well as for use in a
file server application, where the internal serial port can transmit error information via a modem to another system. They also make a high-speed buffered
parallel port adapter.

Best Power Technology, Inc.

P.O. Box 280
Necedah, WI 54646
(608)565-7200
(800)356-5794
(608)565-2221 FAX

Manufactures an excellent line of computer power protection
equipment from high-end Ferroresonent UPS systems to Line
Conditioners and Standby Power Protection systems.

Bitstream, Inc.

215 1st Street
Cambridge, MA 02142
(617)497-6222
(800)522-3668

Manufactures fonts and font software.

Black Box Corporation

P.O. Box 12800
Pittsburgh, PA 15241
(412)746-5530

Manufactures and distributes a variety of communications products including
network adapters, cables, and connectors for a variety of applications.

Boca Research, Inc.

6413 Congress Avenue
Boca Raton, FL 33487-2841
(407)997-6227
(407)241-8088 Technical Support
(407)997-0918 FAX
(407)241-1601 BBS

Manufactures a low-cost line of adapter card products for
IBM-compatibles.

Bondwell Industrial Company, Inc.

47485 Seabridge Drive
Fremont, CA 94538
(415)490-4300

Manufactures a line of laptop systems.

Borland International

1800 Green Hills Road
Scotts Valley, CA 95066
(408)439-1411
(800)331-0877
(408)438-8400 Technical Support
(408)439-9344 FAX
(408)431-5096 BBS

Software manufacturer that features Turbo language products,
Paradox, as well as dBASE IV, acquired from Ashton-Tate.

Boston Computer Exchange

55 Temple Place
Boston, MA 02111
(617)542-4414

A broker for used IBM and compatible computers.

Bracking, Jim

967 Pinewood Drive
San Jose, CA 95129
(408)725-0628

Manufactures the HDtest hard disk test and format program. This program,
distributed as shareware, is excellent for testing and educational use.

Brightbill-Roberts

120 E. Washington Street
#421
Syracuse, NY 13202
(315)474-3400
(800)444-3490

Manufactures the ShowPartner FX presentation graphics program.

Buerg, Vernon D.

139 White Oak Circle
Petaluma, CA 94952
(707)778-1811
(707)778-8728 FAX
(707)778-8944 BBS

Manufactures an excellent line of utility programs including the popular LIST
program. Buerg Software is distributed through BBS systems and CompuServe.

Bureau of Electronic Publishing

141 New Road
Parsippany, NJ 07054
(201)808-2700
(800)828-4766

Distributes and publishes software on CD-ROM disks.

Byte Information Exchange (BIX)

One Phoenix Mill Lane
Peterborough, NH 03458
(603)924-7681

An on-line computer information and messaging system.

Byte Magazine

One Phoenix Mill Lane
Peterborough, NH 03458
(603)924-9281
(617)861-9764 BBS

A monthly magazine covering all lines of microcomputers.

C. Itoh Electronics, Inc.

19300 S Hamilton Avenue
Box 9116
Torrance, CA 90508
(213)327-9100

Manufactures PC printers and other peripherals.

Cable Connection

557 Salmar Avenue
Suite B
Campbell, CA 95008
(408)379-9224

Manufactures a variety of cable, connector, and switch products.

Cables To Go

26 W. Nottingham
Suite 200
Dayton, OH 45405
(513)275-0886
(800)826-7904

Manufactures a variety of cable, connector, and switch products.

Cache Computers, Inc.
46600 Landing Parkway
Fremont, CA 94538
(510)266-9922

Manufactures a line of 386 and 486 motherboards.

Cal-Abco
6041 Variel Avenue
Woodland Hills, CA 91367
(818)704-7733
(800)669-2226

Distributes computer systems and peripherals.

Canon USA, Inc.
One Canon Plaza
Lake Success, NY 11042
(516)488-6700
(800)221-3333
(516)354-5805 FAX
(516)488-6528 BBS

Manufactures a line of printer and video equipment as well as floppy drives.
Supplies floppy drives to Compaq and IBM.

Casio, Inc.
15 Gardner Road
Fairfield, NJ 07006
(201)575-7400

Manufactures personal data systems and digital watches.

Central Point Software, Inc.
15220 NW Greenbrier Parkway
Beaverton, OR 97006-9937
(503)690-8088
(800)445-4208
(503)690-8083 FAX
(503)690-6650 BBS

Manufactures the PC Tools, Copy II PC, and Central Point Backup software.
Central Point supplies many of the utilities found in IBM and MS-DOS 5.0 and
higher.

Chemtronics, Inc.
8125 Cobb Center Drive
Kennesaw, GA 30144
(404)424-4888
(404)424-4267 FAX

Manufactures and sells a complete line of computer and electronic grade chemicals, materials, and supplies.

Cherry Electrical Products
3600 Sunset Avenue
Waukegan, IL 60087
(708)662-9200

Manufactures a line of high-quality keyboards for IBM-compatible systems.

Chicago Case Company
4446 S. Ashland Avenue
Chicago, IL 60609
(312)927-1600

Manufactures equipment-shipping and travel cases.

Chinon America, Inc.
660 Maple Avenue
Torrance, CA 90503
(213)533-0274
(800)441-0222

Manufactures a line of floppy disk and CD-ROM drives.

Chips & Technologies, Inc.
3050 Zanker Road
San Jose, CA 95134
(408)434-0600
(800)944-6284

Manufactures specialized chip sets for compatible motherboard manufacturers.

Ci Design Company
1711 Langley Avenue
Irvine, CA 92714
(714)261-5524

Manufactures custom-made 3 1/2-inch drive mounting kits used by Toshiba, Panasonic, and NEC for their drive products. Also makes drive faceplates, enclosures, and custom cable assemblies.

Cipher Data Products, Inc.
10101 Old Grove Road
San Diego, CA 92131
(619)578-9100
(800)424-7437

Manufactures a line of tape-backup products. Also supplies
tape-backup systems to IBM.

Ciprico, Inc.
2955 Xenium Lane
Minneapolis, MN 55441
(612)559-2034
(800)727-4669

Manufactures high-performance SCSI host adapters.

Citizen America Corporation
2450 Broadway
Suite 600
Santa Monica, CA 90404
(310)453-0614
(800)556-1234
(310)453-2814 FAX
(310)453-7564 BBS

Manufactures a line of printers and floppy disk drives.

CMD Technology, Inc.
1 Vanderbilt
Irvine, CA 92718
(714)454-0800
(800)426-3832
(714)455-1656 FAX

Manufactures EISA adapters, PCI and VL-Bus IDE and SCSI disk adapters.

CMS Enhancements, Inc.
2722 Michelson Drive
Irvine, CA 92715
(714)222-6000

Distributes a variety of system and peripheral products, and
specializes in hard disk drives.

Colorado Memory Systems, Inc.

800 S. Taft Avenue
Loveland, CO 80537
(303)669-8000
(800)346-9881
(303)667-0997 FAX
(303)635-0650 BBS

Manufactures tape-backup subsystems specializing in QIC-80
and QIC-40 systems that attach through an interface card,
floppy controller, or parallel port connection.

Columbia Data Products

1070B Rainer Drive
Altamonte Springs, FL 32714
(407)869-6700
(407)862-4725 FAX
(407)862-4724 BBS

Manufactures SCSI drivers for Western Digital FASST host adapters.

Comb

720 Anderson Avenue
Street Cloud, MN 56372
(612)654-4800
(800)328-0609

Liquidates and distributes a variety of discontinued products,
including PC-compatible systems and peripherals.

Compaq Computer Corporation

 20555 State Hwy.
Suite 249
Houston, TX 77070
(713)370-0670
(800)231-0900
(800) 345-1518 Technical support
(713) 374-1518 BBS

Manufactures high-end IBM-compatible computer systems.

CompUSA, Inc.

15151 Surveyor
#A
Addison, TX 75244
(214)702-0055
(800)932-2667

Computer retail superstore and mail-order outlet.

CompuServe Information Service (CIS)
5000 Arlington Centre Boulevard
Columbus, OH 43220
(614)457-8600
(800)848-8199

Largest on-line information and messaging service; offers
manufacturer- and vendor-sponsored forums for technical support.

Computer Component Source, Inc.
135 Eileen Way
Syosset, NY 11791-9022
(516)496-8727
(800)356-1227
(516)496-8984 FAX
(800)926-2062 FAX

Distributes a large number of computer components for repair. Specializes in
display parts such as flyback transformers and other components.

Computer Hotline Magazine
15400 Knoll Trail
#500
Dallas, TX 75248
(214)233-5131
(800)866-3241

Publication featuring advertisers offering excellent sources of
replacement and repair parts, as well as new and used equipment
at wholesale prices.

Computer Reseller News Magazine
CMP Publications, Inc.
600 Community Drive
Manhasset, NY 11030-3875
(516)562-5000
(516)562-5468

An excellent industry trade weekly news magazine featuring news for computer professionals involved in value-added reselling of computer equipment.
Subscriptions are free to those who qualify.

Computer Retail Week Magazine
CMP Publications, Inc.
600 Community Drive
Manhasset, NY 11030-3875
(516)562-5000
(516)562-5468

An excellent industry trade weekly news magazine featuring news for computer superstores, mass merchants, and retailers. Subscriptions are free to those
who qualify.

Computer Shopper Magazine

5211 S. Washington Avenue
Titusville, FL 32780
(305)269-3211

Monthly magazine for experimenters and bargain hunters that
features a large number of advertisements.

Computer Technology Review Magazine

West World Productions, Inc.
924 Westwood Blvd.
Suite 650
Los Angeles, CA 90024-2910
(213)208-1335

An excellent monthly technical magazine for systems integrators, Value Added
Resellers, and Original Equipment Manufacturers. Subscriptions are free to
those who qualify.

Comtech Publishing Ltd.

P.O. Box 12340
Reno, NV 89510
(702)825-9000
(800)456-7005
(702)825-1818 FAX

Manufactures dSalvage Professional, the best and most comprehensive xBASE
data-recovery and file repair software available.

Connector Resources Unlimited (CRU)

1005 Ames Avenue
Milpitas, CA 95035
(408)942-9077

Manufactures a large variety of disk enclosures, mounting kits, cables, and
connectors for IBM and Mac systems.

Conner Peripherals, Inc.

3081 Zanker Road
San Jose, CA 95134
(408)456-4500
(800)275-4642
(408)456-3388 Technical Support
(408)456-4501 FAX
(800)4CONNER (426-6637) FAXback Information System
(408)456-4415 BBS

Manufactures 3 1/2-inch IDE and SCSI hard disk drives. Partly owned by
Compaq, and supplies most of Compaq's hard drives.

Core International, Inc.
7171 North Federal Hwy.
Boca Raton, FL 33487
(407)997-6055
(407)241-2929 BBS

Distributes a variety of different manufacturers' hard disk drives including
Seagate and Western Digital.

Corel Systems, Inc.
1600 Carling Avenue
Ottawa, ONT, K1Z8R7
(613)728-8200
(800)836-7874
(613)728-9790 FAX
(613)728-4752 BBS

Manufactures the CorelDRAW! graphics program as well as Corel SCSI, a SCSI
driver kit featuring drivers for a variety of SCSI host adapters and devices.

Creative Labs, Inc.
2050 Duane Avenue
Santa Clara, CA 95054
(408)428-6600
(800)544-6146
(408)428-6622 Technical Support
(408)428-6011 FAX
(408)428-6660 BBS

Manufactures the Soundblaster series audio cards for multimedia and sound
applications.

CS Electronics
1342 Bell Avenue
Tustin, CA 92680
(714)259-9100
(714)259-0911 FAX

Manufactures a very high-quality line of disk and tape drive cables, specializing in SCSI-1, SCSI-2, and SCSI-3 applications. They offer custom lengths,
connectors, and impedances for a proper match with an existing installation
and use the highest quality raw cable available.

Cumulus Corporation
23500 Mercantile Road
Cleveland, OH 44120
(216)464-2211
(216)464-3019 BBS

Manufactures processor-upgrade products and clone systems.

Curtis Manufacturing Co, Inc.

30 Fitzgerald Drive
Jaffrey, NH 03452
(603)532-4123
(800)548-4900

Manufactures a line of computer accessories, cables, and toolkits.

Cyrix Corporation

2703 N. Central Expressway
Richardson, TX 75080
(214)234-8387
(800)327-6284
(214)699-9857 FAX

Manufactures fast Intel-compatible processors and math copro-cessors for 286-, 386SX-, and 386DX-based systems. One product they make is the 486DRx2, a clock doubled 486 processor that is pin compatible with the Intel 386DX, and which can be used to upgrade existing 386DX systems.

Dak Industries, Inc.

8200 Remmet Avenue
Canoga Park, CA 91304
(818)888-8220
(800)325-0800
(818)715-7153 BBS

Liquidates and distributes a variety of discontinued and/or unique products, including PC compatible systems and peripherals.

Dallas Semiconductor

4401 S. Beltwood Parkway
Dallas, TX 75244
(214)450-0400

Manufactures real-time clock and nonvolatile RAM modules used by a number of OEMs including IBM, Compaq, and others.

Damark International, Inc.

7101 Winnetka Avenue North
Minneapolis, MN 55429
(800)729-9000

Liquidates and distributes a variety of discontinued products, including PC-compatible systems and peripherals.

Data Depot

1710 Drew Street
Clearwater, FL 34615-2151
(813)446-3402
(800)275-1913
(800)SOS-DIAGnostics (767-3424)
(813)443-4377 FAX

Manufactures the PocketPOST diagnostics card for ISA and EISA
systems, as well as several other excellent diagnostics hardware
and software products.

Data Spec

20120 Plummer Street
Chatsworth, CA 91311
(818)993-1202
(800)431-8124

Manufactures a complete line of switch boxes for parallel, serial, video, and
many other connections.

Data Technology Corporation (DTC)

1515 Centre Pointe Drive
Milpitas, CA 95035-8010
(408)942-4000
(408)942-4027 FAX
(408)942-4197 BBS

Manufactures a complete line of hard disk controllers for ISA and EISA bus
systems.

Datastorm Technologies, Inc.

3212 Lemone Boulevard
Columbia, MO 65205
(314)443-3282
(314)443-3282 BBS

Manufactures ProCOMM and ProCOMM Plus communications software.

Dell Computer Corporation

9505 Arboretum Boulevard
Austin, TX 78759
(512)338-4400
(800)426-5150
(512)338-8528 BBS

Manufactures a line of low-cost, high-performance, IBM-compatible computer
systems.

DiagSoft, Inc.
5615 Scotts Valley Drive
Suite 140
Scotts Valley, CA 95066
(408)438-8247
(800)342-4763
(408)438-7113 FAX

Manufactures the QAPlus user-level PC diagnostics software, as well as the high-end QAPlus/FE (Field Engineer) software, which is an excellent program that includes complete high-resolution floppy drive testing and the Power Meter benchmarking utility.

Digi-Key Corporation
701 Brooks Ave. South
P.O. Box 677
Thief River Falls, MN 56701-0677
(800)344-4539
(218)681-3380 FAX

Sells an enormous variety of electronic and computer components, tools, and test equipment. Publishes a complete catalog listing all items.

Digital Research, Inc.
70 Garden Court
Monterey, CA 93942
(408)649-2893
(800)848-1498
(408)649-3443 BBS

Manufactures the DR DOS operating system.

Direct Drives
1107 Euclid Lane
Richton Park, IL 60471
(708)481-1111

Distributes an incredible selection of hard disk drives and controllers. Also publishes the *Hard Drive Buyer's Resource Guide*, the most comprehensive and accurate listing of drive and controller specifications available.

Distributed Processing Tech. (DPT)
140 Candace Drive
Maitland, FL 32751
(407)830-5522
(407)831-6432 BBS

Manufactures high-performance caching SCSI host adapters.

Diversified Technology

112 E. State Street
Ridgeland, MS 39158
(201)891-8718
(800)443-2667

Manufactures industrial and rack-mount PC-compatible systems as well as a
variety of backplane-design CPU boards and multifunction adapters.

DTK Computer, Inc.

17700 Castleton Street
Industry, CA 91748
(818)810-8880
(818)333-6548 BBS

Manufactures PC-compatible systems and BIOS software.

Dukane Corporation

2900 Dukane Drive
St. Charles, IL 60174
(708)584-2300
(708)584-5156 FAX

Manufactures the best Audio Visual overhead projectors on the market today.
They specialize in portable high brightness units designed for LCD panel
projection applications.

Dynatech Computer Power, Inc.

5800 Butler Lane
Scotts Valley, CA 95066
(408)438-5760
(800)638-9098

Manufactures a line of computer power-protection devices.

Edmund Scientific

101 E. Gloucester Pike
Barrington, NJ 08007
(609)573-6250

Supplies scientific supplies including optical equipment and components, test
equipment, and a variety of electronic components and gadgets. Their catalog
is an experimenter's dream!

Electronic Buyers' News **Magazine**

CMP Publications, Inc.
600 Community Drive
Manhasset, NY 11030-3875
(516)562-5000
(516)562-5468

An excellent industry trade weekly magazine featuring news and information for those involved in electronics purchasing, materials, and management. Subscriptions are free to those who qualify.

Electronic Engineering Times **Magazine**

CMP Publications, Inc.
600 Community Drive
Manhasset, NY 11030-3875
(516)562-5000
(516)562-5468

An excellent industry trade weekly news magazine featuring news for engineers and technical managers. Subscriptions are free to those who qualify.

Electronic Products **Magazine**

Hearst Business Communications, Inc.
645 Stewart Ave.
Garden City, NY 11530
(516)227-1300
(516)227-1444 FAX

An excellent industry trade magazine featuring engineering type information on electronic and computer components and in-depth technical articles. Subscriptions are free to those who qualify.

Elek-Tek, Inc.

7350 North Linder Avenue
Skokie, IL 60077
(708)677-7660
(800)395-1000

Computer retail superstore offering a large selection of brand-name equipment at discount pricing.

Emerson Computer Power

15041 Bake Parkway
#L
Irvine, CA 92718
(714)380-1005
(800)222-5877

Manufactures a line of computer power-protection devices.

Endl Publications
14426 Black Walnut Court
Saratoga, CA 95070
(408)867-6642

Publishes SCSI technical documentation such as *The SCSI Bench Reference* and *The SCSI Encyclopedia*.

Epson America, Inc. OEM Division
20770 Madrona Avenue
Torrance, CA 90509-2842
(213)782-0770
(213)782-5220 FAX
(800)922-8911 FAXback Information Line
(408)946-8777 BBS

Manufactures printers, floppy disk drives, and complete PC-compatible systems.

Everex Systems, Inc.
48431 Milmont Drive
Fremont, CA 94538
(415)498-1111
(800)922-8911
(510)683-2984 BBS

Manufactures PC-compatible systems and peripherals.

Exabyte Corporation
1685 38th Street
Boulder, CO 80301
(303)447-7359

Manufactures high-performance 8mm tape-backup systems.

Excel, Inc.
2200 Brighton-Henrietta Townline Road
Rochester, NY 14623
(716)272-8770
(800)624-2001

Distributes refurbished IBM PC, XT, AT, and PS/2 systems as well as printers, modems, displays, and so on.

Fedco Electronics, Inc.
184 W. 2nd Street
Fond du Lac, WI 54936
(414)922-6490
(800)542-9761

Manufactures and supplies a large variety of computer batteries.

Fessenden Technologies

116 N. 3rd Street
Ozark, MO 65721
(417)485-2501

Service company that offers hard disk drive and monitor repair and reconditioning. Also offers floppy disk and hard disk test equipment.

Fifth Generation Systems, Inc.

10049 N. Reiger Road
Baton Rouge, LA 70809
(504)291-7221
(800)873-4384
(504)295-3344 BBS

Manufactures a variety of software utility products including
FASTBACK, the Mace Utilities, and the Brooklyn Bridge.
Recently acquired by Symantec.

Fluke, John Manufacturing Company, Inc.

P.O. Box 9090
Everett, WA 98206-9090
(206)347-6100
(800)443-5853
(206)356-5116 FAX

Manufactures a line of high-end digital troubleshooting tools including the
9000 series products that are designed to troubleshoot PC motherboards down
to the component level. These systems are used by many motherboard manufacturers for design and manufacturing troubleshooting.

Forbin Project

P.O. Box 702
Cedar Falls, IA 50613
(319)266-0543

Manufactures the Qmodem communications software.

Fujitsu America, Inc.

3055 Orchard Drive
San Jose, CA 95134
(408)432-1300
(800)626-4686
(408)944-9899 BBS

Manufactures a line of high-capacity hard disk drives.

Future Domain Corporation

2801 McGaw Avenue
Irvine, CA 92714
(714)253-0400
(714)253-0913 FAX
(714)253-0432 BBS

Manufactures a line of high-performance SCSI host adapters and software.

Gateway 2000

610 Gateway Drive
North Sioux City, SD 57049
(605)232-2000
(800)523-2000
(605)232-2109 BBS

Manufactures a popular line of PC-compatible systems sold by mail order.
Their systems primarily use Micronics Motherboards, Phoenix BIOS, and
industry-standard form factors.

Gazelle

305 North 500 West
Provo, UT 84601
(801)377-1288
(800)RUN-FAST (786-3278)
(801)373-6933 FAX

Manufactures the Optune disk defragmenter and disk performance utility
program.

GigaTrend, Inc.

2234 Rutherford Road
Carlsbad, CA 92008
(619)931-9122

Manufactures high-capacity tape drives.

Global Engineering Documents

15 Inverness Way East
Englewood, CO 80112-5704
(303)792-2181
(800)854-7179
(303) 792-2192 FAX

A source for various ANSI and other industry standard documents, including
SCSI-1, 2, and 3, ATA IDE, ESDI, and many others. Unlike ANSI, they sell draft
documents of standards that are not yet fully ANSI approved.

Globe Manufacturing, Inc.

1159 Route 22
Mountainside, NJ 07092
(908)232-7301
(800)227-3258

Manufactures assorted PC adapter card brackets.

Golden Bow Systems

842 B. Washington Street
San Diego, CA 92103
(619)298-9349
(800)284-3269

Manufactures VOPT, the best and fastest disk optimizer software available.

GoldStar Technology, Inc.

3003 N. First Street
San Jose, CA 95134
(408)432-1331
(408)432-0236 BBS

Manufactures a line of PC systems, monitors, and fax machines.

GRACE Electronic Materials

77 Dragon Court
Woburn, MA 01888
(617)935-4850
(617)933-4318 FAX

Manufactures thermally conductive tapes and heat sinks.

Great Falls Computer Corp.

505 Innsbruck Ave.
Great Falls, VA 22066
(703)759-5570
(703)759-7152 FAX

A service company specializing in computer repair and data
recovery.

GSI (Great Software Ideas), Inc.

17951-H Skypark Circle
Irvine, CA 92714-6343
(714)261-7949
(800)486-7800
(714)757-1778 FAX

Manufactures an extremely flexible and powerful line of IDE adapters and floppy controllers, including units with security locks, and support for 2.88M drives. Also offers complete 2.88M drive upgrade kits. Their IDE controllers have a flexible on-board BIOS that allows them to coexist with other drive interfaces.

Harbor Electronics

650 Danbury Road
Ridgefield, CT 06877
(203)438-9625
(203)431-3001 FAX

Manufactures a line of high-quality SCSI-1, -2, and -3 interconnect cables.

Hauppauge Computer Works, Inc.

91 Cabot Court
Hauppauge, NY 11788
(516)434-1600
(800)443-6284

Manufactures upgrade motherboards for PC-compatible systems.

Hayes Microcomputer Products

P.O Box 105203
Atlanta, GA 30348
(404)840-9200
(800)874-2937
(404)446-6336 BBS

Manufactures a complete line of modems.

Heathkit

Heath Company
Benton Harbor, MI 49022
(616)982-3411
(800)253-0570

Manufactures various electronic device kits assembled by the purchaser. Has incredible kits for learning electronics and computer design. Also sells Zenith computers and technical documentation.

Hermann Marketing

1400 North Price Road
St. Louis, MO 63132-2308
(800)523-9009
(314)432-1818 FAX

Distributes a line of "Uniquely Intel" products and accessories. My favorites are the T-shirts, coffee cups, and especially the keychains containing actual Intel 386DX and 486DX processors encased in clear plastic.

Hewlett-Packard

16399 W. Bernardo Drive
San Diego, DA 92127
(619)592-4522
(800)333-1917 HP FIRST (Fax Information Retrieval System)
(208)344-4809 HP FIRST (Fax Information Retrieval System)

Manufactures an extensive line of excellent printers and
PC-compatible systems.

Hewlett-Packard, Disk Memory Division

11413 Chinden Boulevard
Boise, ID 83714
(208)323-6000

Manufactures high-capacity 3 1/2-inch hard disk drives.

Hitatchi America, Ltd.

50 Prospect Avenue
Tarrytown, NY 94005
(914)332-5800

Manufactures computer peripherals, including hard disks and
LCD devices.

Honeywell, Inc.

4171 North Mesa
Building D
El Paso, TX 79902
(915)543-5146
(800)445-6939

Manufactures a variety of high-quality keyboards and mice for
PC-compatible systems. The Honeywell mouse uses revolutionary new technology that never needs cleaning and works on any surface, unlike traditional
ball and roller mice.

Hyundai Electronics America

166 Baypointe Parkway
San Jose, CA 95134
(408)473-9200
(800)544-7808

Manufactures PC-compatible systems.

IBM Desktop Software

472 Wheelers Farm Road
Milford, CT 06460
(800)426-7699

Supports IBM PC applications software such as DisplayWrite and
PC Storyboard.

IBM National Distribution Division (NDD)

101 Paragon Drive
Montvale, NJ 07645
(800)426-9397

Manufactures and supports IBM DOS and OS/2.

IBM OEM Division

1133 Westchester Avenue
White Plains, NY 10604
(914)288-3000

Manufactures and distributes IBM products such as high-capacity
3 1/2-inch hard disk drives, networking and chip set products.

IBM Parts Order Center

P.O. Box 9022
Boulder, CO 80301
(303)924-4100 Orders
(303)924-4015 Part Number ID and Lookup

IBM's nationwide service parts ordering center.

IBM PC Company

11400 Burnet Road
Austin, TX 78758
(512)823-2851
(800)IBM-3333
(800)426-7015 IBM PC Co. Factory Outlet
                        (discontinued/used equipment)
(800)426-4329 IBM FAX Information Service (FAXback system)
(800)426-3395 IBM Tech Support FAX Information (FAXback system)
(919)517-0001 IBM National Support Center BBS
(919)517-0095 IBM NSC BBS Status Line (voice)

Manufactures and supports IBM's PS/2, PS/Valuepoint, and PS/1
products.

IBM PC Direct

3039 Cornwallis Road
Building 203
Research Triangle Park, NC 27709-9766
(800)IBM-2YOU (426-2968)
(800)465-7999 Canada
(919)517-2050 FAX

IBM PC Company direct mail-order catalog sales division. They sell IBM and
approved third-party systems and peripherals at a discount and publish a
catalog listing all items.

IBM Personal Systems Technical Solutions Magazine

The TDA Group
P.O. Box 1360
Los Altos, CA 94023-1360
(800)551-2832
(415)948-4280 FAX

Publishes an excellent bimonthly magazine covering IBM Personal Computer
systems and software.

IBM Technical Directory

P.O. Box 2009
Racine, WI 53404
(414)633-8108
(800)426-7282

The source for books, reference manuals, documentation, software toolkits,
and language products for IBM systems.

Illinois Lock

301 West Hintz Road
Wheeling, IL 60090-5754
(708)537-1800
(708)537-1881 FAX

Manufactures keylocks used in many different IBM and IBM
compatible computer systems.

InfoChip Systems, Inc.

2840 San Tomas Expressway
Santa Clara, CA 95051
(408)727-0514
(800)447-0200
(408)727-2496 BBS

Manufactures the Expanz data-compression coprocessor products.

InfoWorld Magazine

375 Cochituate Road
Framingham, MA 01701
(508)879-0446

Publishes *InfoWorld* magazine, featuring excellent product reviews.

Inline, Inc.

625 S. Palm Street
La Habra, CA 90631
(213)690-6767
(800)882-7117

Manufactures a complete line of video-connection accessories
including distribution amplifiers, scan converters, line drivers,
projector interfaces, and cables.

Inmac

2951 Zanker Road
San Jose, CA 95134
(408)435-1700

Distributes a large variety of computer supplies, including floppy disks and
cables.

Integrated Information Technology (IIT)

2445 Mission College Boulevard
Santa Clara, CA 95054
(408)727-1885
(800)832-0770

Manufactures fast Intel-compatible math coprocessors for
286-, 386SX-, and 386DX-based systems.

Intel Corporation

3065 Bowers Avenue
Santa Clara, CA 95051
(408)765-8080
(800)548-4725

Manufactures microprocessors used in IBM and compatible systems.
Also makes a line of memory and accelerator boards.

Intel PC Enhancement Operations

5200 NE Elam Young Parkway
Hillsboro, OR 97124
(503)629-7354
(800)538-3373
(503)645-6275 BBS

Manufactures a variety of PC upgrade products and expansion boards including Overdrive CPU upgrades, AboveBoard memory adapters, SIMM memory modules, and modems.

Interface Group

300 First Avenue
Needham, MA 02194
(617)449-6600

Produces the annual COMDEX/Fall and COMDEX/Spring computer shows.

International Electronic Research Corp. (IERC)

135 W. Magnolia Boulevard
Burbank, CA 91502
(213)849-2481
(818)848-8872 FAX

Manufactures a line of excellent CPU heat sink products including clip-on, low-profile models, especially for 486 and Pentium processors that do not require a special socket.

Intex Solutions, Inc.

35 Highland Circle
Needham, MA 02194
(617)449-6222
(617)444-2318 FAX

Manufactures and distributes software, especially Lotus enhancement products such as the Rescue Plus Lotus spreadsheet Data Recovery program. Rescue is the most comprehensive and capable data recovery program for Lotus spreadsheet files.

Iomega Corporation

1821 West 4000 South
Roy, UT 84067
(801)778-1000
(800)456-5522
(801)778-4400 BBS

Manufactures the Bernoulli box removable-cartridge drive.

IQ Technologies, Inc.

22032 23rd Drive SE
Bothell, WA 98021
(206)483-3555
(800)752-6526

Manufactures PC interconnect cables and devices, including the SmartCable RS232 devices.

Irwin Magnetic Systems, Inc.

2101 Commonwealth Boulevard
Ann Arbor, MI 48105
(313)930-9000
(800)421-1879
(313)930-9380 BBS

Manufactures a line of tape-backup products ranging from DC-2000 to DAT and 8mm units. Also supplies IBM with some tape-backup systems.

Jameco Computer Products

1355 Shoreway Road
Belmont, CA 94002
(415)592-8097

Supplies computer components, parts, and peripherals by way of mail order.

JDR Microdevices

2233 Branham Lane
San Jose, CA 95124
(408)559-1200
(800)538-5000
(408)559-0253 BBS

A vendor for chips, disk drives, and various computer and electronic parts and components.

Jensen Tools

7815 S. 46th Street
Phoenix, AZ 85044
(602)968-6231
(800)426-1194

Supplies and manufactures high-quality tools and test equipment.

Kalok Corporation

1289 Anvilwood Avenue
Sunnyvale, CA 94089
(408)747-1315

Manufactures a line of low-cost 3 1/2-inch hard disk drives.

Kenfil Distribution

16745 Saticoy Street
Van Nuys, CA 91406
(818)785-1181

A major software distributor.

Kensington Microware, Ltd.
251 Park Avenue South
New York, NY 10010
(212)475-5200
(800)535-4242

Manufactures and supplies computer accessories.

Key Tronic Corporation
North 4424 Sullivan Road
Spokane, WA 99216
(509)928-8000
(800)262-6006

Manufactures and supplies low-cost PC-compatible keyboards.
Supplies Compaq with keyboards.

Kingston Technology Corporation
17600 Newhope Street
Fountain Valley, CA 92708
(714)435-2600
(800)835-6575
(714)435-2699 FAX

Manufactures an excellent line of direct processor upgrade modules for 286 and
386 IBM and Compaq systems, as well as the slot-based MCMaster bus master
processor upgrade card for Micro Channel systems. They also sell numerous
SIMM memory modules and disk upgrades for other systems.

Labconco Corporation
8811 Prospect
Kansas City, MO 64132
(816)333-8811
(800)821-5525
(816)363-0130 FAX

Manufactures a variety of clean room cabinets and clean benches for use in
hard disk drive and other sensitive component repair.

Landmark Research International
703 Grand Central Street
Clearwater, FL 34616
(813)443-1331
(800)683-6696

Manufactures the excellent Service Diagnostics PC diagnostics program, as well
as the Kickstart diagnostics adapter cards. Known also for the Landmark System
Speed Test program.

Laser Magnetic Storage

4425 Arrowswest Drive
Colorado Springs, CO 80907
(719)593-7900
(800)777-5764

Manufactures a variety of optical disk products.

Lexmark

740 New Circle Road
Lexington, KY 40511
(606)232-6814
(606)232-5653 BBS

Manufactures IBM keyboards and printers for retail distribution. Spun off from IBM in 1991, now sells to other OEMs and distributors.

Liuski International, Inc.

10 Hub Drive
Melville, NY 11747
(516)454-8220
(800)347-5454

Hardware distributor that carries a variety of peripherals and systems.

Longshine Computer, Inc.

2013 N. Capitol Avenue
San Jose, CA 95132
(408)942-1746

Manufactures various PC adapters including floppy disks, hard disks, SCSI, Token Ring, and Ethernet.

Lotus Development Corporation

55 Cambridge Parkway
Cambridge, MA 02142
(617)577-8500
(800)343-5414

Manufactures Lotus 1-2-3, Symphony, and Magellan software.

LSI Logic, Inc.

1551 McCarthy Boulevard
Milpitas, CA 95035
(408)433-8000

Manufactures motherboard logic and chip sets.

Manzana Microsystems, Inc.

P.O. Box 2117
Goleta, CA 93118
(805)968-1387

Manufactures floppy disk upgrade subsystems and controllers.

Mastersoft, Inc.

6991 E. Camelback Road
Scottsdale, AZ 85251
(602)277-0900
(800)624-6107

Manufactures Word for Word, a word processing file-conversion program.

Maxell Corporation of America

22-08 Route 208
Fair Lawn, NJ 07410
(201)795-5900
(800)533-2836

Manufactures magnetic media products including disks and tape cartridges.

Maxi Switch, Inc.

2901 East Elvira Road
Tuscon, AZ 85706
(602)294-5450
(602)294-6890 FAX

Manufactures a line of high-quality PC keyboards, including some designed for harsh or industrial environments. Maxi Switch keyboards are used by many compatible system manufacturers including Gateway 2000.

Maxoptix

2520 Junction Avenue
San Jose, CA 95134
(408)954-9700
(800)848-3092

Manufactures a line of optical WORM and magneto-optical drives. Joint venture with Maxtor Corporation and Kubota Corporation.

Maxtor Corporation

211 River Oaks Parkway
San Jose, CA 95134
(408)432-1700
(800)262-9867
(303)678-2222 BBS (2400 bps)
(303)678-2020 BBS (9600+ bps)

Manufactures a line of large-capacity, high-quality hard disk drives.

Maynard Electronics, Inc.

36 Skyline Drive
Lake Mary, FL 32746
(407)263-3500
(800)821-8782
(407)263-3502 BBS

Manufactures a line of tape-backup products.

McAfee Associates

4423 Cheeney Street
Santa Clara, CA 95054
(408)988-3832
(408)988-4044 BBS

Manufactures the SCAN virus-scanning software, which is
nonresident and updated frequently to handle new viruses
as they are discovered.

McGraw-Hill, Inc.

Princeton Road N-1
Highstown, NJ 08520
(619)426-5000
(800)822-8158

Publishes technical information and books.

McTronic Systems

7426 Cornwall Bridge Lane
Houston, TX 77041-1709
(713)462-7687

Manufactures the excellent Port Finder serial and parallel port diagnostic and
utility program. This is a shareware utility available direct from them as well as
through downloading from the IBMHW forum on CompuServe.

Megahertz Corporation

4505 S. Wasatch Boulevard
Salt Lake City, UT 84124
(801)272-6000
(800)527-8677

Manufactures laptop modems and external network adapters.
Also makes AT-speedup products.

Memorex Computer Supplies

1200 Memorex Drive
Santa Clara, CA 95050
(408)957-1000

Manufactures a line of computer disk media, tape cartridges,
and various other supplies.

Mentor Electronics, Inc.

7560 Tylor Boulevard
#E
Mentor, OH 44060
(216)951-1884

Supplies surplus IBM PC (10/27/82) ROM BIOS update chips.

Merisel

200 Continental Boulevard
El Segundo, CA 90245
(213)615-3080
(800)645-7778

A large distributor of PC hardware and software products from many
manufacturers.

Meritec

1359 West Jackson Street
P.O. Box 8003
Painesville, OH 44077
(216)354-3148
(216)354-0509 FAX

Manufactures a line of SCSI 8-bit to 16-bit (Wide SCSI) adapters in a variety of
configurations. These adapters allow Wide SCSI devices to be installed in a
standard 8-bit SCSI bus and vice versa.

Merritt Computer Products, Inc.

5565 Red Bird Center Drive
#150
Dallas, TX 75237
(214)339-0753

Manufactures the SafeSkin keyboard protector.

Methode Electronics, Inc.

DataMate Division
7444 W. Wilson Ave.
Chicago, IL 60656
(708)867-9600
(708)867-3149 FAX

Manufactures and sells a complete line of SCSI terminators.

Micro 2000, Inc.

1100 E. Broadway
Third Floor
Glendale, CA 91205
(818)547-0125

Manufactures the MicroScope PC diagnostics program as well as the
POSTProbe ISA, EISA, and MCA POST diagnostics card. Is extending 25 percent
discount to anyone who mentions this book when purchasing.

Micro Accessories, Inc.

2012 Hartog Drive
San Jose, CA 95131
(408)441-1242
(800)777-6687

Manufactures a variety of cables and disk-drive mounting brackets and accessories, including PS/2 adapter kits.

Micro Channel Developers Association

2 Greenwich Plaza
#100
Greenwich, CT 06830
(203)622-7614

An independent organization that facilitates evolution of the
Micro Channel Architecture. Resolves technical issues related
to the MCA bus.

Micro Computer Cable Company, Inc.

12200 Delta Drive
Taylor, MI 48180
(313)946-9700
(313)946-9645 FAX

Manufactures and sells a complete line of computer cables,
connectors, switchboxes, and cabling accessories.

Micro Design International

6985 University Boulevard
Winter Park, FL 32792
(407)677-8333
(800)241-1853

Manufactures the SCSI Express driver software for integration of SCSI peripherals in a variety of environments.

Micro House International

4900 Pearl East Circle
Suite 101
Boulder, CO 80301
(303)443-3389
(800)926-8299
(303)443-3323 FAX
(303)443-9957 BBS

Publishes the *Encyclopedia of Hard Disks*, an excellent reference book that shows hard disk drive and controller jumper settings.

Micro Solutions, Inc.

132 W. Lincoln Hwy.
DeKalb, IL 60115
(815)756-3411
(815)756-9100 BBS

Manufactures a complete line of floppy controllers and subsystems including 2.88M versions. Also offers floppy drive and tape-backup systems that run from a standard parallel port, using no expansion slots.

Microcom, Inc.

500 River Ridge Drive
Norwood, MA 02062
(617)551-1000
(800)822-8224

Manufactures error-correcting modems and develops the MNP communications protocols.

MicroComputer Accessories, Inc.

5405 Jandy Place
Los Angeles, CA 90066
(213)301-9400
(800)821-8270

Manufactures a variety of computer and office accessories.

Micrografx, Inc.

1303 E. Arapaho
Richardson, TX 75081
(214)497-6431
(800)733-3729

Manufactures the Micrografx Designer, Draw Plus, and Charisma software.
Specializes in Windows and OS/2 development.

Microid Research, Inc.

2336 Walsh Ave
Suite D
Santa Clara, CA 95051
(408)727-6991
(408)727-6996 FAX

Manufactures the MR BIOS, one of the most flexible and configur-able BIOS
versions available. They have versions available for a variety of different chip
sets and motherboards.

Microlink/Micro Firmware, Inc.

330 West Gray St.
Suite 170
Norman, OK 73069-7111
(405)321-8333
(800)767-5465
(405)321-3553 BBS

The largest distributor of Phoenix ROM BIOS upgrades. Develops custom
versions for specific motherboards and supplies many other BIOS vendors with
products.

Micron Technologies

2805 E. Columbia Road
Boise, ID 83706
(208)368-3900
(800)642-7661
(208)368-4530 BBS

Manufactures various memory chips, SIMMs, and memory boards, as well as a
line of IBM-compatible systems.

Micronics Computers, Inc.

232 E. Warren Avenue
Fremont, CA 94539
(510)651-2300
(510)651-6837 BBS

Manufactures PC-compatible motherboards and complete laptop and portable
systems. Micronics motherboards feature the Phoenix BIOS.

Micropolis Corporation
21211 Nordhoff Street
Chatsworth, CA 91311
(818)709-3300
(800)395-3000
(818)709-3310 BBS

Manufactures a line of high-capacity 5 1/4- and 3 1/2-inch hard disk drives.

Microprocessors Unlimited, Inc.
24000 S. Peoria Avenue
Beggs, OK 74421
(918)267-4961

Distributes memory chips, SIMMs, math coprocessors, UART chips, and other integrated circuits.

Microscience International Corporation
90 Headquarters Drive
San Jose, CA 95134
(408)433-9898
(800)334-3595

Manufactures hard disk drives.

Microsoft Corporation
One Microsoft Way
Redmond, WA 98052-6399
(206)882-8080
(800)426-9400
(206)936-6735 BBS

Manufactures MS-DOS, Windows, Windows NT, and a variety of applications software.

MicroSystems Development (MSD)
4100 Moorpark Avenue
Suite 104
San Jose, CA 95117
(408)269-4000
(408)296-5877 FAX
(408)296-4200 BBS

Manufactures the Port Test serial and parallel diagnostics test kit and the Post Code Master POST diagnostics card.

MicroWay, Inc.
Research Park
Box 79
Kingston, MA 02364
(508)746-7341

Manufactures a line of accelerator products for IBM and compatible systems.
Also specializes in math coprocessor chips, math chip accelerators, and
language products.

Mitsubishi Electronics America, Inc.
991 Knox Street
Torrence, CA 90502
(213)217-5732
(800)843-2515
(213)324-3092 BBS

Manufactures monitors, printers, hard disks, and floppy disk storage products.

Motor Magazine
Hearst Corporation
645 Stewart Ave
Garden City, NY 11530
(516)227-1300
(800)AUTO-828
(516)227-1444 FAX

The essential trade magazine for the automotive technician,
including troubleshooting tips and service product information. Subscriptions
are free to those who qualify.

Motorola, Inc.
6501 William Cannon Drive West
Austin, TX 78735
(512)891-2000

Manufactures microprocessors, memory components, real-time clocks, controller chips, and so on.

Mountain Network Solutions, Inc.
240 Hacienda Avenue
Campbell, CA 95008
(408)379-4300
(800)458-0300
(408)438-2665 BBS

Manufactures tape drives and backup subsystems including hardware and
software.

Mueller Technical Research

21718 Mayfield Lane
Barrington, IL 60010-9733
(708)726-0709
(708)726-0710 FAX

You found me! I run a service company that offers the best in PC hardware
and software technical seminars and training, specializing in PC hardware and
software troubleshooting and data recovery. My CompuServe ID is 73145,1566
(Scott Mueller).

Mustang Software

3125 19th Street
#162
Bakersfield, CA 93301
(805)395-0223
(800)999-9619
(805)395-0650 BBS

Manufactures Wildcat! BBS software.

Mylex Corporation

34551 Ardenwood Boulevard
Fremont, CA 94555
(510)796-6100
(800)446-9539

Manufactures high-performance ISA and EISA motherboards and SCSI host
adapters.

National Semiconductor Corporation

2900 Semiconductor Drive
Santa Clara, CA 95052
(408)721-5151
(408)245-0671 BBS

Manufactures a variety of chips for PC circuit applications. Known especially
for its UART chips.

NCL America, Inc.

1221 Innsbruck Drive
Sunnyvale, CA 94086
(408)734-1006

Manufactures high-performance SCSI host adapters.

NCR Microelectronics

1635 Aeroplaza
Colorado Springs, CO 80916
(719)596-5795
(800)334-5454
(719)574-0424 BBS

Manufactures a variety of integrated circuits for PC systems including SCSI protocol chips used by many OEMs. They also sponsor the SCSI BBS, an excellent source for standard documents covering SCSI, IDE, and other interfaces.

NEC Technologies, Inc.

1414 Massachusetts Avenue
Boxborough, MA 01719
(508)264-8000
(800)632-4636
(708)860-2602 BBS

Manufactures Multisync monitors, CD-ROM drives, video adapters, printers, and other peripherals as well as complete PC-compatible systems.

Northgate Computer Systems, Inc.

7075 Flying Cloud Drive
Eden Prairie, MN 55344
(800)548-1993

Manufactures PC-compatible systems sold through mail order.

NovaStor Corporation

30961 Agoura Rd.
Suite 109
Westlake Village, CA 91361
(818)707-9900
(818)707-9902 FAX

Manufactures the Novaback tape backup software for SCSI Tape drives. Supports 8mm, 4mm (DAT), 1/4-inch cartridge (QIC), IBM 3480, and 9-track tape drives.

Novell, Inc.

122 E. 1700 South
Provo, UT 84601
(801)379-5900
(800)526-7937
(801)429-3030 BBS

Manufactures the NetWare LAN operating system.

Okidata

532 Fellowship Road
Mount Laurel, NJ 08054
(609)235-2600
(800)654-3282
(800)283-5474 BBS

Manufactures printers and modems.

Olivetti

765 US Hwy. 202
Somerville, NJ 08876
(201)526-8200

Manufactures Olivetti and many AT&T PC systems.

Ontrack Computer Systems, Inc.

6321 Bury Drive
Suites 15-19
Eden Prairie, MN 55346
(612)937-1107
(800)752-1333
(612)937-2121 Technical Support
(612)937-5161 Ontrack Data Recovery
(800)872-2599 Ontrack Data Recovery
(612)937-5750 FAX
(612)937-0860 BBS (2400bps)
(612)937-8567 BBS (9600+bps)

Manufactures the Disk Manager hard disk utilities for PC, PS/2, and
Macintosh. Disk Manager is the most comprehensive and flexible low-level
format program available, supporting even IDE drives. Also provides extensive
data recovery services.

Orchid Technology

45365 Northport Loop West
Fremont, CA 94538
(510)683-0300
(800)767-2443
(510)683-0329 BBS

Manufactures a line of video and memory board products for IBM and compatible systems.

Osborne/McGraw Hill

2600 10th Street
Berkeley, CA 94710
(415)549-6618
(800)227-0900

Publishes computer books.

Pacific Data Products

9125 Rehco Road
San Diego, CA 92121
(619)552-0880
(619)452-6329 BBS

Manufactures the Pacific Page XL and PacificPage PE Postscript
compatible enhancement products for HP LaserJet printers.

Pacific Magtron, Inc.

568-8 Weddell Drive
Sunnyvale, CA 94089
(408)774-1188

Manufactures hard disk drives.

Packard Bell

9425 Canoga Avenue
Chatsworth, CA 91311
(818)886-4600
(800)733-4411
(818)773-7207 BBS

Manufactures an excellent line of low-cost PC-compatible computer systems.

Panasonic Communications & Systems

2 Panasonic Way
Secaucus, NJ 07094
(201)348-7000
(800)233-8182
(201)863-7845 BBS

Manufactures monitors, optical drive products, floppy drives,
printers, and PC-compatible laptop systems.

Parts Now, Inc.

810 Stewart Street
Madison, WI 53713
(608)276-8688
(800)233-8182

Sells a large variety of laser printer parts for HP, Apple, Canon, and other laser
printers using Canon engines.

PC Connection

6 Mill Street
Marlow, NH 03456
(603)446-7721
(800)800-5555

Distributes many different hardware and software packages by way of mail order.

PC Magazine

One Park Avenue
New York, NY 10016
(212)503-5446

Magazine featuring product reviews and comparisons.

PC Power & Cooling, Inc.

5995 Avenida Encinas
Carlsbad, CA 92008
(619)931-5700
(800)722-6555
(619)931-6988

Manufactures a line of high-quality, high-output power supplies for IBM and compatible systems, including Compaq. Known for high-power output and quiet fan operation.

PC Repair Corporation

2010 State Street
Harrisburg, PA 17103
(717)232-7272
(800)727-3724

Service company and parts distributor that performs board repair of IBM PCs and PS/2s, printers, and typewriters as well as Compaq systems repair. Also offers an extensive parts line for these systems.

PC Week Magazine

10 Presidents Landing
Medford, MA 02155
(617)693-3753

Weekly magazine featuring industry news and information.

PC World Magazine

375 Chochituate Road
Framingham, MA 01701
(508)879-0700
(800)435-7766

A monthly magazine featuring product reviews and comparisons.

PC-Kwik Corporation

15100 S.W. Koll Parkway
Beaverton, OR 97006-6026
(503)644-5644
(800)759-5945
(503)646-8267 FAX

Formerly Multisoft, PC-Kwik manufactures the PC-Kwik Power Pak system performance utilities, Super PC-Kwik disk cache, and WinMaster Windows utility programs.

PC-SIG/Spectra Publishing

1030 E. Duane Avenue
#D
Sunnyvale, CA 94086
(408)730-9291
(800)245-6717

Publishes public-domain software and shareware available on CD-ROM.

PCI Special Interest Group

5200 N.E. Elam Young Parkway
Hillsboro, OR 97124
(503)696-2000
(800)433-5177
(503)693-0920 FAX

An independent group that owns and manages the PCI (Peripheral Component Interconnect) local bus architecture.

PCMCIA—Personal Computer Memory Card International Association

1030G East Duane Avenue,
Sunnyvale, CA 94086
(408)720-0107

An independent organization that maintains the PCMCIA bus standard for credit-card-sized expansion adapters.

Philips Consumer Electronics

One Philips Drive
Knoxville, TN 37914
(615)521-4366

Manufactures Magnavox PCs, monitors, and CD-ROM drives.

Phoenix Technologies, Ltd.

846 University Avenue
Norwood, MA 02062
(617)551-4000

Manufactures IBM-compatible BIOS software for a number of ISA, EISA, and MCA systems.

Pivar Computing Services, Inc.

165 Arlington Heights Road
Buffalo Grove, IL 60089
(708)459-6010
(800)266-8378   .

Service company that specializes in data and media conversion.

PKWare, Inc.

9025 N. Deerwood Drive
Brown Deer, WI 53223
(414)354-8699
(414)354-8559 FAX
(414)354-8670 BBS

Manufactures the PKZIP, PKUNZIP, PKLite, and PKZMENU data compression software. Widely used on BBS systems and by manufacturers for software distribution.

Plus Development Corporation

1778 McCarthy Boulevard
Milpitas, CA 95035
(408)434-6900
(800)624-5545
(408)434-1664 BBS

Manufactures the Plus Hardcard product line. A division of Quantum Corporation.

Priam Systems Corporation

1140 Ringwood Court
San Jose, CA 95131
(408)441-4180
(408)434-1646 BBS

Provides service and repair for Priam drives; original Priam has gone out of business.

Processor Magazine

P.O. Box 85518
Lincoln, NE 68501
(800)247-4880

Publication that offers excellent sources of replacement and repair parts, as well as new equipment at wholesale prices.

Programmer's Shop

90 Industrial Park Road
Hingham, MA 02043
(617)740-2510
(800)421-8006

Distributes programming tools and utility software.

PTI Industries

269 Mount Hermon Road
Scott Valley, CA 95066
(408)438-3900

Manufactures a line of computer power-protection devices.

Public Brand Software

P.O. Box 51315
Indianapolis, IN 46251
(317)856-7571
(800)426-3475

Publishes a public domain and shareware library.

Public Software Library

P.O. Box 35705-F
Houston, TX 77235
(713)524-6394
(800)242-4775

Top-notch distributor of high-quality public domain and shareware software. Its library is the most well researched and tested available. Also offers an excellent newsletter that reviews the software.

Quadram

One Quad Way
Norcross, GA 30093
(404)923-6666
(404)564-5678 BBS

Manufactures a line of adapter boards and upgrades for IBM and compatible systems.

Quaid Software Limited

45 Charles Street East
Third Floor
Toronto, ON, M4Y1S2,
(416)961-8243

Manufactures the Quaid Copywrite disk copy program and other disk utilities.

Qualitas, Inc.

7101 Wisconsin Avenue
#1386
Bethesda, MD 20814
(301)907-6700
(301)907-8030 BBS

Manufactures the 386Max and BlueMax memory-manager utility programs.

Quantum Corporation

500 McCarthy Boulevard
Milpitas, CA 95035
(408)894-4000
(408)434-1664 BBS

Manufactures a line of 3 1/2-inch hard disk drives. Supplies drives to Apple
Computer.

Quarter-Inch Cartridge Drive Standards, Inc. (QIC)

311 East Carrillo Street
Santa Barbara, CA 93101
(805)963-3853
(805)962-1541 FAX

An independent industry group that sets and maintains Quarter Inch Cartridge (QIC) tape drive standards for backup and archiving purposes.

Quarterdeck Office Systems

150 Pico Boulevard
Santa Monica, CA 90405
(213)392-9851
(213)396-3904 BBS

Manufactures the popular DESQview, QEMM, and QRAM memory-manager
products.

Que Corporation

201 West 103rd Street
Indianapolis, IN 46290
(317)581-3500
(800)428-5331 Order Line
(800)448-3804 Sales FAX

Publishes the highest-quality computer applications software and hardware books in the industry, including this one!

Qume Corporation

500 Yosemite Drive
Milpitas, CA 95035
(408)942-4000
(800)223-2479

Manufactures a variety of peripherals including displays, printers, and printer supplies such as toner cartridges. Qume owns DTC, a disk controller manufacturer.

Radio Shack

Division of Tandy Corporation
1800 One Tandy Center
Fort Worth, TX 76102
(817)390-3011
(817)390-2774 FAX

Manages the Radio Shack electronics stores, which sell numerous electronics devices, parts, and supplies. Also manufactures a line of PC-compatible computers and computer accessories and supplies.

Rancho Technology, Inc.

8632 Archibald Avenue
#109
Rancho Cucamonga, CA 91730
(714)987-3966

Manufactures an extensive line of SCSI products including host adapters for ISA, EISA, and MCA bus systems, SCSI extenders, and interface software.

Renasonce Group, Inc.

5173 Waring Road
Suite 115
San Diego, CA 92120
(619)287-3348
(619)287-3554 FAX

Manufactures the excellent InfoSpotter system inspection and diagnostics program, as well as RemoteRX and the Skylight Windows troubleshooting program.

Reply Corporation

4435 Fortran Drive
San Jose, CA 95134
(408)942-4804
(800)955-5295
(408)942-4897 FAX

Designs and sells an exclusive line of complete 386 and 486 mother-board upgrades for IBM PS/2 systems including the Model 30, 30-286, 50, 55, 60, 65, 70, and 80. These are complete new motherboards with integrated local bus SVGA adapters, Pentium Overdrive support, 2.88M floppy controller, Flash BIOS, built-in ATA IDE adapter, support for up to 32M of motherboard memory, and numerous other features. These upgrade boards are actually manufactured for Reply by IBM and are fully IBM compatible.

Rinda Technologies, Inc.

5112 N. Elston Ave.
Chicago, IL 60630
(312)736-6633

Manufactures the DIACOM General Motors and Chrysler automotive diagnostics and troubleshooting software. DIACOM includes a hardware adapter that connects your PC directly to the automobile diagnostics connector through a parallel port on your system, and essentially converts your PC into a professional SCAN tool. Vehicle data then can be observed live or stored for analysis and troubleshooting.

Rotating Memory Repair, Inc.

23382-J Madero Road
Mission Viejo, CA 92691
(714)472-0159

Repair company that specializes in hard drive and floppy drive repair. Also repairs power supplies and displays.

Rotating Memory Services

4919 Windplay
El Dorado Hills, CA 95630
(916)939-7500

Repair company that specializes in hard disk drives.

Rupp Corporation

7285 Franklin Avenue
Los Angeles, CA 90046
(213)850-5394

Manufactures the FastLynx program, which performs system-to-system transfers over serial or parallel ports.

Safeware Insurance Agency, Inc.

2929 N. High Street
Columbus, OH 43202
(614)262-0559
(800)848-3469

Insurance company that specializes in insurance for computer
equipment.

SAMS

201 West 103rd Street
Indianapolis, IN 46290
(317)581-3500

Publishes technical books on computers and electronic equipment.

Seagate Technology

920 Disc Drive
Scotts Valley, CA 95066
(408)438-6550
(408)429-6356 FAX
(408)438-8111 Sales
(800)468-3472 Service
(405)491-6260 Service
(405)491-6261 Service FAX
(408)438-2620 FAXback Information
(408)438-8771 BBS

The largest hard disk manufacturer in the world. Offers the most extensive
product line of any disk manufacturer, ranging from low-cost units to the
highest-performance, -capacity, and -quality drives available.

Service News Magazine

United Publications, Inc.
38 Lafayette St.
P.O. Box 995
Yarmouth, ME 04096
(207)846-0600
(207)846-0657 FAX

An excellent monthly newspaper for computer service and support personnel,
featuring articles covering PC service and repair products. Subscriptions are
free to those who qualify.

SGS-Thomson Microelectronics/Inmos

1000 E. Bell Road
Phoenix, AZ 85022
(602)867-6100

Manufactures custom chip sets, and has been licensed by IBM to produce IBM-
designed XGA chip sets for ISA, EISA, and MCA bus systems.

Sharp Electronics Corporation

Sharp Plaza
Mahwah, NJ 07430-2135
(201)529-8200
(201)529-8731 Sales Hotline
(201)529-9636 FAX

Manufactures a wide variety of electronic and computer equipment including the best LCD monochrome and Active Matrix color displays and panels, as well as scanners, printers, and complete laptop and notebook systems.

Shugart Corporation

9292 Jeronimo Road
Irvine, CA 92714
(714)770-1100

Manufactures hard disk, floppy disk, and tape drives.

Sigma Data

Scytheville Row
P.O. Box 1790
New London, NH 03257
(603)526-6909
(800)446-4525
(603)526-6915 FAX

Distributes a complete line of SIMM memory modules, hard drive, and processor upgrades. They are the sole distributor of a unique line of "Hyperace" direct processor upgrades for 286- and 386-based IBM PS/2 systems, including the Model 50, 60, 70 P70, and 80 systems. They also have a line of ATA IDE adapters and no slot hard disk upgrades for IBM PS/2 systems as well.

Silicon Valley Computer

441 N Whisman Road
Building 13
Mountain View, CA 94043
(415)967-1100
(415)967-0770 FAX
(415)967-8081 BBS

Manufactures a complete line of IDE interface adapters, including a unique model that supports 16-bit IDE (ATA) drives on PC and XT systems (8-bit ISA bus) and models including floppy drive support, as well as serial and parallel ports.

SMS Technology, Inc.

550 E. Brokaw Road
Box 49048
San Jose, CA 95161
(408)954-1633
(510)964-5700 BBS

Manufactures the OMTi disk controllers, formerly known as
Scientific Micro Systems.

SofTouch Systems, Inc.

1300 S. Meridian
Suite 600
Oklahoma City, OK 73108-1751
(405)947-8080
(405)632-6537 FAX

Manufactures the GammaTech Utilities for OS/2, which can undelete and
recover files running under OS/2 even on an OS/2 HPFS partition.

Sola Electric

1717 Busse Road
Elk Grove, IL 60007
(708)439-2800
(800)289-7652

Manufactures a line of computer power-protection devices.

Sonera Technologies

P.O. Box 565
Rumson, NJ 07760
(908)747-5355
(800)932-6323
(908)747-4523 FAX

Manufactures the DisplayMate video display utility and diagnostics program.
DisplayMate displays exercises, troubleshoots, and diagnoses video display
adapter and monitor problems.

Sony Corporation of America

Sony Drive
Park Ridge, NJ 07656
(201)930-1000

Manufactures all types of high-quality electronic and computer equipment
including displays and magnetic- and optical-storage devices.

Specialized Products Company

3131 Premier Drive
Irving, TX 75063
(214)550-1923
(800)527-5018

Distributes a variety of tools and test equipment.

Sprague Magnetics, Inc.

15720 Stagg Street
Van Nuys, CA 91406
(818)994-6602
(800)553-8712

Manufactures a unique and interesting magnetic developer fluid that can be used to view sectors and tracks on a magnetic disk or tape. Also repairs tape drives.

Stac Electronics

5993 Avenida Encinas
Carlsbad, CA 92008
(619)431-7474
(800)522-7822
(619)431-5956 BBS

Manufactures the Stacker real-time data-compression adapter and software for OS/2 and DOS.

Standard Microsystems Corporation

35 Marcus Boulevard
Hauppauge, NY 11788
(516)273-3100
(800)992-4762

Manufactures ARCnet and EtherNet network adapters.

Star Micronics America, Inc.

200 Park Avenue
Pan Am Building
#3510
New York, NY 10166
(212)986-6770
(800)447-4700

Manufactures a line of low-cost printers.

STB Systems, Inc.
1651 N. Glenville
Richardson, TX 75085
(214)234-8750
(214)437-9615 BBS

Manufactures various adapter boards, and specializes in a line of high-resolution VGA video adapters.

Storage Dimensions, Inc.
2145 Hamilton Avenue
San Jose, CA 95125
(408)879-0300
(800)765-7895
(408)944-1220 BBS

Distributes Maxtor hard disk and optical drives as complete subsystems. Also manufactures the Speedstore hard disk utility software.

Symantec Corporation
10201 Torre Avenue
Cupertino, CA 95014
(408)253-9600
(800)441-7234
(408)973-9598 BBS

Manufactures a line of utility and applications software featuring the Norton Utilities for IBM and Apple systems.

SyQuest Technology
47071 Bayside Parkway
Fremont, CA 94538
(415)226-4000
(800)245-2278
(415)656-0470 BBS

Manufactures removable-cartridge hard disk drives.

Sysgen, Inc.
556 Gibraltar Drive
Milpitas, CA 95035
(408)263-4411
(800)821-2151
(408)946-5032 BBS

Manufactures a line of tape-backup storage devices.

Sytron

134 Flanders Road
P.O. Box 5025
Westboro, MA 01581-5025
(508)898-0100
(800)877-0016
(508)898-2677 FAX

Manufactures the SyTOS tape-backup software for DOS and OS/2, the most widely used tape software in the industry.

Tadiran

2975 Bowers Avenue
Santa Clara, CA 95051
(408)727-0300

Manufactures a variety of batteries for computer applications.

Tandon Corporation

405 Science Drive
Moorpark, CA 93021
(805)523-0340

Manufactures IBM-compatible computer systems and disk drives. Supplied to IBM most of the full-height floppy drives used in the original PC and XT systems.

Tandy Corporation/Radio Shack

1800 One Tandy Center
Fort Worth, TX 76102
(817)390-3700

Manufactures a line of IBM-compatible systems, peripherals, and accessories. Also distributes electronic parts and supplies.

Tatung Company of America, Inc.

2850 El Presidio Street
Long Beach, CA 90810
(213)979-7055
(800)827-2850

Manufactures monitors and complete compatible systems.

TCE Company

35 Fountain Square
5th Floor
Elgin, IL 60120
(708)741-7200
(800)383-8001
(708)741-1801 FAX

Manufactures an IDE drive formatter specifically for Conner Peripherals drives
called "The Conner," consisting of a special hardware connector that plugs
into the diagnostics port on Conner IDE drives, as well as special software to
format the drive. They also specialize in power supply and power line monitoring and test equipment, and make one of the best PC power supply test machines available.

TDK Electronics Corporation

12 Harbor Park Drive
Port Washington, NY 11050
(516)625-0100

Manufactures a line of magnetic and optical media including disk and tape
cartridges.

Teac America, Inc.

7733 Telegraph Road
Montebello, CA 90640
(213)726-0303

Manufactures a line of floppy and tape drives, including a unit that combines
both 3 1/2-inch and 5 1/4-inch drives in one half-height package.

Tech Data Corporation

5350 Tech Data Drive
Clearwater, FL 34620
(813)539-7429
(800)237-8931

Distributes computer equipment and supplies.

Tech Spray, Inc.

P.O. Box 949
Amarillo, TX 79105-0949
(806)372-8523

Manufactures a complete line of computer and electronic cleaning chemicals
and products.

Tecmar, Inc.

6225 Cochran Road
Solon, OH 44139
(216)349-0600
(800)344-4463
(216)349-0853 BBS

Manufactures a variety of adapter boards for IBM and compatible systems.

Thermalloy, Inc.

2021 W. Valley View Lane
P.O. Box 810839
Dallas, TX 75381-0839
(214)243-4321
(214)241-4656 FAX

Manufactures a line of excellent CPU heat sink products, including versions with built-in fan modules.

Toshiba America, Inc.

9740 Irvine Boulevard
Irvine, CA 92718
(714)583-3000
(800)999-4823
(714)837-2116 BBS

Manufactures a complete line of 5 1/4- and 3 1/2-inch floppy and hard disk drives, CD-ROM drives, display products, printers, and a popular line of laptop and notebook IBM-compatible systems.

TouchStone Software Corporation

2130 Main Street
Suite 250
Huntington Beach, CA 92648
(714)969-7746
(800)531-0450
(714)960-1886 FAX

Manufactures the CheckIt user level and CheckIt Pro Deluxe high-end PC diagnostics and troubleshooting programs. CheckIt Pro Deluxe also includes their excellent CheckIt Sysinfo environmental diagnostics program.

Trantor Systems, Ltd.

5415 Randall Place
Fremont, CA 94538
(510)770-1400
(415)656-5159 BBS

Manufactures the MiniSCSI and MiniSCSI Plus Parallel Port SCSI adapters, including hard disk and CD-ROM drivers for a variety of devices.

Traveling Software, Inc.

18702 N. Creek Parkway
Bothell, WA 98011
(206)483-8088
(800)662-2652

Manufactures the LapLink file-transfer program for PC and Mac systems as well as several other utility programs.

Tripp Lite Manufacturing

500 N. Orleans
Chicago, IL 60610
(312)329-1777

Manufactures a complete line of computer power-protection devices.

Tseng Labs, Inc.

10 Pheasant Run
Newtown Commons
Newtown, PA 18940
(215)968-0502

Manufactures video controller chip sets, BIOS, and board design for OEMs.

U.S. Robotics, Inc.

8100 N. McCormick Boulevard
Skokie, IL 60076
(708)982-5010
(800)982-5151
(708)982-5092 BBS

Manufactures a complete line of modems and communications products. Its modems support more protocols than most others, including v.32bis, HST, and MNP protocols.

Ultra-X, Inc.

P.O. Box 730010
San Jose, CA 95173-0010
(408)988-4721
(800)722-3789
(408)988-4849 FAX

Manufactures the excellent QuickPost PC, QuickPost PS/2, and Racer II diagnostic cards, as well as the Quicktech and Diagnostic Reference software packages. The Racer II is one of the most complete troubleshooting hardware cards on the market today.

Ultrastor Corporation

15 Hammond Street
#310
Irvine, CA 92718
(714)581-4100

Manufactures a complete line of high-performance ESDI, SCSI, and IDE disk controllers for ISA and EISA bus systems.

UNISYS

Township Line and Union Meeting Roads
Blue Bell, PA 19424
(215)542-2691
(800)448-1424

Manufactures PC-compatible systems that are part of the government Desktop IV contract.

Universal Memory Products

1378 Logan Avenue
#F
Costa Mesa, CA 92626
(714)751-9445
(800)678-8648

Distributes memory components including chip and SIMM modules.

Upgrades Etc.

15251 NE 90th Street
Redmond, WA 98052
(818)884-6417
(800)541-1943

Distributes AMI, Award, and Phoenix BIOS upgrades.

V Communications, Inc.

4320 Stevens Creek Boulevard
#275
San Jose, CA 95129
(408)296-4224

Manufactures the Sourcer disassembler and other programming tools.

Varta Batteries, Inc.

300 Executive Boulevard
Elmsford, NY 10523
(914)592-2500

Manufactures a complete line of computer batteries.

Verbatim Corporation
1200 WT Harris Boulevard
Charlotte, NC 28262
(704)547-6500

Manufactures a line of storage media including optical and magnetic disks and tapes.

VESA—Video Electronic Standards Association
2150 North First St.
Suite 440
San Jose, CA 95131-2029
(408)435-0333
(408)435-8225 FAX

An organization of manufacturers dedicated to setting and maintaining video display, adapter, and bus standards. They have created the VESA video standards as well as the VESA Video local bus (VL-Bus) standard.

Visiflex Seels
16 E. Lafayette Street
Hackensack, NJ 07601
(201)487-8080

Manufactures form-fitting clear keyboard covers and other computer accessories.

VLSI Technology, Inc.
8375 S. River Parkway
Tempe, AZ 85284
(602)752-8574

Manufactures chip sets and circuits for PC-compatible motherboards and adapters. IBM uses these chip sets in some of the PS/2 system designs.

Volpe, Hank
P.O. Box 43214
Baltimore, MD 21236
(410)256-5767
(410)256-3631 BBS

Manufactures the Modem Doctor serial port and modem diagnostics program.

Walling Company
4401 S. Juniper
Tempe, AZ 85282
(602)838-1277

Manufactures the DataRase EPROM eraser, which can erase as many as four EPROM chips simultaneously using ultraviolet light.

Wang Laboratories, Inc.

One Industrial Avenue
Lowell, MA 01851
(508)656-1550
(800)225-0654

Manufactures a variety of PC-compatible systems including some with MCA
bus slots.

Wangtek, Inc.

41 Moreland Road
Simi Valley, CA 93065
(805)583-5525
(800)992-9916
(805)582-3370 BBS

Manufactures a complete line of tape-backup drives including QIC, DAT, and
8mm drives for ISA, EISA, and MCA bus systems.

Warshawski/Whitney & Co.

1916 S. State Street
Chicago, IL 60680
(312)431-6100

Distributes an enormous collection of bargain-priced tools and equipment. Its
products are primarily for automotive applications, but many of the tools have
universal uses.

Washburn & Co.

3800 Monroe Avenue
Pittsford, NY 14534
(716)248-3627
(800)836-8026

The largest distributor of AMI BIOS and AMI motherboard products, known
for providing very high-end technical information and support.

Watergate Software

2000 Powell Street
Suite 1200
Emeryville, CA 94608
(510)596-1770
(510)653-4784 FAX

Manufactures the excellent PC Doctor diagnostics program for PC troubleshooting and repair.

Wave Mate, Inc.

2341 205th Street
#110
Torrance, CA 90501
(213)533-8190

Manufactures a line of high-speed replacement motherboards for IBM and compatible systems.

Weitek Corporation

1060 E. Arques
Sunnyvale, CA 94086
(408)738-8400

Manufactures high-performance math coprocessor chips.

Western Digital Corporation

8105 Irvine Center Drive
Irvine, CA 92718
(714)932-5000
(800)832-4778
(714)753-1234 BBS (2400bps)
(714)753-1068 BBS (9600+bps)

Manufactures many products including IDE and SCSI hard drives; SCSI and ESDI adapters for ISA, EISA, and MCA bus systems; and EtherNet, Token Ring, and Paradise video adapters. Supplies IBM with IDE and SCSI drives for PS/2 systems.

Windsor Technologies, Inc.

130 Alto Street
San Rafael, CA 94901
(415)456-2200
(415)456-2244 FAX

Manufactures PC Technician, an excellent high-end, technical-level PC diagnostics and troubleshooting program.

WordPerfect Corporation

1555 N. Technology Way
Orem, UT 84057
(801)225-5000
(800)451-5151
(801)225-4414 BBS

Manufactures the popular WordPerfect word processing program.

WordStar International, Inc.
201 Alameda del Prado
Novato, CA 94949
(415)382-8000
(800)227-5609

Manufactures the WordStar and WordStar 2000 programs.

Wyse Technology
3471 N. First Street
San Jose, CA 95134
(408)473-1200
(800)438-9973
(408)922-4400 BBS

Manufactures PC-compatible systems and terminals.

Xebec
3579 Gordon
Carson City, NV 89701
(702)883-4000
(702)883-9264 BBS

Manufactures ISA disk controllers originally used by IBM in the XT.

Xerox Corporation
Xerox Square
Rochester, NY 14644
(716)423-5078

Manufactures the Ventura desktop publishing software, as well as an extensive
line of computer equipment, copiers, and printers.

Xidex Corporation
5100 Patrick Henry Drive
Santa Clara, CA 95050
(408)970-6574

Manufactures disk and tape media.

Xircom
26025 Mureau Road
Calbasas, CA 91302
(818)878-7600
(800)874-7875
(818)878-7618 BBS

Manufactures external Token Ring and EtherNet adapters that attach to a
parallel port.

Y-E Data America, Inc.

3030 Business Park Drive
#1
Norcross, GA 30071
(404)446-8655

Manufactures a line of floppy disk drives, tape drives, and printers. Supplied
5 1/4-inch floppy drives to IBM for use in XT, AT, and PS/2 systems.

Zenith Data Systems

2150 E. Lake Cook Road
Buffalo Grove, IL 60089
(708)699-4800
(800)553-0331

Manufactures a line of IBM-compatible systems.

Zeos International, Ltd.

530 5th Avenue NW
St. Paul, MN 55112
(612)633-4591
(800)423-5891

Manufactures a line of good, low-cost PC-compatible ISA and EISA bus systems
sold by way of mail order.

Index

Symbols

G

H

F

I

Q

U

W

X

Y-Z